SHAKESPEARE AND THE RISE
OF THE EDITOR

Sonia Massai's central claim in this book is that the texts of early printed editions of Renaissance drama, including Shakespeare's, did not simply 'degenerate' or 'corrupt' over time, as subsequent editions were printed using their immediate predecessor as their basis. By focusing on early correctors of dramatic texts for the press, this book identifies a previously overlooked category of textual agents involved in the circulation of early English drama in print and challenges the common assumption that the first editor of Shakespeare was Nicholas Rowe, who published his edition of Shakespeare's *Works* in 1709. This study offers the first sustained account of a 'prehistory' of editing from the rise of English drama in print at the beginning of the sixteenth century to the official rise of the editorial tradition of Shakespeare at the beginning of the eighteenth century. Massai's argument forces us to consider that our understanding of what editing is and what it should do may be at odds with early modern understandings of the text of printed playbooks as both imperfect and continually and progressively perfectible.

SONIA MASSAI teaches Shakespeare and Renaissance Studies at King's College London. She is the editor of *World-Wide Shakespeares: Local Appropriations in Film and Performance* (2005). Her essays have appeared in many books and journals, including *The Blackwell Companion to Shakespeare and the Text* (2007), *Textual Performances* (Cambridge, 2004), *Shakespeare Survey, Studies in English Literature* and *New Theatre Quarterly*.

SHAKESPEARE AND THE RISE OF THE EDITOR

SONIA MASSAI

CAMBRIDGE
UNIVERSITY PRESS

CAMBRIDGE
UNIVERSITY PRESS

University Printing House, Cambridge CB2 8BS, United Kingdom

Cambridge University Press is part of the University of Cambridge.

It furthers the University's mission by disseminating knowledge in the pursuit of education, learning and research at the highest international levels of excellence.

www.cambridge.org
Information on this title: www.cambridge.org/9780521878050

© Sonia Massai 2007

First published 2007

A catalogue record for this publication is available from the British Library

ISBN 978-0-521-87805-0 Hardback
ISBN 978-0-521-28727-2 Paperback

For Bianca, Cosimo,
Elda and Giulio

Contents

List of illustrations and tables   *page* viii
Acknowledgements   x

Introduction   1

PART I   THE RISE OF ENGLISH DRAMA IN PRINT   39

1   English humanism and the publication of early Tudor drama   41

2   Italian influences on the publication of late Tudor drama   69

PART II   THE RISE OF SHAKESPEARE IN PRINT   89

3   The Wise Quartos (1597–1602)   91

4   The Pavier Quartos (1619)   106

5   The making of the First Folio (1623)   136

6   Perfecting Shakespeare in the Fourth Folio (1685)   180

Conclusion   196

Notes   206
References   235
Index   247

Illustrations and tables

1 Page of text: *The Pedlar's Prophecy*, 1595, STC 25782
  Reproduced by permission of the British Library, London   *page* 15
2 Page of text: *The Downfall of Robert, Earl of Huntingdon*,
  1601, STC 18271
  Reproduced by permission of the British Library, London   16
3 Page of text: *A Knack to Know a Knave*, 1594, STC 15027
  Reproduced by permission of the British Library, London   17
4 Page of text: *Tamburlaine*, 1606, STC 17428a
  Reproduced by permission of the British Library, London   18
5 Page of text: *Orlando Furioso*, 1599, STC 12266
  Reproduced by permission of the British Library, London   19
6 Page of text: *The Malcontent*, 1604, STC 17480
  Reproduced by permission of the British Library, London   20
7 Page of text: *The Maid's Tragedy*, 1638, STC 1680
  Reproduced by permission of the Bodleian Library, Oxford   22
8 Page of text: *Edward I*, 1593, STC 19535
  Reproduced by permission of the British Library, London   23
9 Page of text: *Othello*, 1622, STC 22305
  Reproduced by permission of the Huntington Library,
  San Marino, California   25
10 Page of text: *Othello*, 1622, STC 22305
  Reproduced by permission of the Huntington Library,
  San Marino, California   26
11 Page of text: *Othello*, 1622, STC 22305
  Reproduced by permission of the Huntington Library,
  San Marino, California   27
12 Page of text: *Othello*, 1622, STC 22305
  Reproduced by permission of the Huntington Library,
  San Marino, California   28

13 Page of text: *Othello*, 1622, STC 22305
Reproduced by permission of the Huntington Library,
San Marino, California 29

14 Woodcut: From Thomas More's *Utopia*, 3rd edition, 1518, by
Ambrosius Holbein
Reproduced by permission of the Cambridge University Library 50

15 Painting: *Portrait of Erasmus*, by Quentin Massys, 1517
Reproduced by permission of Royal Enterprises, London 52

16 Painting: *Portrait of Peter Giles*, by Quentin Massys, 1517
Reproduced by permission of the Koninklijk
Museum, Antwerp 53

17 Page of text: *Fulgens and Lucrece*, 1512–16?, STC 17778
Reproduced by permission of the Huntington Library,
San Marino, California 63

18 Page of text: *Fulgens and Lucrece*, 1512–16?, STC 17778
Reproduced by permission of the Huntington Library,
San Marino, California 65

19 Page of text: *Fulgens and Lucrece*, 1512–16?, STC 17778
Reproduced by permission of the Huntington Library,
San Marino, California 66

20 Page of text: *Richard II*, 1597, STC 22307
Reproduced by permission of the Huntington Library,
San Marino, California 94

Tables

3.1 Books published by Andrew Wise (1593–1602) 96
4.1 The 'Pavier Quartos' (1619) 107

Acknowledgements

This book would not have been written if one day in the now distant summer of the year 2000 Thomas L. Berger had not taken the time to discuss my recent work on Nahum Tate over lunch and had not encouraged me to find other 'editors' of Shakespeare before the publication of Nicholas Rowe's edition of Shakespeare's *Works* in 1709. Long before and since then Professor Berger had been and has continued to be one of the most inspiring teachers and scholars I have had the pleasure to work with. Thank you, Tom! I am also greatly indebted to other colleagues who have kindly read my book, and to Margaret Jane Kidnie and James Purkis in particular, who read the entire typescript at the most inconvenient of times, between Christmas and New Year's Eve 2005. They generously spared the time to give me invaluable feedback which has helped me refine and adjust some of the theories and arguments I explore in this book. I am also deeply grateful to John Jowett, who read my chapter on the 'Pavier Quartos' and an earlier version of my chapter on 'The making of the First Folio'.

My book has also benefited from the responses which I have had over the years from various people who attended conference presentations and seminar papers of extracts drawn from several of its chapters. I am therefore grateful to colleagues who have invited me to present my work at several events. Most recently, Jason Scott-Warren, who invited me to speak at the Graduate Seminar in Cambridge in October 2006; Helen Smith and Louise Wilson, who organized a terrific conference on 'Renaissance Paratexts' at the University of York in July 2006, where I had the pleasure to respond to the helpful comments and questions raised by, among others, Randall McLeod, Bill Sherman, Cathy Shrank, and my panel chair, Emma Smith; and Tarnya Cooper, curator at the National Portrait Gallery, and organizer of the 'Searching for Shakespeare' 2006 exhibition and related events, including a two-day conference where I was invited to speak about the Wise Quartos (chapter 3) and the Pavier Quartos (chapter 4). I have been particularly fortunate to be able to present versions of almost all the other chapters in this book at other seminars and conferences over the last six years. In chronological order, I presented my work on the Fourth Folio text of *Coriolanus* at the London Renaissance Seminar in January 2001 (this specific session was organized by my colleague Gordon McMullan, and other speakers included Ann Thompson and Eric Rasmussen, whom I first met on this memorable occasion) and a case-study on John Wolfe and Richard Jones, now included in chapter 2, at a seminar organized by Laurie Maguire for the International Shakespeare Conference, held at Stratford-upon-Avon in August 2002. Also in 2002 I presented a shorter paper focused only on John Wolfe at the 'Renaissance Go-Betweens' Conference, held at the Shakespeare Library, University of Munich, and organized, among others, by Andreas Hoefele, who kindly invited me to attend this most enjoyable event. The London Renaissance Seminar once again proved to be an exciting forum for a challenging discussion of extracts from chapter 1, when I was invited to present another paper in March 2003. This session was also organized by Gordon McMullan. The Early Modern Seminar Series at the University of Reading afforded another thoroughly enjoyable and very useful opportunity to present my work on the Wise Quartos now included in chapter 3. My heartfelt thanks to the organizer of this Seminar Series, Ralph Houlbrook, for inviting me to speak there in December 2004.

If the support of colleagues, teachers and friends in the field of Shakespeare studies has been crucially important to me since I started working on this book, the guidance I have been generously offered by the curatorial staff at the British Library, where I have carried out most of my research, has been equally vital for my work. Giles Mandelbrote has been particularly generous and patient and has answered many questions, especially about the book trade in early modern London, which was a largely new field for me when I first started working on this book.

The generosity of research-funding institutions has also greatly contributed to the completion of this project. Particularly crucial was the funding made available by the Arts and Humanities Research Council and by the British Academy to cover for the costs of replacing my teaching during the research leave which allowed me to complete this book and travel expenses to one other conference, hosted by the Shakespeare Association of America in New Orleans in 2004. (My thanks also to the organizers of the seminar I attended at this conference, Eric Rasmussen and Bernice Kliman, who gave me encouraging feedback on the section devoted to establishing Thomas Heywood's attitude to dramatic publication, which is now included in chapter 5.)

Further, I would like to thank Sarah Stanton at Cambridge University Press, for her generous help and support over the last two years, Susan Beer, Jo Breeze and Becky Jones, who kindly and patiently assisted me as this book was prepared for the press, and the anonymous readers who made very useful and extensive comments on the first draft of this book. And finally, I am grateful for permission to reproduce an earlier version of the first half of chapter 6, which was published in *Shakespeare Survey* 55 (2002), 260-75, and a section of chapter 2, which was published in Andreas Höfele and Werner von Koppenfels (eds.), *Renaissance Go-Betweens: Cultural Exchange in Early Modern Europe* (Berlin and New York: Walter de Gruyter, 2005), 104–18.

Introduction

'Lear.　How, nothing can come of nothing, speake againe.'[1]

The publication of *The works of Mr. William Shakespear; in six volumes . . . Revis'd and corrected, with an account of the life and writings of the author. By N. Rowe, Esq* (1709) marked the official beginning of a long and influential editorial tradition. The unprecedented appearance of the name of the editor alongside the name of the author on the title page of a printed collection of English plays signalled the rise of a self-conscious proprietary stance towards the dramatic text: whereas seventeenth-century readers had been encouraged to buy *Mr. William Shakespeares Comedies, Histories, & Tragedies. Published according to the True Originall Copies* in the four Folio editions of 1623, 1632, 1663–4, and 1685, readers willing to invest in the new collected edition of Shakespeare's works in 1709 were duly informed that what they were purchasing was Nicholas Rowe's 'Shakespeare'. Rather than an authorizing point of origin, the name of the author was now associated with a material body of works owned by the Tonsons publishing cartel throughout the best part of the eighteenth century. While 'Shakespeare' remained under the control of these 'grand possessors', a long line of editors was commissioned to prepare their own versions of Shakespeare's texts, which unfailingly challenged and claimed to supersede their immediate predecessors. Several studies have charted the development of eighteenth-century editorial theories and practices[3] and have reinforced the assumption that 1709 represented a genuine starting point, before which Shakespeare's texts had gradually deteriorated through the accumulation of accidental corruption in the printing house. The purpose of this book is to challenge this evolutionary understanding of the transmission of 'Shakespeare' in print. While acknowledging 1709 as a crucial watershed in the editorial tradition, this book shows that the conscious editorial manipulation of Shakespeare's dramatic texts had started well before Nicholas Rowe's edition, albeit informed by radically different views about what constituted an 'authoritative' text. What is significant is the *discontinuity*, rather than the *absence*, of editorial practices between the rise of Shakespeare in print and Rowe's edition of 1709.

Instances of editorial intervention in sixteenth- and seventeenth-century editions of Shakespeare have not gone completely unnoticed. However, the general tendency has been to focus on exceptional examples which can best be understood as precursors of the editorial tradition associated with eighteenth-century editors. For example, conjectural emendations in the Douai Manuscript (1694–5, Douai Public Library MS 7.87), which includes transcripts of *Twelfth Night, As You Like It, The Comedy of Errors, Romeo and Juliet, Julius Caesar* and *Macbeth*, were described by G. Blakemore Evans as 'show[ing] considerable intelligence in dealing with corrupt or difficult passages' (1962: 165). Rather than regarding these emendations as representative of late seventeenth-century editorial practices, Blakemore Evans understood them as 'readings which . . . anticipate the emendations proposed by the later eighteenth- and nineteenth-century editors of Shakespeare' (1962: 166). Similarly, having established what categories of variants in the First Folio of 1623 can be ascribed to Ralph Crane, scrivener to the King's Men in the late 1610s and early 1620s, T. H. Howard-Hill concluded that '[Crane's] involvement with the First Folio was so extensive and of such a kind that it is [he] rather than the playwright Nicholas Rowe whom we should acknowledge as the first person to confront the problems of translating Shakespeare's plays from stage to the study' (1992: 129). Several scholars have also noted how some seventeenth-century editions of Shakespeare drew on earlier editions to supplement the shortcomings of their source-text. Thomas L. Berger, for example, regards the 1630 Quarto edition of *Othello* as 'the first "conflated" text of [the play], probably the first consistently conflated text of any Shakespearian play' (1988: 145). More controversially, Jonathan Goldberg has argued that while the First Quarto of *Romeo and Juliet* reflects a theatrical version of the play, the Second Quarto may not be closer to the fuller version of the play as intended by its author but the product of editorial conflation of the First Quarto and a manuscript preserving authorial and non-authorial 'second thoughts and alternatives' (1994: 187).[4] While essential in advancing our understanding of the variety of editorial intervention which contributed to the rise of Shakespeare in print before 1709, these studies are informed by a teleological desire which foregrounds familiar (and therefore *properly* editorial) strategies at the expense of the much wider and more representative textual practices explored in this book.

The editorial tradition ushered in by Rowe at the beginning of the eighteenth century did not rise out of a textual and bibliographical vacuum. In her study on the interrelation between theatrical and print cultures, Julie Stone Peters has helpfully stressed that editorial strategies for the correction of vernacular drama were not unknown in the sixteenth and seventeenth centuries and that the invention of the movable type modified pre-existing methods of editorial intervention devised for the transmission of manuscript texts during the medieval period. More specifically, Peters has identified a link between the opportunities offered by the new technology and the desirability of new standards of textual accuracy: 'print was driven by the scholarly need for well-edited texts; editing was driven by the commercial possibilities the press provided' (2000: 131). The need for well edited texts extended to classical drama, which was made newly available in scholarly editions by Continental editors and publishers. In turn, as Peters continues, '[f]rom their work and the general culture of textual production, principles of textual editing (or at least its claims) filtered into ordinary dramatic publication' (2000: 131). It is well known that such claims became increasingly common on the title pages of English printed playbooks, which often boast of being 'newly corrected and amended'. However, whether such claims represent a mere marketing ploy which gestured towards Continental editorial practices or whether they generally suggest a genuine attempt to correct the text remains largely to be established. Even more importantly, no systematic study has so far identified the principles which informed the intervention of early modern correctors who prepared dramatic copy for the press.

A systematic study of editorial practices in the sixteenth and seventeenth centuries has traditionally been hindered by a drastic lack of documentary evidence. A recent survey of extant manuscript and printed texts used in the printing house to set up known editions of early modern books includes no dramatic titles (Moore 1992).[5] However, the lack of documentary evidence showing the extent to which dramatic copy may have been annotated in preparation for the press should not by itself rule out the occurrence of such practice. Circumstantial evidence suggests that

annotation of manuscript or printed dramatic copy prior to its transmission into print was in fact far from uncommon and that it was generally
valued as a good selling point by early modern publishers.[6] The most
explicit reference to this practice occurs in the stationers' address to the
reader in the second edition of Beaumont and Fletcher's *Comedies and
Tragedies* (Wing B1582, 1679):

> Courteous Reader, THE First Edition of these Plays in this Volume having found
> that Acceptance as to give us Encouragement to make a Second Impression, we
> were very desirous they might come forth as Correct as might be. And we were very
> opportunely informed of a Copy which an ingenious and worthy Gentleman had
> taken the pains (or rather the pleasure) to read over; wherein he had all along
> Corrected several faults (some very gross) which had crept in by the frequent
> imprinting of them. His Corrections were the more to be valued, because he had
> an intimacy with both our Authors, and had been a Spectator of most of them
> when they were Acted in their life-time. This therefore we resolved to purchase at
> any Rate; and accordingly with no small cost obtain'd it. (A1 5–16)

According to Fredson Bowers, this unusually detailed account of the origin
of the corrections introduced in the second edition of Beaumont and
Fletcher's *Comedies and Tragedies* is corroborated by the fact that some of
its variants seem to stem from 'educated guesses' rather than from consultation of a different textual witness unknown to us (Bowers 1966–96: III
242). Also of special interest in this passage are the publishers' willingness to
invest in an annotated copy of the First Folio of 1647 and their decision to
advertise the origin of such copy to attract prospective readers.

Dedications and addresses to the reader prefaced to early modern
printed playbooks confirm that the annotation of the printer's copy for
the press was widely recognized as a desirable practice. Sir Aston Cokayne,
for example, tells his readers about his efforts to prevent the impression of
his *Trappolin Suppos'd a Prince* from a defective copy, after failing to stop
an incomplete version of his earlier play, *The Obstinate Lady*, from reaching
the press:

> I was fearful my *Trappolin*, and other Poems should have run the like mis-
> fortune; and therefore made a diligent enquiry after them, and when I had
> found them out could not get them delivered without parting with some
> money, and promising my honest friend Mr. *W. Godbid* (after I had afforded
> them some small correction) I would bestow them on him, (with my consent) for
> the Press. (Wing C4898, 1658, A3v 18–20, A4r 1–10)

Authors were not the only party with an interest in advertising the origin of
the printer's copy. Publishers of playbooks were similarly anxious to vouch

for its quality and were far more likely to blame printers than authors for the shortcomings of the printed text which was set from it. A good example of this type of allusion to the printer's copy can be found in a 'Postscript' to *Comedies, Tragi-Comedies, With other Poems, by Mr William Cartwright*, where the publisher Humphrey Moseley stresses that '[t]he Printer's faults (such as they are) must lye at his own door; for the written Coppy was very exact' (Wing C709, 1651, 4*6 18–20).

The practice of annotating a manuscript or printed copy for the press was not only common but also distinctive enough to warrant the use of specific terminology to distinguish it from other editorial activities. If starting from the beginning of the nineteenth century the verb 'to perfect' was used specifically in typography to mean 'to complete the printing of a sheet of a book, etc. by printing the second side' (*OED* v.1.b), in the sixteenth and seventeenth centuries it meant both 'to bring to completion' (*OED*, v.1.a) and 'to make perfect or faultless' (*OED* v.3), and was often used to indicate the process of getting a manuscript or printed text ready for its (re)transmission into print.

The paratextual materials prefaced to early modern dramatic and non-dramatic printed books provide examples of both usages. In 1590, a publisher's address in Henry Smith's *A Sermon of the benefite of Contentation. ... Taken by Characterie* (STC 22693) confirms that the printer's copy had reached the press without the author's permission, the word 'characterie' in the title indicating one of the most popular methods of stenography regularly used at the end of the sixteenth century to transcribe sermons as they were preached. A year later Smith revised and fleshed out the version preserved in the 1590 edition. In his address to the reader he conveniently specifies that his revision consisted both in perfecting the matter, that is in providing passages that had been accidentally omitted in the first edition, and in correcting typographical errors: 'HEaring how fast this Sermon hath uttered, and yet howe misarablye it hath bin abused in Printing, as it were with whole lims cut off at once, and cleane left out, I haue taken a little paines (as my sicknesse gaue me leaue) both to perfit the matter, and to correct the print' (STC 22696.5, 1591, A2r 2–14). Similarly, Nicholas Ling, the publisher who compiled and edited several collections of aphorisms, common-places and proverbs, including *Politeuphuia* (STC 15685, 1597), addresses his dedicatee by proudly announcing that 'what you seriously began long since, and haue alwaies beene very careful for the full perfection of, at length thus finished, ... I present you with' (A2r, 5–11). If these two examples show how the verb 'to perfect' was currently used to mean 'to complete, to finish', other examples indicate that the same verb was also used to mean 'to correct, to make perfect or faultless' and was applied specifically to the preparation of the printer's copy for the press. Theophilus Lavender, the compiler of *The Trauels of foure English men and preacher into Africa ...* (STC 3052, 1612), specifically distinguishes desirable additions from the perfecting of errors, thus reversing the distinction set up by Henry Smith in the revised edition of his *The Benefite of Contentation*: 'the publishing hereof without the Authors consent, may perhaps be an inducement vnto him to enlarge this discourse, by adding thereunto the diuersities of Religions in those Countries, ... and by perfiting any thing which herein shall be thought imperfect' (B2r 18–24).

Allusions to the 'perfection' of the printer's copy can also be found in early modern printed playbooks. Sometimes the verb 'to perfect' is used ambiguously, and it is impossible to gather from the context whether it is used to mean 'to complete' or 'to correct'. George Chapman, for example, having reassured the dedicatee of his *The Widow's Tears, A Comedy* (STC 4994, 1612) that '[o]ther Countrie men haue thought the like [that is, playbooks] worthie of Dukes and Princes acceptations', promises to 'select, and perfect, out of my other Studies, that may better expresse me' (A2r 8–10, 20–1). In this instance, 'to perfect' could mean either 'to finish' or 'to correct'. Fortunately, other early modern dramatic paratexts are far more explicit when it comes to describing the process whereby the printer's copy was prepared for the press. In 1576, the printer and publisher Richard Jones prefaced his edition of *The Princelye Pleasures, at the Courte at Kenelwoorth*[7] with an address to the reader where the phrase 'perfect Copies' clearly means 'complete':

I thought meete to trye by all meanes possible if I might recouer the true Copies of the same [that is, the entertainment at Kenilworth], to gratifye all suche as had requyred them at my handes, or might hereafter bee styrred with the lyke desire. And in fine I haue with much trauayle and paine obtained the very true and perfect Copies, *of all that were there presented.* (my emphasis, Greg 1939–59: 1195)

In Whetstone's *Promos and Cassandra* (STC 25347, 1578), also printed and published by Richard Jones two years later, both author and publisher refer to the preparation of the manuscript copy of this play for the press. In his dedicatory epistle, George Whetstone uses the adjective 'vnperfect' to explain how his personal circumstances prevented him from correcting the text of this comedy before it was handed over to Jones:

Syr, ... of late I perused diuers of my vnperfect workes, fully minded to bestowe on you, the trauell of some of my forepassed time. But (resolued to accompanye, the aduenturous Captaine, Syr *Humphrey Gylbert*, in his honorable voiadge,) I found my leysure too littel, to correct the errors of my sayd workes. So that (inforced) I lefte them disparsed, amonge my learned freendes, at theyr leasure, to polish, if I faild to returne. (A2r 5–16)

Whetstone makes clear that the process of transferring a manuscript work into print involved a specific stage during which an 'vnperfect' work was 'polished' and corrected. Richard Jones added an address to the reader, which reinforces the impression that both authors and publishers regarded a manuscript copy as deficient, if the author had been unable to perfect it:

GEntle Reader, this labour of Maister Whetstons, came into my handes, in his fyrst coppy, whose leasure was so lyttle (being then readie to depart his country) that he had no time to worke it a new, nor to geue apt instructions, to prynte so difficult a worke, beyng full of variety, both matter, speache, and verse . . . so that, if I commit an error, without blaming the Auctor, amend my amisse. (A3v 2–11)

Jones's address is also useful to establish that if the author was not available to perfect his work, it was still preferable for another willing agent, including the publisher, to correct it in preparation for the press rather than to print the author's 'fyrst coppy'.[8]

The desirability of editorially annotated copy over an imperfect one emerges both in single and in collected editions of early modern playbooks. The 1591 edition of Lyly's *Endymion, the Man in the Moon* (STC 17050) includes an address to the reader, where the publisher[9] explains that '[s]ince the Plaies in Paules were dissolued, there are certaine Commedies come to my handes by chaunce, vvhich were presented before her Maiestie at seuerall times by the children of Paules', and that 'if any place [*Endymion*] shall dysplease, I will take more paines to perfect the next' (A2r 3–11). The publisher's emphasis on aspects of this play that may 'displease' its readers rather than errors, along with the fact that the text of this play is exceptionally good,[10] may suggest that the manuscript copy did not require the intervention of a correcting hand, but may have elicited the publisher's intervention as a censoring agent. Far more explicit is the reference to the perfection of copy in the well-known and often quoted dedicatory epistle signed by Heminge and Condell included in Shakespeare's First Folio of 1623 (STC 22273).[11] Although Heminge and Condell inform their readers that they have acted as the custodians of Shakespeare's works and they are now simply presenting them to two worthy patrons – 'We haue but collected them, and done an office to the dead, to procure his Orphanes, Guardians' (A2v 5–6) – later on in the same epistle they specify that 'it hath bin the height of our care, vvho are the Presenters, to make the present worthy of your H.H. by the perfection' (A2v 11–13). The final sentence confirms that the printer's copy of Shakespeare's works as they appear in the First Folio had been prepared for the press and that Heminge and Condell take at least nominal responsibility for it: 'we most humbly consecrate to your H.H. these remaines of your seruant Shakespeare; that what delight is in them, may be euer your L.L. the reputation his, & the faults ours' (A2v 20–3).

The last four examples show that editorial annotation of copy seems to have been deemed not only acceptable but desirable even when the author was unavailable to act as the 'exequutor of his owne writings' (A2r 27–8). However, further examples show that if 'to perfect' meant 'to complete' rather than 'to correct' then the identity of the annotator did make a difference. Towards the end of the Interregnum, publishers of English drama became particularly eager to stress that their function was to preserve, rather than to perfect, the legacy of playwrights who had not survived the recent period of profound political changes and the closure of the theatres. When Humphrey Moseley published *The Last Remains of Sr John Suckling* in 1659, he lamented both the author's death and the blow inflicted on the court culture within which his works had first been conceived and enjoyed. Moseley was however comforted by the happy arrangement which ensured the survival of Suckling's works before he was forced to go abroad. As he explains to his readers,

> being sequestred from the more serene Contentments of his native Country, [Suckling] first took care to secure the dearest and choisest of his Papers in the several Cabinets of his Noble and faithful Friends; and among other Testimonies of his worth, these elegant and florid Peeces of his Fancie were preserved in the custody of his truly honorable and vertuous Sister, with whose free permission they were transcribed, and now published exactly according to the Originals. This might be sufficient to make you acknowledge that these are the real and genuine Works of Sir *John Suckling*. (Wing s6130, A2v 3–19, A3r 1–2)

The moral integrity of the preservers of Suckling's works, 'his Noble and faithful Friends' and 'his truly honorable and vertuous Sister', is metonymically transferred to the printer's copy to guarantee its authenticity. Moseley seems particularly keen to celebrate the fact that copies of Suckling's works survived, unscathed, the temporary usurpation of legitimate political authority. A further address to the reader prefaced to the one dramatic work included by Moseley in his collection, namely Suckling's *The Sad One: A Tragedy*,[12] usefully contrasts the use of the terms 'imperfect' (that is 'erroneous' or 'faulty') and 'unfinish'd', to emphasize the fact that albeit 'unfinish'd', Suckling's copy required no annotating or perfecting hand to prepare it for the press:

> I Hope I shall not need to crave your pardon for publishing this Dramatick Piece of Sir *John Suckling*, (Imperfect I cannot say, but rather unfinish'd) there being a kind

of Perfection even in the most deficient Fragments of this incomparable *Author*. To evince that this Copy was a faithful Transcript from his own handwriting, I have said enough in my former Epistle, and I thought it much better to send it into the world in the same state I found it, without the least addition, then procure it supplied by any other Pen. (A2r 3–11, A2v 1–7)

When, as in this instance, 'to perfect' means 'to supplement' by means of additions supplied by a different agent, then the incomplete fragment is regarded as a preferable alternative.

Also in 1659, Andrew Crooke and Henry Brome published a collection of *Five New Plays* by Richard Brome (Wing B4872) and prefaced it with an address to the reader which places a strong emphasis on their direct descent from authorial manuscripts: '[a]s for the *Stationers*, they bring these *Poems* as they had them from the *Author*, not suffering any false or busy hand to adde or make the least mutilation; having been more watchful over the Printers common negligence, than such work as this hath usually obtained' (A5v 8–15). The publishers' allusion to interference with authorial copy as a 'mutilation' inflicted on the sovereign body of the author's work reminds readers in the late 1650s of other outrageous acts of desecration of legitimate authority. A further allusion to the desirability of publishing five pre-revolutionary comedies in the late 1650s – 'for (a man would think) we have had too many *Tragedies*' (A3v 11–13) – reinforces the link, as in Moseley's edition of Suckling's works, between political and textual crimes which threaten the purity of genealogical and stemmatic lines of descent.

The later date of Suckling's and Brome's collections would seem to suggest a temporal shift in attitudes toward non-authorial preparation of dramatic copy for the press. However, while the emphasis placed on the link between the dead authors and their works is certainly in keeping with emergent models of singular and proprietary authorship,[13] the desirability of authoritative texts and of non-authorial annotation of copy are not mutually exclusive, as shown by a further reference to the quality of the printer's copy in the stationers' address to the reader prefaced to the second edition of Beaumont and Fletcher's *Comedies and Tragedies*. Having explained how the plays included in the first edition of 1647 had been annotated by a 'worthy Gentleman [who] had taken the pains (or rather the pleasure) to read over', the stationers proceed to advertise their new edition as 'incorrupt and genuine' (A1v 4–5), thus indicating that non-authorial correction (as opposed to completion) of the printer's copy was not seen as spurious interference.

More generally, while non-authorial completion or revision of an authoritative, though fragmentary, copy was increasingly regarded as detrimental tampering, non-authorial preparation of dramatic copy for the press was valued both when it corrected a manuscript draft of a work which the author had failed to perfect and when it corrected imperfections which had found their way into earlier editions then used as printer's copy for later re-issues. Whether carried out by the author or by an annotator, the perfection of the printer's copy was seen as a necessary stage in the process of transmission of both dramatic and non-dramatic texts through the press. Preparation for the press was even described by Sir Aston Cokayne as a proper process, or 'method', specifically intended to negotiate the transmission of his dramatic works from manuscript to print: 'I have made some progress into a Play, to be called the Tragedy of *Ovid*, which (if my *Obstinate Lady*, and *Trappolin* take) I may be encouraged to perfect, and present to you hereafter, with some other things that are not yet put into method, fit for the Press' (*Small Poems of Divers Sorts* WING C4898, 1658, A5v 5–13).

To sum up, the allusions to preparation of copy in early modern printed playbooks collectively suggest that the widely held assumption, according to which dramatic texts printed more than once before 1709 simply deteriorated through the accumulation of new typographical errors as they were repeatedly submitted to the press, needs to be carefully revisited.[14]

'PUTTING INTO METHOD FIT FOR THE PRESS': OR, HOW DRAMATIC COPY WAS PREPARED FOR THE PRESS

The allusions to the perfection of dramatic copy surveyed above usefully foreground annotating readers as a previously overlooked category of textual agents involved in the transmission of English drama into print. However, they shed little light on their impact on the actual readings preserved by early printed playbooks. Since, as mentioned above, no manuscript or printed copies used to set up extant editions of early English drama have survived, the best way to establish how dramatic texts were perfected for the press is to identify patterns of textual variation in plays which were printed more than once, especially when they claim to be 'newly perused and amended' on their title pages. The case studies included in the second part of this book accordingly focus on the evolution of the texts of a selection of Shakespeare's plays as they were repeatedly reprinted during the late sixteenth and the seventeenth centuries, and not on their transmission from manuscript to print.

Among the first printed playbooks to advertise editorial intervention on their title pages and to survive in more than one edition are the third quarto of *1 Henry IV* and the third quarto of Shakespeare's *Richard III*, which were published by Andrew Wise in 1599 and 1602. The Shakespearean quartos published by Wise are discussed in detail in chapter 3 below. What is worth mentioning here is the type of substantive variants which found their way into the third quartos of *1 Henry IV* and *Richard III*. The latter, which is advertised on its title page as being 'Newly augmented, by William Shakespeare', adds five new stage directions and modifies two, while the former, which is advertised on its title page as being 'Newly corrected by W. Shakespeare', corrects a mis-assigned speech prefix. Also significant is the fact that the second quarto of *Richard III* adds two lines of dialogue, although no editorial pledge is included in its title page.

Collectively these three quartos introduce corrections which affect speech prefixes, stage directions and the text of the dialogue. This type of corrections resembles the changes introduced in other editions where the paratexts advertise the intervention of an annotating reader. One good example is the second edition of Beaumont and Fletcher's *Comedies and Tragedies* (1679), where local variants, as mentioned above, are believed to stem from 'educated guesses' rather than from consultation of a different textual witness (Bowers 1966–96: III 242). One of these plays is *A Wife for a Month*. Its Cambridge editor, Robert Kean Turner, argues that the corrections in the 1679 text required access to no other version than the first edition of 1647: 'several . . . alterations', he explains, 'are shrewd and apparently right, but none seems beyond the capacity of a thoughtful reader' (Bowers 1966–96: VI 366). The corrections in the 1679 text of this play are sporadic and target missing or misleading stage directions, missing or mis-assigned speech prefixes and non-sensical readings in the dialogue. More specifically, two stage directions are added at 3.2.118 and 3.2.119, and another is modified at 3.3.0.1,[15] a missing stage direction and a missing speech prefix are added at 4.2.3, another stage direction is modified to add a character involved in the action at 1.2.49, and a reading in the dialogue is improved so that 'face' is replaced by 'fann' in Frederick's line 'hold your fann between, you have eaten Onions' at 4.2.15.

What the corrections in the Shakespearean quartos published by Wise and in the second edition of *A Wife for a Month* have in common is that they imply some familiarity with the fictive world of the play. As such they cannot be safely attributed to agents associated with the printing house, because, as indicated by Joseph Moxon's tract on the *Art of Printing* (1683–4), compositors and printing house correctors focused on spelling, pointing (or punctuation) and typographical inaccuracies, and not on inconsistencies in speech prefixes, stage directions and dialogue.

According to Moxon, a corrector should be 'well skilled in Languages . . . very knowing in Derivations and Etymologies of Words, [and] very sagacious in *Pointing*'. In other words, the corrector was expected to improve the formal qualities of the text by paying special attention to the spelling of foreign or unusual words and to '*Pointing, Italicking*, [and] *Capitalling*' (Moxon 1958: 246–7), or what W. W. Greg would call 'accidentals'. Even when advising authors on how best to prepare copy for the press, Moxon is solely concerned with the formal accuracy of the text:

> it behoves an Author to examine his *Copy* very well e're he deliver it to the *Printer*, and to Point it, and mark it so as the *Compositer* may know what Words to *Set* in *Italick, English, Capitals, &c*. (Moxon 1958: 250)

Nowhere in his tract on the art of printing does Moxon regard the accuracy of the 'signified', or, more specifically, the dramatic consistency of the fictive world of the play, as a concern for the agents involved in correcting and setting the text in the printing house.[16]

Moxon's manual was written at the end of the seventeenth century, and although printing house practices must have evolved during the intervening two centuries since the advent of print, Moxon's description of the task of the compositor and the printing house corrector is corroborated by extant specimens of earlier proof-sheets. The Bridgewater copy of *The First Part of the Contention*, for example, which was printed by Valentine Simmes for Thomas Millington in 1600 (STC 26100, Huntington Library, 79,885), preserves manuscript corrections on the outer forme of sheet B, which were then introduced in other copies of the same edition. Tucker Brooke, who first identified outer B as a proof-sheet, concluded that out of the 'twenty-one distinct changes called for by the manuscript marks, . . . sixteen . . . are mere matters of punctuation, four improve the spelling, and one corrects the spacing' (Brooke 1931: 88).[17] Accordingly, textual scholars tend to focus compositorial studies on accidental variants alone. Don McKenzie, for example, in his study of the second quarto of *The Merchant of Venice* (1619), which was set from the first quarto (1600) by compositor B in William Jaggard's printing shop, established that 'most features of presentation certainly, spellings almost certainly, and punctuation very probably, were the compositor's concern' but that substantive changes in speech prefixes and stage directions were not: '[s]ince they appear to have all the characteristics of planned rather than impromptu editing, I shall assume that substantive changes in stage directions and speech prefix forms were not made by compositor B' (1959: 75–6).

The type and range of corrections introduced in the Shakespearean Quartos published by Wise and in the second edition of *A Wife for a Month* are also radically different from the annotation of theatrical documents used to regulate performance. Extant printed play texts annotated for performance show that theatrical annotators were more likely to add sound and prop cues as well as directions which cleared the stage or signalled the use of props supplied by stage hands, rather than by actors with speaking parts (Baskerville 1932–3: 29–51 and Thomson 1996: 76–210).[18] In other words, theatrical annotators did not intervene to normalize speech prefixes, to alter the dialogue, or to add stage directions unless they involved substantial changes in the stage action. Theatrical agents did generally intervene more frequently and more widely when they prepared manuscript copies for performance. The scribe and book-keeper who copied Henry Glapthorne's *The Lady Mother*, for example, also corrected the dialogue on two occasions and added the missing name of a character to a stage direction (Brown 1959: viii). The intervention of the stage-adapter in Philip Massinger's autograph manuscript of *Believe as You List* is even more extensive, ranging from the addition of stage directions, names of actors, and other indications necessary to make the copy serve for prompt use, to 'corrections in the text', which suggest that 'the stage adapter was charged with the duty of general supervision of the play as it was submitted by Massinger, as well as the especial function of preparing it for the stage' (Sisson 1928: xv, xxi).

The fact that theatrical annotators of printed copy seem not to have interfered with the text of the play may indicate that transmission into print was assumed to have already removed at least some of the most obvious inconsistencies and general untidiness associated with dramatic manuscripts prior to their annotation for performance. However, even theatrical annotators of manuscript copy, who seem to have intervened more often than theatrical annotators of printed copy, paid only cursory attention to the overall quality of the text. As William B. Long points out,

Elizabethan-Jacobean-Caroline theatrical notation was a reaction to a problem, not an end in itself.... There was no marking for regularity or thoroughness, no set group of alterations made to a manuscript once it got to a theater. There was no 'tidying up' or 'regularization'.... None of the theatrical personnel who add notations to the surviving playbooks shows any inclination to clarify, particularize, or regularize either stage directions or speech headings. (1999: 417, 419)

More generally, as noted by Grace Ioppolo, theatrical annotators can hardly be taken to have been directly involved with the preparation of copy for the press: 'any theory that an acting company would have had to prepare or maintain copies eventually suitable for readers', as Ioppolo explains, 'is insupportable from the kind of records kept by [Philip] Henslowe and other theatrical businessmen' (2006: 182).

The closest counterpart to the emendations introduced in the Shakespearean Quartos published by Wise and the second edition of *A Wife for a Month* are manuscript corrections which are preserved in early modern printed playbooks and which pre-date the rise of a proprietary editorial tradition at the beginning of the eighteenth century. Although none of these annotated editions was used as printer's copy for subsequent editions, their manuscript annotations show how an early modern reader would have perfected a dramatic text, that is, what an early modern reader, as opposed to an eighteenth-century or a twenty-first-century editor, would have noticed as demanding emendation.

The most common types of manuscript annotations in early modern printed playbooks are sporadic corrections in the main body of the dramatic text and include: (1) the occasional addition or correction of stage directions; (2) the occasional addition or correction of speech prefixes; and (3) the occasional correction of nonsensical readings in the dialogue. Most isolated corrections are difficult, if not impossible, to date. However, some isolated annotations can be dated thanks to the fact that some letters, which were distinctive of sixteenth- and seventeenth-century secretary hands, fell out of use around the turn of the eighteenth century.

Manuscript annotations in distinctively early hands show that early readers intervened when their familiarity with the fictive world of the play allowed them to spot mis-assigned or missing speech prefixes, when their memories of the play as performed or their understanding of theatrical conventions prompted them to add or edit stage directions, and when their attention was caught by compositorial mistakes in the dialogue. The following are some representative examples. Missing speech prefixes are supplied in copies of *The Pedlar's Prophecy* (STC 25782: 1595, BL C.34.b.37, D2v 36, fig. 1) and the anonymous *The Downfall of Robert, Earl of Huntingdon* (STC 18271: 1601, BL 161.k.70, G3v 6 and G3v 17, fig. 2). A missing character – 'and Honesty' – is added to the opening stage direction – 'Enter King Edgar, bishop Dunston, and Perin a courtier' – in a copy of *A Knack to Know a Knave* (STC 15027: 1594, BL C.34.b.26, A2r 3, fig. 3). Corrections to the dialogue in distinctively early hands can be found in copies of the 1606 edition of Part II of Christopher Marlowe's *Tamburlaine the Great* (STC 17428a: 1606, BL 82.C.22(1), D2v 29, fig. 4), the second edition of *Orlando Furioso* (STC 12266: 1599, BL C.34.h.13, B1r 23, fig. 5) and the second edition of John Marston's *The Malcontent* (STC 17480: 1604, BL C.39.c.25, C4v 19 and C4v 27–8, fig. 6). Corrections introduced by

The Pedlers

And that with the moſt deteſtable Barbarians,
Which here for euer hath their dwellings fixed:
Still you Mariners bring them in daily,
So you may haue pence,
You make your ſelues rich and go gaily,
I would you were as readie to carry them hence.
You would bring in the diuell for pence and groates:
Ye ſhall ſee them one day play their parts gaily,
When we thinke leaſt, they ſhall cut our throates.

Mar. They that wil talke at their pleaſure what they will,
Shail heare againe, that ſhall them diſpleaſe,
But what frantike fooles ſay, it doth not greatly skill,
For your talke doth neither profit nor diſprofit a peace:
But whereas thou laieſt to the charge of Mariners,
That we haue filled the land full of Alians,
Thou belieſt vs, we bring in none but Goſpellers,
And ſuch as we know to be very good Chriſtians.

Ped. Oh holy Ghoſpell, ô tydings of health moſt pure,
Thou art made a cloake to all abhomination,
Vengeance hangeth ouer your head be you ſure,
For miſuſing the word of mans ſaluation,
What miſchieſe and outrage hath bene wrought,
And that vnder the pretence of the Goſpell,
There is no hereſie, no impietie, no ſacriledge on ſought,
And all painted out, with the cullour of the Goſpell.

Arti. Of the Goſpell we do boaſt, and do it profeſſe,
But more honeſt fidelitie is among Turkes,
O the boaſting, the pride, and the fleſhly exceſſe,
Among vs is neither true faith, nor yet good workes.

Tra. Speake of your ſelfe friend, and of no man elſe,
You know no mans conſcience but your owne,
VVe are men of fleſh and blood, and no Angels,
VVhat euery man is, to God it is knowne.

Ped. VVill you haue one word for all?
All. VVhat is that?
Ped. Ye are naught all:

And

1. *The Pedlar's Prophecy,* 1595

The down-fall of Robert

All in one voice, with a confused cry,
In execrations band you bitterly,
Plague followe plague, they cry, he hath vndone
The good Lord Robert, Earle of Huntington:
And then
What then, thou villane? Get thee from my sight.
They that with plagues, plagues wil vpon them light.
 ¶ Enter another seruant.
  Pri. What are your tidings?
  Ser. The Couent of Saint Maries are agreed,
And haue elected, in your Lordshippes place,
Olde father Ierome, who is ffald Lord Prior,
By the newe Archbishoppe.
  Pri. Of Yorke thou meanst.
A vengeance on him, he is my hopes foe.
            Enter a Herald.
  Gilbert de Hood late Prior of Saint Maries,
Our Soueraigne Iohn commandeth thee by mee,
That presently thou leaue this blessed land,
Defiled with the burden of thy sinne.
All thy goods temporall and spirituall,
(With free consent of Hubert Lorde Yorke,
Primate of England and thy Ordinary)
He hath suspended, and vow'd by heauen,
To hang thee vp, if thou depart not hence,
Without delaying or more question:
And that he hath good reason for the same,
He sends this writing firm'd with Warmans hand,
And comes himselfe: whose presence if thou stay,
I feare this Sunne will see thy dying day.
  Pri. O, Warman hath betraid mee: woe is mee.
   ¶ Enter *Iohn*, Queene, *Chester*, *Salsbury*.
  Ioh. Hence with that Prior, sirra do not speake,
My eyes are full of wrath, my heart of wreake:
Let Lester come, his hault hart, I am sure,

                                                Will

2. *The Downfall of Robert, Earl of Huntingdon*, 1601

A merie Knacke to

knowe a Knaue,

Enter King Edgar, bishop Dunston, and Perin a courtier.

and Honesty

King. DVnston, how highlie are we bound to praise
The Eternall God that still prouides for vs,
And giues vs leaue to rule in this our land,
Lyke wise Vaspasian, Romes rich Emperour:
Suppressing sinne, that daylie raignes in vs :
First, murther we rewarde with present death,
And those that doe commit fellonious crimes,
Our lawes of England doe awarde them death:
And hee that doeth dispoyle a Virgins chastitie,
Must lykewise suffer death by lawes decree,
And that decree is irreuocable.
Then as I am Gods Vicegerent heer on earth,
By Gods appointment heere to raigne and rule,
So must I seeke to cut abuses downe,
That lyke to Hydras heades, daylie growes vp one in ano-
And therein makes the land infectious.   (thers place,
Which if with good regard we looke not to,
We shall, lyke Sodom, feele that fierie doome,
That God in Iustice did inflict on them.
    Dunston. Your Graces care herein I much cummend,
And England hath iust cause to praise the Lorde,
That sent so good a King to gouerne them,
Your lyfe may be a Lanterne to the state,
By perfect signe of humilitie.
Howe blest had Sodome bene in sight of God,
If they had had so kinde a Gouernour,
They had then vndoubtedlie escapt that doome,
                          A 2   That

3. *A Knack to Know a Knave,* 1594

The Conqueſt of Tamburlaine

Tam. Iudge by thy ſelfe Theridamas, not me,
For preſently Techelles heere ſhall haſte,
To bid him battaile ere he paſſe to farre,
And loofe more labour then the gaine will quight.
Then ſhalt thou ſee the Scythian Tamburlaine,
Make but a ieſt to win the Perſean crowne.
Techelles, take a thouſand horſe with thee,
And bid him turne his backe to warre with vs,
That onely made him King, to make vs ſports,
We will not ſteale vpon him cowardly,
But giue him warning with more warriours.
Haſt thee Techelles, we will followe thee.
What ſaith Theridamus?
Ther. Go on for me. Exeunt.

Actus. 2. Scæna. 6.
Coſroe, Meander, Ortygius, Menaphon, with other
Souldiours.

Coſ. What meanes this diuelliſh ſhepherd to
With ſuch a gyantly preſumption: (aſpire
To caſt vp hilles againſt the face of heauen,
And dare the force of angry Iupiter.
But as he thruſt them vnderneath the hilles,
and preſt out fire from their burning iawes:
So will I ſend this monſtrous ſlaue to hell,
Where flames ſhall euer feede vpon his ſoule.
Men. Some powers diuine, or elſe infernall, mixt
Their angry ſeedes at his conception:
For he was neuer ſprung of humane race,
Since with the ſpirit of his fearefull pride,
He dare ſo doubtleſly reſolue of rule,
and by profeſſion be ambitious.
Ortig. What God, or fiend, or ſpirit of the earth
Or monſter turned to a manly ſhape.
Or of what mould, or mettle he be made,
What ſtarre or ſtate ſoeuer gouerne him,
Let vs put on our meete incountring mindes,

And

4. *Tamburlaine*, 1606

ORLANDO FVRIOSO.

Sith fathers will hangs on his daughters choyce,
And I as earst Princesse Andromache,
Seated amidst the crue of Priams sonnes,
Haue libertie to chuse where best I loue;
Must freely say, for fancie hath no fraud,
That farre vnworthy is Angelica
Of such as deigne to grace her with their loues.
The Souldan with his seate in Babylon,
The Prince of Cuba and of Mexico,
Whose wealthy Crownes might win a womans wil;
Yong Brandemart master of all the Iles,
Where Neptune planted hath his treasurie :
The worst of these men of so high import,
As may command a greater Dame then I.
But Fortune or some deepe inspiring fate,
Venus or els the bastard brat of Mars,
Whose bowe commands the motions of the minde,
Hath sent proud loue to enter such a plea,
As nonsutes all your Princely euidence,
And flat commands that maugre maiestie,
I chuse Orlando, Countie Palatine.
Rodam. How likes Marsillus of his daughters choice?
Marsillus. As fits Marsillus of his daughters spouse.
Rodamant. Highly thou wrong'st vs, King of Affrica,
To braue thy neighbour Princes with disgrace,
To tye thine honour to thy daughters thoughts,
Whose choyce is like that Greekish giglots loue,
That left her Lord, Prince Menelaus,

B   And

5. *Orlando Furioso*, 1599

MALECONTENT.

SCENA TERTIA.

Enter Duke Pietro, *Count* Celfo, *Count* Equato,
Bilioſo, Ferrard, *and* Mendoza.

Piet. The night growes deepe and fowle, what houre iſt?
Celſo. Vpon the ſtroake of twelue.
Mal. Saue yee Duke.
Piet. From thee, begone I do not loue thee, let me ſee
thee no more, we are diſpleaſd.
Mal. Why God buy thee, heauen heare my curſe,
May thy wife and thee liue long together.
Piet. Be gone ſirra.
Mal. When *Arthur* ſtrſt in Court began, — *Agamemnon*
Menelaus—was euer any Duke a *Cornuto* ?
Piet. Begon hence.
Mal. What religion wilt thou be of next?
Mend. Out with him.
Mal. With moſt ſeruile patience time will come,
When wonder of thy error will ſtrike dumbe,
Thy befeld ſence, ſlaues I fauour, I marry ſhall he, riſe,
„*Good God how ſubtile Hell doth flatter vice,*
„*Mount him aloſt, and makes him ſeeme to flie,*
„*As foule the* Tortois *mockt: who to the skie,*
„*T b' ambitious ſhell fiſh raiſ'd t b' end of all,*
„*Is onely that from height he might dead fall*   *Exit*
Piet. It ſhall be ſo.
Mend. It muſt be ſo, for where great States reuenge,
„ Tis requiſite, the parts with pietie
„ And ſoft reſpect forbeares, be cloſely dogd,
„ Lay one into his breaſt ſhall ſleepe with him,
„ Feede in the ſame diſh, run in ſelfe faction,
„ Who may diſcouer any ſhape of danger,
„ For once diſgrac'd, diſplaied in offence,
„ It makes man bluſhleſſe, and man is (all confeſſe)
           More

6. *The Malcontent,* 1604

early readers are sporadic and yet, at times, quite ingenious. The annotator of *Orlando Furioso*, for example, radically changes the sense of Marsillus's reply to Rodamant's question – 'How likes Marsillus of his daughters choice?' (B1r 22) – by shifting the emphasis from Orlando's eligibility as a son-in-law – 'As fits Marsillus of his daughters spouse' – to his confidence in his daughter's sound judgement – 'As fits Marsillus daughter of her spouse.' Similarly, the annotator of *The Malcontent* introduces corrections, which would only attract the attention of a careful reader. At C4v 27–8, for example, the annotator changes 'with' to 'which' and 'loft' to 'soft' in order to clarify the meaning of two obscure lines: 'Tis requisite, the parts with pietie / And loft respect forbeares, be closely dogd'. Although the annotator's intervention may not restore or clarify the text of this section of the dialogue, the proposed emendations effectively change lines whose original sense is far from obvious.

Rare instances of manuscript corrections which can be attributed to eminent seventeenth-century readers confirm that their intervention was prompted by their familiarity with the fictive world of the play. One example is a copy of George Chapman's *The Conspiracy and Tragedy of Charles, Duke of Byron* (STC 4969, 1625), which was densely annotated by Philip Herbert, Earl of Pembroke and Lord Chamberlain between 1626 and 1641. Herbert's annotations do not only provide a vivid political commentary which relates the action set in the French Court to the contemporary Court of Charles I, but they also emend several mistakes in the dialogue. As A. H. Tricomi has noticed, '[Herbert] is a careful, attentive reader [who] in several places emends the printed text like an editor' (1986: 335). King Charles himself annotated a copy of the fourth quarto of Francis Beaumont and John Fletcher's *The Maid's Tragedy* (STC 1680, 1638), which is bound with eight other plays in a single volume now in the holdings of the Bodleian Library (Malone 217). Like Herbert's, the King's annotations fall into two categories: straightforward corrections – one missing speech prefix is added on C1r 28 and two wrong ones are emended on H3v 35–6 (fig. 7) – and two additional speeches in 4.2.[19]

Some early modern playbooks preserve clusters of manuscript corrections, which, like the isolated corrections examined above, target missing or misleading stage directions, missing or mis-assigned speech prefixes, and non-sensical readings in the dialogue. A copy of George Peele's *Edward I*, for example, preserves a selection of manuscript corrections, including the emendation of two speech prefixes and the addition of a missing one (STC 19535: 1593, BL C.34.d.52, D2r 20, 25, fig. 8, and G1r 8, 9), the insertion of a

To thanke a man for pardoning of a crime
I never knew.

Kin. No: to insinuat your knowledge, but to shew you
my errors are every where, you meant to kill me, and get the
fort to scape.

Mel. Pardon me Sir, my blamenesse will be pardoned,
you preserve
A race of idle people here about you,
Eaters, and talkers, to defame the worth
Of those that doe things worthy, the man that uttered this
Had perish'd without food, bee't who it will,
But for this arme that fed him from the Foe.
And if I thought you gave a faith to this,
The plainnesse of my nature would speake more,
Give me a pardon (for you ought to doo't)
To kill him that spake this.

Cal. I that will be the end of all,
Then I am fairely paide for all my care and service.

Mel. That old man, who calls me enemy, and of whom I
(Though I will never much my hate so low,)
Have no good thought, would yet I thinke excuse me,
And sweare he thought me wrong'd in this.

Cal. Who I, thou shameles Fellow, didst thou not speake
to me of it thy selfe?

Mel. O then it came from him.

Cal. From me, who should it come from but from me?

Mel. Nay I beleeve your mallice is enough,
But I'm lost my anger, Sir I hope
You are well satisfied.

King. Lisip. cheare Amintor & his Lady, theres no found
Comes from you, I will come and doo't my selfe.

Amin. You have done already Sir for me I thanke you.

Kin. Melantius I doe credit this from him,
How slieght so ere you ma'kt.

Cal. Tis strange you should.

Cal. To strange he should beleeve an old mans word,
That nere lied in his life.

Mel.

Mel. I taake not to thee,
Shall the wild words of this distempered man,
Frenticke with age and sorrow, make a breach
Betwixt your Majestie and me? twas wrong
To hearken to him, but to credit him
As much, at least, as I have power to beare,
But pardon me, whilst I speake onely truth,
I may commend my selfe —— I have bestow'd
My carelesse blood with you, and should be loth
To thinke an action that would make me lose
That, and my thanks too: when I was a boy
I thrust my selfe into my Countries cause,
And did a deed, that pluckt five yeares from time,
And fill'd me man then, and for you my King
Your fable ha all have fed by vertue of my arme,
This sword of mine hath plowd the ground,
And reapt the fruit in peace;
And you your selfe have liv'd at home in ease:
So terrible I grew, that without swords
My name hath fetcht you conquest, and my heart
And limmes are fill'd the fame, my will is great
To doe you service: let me not be paid
With such a strange distrust.

King. Melantius, I hold it great injustice to beleeve
Thine enemie, and did not, if I did,
I doe not, let that satisfie: what fricke
With sadnesse all? more wine.

Cal. A few faire words have overthrowne my truth; *aside.*
Ah! art a Villaine.

Mel. Why thou wert better let me have the fort,
Dotard, I will disgrace thee thus for ever,
There shall no credit lie upon thy words;
Thinke better and deliver it.

Cal. My L rge, hees at me now agen to doe it, speake,
Denie it if thou canst, examine him
Whilst he is hot, for if he coole agen,
Hee will forsweare it.

King.

of *Edward I. Longshankes*.

Tell them the Chaines that *Mulciber* erst made,
To trie *Prometheus* lims to *Caucasus*,
Nor furies phanges shal hold me long from her,
But *I* will haue her from the vsurpers tent,
My beautious *Elinor* : if ought in this,
If in this case thy wit may boote thy friends,
Expres it then in this, in nothing els.

   Dauid. I theres a Carde that puts vs to our trumpe,
For might *I* see the starre of Leisters loines,
I were enough to darken and obscure,
This *Edwards* glorie, fortune, and his pride :
First hereof can I put you out of doubt,
Lord *Mortimor* of the king hath her in charge,
And honourable intreates your *Elinor*,
Some thinkes he praies *Lluellen* were in heauen,
And thereby hopes to coache his loue on earth.

   Lluel. No, where *Lluellen* mounts, there *Ellen* flies,
Inspeakeable are my thoughts for her,
Shee is not from me in death to be diuorst.

   Dauid. Go to, it shall be so, so shall it be,
Edward is full resolued of thy faith,
So are the English lords and Barons all:
Then what may let thee to intrude on them,
Some new found stratagem to feele their wit,
It is enough : *Meredeth* take my weapons,
I am your prisoner, say so at the least,
Go hence, and when yon parle on the walles,
Make shew of monstrous tirannie you intend,
To execute on me, as on the man,
That shamefullie rebels gainst kin and kinde:
And least thou haue thy loue, and make thy peace,
With such conditions as shall best concerne,
Dauid must die say thou a shamefull death,
Edward perhaps with ruthe and pittie moou'd,
Will in exchange yeelde *Elinor* to thee,
And thou by me shalt gaine thy hearts desire.

   Lluel. Sweetely aduized *Dauid*, thou blessest me,

D 2

My

8. *Edward I*, 1593

qualifying preposition in a stage direction – '*On the walles enter* [to] *Longshankes* …' – which would otherwise replicate an earlier one – '*Enter Longshankes, Sussex, and others*' (D2v 4, II) – and one correction in the dialogue (H1r I). The annotating hand responsible for these corrections seems early, as suggested by the prefix added on D2r (fig. 8). However, there is nothing specifically early modern about the other annotations added by the same hand. Dating this set of annotations is therefore difficult. Conversely, the annotations added by one or two hands to a copy of the first edition of *Othello* held at the Huntington Library and reproduced in Michael J. B. Allen and Kenneth Muir's *Shakespeare's Plays in Quarto* (Allen and Muir 1981) are distinctively early modern. The same early hand added at least four directions – 'A/side/to him/selfe' (E1r 9–5 up, fig. 9), 'Lets fall the / napkine' (H1v 9/10), 'othello kneeles' (H3v 9 up, fig. 10), and 'he strikes her' (K2v 17) – and three corrections in the dialogue – the 's' in 'meslt' is inked over and the corrected reading 'melt' is added underneath (D2v I up, fig. II), 'loues' is blotted out and 'hates' is added in the margin (G3v 10 up, fig. 12), and 'Not' in 'Not hot and moist' is crossed out and replaced by 'both', which is also added in the margin (H4v 12, fig. 13). Another early hand added a further correction to the dialogue by inserting 'without remorce' and a caret mark between 'be' and 'remorce' underneath Iago's line 'And to obey, shall be remorce' at H3v I up (fig. 10). Similarities in the colour and thickness of the ink suggest that the same hand also added a missing speech prefix (G4v I up).

The range of manuscript corrections introduced in annotated printed playbooks is representative of, but not unique to, the type of intervention associated with early modern annotating readers. While, as explained above, the impact of printing house and theatrical agents on the text of printed playbooks is radically different, the intervention of correcting authors[20] and annotating readers reveals intriguing similarities. One interesting example of a correcting author is provided by Philip Massinger, who annotated the Foljambe copy of *The Duke of Milan*, which is now part of the Dyce collection at the National Art Library at the Victoria and Albert Museum, and eight further copies of his plays, printed between 1624 and 1632 and once bound together in a presentation volume (Greg 1924–5: 59–61 and Simpson 1935: 26). Commenting on Massinger's annotations in *The Duke of Milan*, Greg pointed out that 'beyond their immediate importance for the restoration of the text, these corrections have a bibliographical interest as showing, in one instance at least, the degree of accuracy which an unaided compositor was able to attain in the opinion of the author whose work he was setting

The Moore of Venice.   · 25

For euen her folly helpt her, to a haire.

 Def. These are old paradoxes, to make fooles laugh i'the Alehouse,
What miserable praise hast thou for her,
That's foule and foolish?

 Iag. There's none so foule, and foolish thereunto,
But does foule prankes, which faire and wise ones doe.

 Defd. O heauy ignorance, that praises the worst best : but what
praise couldst thou bestow on a deseruing woman indeed? one,
that in the authority of her merrits, did iustly put on the vouch of
very malice it selfe?

 Iag. She that was euer faire, and neuer proud,
Had tongue at will, and yet was neuer lowd,
Neuer lackt gold, and yet went neuer gay,
Fled from her wish, and yet said, now I may :
She that being angred, her reuenge being nigh,
Bad her wrong stay, and her displeasure flye;
She that in wisedome, neuer was so fraile ,
To change the Codshead for the Salmons taile.
She that could thinke, and ne're disclose her minde,
She was a wight, if euer such wight were.

 Def. To doe what ?

 Iag. To suckle fooles, and chronicle small Beere.

 Def. O most lame and impotent conclusion:
Doe not learne of him *Emillia*, tho he be thy husband;
How say you *Cassio*, is he not a most prophane and liberall
Counsellour?

 Cas. He speakes home Madam, you may rellish him
More in the Souldier then in the Scholler.

 Iag. He takes her by the palme; I well sed, whisper : as little a
webbe as this will ensnare as great a Flee as *Cassio*. I smile vpon
her, doe : I will catch you in your owne courtesies: you say true,
tis so indeed. If such trickes as these strip you out of your Leiute-
nantry, it had beene better you had not kist your three fingers so oft,
which now againe, you are most apt to play the sir in : good , well
kist, an excellent courtesie ; tis so indeed: yet againe, your fingers at
your lips? Would they were Clisterpipes for your sake.--- The
Moore, I know his Trumpet.   *Trumpets within.*
     E   *Enter*

9. *Othello*, 1622

Oth. But this denoted a fore-gone conclusion,

Iag. Tis a shrewd doubt,tho it be but a dreame,

And this may helpe to thicken other proofes.

That doe demonstrate thinly.

Oth. I'le teare her all to peeces.

Iag. Nay,but be wise,yet we see nothing done,

She may be honest yet,tell me but this,

Haue you not sometimes seene a handkercher,

Spotted with strawberries in your wiues hand.

    Oth. I gaue her such a one,twas my first gift.

    Iag. I know not that,but such a handkercher,

I am sure it was your wiues,did I to day

See *Cassio* wipe his beard with.

    Oth. Ift be that.

    Iag. If it be that,or any▪was hers,

It speakes against her,with the other proofes.

    Oth. O that the slaue had forty thousand liues,

One is too poore,too weake for my reuenge :

Now doe I see tis time,looke here *Iago*,

All my fond loue,thus doe I blow to heauen,-- tis gone.

Arise blacke vengeance,from thy hollow Cell,

Yeeld vp O loue thy crowne,and harted Throne,

To tirranous hate,swell bosome with thy fraught,

For tis of Aspecks tongues.

    Iag. Pray be content.   *he kneeles.*

    Oth. O blood,*Iago*,blood.

    Iag. Patience I say,your mind perhaps may change.

    Oth. Neuer :

In the due reuerence of a sacred vow,   *othello kneeles*

I here ingage my words.

    Iag. Doe not rise yet :

Witnesse you euer-burning lights aboue,

You Elements that clip vs roundabout,   *Iago kneeles:*

Witnesse that here,*Iago* doth giue vp

The excellency of his wit,hand,heart,

To wrong'd *Othello's* seruice : let him command,

And to obey,shall be remorce,   *with out remorse*

                                                                     Whit

10. *Othello*, 1622

20   The Tragedy of Othello

And it is thought abroad, that twixt my sheetes
Ha's done my office; I know not, if't be true ---
Yet I, for meere suspition in that kind,
Will doe, as if for surety: he holds me well,
The better shall my purpose worke on him.
Cassio's a proper man, let me see now,
To get his place, and to make vp my will,
A double knauery --- how, how, --- let me see,
After some time, to abuse *Othelloe's* eare,
That he is too familiar with his wife:
He has a person and a smooth dispose,
To be suspected, fram'd to make women false:
The Moore a free and open nature too,
That thinkes men honest, that but seemes to be so:
And will as tenderly be led bit'h nose --- as Asses are:
I ha't, it is ingender'd: Hell and night
Must bring this monstrous birth to the worlds light.

                                                    Exit.

                    Actus 2.

                    Scœna 1.

        Enter Montanio, *Gouernor of* Cypres, *with*
                two other Gentlemen.

                Montanie.

VVHat from the Cape can you discerne at Sea?
        1 *Gent.* Nothing at all, it is a high wrought flood,
I cannot twixt the hauen and the mayne
Descry a saile.
    Mon. Me thinkes the wind does speake aloud at land,
A fuller blast ne're shooke our Battlements:
If it ha ruffiand so vpon the sea,
What ribbes of Oake, when the huge mountaine melt,

                                                        Can

11. *Othello,* 1622

46   *The Tragedy of* Othello

If thou but thinkeſt him wrongd, and makeſt his eare
A ſtranger to thy thoughts.
   Iag. I doe beſeech you,
Though I perchance am vicious in my gheſſe,
As I confeſſe it is my natures plague,
To ſpy into abuſes, and oft my iealouſie
Shapes faults that are not; I intreate you then,
From one that ſo imperfeƈtly conieƈts,
You'd take no notice, nor build your ſelfe a trouble,
Out of my ſcattering, and vnſure obſeruance;
It were not for your quiet, nor your good,
Nor for my manhood, honeſty, or wiſedome,
To let you know my thoughts,
   Oth. Zouns.
   Iag. Good name in man and woman's deere my Lord;
Is the immediate Iewell of our ſoules :
Who ſteales my purſe, ſteals traſh, tis ſomething, nothing,
Twas mine, tis his, and has bin ſlaue to thouſands :
But he that filches from me my good name,
Robs me of that, which not inriches him,
And makes me poore indeed.
   Oth. By heauen I'le know thy thought.
   Iag. You cannot, if my heart were in your hand,
Nor ſhall not, whilſt tis in my cuſtody :
O beware iealouſie.
It is the greene eyd monſter, which doth mocke
That meate it feedes on. That Cuckold liues in bliſſe,
Who certaine of his fate, loues not his wronger :
But oh, what damned minutes tells he ore,
Who dotes, yet doubts, ſuſpeƈts, yet ſtrongly loues.
   Oth. O miſery.
   Iag. Poore and content is rich, and rich enough,
But riches, fineleſſe, is as poore as winter,
To him that euer feares he ſhall be poore :
Good God, the ſoules of all my tribe defend
From iealouſie,
   Oth. Why, why is this ?

                                          Thinkſt

12. *Othello*, 1622

56   *The Tragedy of* Othello

Desd. Who he? I thinke the Sun where he was borne,
Drew all such humors from him.   *Enter* Othello.
    Em. Looke where he comes.
    Def. I will not leaue him now,
Let *Cassio* be cald to him: how is it with you my Lord?
    Oth. Well my good Lady: O hardnesse to dissemble:
How dee you *Desdomona?*
    Def. Well,my good Lord.
    Oth. Giue me your hand, this hand is moist my Lady.
    Def. It yet has felt no age,nor knowne no sorrow.
    Oth. This argues fruitfulnesse and liberall heart,
Not hot and moist,this hand of yours requires
A sequester from liberty: fasting and praying,
Much castigation, exercise deuout;
For heere's a young and swetting diuell here,
That commonly rebels: tis a good hand,
A franke one.
    Def. You may indeed say so,
For twas that hand that gaue away my heart.
    Oth. A liberall hand,the hearts of old gaue hands,
But our new herraldry is hands, not hearts.
    Def. I cannot speake of this,come,come,your promise.
    Oth. What premise chucke?
    Def. I haue sent to bid *Cassio* come speake with you.
    Oth. I haue a salt and sullen rhume offends me,
Lend me thy handkercher,
    Def. Here my Lord.
    Oth. That which I gaue you.
    Def. I haue it not about me.
    Oth. Not.
    Def. No faith my Lord.
    Oth. Thats a fault: that handkercher
Did an *Egyptian* to my mother giue,
She was a charmer,and could almost reade
The thoughts of people;she told her while she kept it,
T'would make her amiable,and subdue my father
Intirely to her loue :

         Or

13. *Othello,* 1622

up' (Greg 1923–24: 209–10). In other words, these corrections collectively show what Massinger deemed worth emending, thus providing an interesting counterpart to the corrections introduced by early annotating readers. Although quantitatively more extensive, Massinger's corrections left many mistakes unaltered. Besides, as well as tampering with spelling and punctuation, Massinger provided a few missing speech prefixes,[21] edited a stage direction,[22] and corrected several misreadings in the dialogue.[23]

The number, rather than the quality, of the emendations introduced by Massinger would seem to suggest that annotating readers can be distinguished from correcting authors by the relative infrequency of their intervention. However, at least one other early modern playwright made little effort to check the text of one of his plays for accuracy, as he contributed to the preparation of manuscript copies for sale or presentation: as Trevor Howard-Hill observes, besides acting as a transcribing author,[24] by adding many 'new refinements into any transcript that came to hand' (1993: 5), 'Middleton's single correction in the six manuscripts of [*A Game at Chess*] consists of the addition of a line . . . written in carelessly without indication of the speaker, in the vicinity of a correction made in another hand' (1987: 312).[25] Interestingly, five further corrections to the dialogue and to one stage direction were carried out by other unidentified hands (Howard-Hill 1993: 3).

It therefore follows that it may not be possible to distinguish the intervention of a correcting author from an annotating reader, unless the inclusion of paratextual materials sheds light on the circumstances surrounding dramatic publication or the correcting author also acted as a reviser or adapter of his own work, and changed other aspects of the text as he was cursorily emending it. More generally, the perfection of play texts set from printed copy during the sixteenth and the seventeenth centuries seems function- rather than agent-specific. This is why I believe that correctors of early modern dramatic copy for the press are best described as 'annotating readers'. First of all, this phrase highlights the fact that, whether correcting authors, publishers or gentlemen readers, these agents share a distinctive level of familiarity with the fictive world of the play as *readers*, which sets them apart from printing house and theatrical agents. Furthermore, this phrase draws attention to the fact that preparation of dramatic copy for the press was carried out by a variety of agents whose identity can seldom be established and therefore sharpens our sense of the level of indeterminacy of the attribution of sporadic corrections, which is intrinsic to the bibliographical make-up of early modern printed playbooks.

'GENTLE CORRECTORS': EDITORIAL AGENTS BEFORE 1709

As well as establishing how play texts were prepared for the press, this book identifies publishers as a major category of annotating readers or procurers of annotated copy. Generally, though, the identity of specific annotators can be determined only on the relatively rare occasions when the paratext discusses the printer's copy and the agent(s) involved in its annotation. The prevalent anonymity of these textual agents partly explains why their contribution has been systematically overlooked. However, other reasons seem equally significant. Another possible explanation is the privileging of authorial agency over other types of agents involved in the process of transmission of early modern play texts into print. It is well known how New Bibliographical methods, such as Greg's 'Rationale of Copy-text' (1950–1: 19–36), and New Bibliographical categories, such as A. W. Pollard's distinction between 'good' and 'bad' quartos (Pollard 1909), were specifically devised to help editors establish what extant printed version of a play text was closer to the work as intended by its author. Although New Bibliographical methods and categories have been repeatedly qualified by recent generations of textual scholars, the primacy of authorial agency lingers on. Tellingly, a recent development in the field of Shakespeare textual studies has led the scholarly community to consider the possibility that Shakespeare did not only write with the stage and the page in mind (Erne 2003), but that he may also have instructed his printers on matters of layout and expressive typography (Woudhuysen 2004: 69–100). While salutary in helping us redress our understanding of Shakespeare's investment in theatrical *and* print cultures, a renewed emphasis on 'Shakespeare as literary dramatist' has reinforced the optimistic assumption championed by the New Bibliography, according to which a direct line of transmission connected the author to the authorized editions of his works. Paradoxically, this new understanding of Shakespeare's attitude towards print culture shifts our attention back to what Paul Werstine calls an 'increasingly engorged author-function', which '[eats] up the army of . . . extra authorial agents' who actively contributed to the production of early modern printed texts as material artifacts (Werstine 1996: 50).

Another possible explanation for the neglect suffered by early modern correctors of dramatic copy is the perceived lack of documentary evidence. As Fredson Bowers explained while reviewing Greg's 'Rationale of Copy-text', 'if . . . [an editor] can be given a theoretical basis for believing that what he can neither detect nor measure cannot have existed, . . . [he] is spared having to take account of quite unassessable evidence' (Bowers 1978: 112).

In other words, while focusing on authorial or theatrical intentions worth preserving and typographical and editorial accidents in need to be purged and removed from modern editions gives an editor a clear and achievable strategy of intervention, contemplating the contribution of annotating agents who silently introduced sporadic corrections in the printer's copy complicates both our sense of what constitutes an 'authoritative' (as opposed to an 'authorial') text and our understanding of the role of the modern editor.

The effacement of early modern correctors of dramatic copy may also be due to the fact that most of the ones we can identify were publishers and that Shakespeare textual scholars and editors have traditionally questioned their moral and professional integrity. The theory of literary piracy perpetrated by the stationers who published Shakespeare's dramatic works during his lifetime dates as far back as the eighteenth century.[26] This theory was reinforced by the work of late twentieth-century scholars interested in the pre-history of copyright, who tended to represent the working relations between early modern authors and their publishers as oppositional.[27] Furthermore, allusions to the unauthorized sale of reported play texts, such as the often quoted prologue added to the 1639 quarto edition of *If You Know Not Me, You Know Nobody, Part I* (STC 13335), where Thomas Heywood explains that 'some by Stenography, drew / The Plot: put it in print, scarce one word true' (A2r 12–13), have often been used to argue that the phenomenon of literary piracy was widespread and that it affected the transmission of early modern play texts into print, including Shakespeare's early quarto editions. Heminge and Condell's famous claim in the dedicatory epistle prefaced to Shakespeare's Folio of 1623, according to which the Folio replaced earlier editions set up from 'stolne and surreptitious' copies, has similarly been taken to mean that *all* previous editions had been published without Shakespeare's or his company's consent. Pollard was among the first scholars to qualify this assumption. His influential distinction between 'good' and 'bad' quartos allowed him to 'redeem' some of the quarto editions pre-dating the Folio and their publishers. In a memorable passage he explains why the majority of early modern publishers should be cleared of the blot of fraud and thievery:

It may be most freely and willingly admitted that the theory that anyone could steal and print an Elizabethan play and obtain copyright in it by paying sixpence to the Stationers' Company, to the exclusion of the author and his assigns, does not conflict with the official functions either of the Censors of the Press or of the Stationers' Company. Neither the one nor the other were legally bound to show any consideration to authors. What the theory, when extended to cover not an isolated instance but a whole series of depredations, conflicts with is common sense and the English character. It is understood that in this happy land if various people in authority, from His Majesty the King downwards, did all the things they are legally entitled to, the Constitution would be in a sad plight. But these mysterious possibilities remain unfilled, and while they are unfulfilled no one troubles to obtain paper guarantees against them with the result that future historians will perhaps gravely argue that of course they happened. (1909: 10)

Pollard's trust in 'common sense' and 'the English character' is touching but hardly bears rigorous scrutiny. However, his views were indeed substantiated towards the end of the twentieth century by scholars who had a better understanding of the economics of the book trade.[28] One major advancement in the field of Shakespeare textual studies stemmed from Peter Blayney's realisation that the profit margins from the publication of play texts were not so good as previous scholars had assumed and that it was therefore safer to conclude that 'few early modern stationers ever imagined that the best way to make a quick fortune was to wrest – honestly or otherwise – a play or two from the supposedly protective clutch of an acting company' (1997: 389).

Blayney's conclusions were recently challenged by Alan Farmer and Zachary Lesser, who argued that printed playbooks 'turned a profit more reliably than most other types of books, and this profit would not have been paltry, as many have claimed, but rather would have been fairly typical for an edition of books' (2005: 6). The debate about the financial viability of dramatic publication is still ongoing.[29] It is however worth stressing that Farmer and Lesser have not contested Blayney's major argument according to which few London stationers would have been willing to venture into dramatic publication, let alone invest into 'maimed and surreptitious' copies of commercial play texts. Farmer and Lesser have rather pointed out that, although printed playbooks represented a profitable undertaking, not all London stationers would choose to publish them:

With a play, a publisher stood a far greater chance of earning the increased profits accruing from reprints than he did with the average speculative book ... This is not to say that all publishers wanted to publish plays, nor that every play was of equal interest to those publishers; early modern stationers tended to specialize in the kinds of books they published, playbooks included. Some stationers seem to have refused to deal with plays at all, whether because of personal moral objections, ..., or because they felt that plays did not fit their specialty and so would not sell well *for them*, regardless of the demand for plays in general. And even those stationers who did deal in plays did not simply publish every play that became available to them. (2005: 20–1)

Whether relatively more or less profitable than other books, printed play-books clearly represented a specialist type of publication. Moreover, as I will argue later on in this book, those stationers who chose dramatic publication over other types of books often did so because they had well-established connections with the world of the commercial theatre. These connections in turn suggest that those stationers who invested in dramatic publication, far from being literary pirates, were likely to receive the manuscript copies from which their editions were set either directly from the author or by members of his company.

Besides benefiting from the fresh insights gained through an interdisciplinary approach to textual studies and the book trade, our current understanding of the role of the early modern publishers has also been affected by changing views on the rise of dramatic authorship. While the Foucauldian paradigm led scholars in the 1980s to envisage the birth of the dramatic author as the product of censorship,[30] the sociological approach to textual and bibliographical studies championed, among others, by Don McKenzie, Jerome McGann and Roger Chartier, has encouraged a younger generation of scholars to understand early modern dramatic authorship as the effect of specific modes of textual production. According to Douglas Brooks, for example, 'the printing of plays facilitated the commodification of dramatic authorship and generated, consequently, an intensifying preoccupation with individualized authorial agency' (Brooks 2000: xiii–xiv). Focusing specifically on the significance of the prefatory materials included in Shakespeare's and Beaumont and Fletcher's Folio editions of 1623 and 1647, Margreta de Grazia, Leah Marcus and Jeffrey Masten have similarly commented on the 'immense amount of cultural work involved in converting … texts written for the theatre … into volumes that could organize texts under a single patronymic' (Masten 1997: 119–20).[31] Refreshing and innovative is Zachary Lesser's contribution to recent studies on publishers of early modern drama as specialist readers 'who tailor[ed] their products to meet commercial demands [while], at the same time, shaping future demand' for specific types of plays. Like de Grazia, Marcus, Brooks and Masten, Lesser envisages dramatic publishers as agents actively engaged not only in the material transmission of play texts but also in their ideological reception:

We cannot analyze the ways in which books were marketed and sold, as though their meanings were predetermined and stable, without simultaneously discussing the shaping role of the book trade in creating these meanings. The publisher does not merely bring a commodity to market but also imagines, and helps to construct, the purchasers of that commodity and their interpretations of it. (2004: 17)

In his forthcoming book on Edward Blount, one of the publishers of Shakespeare's First Folio of 1623, Gary Taylor also points out that early modern publishers played a key role as specialist readers, since their ability to market playbooks depended on the extent to which other booksellers and ordinary readers credited their judgement as critics and guarantors of the literary quality of the books they chose to publish.

While this group of scholars has helped us understand how publishers, as owners and readers of copy and chief investors in publishing ventures, played an active role in the making of printed playbooks and their reception, they have not considered their practical impact on the evolution of the texts of printed playbooks prior to the 'official' rise of Shakespeare editorial tradition in 1709. My book addresses this blind spot in current textual and bibliographical studies on Shakespearean and early modern drama by focusing on those publishers who did not only decide to invest in dramatic publication, but also committed themselves to the perfection of dramatic copy as annotators or procurers of annotated copy.

The first part of this book explores the rise of pre-Shakespearean drama in print by investigating two groups of publishers, namely John and William Rastell and Richard Jones, who were respectively responsible for ushering English interludes and English commercial drama into print at the beginning and at the end of the sixteenth century. This section of the book establishes what prompted these stationers to publish English drama even before their enterprising ventures created a market for it and the extent to which they invested in the preparation of dramatic copy for the press. Although different in important respects, the editorial and philological traditions associated with classical and vernacular humanism are identified in this part of the book as the main sources of the editorial impulse which led these early publishers of English drama to invest in the accuracy of their texts.

The first chapter in Part I focuses on John and William Rastell, who were almost single-handedly responsible for the rise of English drama in print as publishers of most of the extant early Tudor interludes dating from the mid-1510s to the mid-1530s. This chapter establishes that the impetus which drove the Rastells to commit dramatic works to print was strongly pedagogical and that their printing shops were the closest English counterparts to humanist presses on the Continent thanks to their collaboration with Thomas More and other members of his social and cultural circle. This chapter pays special attention to how Erasmus's editorial activities in Continental Europe affected the literary activities of More's circle in London and the dramatic output of John and William Rastell's presses.

The second chapter in Part I builds on recent assessments of Richard Jones's self-conscious and interventionist style as a publisher (Melnikoff 2001) by relating his publishing career to that of another 'adventurous' London stationer, John Wolfe. Though often branded as 'unruly' and 'disreputable' because of their opposition to profitable patents and printing privileges, publishers like Jones and Wolfe eventually managed to become successful stationers thanks to their remarkable ability to carve a niche in the market by targeting small groups of literary-minded readers. Wolfe, who may have trained in Italy for a few years, printed and published some of the best known masterpieces of the Italian Renaissance, which appealed to the Italian-speaking community at the court of Elizabeth I and to the growing numbers of religious émigrés fleeing from the intellectual and political extremism of the Counter-Reformation. Similarly, Jones addressed most of his books to a specific group of readers, the genteel members of the Inns of Court, who not only supported Jones's business as paying customers but often procured copy and prepared it for press. Collectively, the two chapters in Part I chart the shift from the humanist impulse to publish dramatic works as a pedagogical venture to the commercial impulse to publish dramatic works to satisfy a small but not insignificant literary readership.

Part II is devoted to a re-assessment of textual variation in the early quarto and folio editions of Shakespeare in the light of the categories of variants attributed to early modern correctors in this Introduction and in Part I. The first chapter in Part II deals with Andrew Wise, one of the first publishers who invested in Shakespeare and published as many as five of his plays between 1597 and 1602, including multiple editions of *Richard II, Richard III* and *1 Henry IV.* The popularity of the Shakespearean Quartos published by Wise and the frequency with which he issued them are genuinely exceptional, so much so that some scholars have assumed that the Chamberlain's Men must have established a regular professional relationship with him (Erne 2003: 87–8; Gurr 2003: 185). This chapter identifies a further connection between Wise and the Chamberlain's Men and considers the possibility that Wise, like Richard Jones, may have been an interventionist publisher who personally committed to the preparation of dramatic copy for the press or actively sought annotated copy prior to re-issuing Shakespeare's popular history plays. Ultimately, though, this chapter refrains from firmly identifying Wise as the incontrovertible source of the corrections which found their way into his Shakespearean editions and tests this hypothesis against the alternative theory that Shakespeare rather than Wise may have added them.

The next chapter in Part II challenges the popular narrative according to which Thomas Pavier, the most significant investor in Shakespeare in print between his death in 1616 and the publication of the First Folio in 1623, attempted to defraud the King's Men and his fellow stationers by publishing ten unauthorized editions of Shakespearean and apocryphal plays in 1619, which are better known as the 'Pavier Quartos'. After explaining why this popular narrative is untenable, this chapter provides an alternative explanation to account for the fact that Pavier first decided to publish these ten plays as a collection but then published them separately and with a bizarre mixture of accurate and false imprints on their title pages. Special attention is also paid to the level of editorial intervention in these editions, which is consistent with the quality and range of textual variation in Pavier's earlier dramatic editions and not dissimilar from the local changes and corrections which found their way into the Wise Quartos. Rather than a fraudster, Pavier therefore seems to have been another enterprising publisher, who did not only anticipate the plan to publish a collected edition of Shakespeare's dramatic works but also took great care to improve the quality of the texts of the plays he published in 1619.

In 'The Making of the First Folio' I argue that at least some of the First Folio plays set from printed copy were not annotated through sporadic consultation of theatrical manuscripts, as posited, among others, by the editors of the influential Oxford edition of *The Complete Works* (1986), but by annotating readers who may include professional correctors associated with John Smethwick, one of the two less prominent members of the Folio syndicate. This chapter shows that, as with the Wise and the Pavier Quartos, editorial intervention during the preparation of printed copy for some First Folio plays cannot be discounted. If the chapter on the Wise Quartos questions the myth of a direct link between the author and at least some of the 'good' quartos that preceded the First Folio, this chapter challenges another strong myth, that of a link between some of the texts included in this edition and the 'true and originall' copies of the theatrical manuscripts preserved by the King's Men.

The last chapter rejects the assumption that the textual variants accumulated by Shakespeare's texts as they were repeatedly reprinted throughout the seventeenth century stem from compositorial tampering and the occasional intervention of printing house correctors. After reviewing the findings of other scholars who have examined textual variation in a range of seventeenth-century Shakespearean editions, this chapter focuses on Henry Herringman and his edition of the Fourth Folio of 1685. From the beginning of his extraordinary career in dramatic and literary publishing,

Herringman relied on the editorial services of some of the most prominent literary figures of his time, including John Dryden. After selling the retailing side of his business in 1684, Herringman may have personally taken care of the editorial work involved in the publication of his subsequent Folio collections, including Shakespeare's, thus anticipating the efforts of a far greater editor-publisher, Jacob Tonson. However, internal evidence drawn from the text of *Coriolanus* as it appears in the Fourth Folio suggests that Nahum Tate is another likely source of the corrections in this edtion.

This final chapter also reflects on how the strategies of editorial intervention studied in this book relate to eighteenth-century editorial approaches associated with professional scholars and gentlemen readers who started to identify themselves as 'editors' of Shakespeare. This chapter in turn leads to the Conclusion, where I explain what implications my findings about sixteenth- and seventeeth-century 'correctors' of Shakespeare have for modern editors, who generally regard Nicholas Rowe as the initiator of a tradition which still informs their thinking about early modern play texts and the ways in which these texts are re-presented to the modern reader.

PART I

The rise of English drama in print

English humanism and the publication
of early Tudor drama

Henry Medwall's *Fulgens and Lucrece* (STC 17778, 1512–16?) is renowned among scholars of early modern drama for being the earliest English printed playbook. Yet hardly any attention has been devoted to the peculiar circumstances of its publication.[1] *Fulgens and Lucrece* was issued by the only English press which can be described as humanist,[2] both in terms of its output and the social and cultural circle associated with its founder, John Rastell. Thomas More, the most influential representative of English humanist culture in the first quarter of the sixteenth century, was John Rastell's brother-in-law. Henry Medwall had known More since the latter entered Cardinal Morton's household[3] and it was William Rastell, John's eldest son, who printed Medwall's second extant interlude, *Nature* (STC 17779), in 1530. William was also the printer of most of John Heywood's interludes, including *The Play of the Weather* (STC 13305, 1533) and *The Play of Love* (STC 13303, 1534). John Heywood had married William Rastell's sister Joan in 1531 and there are good reasons to believe that the two men were sharing quarters in St Bride's Church Yard, Fleet Street, when William issued Heywood's interludes in the early 1530s (Reed 1923–4: 36). Close family and professional relations and a strong association with English humanist culture define the small group of learned men of letters who were among themselves responsible for writing and printing three quarters of the early Tudor Drama to be committed to print before the mid-1530s.

Except for two editions of *Everyman* and a translation of Terence's *Andria* possibly printed by Richard Pynson,[4] only three other interludes survive in print from the early Tudor period. These are *Hyckescorner* (STC 14039: ?1515–16), *The World and the Child* (STC 25982: 1522), and *The Interlude of Youth* (STC 14111: 1530?–1535) and were all printed by Wynkyn de Worde. The sporadic quality of de Worde's dramatic publications can be gauged against the considerable output of his commercial press, which according to *The Short Title Catalogue* amounts to over eight hundred

editions. Conversely, one in ten and one in five books printed by John and
William Rastell respectively were playbooks. The relative infrequency of
dramatic titles in de Worde's output supports Julie Stone Peters's theory
according to which these three interludes are more likely to have been
commissioned than to have stemmed from de Worde's own initiative or
interests (2000: 27). By the same token, John and William Rastell's
commitment to printing dramatic literature cannot but be regarded as a
self-conscious undertaking.

The fact that the vast majority of extant early Tudor interludes are
clearly the product of a deliberate publishing venture associated with the
humanist presses run by John and William Rastell has tremendous implications for our understanding of the relationship between drama and print
culture in the early modern period. Recent studies have started to redress
what Julie Stone Peters refers to as 'one of those enduring lies so convenient
to the history of progress: that Renaissance dramatists were unconcerned
with the circulation of their work on the page; that the press kept aloof
from the stage and the early stage kept aloof from the press' (2000: 4–5).[5]
The evidence analysed in this chapter shows that the earliest printed secular
plays in English, which initially co-existed with, but ultimately replaced,
the older religious moralities and miracle plays associated with manuscript
and oral cultures, were indeed conceived with both the stage and the page
in mind. Furthermore, a close analysis of the printed texts of a selection of
early Tudor interludes suggests that, despite significant differences, the role
acquired by editing among contemporary humanist scholars had a major
impact on the level of editorial commitment invested in their transmission
into print.

The early modern period ushered in radical changes not only in the way
in which texts were reproduced but also in the way in which they were
edited, annotated and published. By the time Gutenberg's invention of
movable type was adopted by printers in Strasbourg (1458), Bamberg
(1460), Cologne and Subiaco (1465), Rome (1467), Basle (1468), Venice
(1469), Paris (1470) and London (1476),[6] the growing interest in Latin and
Greek literature and culture had led to a revival of philological and textual
studies. Early Italian humanist scholars, such as Francesco Petrarca, Poggio
Bracciolini and Leonardo Bruni, had already started searching ecclesiastical
and private libraries in order to secure authoritative manuscripts or make
fresh transcripts of rare, ancient texts. They had also started collating
and editing the manuscripts they discovered according to sophisticated
editorial methods. In the fourteenth century, Petrarca produced outstanding editions of Cicero, Livy and St Augustine. In the fifteenth century,

Marsilio Ficino translated and edited all of Plato, while Lorenzo Valla proved that the notorious Donation of Constantine, a legal document often invoked to confirm the legitimacy of the temporal power of the Roman Church over Rome and its surrounding territories, was a forgery. By comparing the Vulgate to its Greek source, Valla corrected the New Testament and the Fathers of the Church, a daring display of editorial prowess which was to inspire Desiderius Erasmus, Valla's greatest admirer and most prolific successor north of the Alps. Erasmus, in turn, contributed to the consolidation of the emergent humanist culture in England and the rest of Northern Europe at the beginning of the sixteenth century.[7]

Erasmus and More's friendship was already perceived as proverbial in the early 1590s. In *The Book of Sir Thomas More*, for example, when Erasmus and More meet for the first time, More swaps clothes with his servant in order to test Erasmus's ability to 'distinguishe merit and outward ceremonie' (Greg 1911: lines 750–1). Their encounter effectively captures the jovial spirit of their friendship, which was immortalized in the punning title of Erasmus's *Encomium Moriae*. Other important aspects of their friendship have been carefully investigated. Scholars now agree that Erasmus had a considerable influence on More's unfaltering belief in the revival, as opposed to a divisive reform, of Christianity and on More's scholarly and literary achievements, the most prominent example being the translations of Lucian, which the two friends carried out together over a period of several years.[8] This chapter focuses instead on Erasmus's achievements as an editor and the extent to which his distinctive attitudes towards print culture and textual scholarship affected Thomas More and the humanist circle responsible for printing More's English works, as well as three quarters of the surviving early Tudor interludes. While highlighting the major differences between Erasmus's editorial methods and the Rastells' approach to dramatic publication, this chapter identifies a link between Erasmus's and More's preoccupation with textual accuracy and the Rastells' commitment to producing printed playbooks which would enhance the literary status of vernacular drama.

'LIKE A MODERN HERCULES': ERASMUS'S EDITORIAL LABOURS

Erasmus, the son of a parish priest, rose to prominence as the 'quintessential European man of letters' thanks to his systematic investment in the medium of print and to the network of editorial assistants he recruited in the main printing centres in Northern and Southern Europe (Jardine 1993: 147).[9] By the time Erasmus started collaborating with Johann Froben in Basel, he had already worked with the most important scholar printers in Europe, including Thierry Martens, Josse Bade, better known as Ascentius, and Aldo Manuzio. Most of Erasmus's important editions, such as Rudolph Agricola's *De inventione dialectica* (Martens, 1515), the correspondence of St Jerome (Froben 1516), and his corrected version of the New Testament (Froben 1515), stemmed from his close collaboration with devoted teams of humanist scholars, who worked for him as editors and correctors. Most prominent among them was Beatus Rhenanus, the son of a butcher from Alsace, who, like Erasmus, had risen from obscurity thanks to his scholarly achievements. Rhenanus supervised the impression of most of Erasmus's works issued by Froben's press and provided the first biographical account of Erasmus's life as the editor-in-chief of the collected works published by Froben in 1540, a few years after Erasmus's death.

The support of large editorial networks in the most important printing centres in France, the Low Countries and the Upper Rhein allowed Erasmus to continue the tradition of textual scholarship which had flourished in Italy in the fourteenth century, thus closing the gap between Northern and Southern European humanism. Writing to Thomas Anshelm from Basle on 1 April 1516, Erasmus had explicitly referred to his wish to 'compete with the Italians in [the] field' of textual scholarship, which, Erasmus continues, 'would . . . bring us much more credit than to engage them in barbarous fashion with rocks and iron weapons' (Mynors and Thomson 1976: 267, lines 10–3). Erasmus's appeal to promote civility against barbarism barely hides his competitive determination to outdo his Italian forefathers. His contemporaries were fully aware of Erasmus's belligerent intentions, and often flattered him by proclaiming him the winner. Germain de Brie, for example, who was trying to get Erasmus to visit France in 1517, claimed that 'with no desire to offend . . . the Italians, . . . it is Erasmus . . . alone who wins the palm against all men on both sides of the Alps' (Mynors and Thomson 1977: 318, lines 77–80). Erasmus certainly deserved the palm for his life-long commitment to producing scholarly editions of patristic and classical texts, and, more importantly, for his contribution to the rise of a scholarly and professional editorial tradition within the emergent medium of print.

Erasmus's correspondence offers precious insights into his commitment to rigorous textual scholarship and into the principles which shaped his editorial methods. Often mentioned is Erasmus's arduous search for authoritative copies (Mynors and Thomson 1976: 266, lines 388–90), and the 'labour of comparing together so many volumes [which] is very tedious'

(Mynors and Thomson 1976: 260, lines 183–4). In fact, at times of genuine dejection at the enormity of the editorial task at hand, Erasmus admits that 'no other work brings a man more tedium' (Mynors and Thomson 1976: 262, line 244), along with 'impairment of the eyes, premature old age, and starvation' (Mynors and Thomson 1975: 195, line 13). Another aspect of the editorial function which Erasmus deplores is the self-effacement required of the editor, especially when the text in question is nothing less than the Holy Scriptures. Following in the footsteps of Lorenzo Valla and Jacques Lefèvre (Trapp 1991: 103–4), Erasmus realized that his corrections of the New Testament were going to be met by the open hostility of the majority of theologians and clerics who were used to regarding the Vulgate as *the* word of God. Erasmus understandably dons the monastic cloak of perfect humility when, in the address 'To the Reader' prefaced to the 1515 edition, he claims that his corrections simply 'paved ... a road ... on which in future great theologians can drive more easily with coach and horses ... and display the splendid pageants of their wisdom'. However, a few lines later in the same address, he ventures on dangerous grounds as he describes the pleasure he derives from reforming the Holy Scriptures by going back to their sources. Erasmus's comment that '[f]ruit tastes better that you have picked with your own hands from the mother tree' smacks of editorial hubris in a post-lapsarian world of fallen texts (Mynors and Thomson 1976: 203, lines 161–5 and 179–80). Even more telling is Erasmus's closing remark in the same address: '[a]s for the sweets of fame, so little I am tempted by them that I would not even have set my name to the work, had I not feared that this might reduce its power to do good; for all men suspect a book with no author's name' (Mynors and Thomson 1976: 205, lines 235–8). The fact that the 'book with no author's name' is the Bible, quite literally the word of God, suggests the extent of Erasmus's editorial confidence. At the opposite end of the self-effacing editor, who strives to restore the author's intentions, stands the heroic editor, who, 'like a modern Hercules',[10] fights against 'the monsters of errors' (Mynors and Thomson 1976: 263, line 284) in order to restore the text to its former state of formal integrity. Erasmus often describes his editorial work by comparing it to the strenuous battle under-taken by the Christian soldier to defeat darkness and corruption. 'In the course of the last two years', he writes to Servatus Rogerus in 1514, 'I have, among other things, revised St Jerome's epistles; I have slain with daggers the spurious or interpolated passages, while I have elucidated the obscure parts in my notes' (Mynors and Thomson 1975: 300, lines 161–4). The editor becomes almost god-like in his efforts to resurrect the true reading from a corrupt text. 'I believe', Erasmus claims, 'that the writing of his books cost

Jerome less effort than I spent in the restoring of them, and their birth meant fewer nightly vigils for him than their rebirth for me' (Mynors and Thomson 1976: 262, lines 259–62).

Underlying these two conflicting models of editorship, the self-effacing drudgery of the anonymous editor and the heroic stance of the proprietary editor who reclaims the corrupt text from oblivion or corruption as his own creation, lies a deeply rooted anxiety about issues of authorship, originality and textual accuracy. These issues come into sharper focus when Erasmus and his editorial assistants discuss problems arising from the preparation of the printer's copy for the press. Interestingly enough, these problems are often discussed in short factual exchanges not meant for the wider circulation reserved to dedicatory epistles and formal addresses to the reader. Such exchanges make clear that preparation of copy is normally the prerogative of the author or the editor-in-chief. In a letter to Aldo Manuzio dated 28 October 1507, Erasmus explains that Bade's first edition of his translations of Euripides' *Hecuba* and *Iphigenia* was 'chock-full of errors' and that he wishes Aldo to reprint them for him. 'If you find it convenient to undertake the commission', Erasmus explains, 'I shall furnish you with the corrected copy, which I send by the bearer's hand, free from all obligation' (Mynors and Thomson 1975: 132, lines 40–1). When bad weather and poor health prevented Erasmus from travelling from Bologna to Venice, he wrote to Aldo again, this time to send instructions on how the corrected copy should be printed. 'Perhaps', Erasmus cautiously points out, 'there will be some points on which you will not agree with me, and for this reason I was particularly anxious to visit you in person'. 'There are certain passages, too', he adds, 'where I have dared to diverge from the text before me'. The text translated by Erasmus was Aldo's own 1503 edition of Euripides' *Works*. Fully conscious of departing from the Greek version authorized by Aldo's imprint, Erasmus attempts to disentangle the proprietary claims over the text, which are uneasily shared by its scholarly printer and its translator:

I should very much like to discuss these matters with you face to face . . . But if you find an obvious mistake anywhere, for I am human, you have my permission to alter it at your discretion . . . But if anything seems doubtful, yet defensible – a case where I may seem not so much to have made a slip through error as to have differed from you in opinion – please either leave it, or, if you so desire, even change it: for there is no responsibility that I would not now venture to entrust to my dear Aldus. (Mynors and Thomson 1975: 136, lines 18–27)

Erasmus's proprietary stance towards Euripides' text, which justifies his departures from the authorized version, does not only conflict with the overt objective of his editorial approach, which is to ensure the recovery of authorial intentions, but also with the expertise of the scholar printer who published the authorized version and who is now checking Erasmus's translation before it goes to press.

Similarly interesting is the negotiation of editorial authority between Erasmus and Beatus Rhenanus. In April 1515 Rhenanus writes to Erasmus to announce that Seneca is making 'capital progress' through the press and that 'Nesen is most careful in reading proof'. Rhenanus then admits that he wishes he 'were as successful in emending the text as [Nesen] is "right keen of scent" in sniffing out errors'. Rhenanus is preparing the printer's copy as opposed to correcting proof, and this is clearly perceived as problematic: '[i]n any case, as the copy is still disfigured by many mistakes (as you well know), you are the person whose help it would still need'. The trusty assistant copies one passage before and after emendation to get Erasmus's approval. Since he cannot do the same with all the passages requiring emendation, he laments his lack of confidence and erudition in fulfilling his role as editor: 'I do not like always relying on my judgement, especially extempore, and under pressure from men who cannot stand delay'. 'If only we had an ancient copy', Rhenanus adds, 'there is nothing I should enjoy more than to emend this text in places that are still left uncorrected' (Mynors and Thomson 1976: 79–80, lines 2–6 and 29–32). A second letter sent to Erasmus two weeks later reveals how Rhenanus's self-proclaimed lack of judgement is not the only obstacle preventing him from carrying out his function as editor:

I could wish the copy was cleaner and the reader a little more careful. But he does not detect all the mistakes, nor am I the man, if he sometimes detects them, to set them all to rights, both because my knowledge is so very limited and because to be over-clever in someone else's book has something foolish about it. (Mynors and Thomson 1976: 82, lines 6–10)

'To be over-clever in someone else's book' means to interfere not only with Seneca's lines but also with Erasmus's editorial decisions. The corrector's role is not only to ensure that no new mistakes are allowed to wander into the text as it goes through the press, but also that the intentions of the proprietary editor who reclaims the text of Seneca as his own creation are not tampered with.

Other editors working for Erasmus shared Rhenanus's reluctance to interfere with Erasmus's editorial intentions. Before Nicholas Gerbel joined Erasmus's editorial team in Basle in September 1515, he supervised the impression of Erasmus's *Lucubrationes* at Schürer's press in Strasbourg. Three letters dated August 1515 charter Gerbel's increasing uneasiness about his editorial interventions in Erasmus's text. The first letter shows that Gerbel was appointed as proof-corrector: '[y]our *Lucubrationes*', he is proud to inform Erasmus, 'is being printed just now with more than common diligence, and I work at it as best I can with all my powers' (Mynors and Thomson 1976: 148, lines 30–1). The second letter suggests that Gerbel might be acting beyond his remit: '[I have] put right a few things in it, wherever this could conveniently be done; in such a way, however, as not to go too far from your own corrections' (Mynors and Thomson 1976: 149, lines 7–9). In the third and final letter Gerbel is positively concerned about the legitimacy of his intervention: '[t]here is only one thing I am really afraid of – that you will say I am a poor diviner: in reading your writing I have so often been compelled to guess' (Mynors and Thomson 1976: 168, lines 9–11).

Overall, the editors working for Erasmus only rarely admit that the state of the printer's copy was poor and that they had to rely on their own judgement to 'divine' the right reading. Generally, Erasmus strives to suggest absolute control over preparation of copy, even when the relative authority of variant readings is preserved for the benefit of the discerning reader.[11] Inevitably Erasmus foresees the work of later generations of editors as undermining his own. In the 1515 address 'To the Reader' prefaced to his corrections to the New Testament Erasmus justifies an interesting editorial feature as follows:

After revising the sacred books I added these pointers (so to call them), partly to explain to the reader's satisfaction why each change was made, ... partly in hope of preserving my work intact, that it might not be so easy in future for anyone to spoil a second time what had once been restored with such great exertions. (Mynors and Thomson 1976: 199, lines 48–54)

This proprietary attitude not only towards his own writings but also towards his classical and patristic editions increased as Erasmus approached the end of his prolific career. The preface to his 1526 edition of *The Adages* echoes and reinforces the same wish which Erasmus expressed in 1515: 'If God takes me out of this world, I beg and pray the coming generations to preserve intact what we have restored with so much labour' (quoted in Jardine 1993: 44). The first will drafted by Erasmus in 1527 directs Froben to publish a collected edition of his writings after his death and to appoint an editorial team to oversee its impression. As P. S. Allen has pointed out, 'their instructions were to correct printers' errors, or evident mistakes of the author, after careful consideration; but on no account were they to inter-polate additions of their own' (Allen 1913–15: 317).

Erasmus's pursuit of textual accuracy was overtly supported by his confidence in his ability to restore authorial intentions. However, his obsessive determination to produce definitive editions of his own works and of classical, Biblical and patristic texts suggests the extent to which Erasmus was in fact fully aware that the transmission of a text into print could never be reduced to purely mechanical reproduction and that editorial intervention, albeit overtly self-effacing, did not preserve but produced 'true readings'.

ENCOMIUM ERASMI: ERASMUS'S LEGACY IN THOMAS MORE'S *UTOPIA*

The complex paratextual materials prefaced in slightly variant versions to the four editions of *Utopia* printed in Louvain in 1516, Paris in 1517, and Basle in March and November 1518 indicate that More consciously emulated Erasmus's editorial methods and practices and that he was equally preoccupied by issues of originality and intentionality in relation to the editorial task and the transmission of his works into print. The prefatory matter included in the 1516 edition provides interesting insights into the individual contributions of the several agents involved in the project. Peter Giles, one of Martens' correctors who had known Erasmus for several years, explains his role as annotator as follows:

Only I did see to it that the book included a quatrain written in the Utopian tongue, which Hythloday showed to me after More had gone away. I have prefixed to it the alphabet of the Utopians, and also added to the volume some marginal notes. (Logan, Adams and Miller 1995: 27)

Geldenhauer's role as corrector is not openly acknowledged, although he contributes a six-line poem placed at the end of the volume. The intense collaboration among several named and unnamed parties which went into the publication of the 1516 edition is also significantly downplayed in Desmarez's letter to Giles:

Utopia owes a great deal to Hythloday for marking down this land which ought not to have remained obscure; it owes an even greater debt to the most learned More, whose skilful pencil has drawn it for us so vividly. In addition to both of them, not the least part of the thanks must be shared with you, who will make public both Hythloday's conversation and More's report of it – to no small delight of future readers. (Logan, Adams and Miller 1995: 263)

In Desmarez's account the fictitious traveller Hythloday is described as the source of what is known about Utopia, More as the reporter of Hythloday's

Io. Clemens. Hythlodæus. Tho. Morus. Pet. Aegid.

14. From Thomas More's *Utopia*, 3rd edition, 1518, by Ambrosius Holbein

recollections, and Giles as the corrector. Interestingly, the only authorial and editorial agents identified by Desmarez are also characters in More's narrative, while other collaborators involved in the publication of the first edition of *Utopia*, including Geldenhauer and Erasmus, are not mentioned. Erasmus's name is first associated with *Utopia* on the title page of the 1517 edition, where he appears as the author of the marginal notes, which Giles had claimed as his own in the first edition. Some scholars believe that 'Giles and Erasmus should be considered at least as minor co-authors [and] ... that the marginalia evolved from the discussion of each friend with More' (McKinnon 1971: 12). Alternatively, the editors of the 1995 Cambridge edition speculate that 'perhaps the 1517 edition is wrong' (Logan, Adams and Miller 1995: 27n). However, it is not until the third edition in 1518 that Erasmus is unequivocally associated with *Utopia*, but even then only as the author of an additional commendatory letter sent to Froben where *Utopia* is recommended to the prestigious scholar-printer in Basle as a publishing venture worth undertaking.

Erasmus's absence from the prefatory material of the 1516 edition appears even more conspicuous if one considers not only Erasmus's friendship with More but also the several references to *Utopia* in their correspondence between 1515 and 1517. Perhaps most telling of all is More's letter to Erasmus dated 3 September 1516: 'I send you my book on Nowhere', and, More urges Erasmus, 'you must do what you can for it' (Mynors and Thomson 1977: 66, lines 2–4). According to the Cambridge editors, Erasmus did not only co-ordinate the publication of all four editions of *Utopia*, but, as suggested by More's letter, he also contributed to preparing More's manuscript for the press (Logan, Adams and Miller 1995: 271). Considering the level of collaboration which went into the 1516 and the 1517 editions and that Erasmus asked Froben to appoint Beatus Rhenanus, his main editor in Basel, as the chief supervisor of the 1518 editions, the Cambridge editors go as far as claiming that *Utopia* 'was a corporate product of Erasmus's humanist circle' (Logan, Adams and Miller 1995: 276).

The addition of Erasmus's letter to the 1518 editions acquires further significance when considered alongside the simultaneous appearance of two woodcuts, both by Ambrosius Holbein, Hans Holbein's elder brother. One of them represents an episode recounted in Book I, when More, Hythloday and Giles sit down to discuss the traveller's recollections of Utopia in Giles's garden in Antwerp (fig. 14). Art historian Hans Belting has advanced an intriguing reading of this woodcut, by linking it to Quentin Massys's famous dyptich representing Erasmus and Giles and meant as a present for their friend, Thomas More (figs. 15 and 16).

15. *Portrait of Erasmus*, by Quentin Massys, 1517

According to Belting, the letter held by Giles in his hand and bearing More's handwriting stands for the third absent friend, thus making of the diptych a fictitious triptych. The same private joke would seem to apply to the woodcut included in the 1518 editon of *Utopia*. Although the woodcut reproduces the account of the fictive encounter down to the detail of the 'bench covered with grassy turf' (Logan, Adams and Miller 1995: 47), the woodcut might also immortalize a real-life event. If the three friends were often separated by their public and professional commitments, they might indeed have come together to discuss More's project in the very garden

16. *Portrait of Peter Giles*, by Quentin Massys, 1517

represented in the woodcut (Belting 2002). The Yale editors of More's *Complete Works* believe that Erasmus 'had successively seen his two friends within a few days in Bruges and Antwerp on his way through the Netherlands to Basle' (Surtz and Hexter 1965: 575). Belting is however more inclined to believe that Erasmus, given the timeliness of his journey to Basle during More's stay in the Netherlands, would not have missed the opportunity to introduce More to Giles (Belting 2002). Belting's suggestion that Hythloday's portly figure might stand for Erasmus seems particularly persuasive, given that a sustained blend of reality and fiction is one of the most distinctive features in *Utopia*.

Less convincing is Belting's theory according to which the apparent erasure of Erasmus's collaboration from the narrative, from the woodcut, *and* from the paratextual material was due to an attempt to protect his reputation as a serious writer, at a time when his annotations on the New Testament were prompting negative reactions from the clerical world (Belting 2002). After all, Erasmus was the author of the equally satirical and controversial *Encomium Moriae*. Besides, recent scholarship has questioned the apparently straightforward polemical nature of the divide which the publication of Erasmus's annotations on the New Testament caused between him and his editorial collaborator and Louvain theologian Martin Dorp (Jardine 1993: 119–20). The partial erasure of Erasmus from the woodcut and from the prefatory matter of *Utopia* seems more in keeping with the anxious negotiations between authorial intention and editorial intervention which emerge so vividly from the exchanges between Erasmus and his editorial teams scattered across Continental Europe. A letter from Erasmus to More dated 1 March 1517 confirms that at least some of their contemporaries believed Erasmus to have co-authored *Utopia*. 'I enclose a letter from Marliano', Erasmus writes to More, 'having heard that he suspects the first book of the *Utopia* of coming from me, and I should not like that to get about for nothing is more baseless' (Mynors and Thomson 1977: 271, lines 9–12). And yet More's letter to Giles prefaced to the first edition of *Utopia* ironically refers to Hythloday not only as the source of the recollections which he pencilled down 'so vividly', but also as the ultimate editorial authority without whose support the book was unlikely to withstand public scrutiny:

Therefore I beg you to get in touch with Hythloday ... and make sure that my work contains nothing false and omits nothing true. Perhaps it would be better show him the book itself. If I've made a mistake, there's nobody better qualified to correct me; but even he cannot do it, unless he reads over my book. (Logan, Adams and Miller 1995: 35–6)

Overall, the multiple coded references to Erasmus in the paratext of More's *Utopia* identify Erasmus, albeit obliquely, not only as the source of inspiration of his work, but also as the chief collaborator and editor entrusted with the publication of *Utopia*. Eramus's ghostly presence in the text and in the paratextual materials prefaced to *Utopia* is symptomatic of the same tension between authorial and editorial intentions which emerges from Erasmus's correspondence with his editorial assistants. The authority of the text is once again understood as being simultaneously ensured and threatened by the multiplicity of agents engaged in its transmission.

Thomas More provided a crucial link between Continental and English humanism. More specifically, his familiarity with Erasmus's editorial methods had a crucial impact on the printing and publication of vernacular texts in England. If the paratextual materials prefaced to More's *Utopia* reveal the influence of Erasmus's approach to the establishment of an authoritative text through the simultaneous deployment and effacement of editorial assistants, the paratextual materials prefaced to More's English works provide an inspiring insight into the standards of textual accuracy which he demanded from his printers, who included, most prominently, John and William Rastell.

The title page of the second edition of *A dyaloge of Syr Thomas More* (STC 18085, 1530) informs readers that the text was 'Newly ouersene' by the author. More's involvement in the printing of this edition is confirmed by the addition of two important passages (Campbell 1927: 12), which were prompted by Tyndale's *An answere vnto Sir Thomas Mores dialoge* (STC 24437, 1531), and by authorial corrections in the errata list, which must have been added when More checked the proofs (Simpson 1935: 4). The errata lists appended to *The apologye of syr T. More knyght* (STC 18078, 1533) are similarly suggestive of the level of attention bestowed on the correction of the proofs and of the complex and minute changes which More made at such a late stage during the printing process. Five faults escaped in the first part of *The apologye* are omissions, and the recommended corrections imply either the author's personal involvement or consultation of copy.[12] The list of faults escaped in the second part of *The apologye*, on the other hand, shows the author's unequivocal intervention. Further examples of omissions whose correction requires at least consultation of copy are listed along with a substantial note by the author: 'I haue consydered good readere of late, a place in a Boke of Tindale ... [which] modefyeth ... his olde posycyone agaynst satysfaccyon' (Gg4r 10–13). After explaining the implications of a shift in Tyndale's views on a matter of theological concern, More justifies the unusual insertion of such a long note in the errata list: 'I geue you knowlege therof, bycause I wolde not willyngly in any thynge mysse reherse hym' (Gg4r 20–2). Having gone out of his way to report Tyndale's views faithfully, More hastens to point out that 'as touchyng the sacrament of penaūce, his moderacyon nothynge mendeth his heresy' (Gg4v 5–6).

Matters of theological concerns had prompted More's involvement in the printing of his English works as early as 1523. In his refutation of Luther (STC 18088.5), the second Latin work printed by Pynson, a clearly harassed agent in the printing house, either Pynson himself or his Latin expert Bertula, attaches the following note:

After the work had already been printed, another copy arrived, emended again by the author himself: in this he himself had added many things, had changed many things. And for that reason it happened that many sheets were cut in pieces in order to conform to the author's changes. Moreover, where he added something, we were forced to mark all the things which he had added with the letters from that passage into which they had been inserted ... since we did not find any more convenient method. (quoted in Devereux 1975: 48)

This unusual note is particularly useful because it gives us an indication of how demanding More is likely to have been with the Rastells and how much more careful and willing than Pynson they must have been in meeting his demands. More must have been particularly pleased with William Rastell, given the exceptional accuracy of his presswork. Even Dr Johnson, who lamented the state of the art of printing in the early modern period,[13] praised William's professional skills: 'his works', he claimed, 'are carefully and correctly printed, and may therefore be better trusted than any other edition of the English books of that or the preceding age' (quoted in Campbell 1927: 44).

The preface to *A dyaloge* sheds light on what prompted More's crucial investment in the publication of his English works. This preface is worth quoting at length because of its detailed account of the perceived advantages of the medium of print over oral report or manuscript circulation. Asked by a friend to send his views 'towchynge many suche maters/ as beynge in dede very certayne and owt of doute', but 'nethelesse of late by lewde people put in questyon', More decides to entrust a messenger with his answer. However, he soon changes his mind:

whan I consydered what the maters were/ and howe many great thyngys had ben treated bytwene the messenger and me/ and in what maner [and] fassyon/ al be it I mystrustyd not his good wyll/ and very well trusted his wytte/ his lernynge well seruynge hym to the perceyuynge and reportynge of our communycacyon: yet fyndyng our treatye so dyuerse & so long/ and somtyme suche wyse intrycate/ that my selfe coulde not without labour call it orderly to mynd/ me thought I had not well done/ without wrytynge/ to truste his onely memory/ namely syth some partys of the mater be suche of them selfe/ as rather nede to be attentely redde and aduysed/ than houerly harde and passyd ouer. (2nd edn, STC 18085, b1r lines 18–28)

A written answer ranks above an oral report not because the messenger, or his learning and memory, should not be trusted, but because complex theological matters can be more orderly arranged, and ultimately understood, if they are entrusted to the visual medium of writing rather than to the auricular medium of speech. After opting for a written reply, More's mind is not at rest for long, because he soon realizes that his written answer is not safer than an oral reply from accidental misunderstanding or conscious misinterpretation. Even worse, his manuscript copy can be annotated and then surreptitiously printed, and his views seriously misconstrued:

sone after it was showed me/ that of all my wrytynges were wrytten dyuerse copyes . . .. [M]e thought grete parell myght aryse/ yf some of that company (whiche are confedered and conspyred togyder/ in the sowynge and settynge forth of Luthers pestylent heresyes in this realme) sholde malycyously chaunge my wordes to the worse, & so put in prynte my boke/ framed after theyr fantasyes/ whiche whan I wolde afterwarde reproue and shewe ỹ dyfference/ I myght peraduenture seme for the coloure of my cause/ to haue amended myne owne/ vpon the syght of theyrs. for eschewyng wherof I am now dryuen/ as I say to this thyrde busynes of publyshynge and puttynge my boke in prynte my selfe: wherby theyr enterpryse (yf they sholde any suche intende) shall (I trust) be preuented and frustrate. (biv lines 2–15)

Compared to the circulation of manuscript copy, the author's preparation of copy for the press has an extra advantage. More informs his reader that he did not have the presumption to publish his book before 'studyously submyt[ting]' his copy to the 'examynacyon and iudgment' of learned and wise men (biv lines 27–8). Overall, More finds that print guarantees more control over authorial intentions than speech or manuscript copy.

The preface to *The debellacyon of Salem and Bizance* (STC 18081, 1533) is similarly useful to understand why More was so meticulous and so demanding when he corrected his proofs. *The debellacyon* represents an advanced stage in More and Tyndale's dispute over theological matters, and More draws the reader's attention to the importance of words, and the accuracy with which they should be reported and transmitted:

the pacyfyer [re: Tyndale] hath in some places put in myne owne wordes where yt pleased hym: yet hathe he for the moste parte vsed a prety crafte, to mysse reherse my mater and leue my wordes oute . . . [B]esydes this, the man hath in some places lefte oute some of his owne, & mysse rehersed them/ to make the reader wene, that in the reprouynge theym, I hadde wryten wronge. (a6r lines 4–14)

Unlike Tyndale, More is prepared to quote verbatim not only from his *Apologye* but also from his adversary's work. The reader will thus be able to see how More 'loue[s] the lyght, no lesse thenne thys pacyfyer wolde fayne walke in the darke' (a7r lines 19–21).

The note appended after the errata list is perhaps the most astonishing feature of *The debellacyon*. More turns this lengthy address to 'the chrysten reader' into an opportunity to prove that, unlike Tyndale, he is prepared to admit that he may stumble, and that, when he does, he is willing to reform his text for the sake of truth. The lengthy note might seem utterly excessive in view of the nature of More's oversight. After pointing out that the printer is not to be blamed for such oversight, he does not only direct the reader to the place in the text which needs amending but quotes the faulty sentence at length:

For of trouth not ỹ pacifyer but my selfe was ouersene in that place with a lytle haste, in mysse remembrynge one worde of his. For where as he sayth in the person of Byzance, in the thyrde lefe of Salem and byzance. *I wyl cause yt to be wryten into this dyaloge word for word as yt is come to my handes*: I forgate whan I answered yt that he sayde, *as yt is come!* and toke it as though he sayd as it cometh to myne handes. (z1r 14–24)

The significance of the fact that More's use of the wrong tense prompts a four-page apology cannot be overemphasized. This note effectively suggests the level of editorial commitment that went into the printing of More's English works. More consciously used the medium of print to argue and defend his own convictions against a growing tide of opposition which was coming not only from the quarters of religious dissenters but also from a far more dangerous and formidable adversary, the king himself.

More's investment in the accuracy of the text of his printed works far exceeded a purely philological ideal. It is therefore remarkable that John and William Rastell were entrusted with the daunting task of representing More's intentions in print. How significant is the fact that three quarters of the extant printed interludes from the period were also printed by John and William Rastell? To what extent did Erasmus's and More's investment in textual accuracy and the establishment of an authoritative text affect the Rastells' approach to dramatic publication? The last section of this chapter addresses these questions by closely examining the most prominent features of the dramatic output of their presses. Unfortunately none of the interludes issued by the Rastells' presses survives in multiple editions. As a result, the methodology employed in later chapters, which involves a contrastive analysis of later editions of a play text with their source texts, cannot be applied to the interludes published by the Rastells. However, a close analysis of their printing conventions, layout and the sophisticated literary qualities of the dialogue suggests a continuity of methods and a comparable investment in textual accuracy in the Rastells' approach to dramatic and non-dramatic publication.

JOHN AND WILLIAM RASTELL AS PUBLISHERS OF EARLY
TUDOR INTERLUDES

Although peripheral to the great printing centres on Continental Europe,
John and William Rastell's presses clearly emulated their standards, their
methods and their humanist agenda, which included the publication of
dramatic literature as a pedagogical tool. Humanist textual scholars revived
classical drama, which, as a result, was accorded renewed prominence in
English schools' and universities' curricula from the beginning of the
sixteenth century.[14] Although classical plays started to be acted in English
universities as early as 1510–11, drama was mostly appreciated for the
elegance of its language and its moral implications (Norland 1995: 67–9).
Humanist views on classical drama affected More and his circle of fellow
scholars and friends, who found the native tradition of moral interludes
to be particularly suitable to fulfil similar didactic ends. If the humanist
quality of the dramatic literature produced by the More–Rastell–Heywood
circle has become something of a critical commonplace,[15] more attention
needs to be paid to the influence of the editorial methods and the investment in the medium of print associated with the humanist tradition on the
dramatic output of John and William Rastell's presses. By taking *Fulgens
and Lucrece* (STC 17778, 1512–16) and *The Nature of the Four Elements* (STC
20722, 1520?) as my main examples, I shall argue that, despite significant
differences, the quality of the presswork and the multiplicity of agents
involved in their transmission into print highlight a continuity of methods
and concerns between the dramatic and non-dramatic books published by
the Rastells. In other words, the printing and publication of dramatic texts
seem to have elicited the same level of care and attention which was later
reserved to the other books issued by the Rastells, including More's English
works, and to have benefited from the Rastells' exposure to More and his
humanist circle.

Several typographical and conventional features in the text of *The Four
Elements* suggest that the printing of this interlude was not regarded as a
cheap, hasty, stopgap job, but as an important project, on a level with the
other publications issued by John Rastell's press. T. H. Howard-Hill and
Julie Stone Peters have studied the evolution of dramatic conventions from
pre-print to post-print dramatic manuscripts and early modern printed
drama. Both agree that conventions, such as the presence and position of
stage directions, the format of speech prefixes, or the inclusion of lists of
players and descriptions of the venue of performance, became standard and
immediately recognizable as pertaining to a dramatic text only towards the

end of the sixteenth century (Peters 2000: 24, Howard-Hill 1990a: 143). At
the beginning of the sixteenth century, both manuscript and printed playbooks shared a mixture of what Howard-Hill describes as the 'native' and
the 'classical' methods of setting out dramatic texts (1990a: 112). While the
native method derives from manuscript liturgical drama and bears the
marks of performance by recording entrances, exits, and occasional stage
action, the classical method is 'even more parsimonious with the features
that identify the works as plays' (Howard-Hill 1990a: 133). *Four Elements* is
clearly set out as a dramatic text. Its title-page mentions the time required
by a performance of the full text of the interlude and how to shorten it, if
necessary:

yf ŷ hole matter be plydt wyl conteyne the space of an hour and a halfe/ but yf
ye lyst ye may leue out muche of the sad mater as the messengers pte/ and some
of naturys parte and some of experyens pte & yet the matter wyl depend
conuenyently/ and than it wyll not be paste thre quarters of an hour of length.
(A1r lines 5–11)

A list of characters follows, which reinforces the impression that this text
was meant as a script for future productions, although performance was
more likely to mean 'public recitation' than 'scenic representation with
actors' (Peters 2000: 22). And yet other features of the text of *Four Elements*
make clear that, as Richard Axton puts it, 'it was [Rastell's] practical
concern to treat plays as more than ephemera and to make play texts
available as books to a reading public' (1979: 3). A telling feature is the
index and its prominent position at the bottom of the title page and on its
verso. The index is a list of the 'dyuers matters whiche be in this interlude
conteynyd', that is 'Of the sytuacyon of the.iiii.elements that is to sey the
yerth the water the ayre and fyre/ & of theyr qualytese', 'Of certeyne poynts
of cosmography', 'Of the cause of the ebbe and flode of the see', 'Of the
cause of rayne snowe and hayle', and so on (A1r 17–21; A1v lines 6, 16–17).
The index bestows a literary quality on the text of this merry interlude and
encourages readers not only to use it for public or private recitations but
also for consultation on matters of scientific interest. Another interesting
feature suggests the ambitious nature of Rastell's publishing venture. A
song and a dance on c6v are simply introduced by a descriptive stage
direction – 'Than he syngyth this song & daunyth with all / And euermore
maketh countenaunce accordyng / To the matter & all ŷ other annswer
lyke wyse' (c6v lines 11–13). However, an earlier song at c4v to c6r prompts
the insertion of what is believed to be the 'earliest piece of music printed
from moveable type in one impression known in England . . . at a time

when it was unknown in the country in which it was developed', that is France (Coleman 1971: 17–18, 22). Although the score was clearly going to be useful for performance, it also added tremendous typographical significance to the printed edition of Rastell's interlude, thus suggesting that its transmission into print involved a remarkable level of technical expertise.

By far the most prominent literary feature in the *mise en page* of Rastell's *Four Elements* is the use of pilcrows, or paragraph signs. These conventional signs, which in other sixteenth-century printed playbooks mark changes of speakers, are also used to highlight rhyming patterns, which in turn signal the different social and moral qualities of the characters in the play. The serious, well-meaning and virtuous characters, including the messenger, whose objective is to instruct and guide Humanity, normally speak in rhyme royal stanzas. The rhyming pattern is remarkably regular and is not disrupted by changes of speakers. The paragraph sign is used to highlight the centred names of the speakers but also the first line of each stanza. The entrance of those characters who disrupt Humanity's training also disrupts the rhyming pattern, as regular verse disappears altogether except for the occasional tail-rhyme stanzas. Once Sensual Appetite, the Taverner, or Ignorance gain control over Humanity, the centred names of the characters move to the left margin and appear much more like speech prefixes through being abbreviated. The use of paragraph signs to highlight changes of speakers as opposed to stanza divisions contributes to reinforce the visual difference between dramatic dialogue and the literary exposition of scientific theories or moral truths. Although the ending of this interlude is missing from its unique extant copy, the ultimate containment of the disruptive characters is suggested by a shift of the speakers' names back to their central position and by a resumption of the use of paragraph signs to indicate stanza divisions.

The text of *Fulgens and Lucrece* uses very similar rhyming structures, *mise en page* and typographical conventions. As in *Four Elements*, different rhyming patterns stress differences of rank and distinguish serious matter from comic entertainment. The opening exchange between servants A and B, for example, has an irregular rhyming pattern. However, when B starts elucidating the plot of the interlude, his lines switch to rhyme royal stanzas, thus resembling the prologue normally spoken by a formal character, like the messenger in *Four Elements*. Typographically, the stanza division in B's lines is highlighted by a blank line. As the exchange between A and B resumes, the rhyming pattern is maintained, although it is less regular and stanza divisions are no longer marked by blank lines. At A5r 20, the stage direction 'intrat fulgens dicens' ushers in the Roman father who delivers a twelve-stanza speech, duly arranged so as to increase the reader's appreciation of Fulgens's regular and elegant lines. The rhyming pattern finally breaks when A and B are once again together on stage towards the end of BIV. Another stage direction at B2v 18 – 'Intrat fulgeus lucres & ancilla & dicat' – signals the entrance of the noble Roman father and his virtuous daughter and the resumption of rhyme royal stanzas, thus marking a break from A's speech and its unsophisticated rhyming pattern (AAAB). The regularity with which the verse changes to signal difference in plot and characterization is constant throughout the two parts of the play. Lucrece, whose lines are always impeccably regular, lapses into irregular verse, as she briefly interacts with Ancilla at the bottom of B3v. As in *Four Elements*, when the lower-rank characters use verse, the rhyming pattern is either irregular or predominantly made up of tail-rhyme stanzas. The use of different rhyming patterns is so subtle that when Cornelius, the socially lower but morally superior suitor, joins A and B in Part II he uses tail-rhyme stanzas, but switches to rhyme royal stanzas when he interacts with Lucrece and the other higher-rank characters. Even Lucrece switches to irregular couplets when speaking to A and B, but reverts to rhyme royal stanzas as soon as she is left alone on stage, even for the length of a single stanza, as in E5v.

The typographical features in *Fulgens and Lucrece* and *Four Elements* appear even more distinctive of John Rastell's presswork when compared to the text of the three interludes printed by Wynkyn de Worde in the first quarter of the sixteenth century. The paragraph signs in *Hyckescorner* (STC 14039, *c.* 1515), for example, are used exclusively to highlight speech prefixes, which are placed respectively on the left and the right margin of each consecutive verso and recto page. The verse is irregular throughout, and no effort is invested in the visual arrangement of the dialogue. In *The World and the Child* (STC 25982, 1522), speech prefixes are centred but paragraph signs are still used to highlight changes of speakers, and although some parts of the text are in verse, the layout is not devised to set them apart from the rest of the play. In *Youth*, the latest of the three interludes printed by de Worde (STC 14111, 1530–35), the speech prefixes move again to the left and to the right margins and paragraph signs are used exclusively to highlight speech prefixes, thus showing no evolution in the setting of dramatic texts in de Worde's printing house.

The manuscript annotations added to the only extant complete copy of *Fulgens and Lucrece*, held at the Huntington Library (62599), show that sixteenth-century readers responded to the literary qualities foregrounded by Rastell's use of typographical conventions and cared enough about

The man is madde J trowe
So madde J am that nedis J must
As in this poynt haue my lust
How so euer J doo
Parde ye may do me that request
for why it is but good and honest

Et osculabit.   Intrat A.
A Now a felychip J the beseche
   Set euen suche a patche one my breche
B A wyld sepre thetone
an. Goddis mercy this is he
   That J haue sought so
A Haue ye sought me
an. ye that haue J do
   This gentylman can wytnes bere
   That all this owre J haue stonde here
   Sechyng euen for you
A Haue ye two be togeder so longe
an. ye why not
A Mary then all is wrong
   J fere me so now
B Nay nay here be to many wytnes
   for to make ony syche besynes
   As thou wenest hardely
an. why what is the mannes thought
   Suppose ye that J wolde be nowght
   yf no man were by
B Nay for god y ment not so
   But J wolde no man sholde haue to do
   with you but onely J
an. Haue to do φ a. what call ye that.
   Hyt sowndyth to a thing J wote ner what

17. *Fulgens and Lucrece*, 1512–16?

textual accuracy to emend the text when Rastell's generally high standards momentarily lapsed. The last page of this copy of *Fulgens and Lucrece* bears the inscription 'I am Miles Blomefyldes booke'. According to Alan Nelson, 'this famous sixteenth-century collector of plays ... may have been the corrector' (1980: 28).[16] Most corrections add missing speech prefixes (C6r 2, 5 fig. 17) or signal that speech prefixes are misplaced.[17] Interestingly, both the sixteenth-century corrector and the twentieth-century editor noticed that 'the novelty of the enterprise seems to have given Rastell some difficulties, particularly in respect to speech headings in Part I' (Nelson 1980: 28).

Other corrections not related to speech prefixes focus on anomalies in the rhyming pattern and visual layout of regular stanzas. On A6r (fig. 18), for example, the corrector intervenes to emend the visual arrangement of the second stanza and adds a paragraph sign in order to signal the beginning of the third stanza. Similarly, on B1r (fig. 19), the corrector adds the suffix 'yng' to 'counsell' in order to restore the final couplet of the third rhyme royal stanza. The couplet itself is highlighted by the straight rule drawn above the added suffix. The corrector missed a further irregularity on A6v. An abnormal rhyming pattern in this section of the dialogue must have confused the compositor, who assumed that 'case' in the first line was the opening of a new stanza, while it is in fact the last line of the last stanza on A6r. The visual layout of the next two stanzas is muddled as a result. As pointed out above, the rhyming patterns are normally regular when the Roman characters are speaking, and this sort of irregularity is very rare. This irregularity in the rhyming pattern and, consequently, in the visual layout of several consecutive stanzas, shows how easily the compositor(s) could be misled. By the same token, the clean quality of the text elsewhere suggests careful setting of a clear and well-prepared copy. Also worth noting is the fact that, although the corrector failed to redress the irregularity on A6v, his manuscript corrections to layout and rhyming patterns confirm that he appreciated the importance of these conventions and that he regarded related anomalies in the text of *Fulgens and Lucrece* as worth emending.

The level of attention bestowed on the accurate transmission of the texts of *The Four Elements* and *Fulgens and Lucrece* into print suggests continuity of practices across the dramatic and non-dramatic outputs of the Rastells' presses and the far-reaching influence of humanist editorial traditions. However, the predominantly collaborative nature of dramatic authorship at the beginning of the sixteenth century may account for one important difference between the editorial tradition associated with Erasmus, Thomas More and other contemporary humanist scholars and the Rastells' approach to dramatic publication. Erasmus and More's preoccupation with the preservation or recovery of authorial intentions seems fundamentally at odds with early modern models of dramatic authorship. Representative of the level of collaboration elicited by the composition and publication of early Tudor interludes is *Gentleness and Nobility*, which was probably written by John Heywood in 1523, soon after he arrived in

For the whiche I thank all mighty god of his grace

Than haue I a wyfe of gode condicyon
And right coformable to myn entent
In euery thing that is to be done
And how be it that god hath me not sent
An hayr male whiche were conuenient
My name to cotinew and it to repeyre
yet am I not vtterly deſtitute of an heyre

For I haue a doughter in whom I delight
As for the chefe comfort of myn olde age
And ſurely my ſeyd doughter lucres doth hight
Men ſepth ſhe is as lyke me in viſage
As though ſhe were euyn myn owne ymage
For the whiche cauſe nature doth me force & bynde

The more to fauour and loue here in my mynde
But yet to the principall and grettiſt occaſion
That makyth me to loue her as I do
Is this whiche I ſpeke not of affection
But euyn as the treuth mouith me ther to
Nature hath wrought in my lucres ſo
That to ſpeke of beaute and clere vnderſtanding
I can not thinke in here what ſhold be lakking

And beſides all that yet a gretter thing
whiche is not oft ſene in ſo yong a dameſell
She is ſo diſcrete and ſad in all demeanyng
And therto full of honeſt and verteous counſell
Of here owne mynd that wonder is to tell
The giftes of nature and of eſpeciall grace

18. *Fulgens and Lucrece*, 1512–16?

That my defire is to honour & aduaunce
your doughter lucres if fhe will agree
That I fo poze a man her hufbonde fhuld be.

ful. ¶Ye nede not fyr to vfe thefe wozdis to me
For nou in this cyte knowith better than I
Of what grete birth oz fubftaunce ye be
My doughter lucres is full vnwozthy
Of birth & goodis to loke fo hye
Sauyng that happily her gode côdicyon
May her enable to fuche a pzomocyon

But if this be youre mynde and fuche intent
why do ye not laboure to her therfoze
For me femyth it were ryght expedient
That we know therin her mynde befoze
Oz euer we fhold cômune therof any moze
For if fhe wold to your mynde apply
No man fhalbe fo glad therof as I

coz. ¶Suppofe ye that I dyde not fo begyn
To gete fyzfte her fauoure yes trufte me well.

ful. ¶And what comfozt wolde fhe gyue you therin
coz. ¶By my feyth no grete comfozt to tell
Saue that fhe abideth to haue youre counfell
For as fhe feyth fhe will no thing.
In fuche mater to do with oute your counfell

Noz other wyfe than ye fhalbe contente
And theruppon it was my mynde & defire
To fpeke with you of her foz the fame intent
your gode will in this behalfe to requyre
For I am fo bzent in loues fyze
That no thing may my payne aflake
withoute that ye wyll my cure vndertake

           b.f.

19. Fulgens and Lucrece, 1512–16?

London and around the time he married John Rastell's daughter, Joan. Some scholars believe that the epilogue was written by John Rastell and that the play was printed when William was already working in his father's printing house. The mixture of Latin and English stage directions has also been interpreted as a symptom of collaboration or revision (Axton 1979: 22). Interestingly, later interludes, such as *The Play of the Weather* (STC 13305, 1533) and *The Play of Love* (STC 13303, 1534), which deploy more distinctively classical conventions, such as scant stage directions[18] and regular verse and stanza divisions,[19] include John Heywood's name on their title pages. However, the majority of the Rastells' interludes refrain from privileging one agent – either the 'compiler', or the reviser, or the printer-corrector – over the other members of the Rastells' circle, who collectively contributed to the compilation and the transmission of the first English playbooks into print.

Although the Rastells–More–Heywood circle was exceptional for its strong familial, intellectual and professional connections, the collaborative model of dramatic composition and publication associated with it was not. Recent textual scholars date the rise of singular dramatic authorship towards the end of the sixteenth and the beginning of the seventeenth centuries, when the names of dramatists like Shakespeare and Jonson started to appear on the title pages of plays originally written for the commercial stage.[20] However, compared to other types of literary authorship, playwrighting remained a predominantly collaborative process throughout the sixteenth and the opening decades of the seventeenth centuries. It is therefore hardly surprising that the fraught negotiations between authorial and editorial intentions in relation to the establishment of an authoritative text, which emerge so vividly and so frequently from the paratextual materials prefaced to Erasmus's and More's works, scholarly editions and translations, are altogether absent from printed English playbooks, at least until the rise of named editors of Shakespeare at the beginning of the eighteenth century. What the Rastells inherited from the editorial tradition associated with contemporary humanist scholars like Erasmus and More was a distinctive commitment to textual accuracy.

Twentieth-century editors have remarked on the textual accuracy of the early Tudor interludes issued by the Rastells' presses. According to Greg, 'the original impression of [*Calisto and Melebea*] is by no means a bad piece of printing if we except a few passages . . . [and] the press-work is good' (Greg 1908b: vi). According to editors of *The Play of the Weather*, the 'text is complete with no unclear or missing words' (Robinson 1987: 5) and Heywood himself might have overseen its impression (Canzler 1968: 313).

The textual quality of the interludes printed by John and William Rastell have far-reaching implications for our understanding of the publication of later Tudor and Stuart drama. As Greg Walker has pointed out, 'Jonson's decision to present his plays in a certain textual form, evoking the iconography and rhetoric of other, more prestigious genres, was in many ways simply a repetition of the decisions and practices of the early printers, who began to produce playbooks in a variety of forms almost exactly a hundred years earlier' (Walker 1998: 9).

Overall, the level of editorial attention bestowed on the printing of the interludes issued by John and William Rastell's presses undermines the received notion according to which English printers worked in isolation and never positively compared to their Continental competitors. The publication of English dramatic literature in the early modern period had a discontinuous development, but it certainly got off to an impressive start thanks to the More–Rastell–Heywood circle. Claiming that 'without Erasmus, we would not have had Shakespeare' (Norland 1995: 94) might seem an overstatement.[21] However, it certainly seems true that without Erasmus and the influence of his editorial practices on More and his humanist circle, English printed drama would not have set such an outstanding example, which was to inspire later Tudor dramatists, including Shakespeare.

CHAPTER 2

Italian influences on the publication of late Tudor drama

The publication of early Tudor interludes was brought to an abrupt end by a series of traumatic events in the mid-1530s. William Rastell stopped printing shortly before More's execution in 1535 and his father John died in prison in 1536. An interval of roughly ten years separates the last interlude printed by the Rastells from the next, Heywood's *The Four P's* (STC 13300), which was printed by William Middleton around 1544. English drama was increasingly regulated and its growth stifled during the last years of Henry VIII's reign.[1] Official control tightened under Edward and Mary,[2] and John Bale's interludes were printed abroad while Bale was in exile.[3] Only when Elizabeth came to power did printers like Richard Tottell, Thomas Berthelet and William Copland start printing playbooks again.[4] Elizabeth's personal interest in dramatic performance, pageants and courtly entertainments and her less overtly interventionist approach to the regulation of dramatic activities[5] certainly played a crucial role in the resurgence of late Tudor drama. However, the second most important development in the history of English printed drama since its auspicious beginnings in the early Tudor period was once again triggered by Continental influences, and, more specifically, by the impact of the editorial practices and conventions associated with contemporary Italian drama in print on some enterprising members of the London book trade.

During the first half of the *Cinquecento*, Ariosto, Trissino, Machiavelli, Aretino and Cinthio wrote tragedies and comedies which were to affect the course of modern European drama. Their subject matter was drawn from Italian *novelle* and their structure from the classical models derived from Seneca, Plautus and Terence. Mid-sixteenth-century printers, based mostly in Venice, made these plays available in scholarly editions, which circulated widely throughout the rest of Europe. The advanced level of textual and philological studies in Italy meant that Italian printers could rely on the assistance of professional, scholarly editors. According to Brian Richardson, 'in the latest third of the fifteenth century, the gap between [classical and vernacular textual scholarship] started to narrow ... and the older [vernacular] texts began to be treated with the same care that might be applied to a classical text' (1994: x). Pietro Bembo and Vincenzo Borghini, for example, who had trained under Poliziano and Vettori, two of the most famous classical scholars at the end of the fifteenth century, were regularly employed by Aldo Manuzio in Venice and by the Giunti family in Florence to prepare their vernacular books for the press. By the mid-sixteenth century, more and more professional editors of vernacular texts followed Bembo's and Borghini's example and established regular professional links with specific printing houses. Lodovico Dolce and Girolamo Ruscelli's names, for example, appear frequently on the title pages of books issued by Gabriele Giolito and Giacomo Giglio, two Venetian printers who regularly printed playbooks and exploited the reputation of their editors in order to attract wider readerships.[6]

The circulation of Italian playbooks and their influence on late Tudor literary coteries increased during the second half of the sixteenth century thanks to regular migrations of intellectuals and men of letters from the South of Europe. Particularly significant were the counter-flow of Marian exiles from the Continent, which started soon after Elizabeth's accession, and the growing number of Italian Protestant refugees who came to London to flee the Counter-Reformation in their own country. Prominent literary figures among the Italian exiles who lived and worked in London during Elizabeth's reign include Giovanni Battista Castiglione, John Florio, Giacomo Castelvetro, Petruccio Ubaldini and Scipione Gentili. Castiglione and Florio taught Elizabeth and her courtiers Italian, thus creating a taste for Italian language and literature. Italianate drama, translations and adaptations of Italian plays which combined vernacular sources with classical models of tragedy and comedy became particularly popular at Court and at the Inns of Court starting from the early 1560s. A representative example is *The Tragedie of Tancred and Gismund* (STC 25764, 1591), which was first 'compiled' and staged by the 'Gentlemen of the Inner Temple' in 1567–8. The prologue in this tragedy was inspired by Lodovico Dolce's *Didone* (1547), whereas the subject matter was drawn directly from Boccaccio's *Decameron*, although Antonio Cammelli had first dramatized it in 1499 (Cunliffe 1912: xxxvi, lxxxiv).

Italianate drama soon grew out of fashion, as suggested by Wilmot's decision to 'revive and polish' *Tancred and Gismund* for the press in 1591. His efforts as editor and reviser are usefully described in William Webbe's dedicatory letter to Wilmot:

I cannot sufficiently commend your more then charitable zeale, and scholerly compassion towards him [the text], that haue not only rescued and defended him from the deuouring iawes of obliuion, but vouchsafed also to apparrel him in a new sute at your own charges, wherin he may again more boldly come abroad, and by your permission returne to his olde parents, clothed perhaps not in richer or more costly furniture then it went from them, but in handsomnes & fashion more answerable to these times, wherein fashions are so often altered. (*3v 2–12)[7]

By the mid-1580s, Italianate tragedies and comedies had started to be replaced by courtly drama written specifically for children companies and by royal entertainments. Their legacy, though, was far-reaching. The introduction of blank verse as a standard metre for English drama, traditionally credited to Sackville (Cunliffe 1912: lxxxi), is possibly the best known aspect of that legacy. Less well known is the legacy of Italian and Italianate drama in relation to the printing and publication of late Tudor drama.

'FOLLOWING THE ITALIANS' HUMOUR': THE RISE OF EDITORIAL DISCOURSE IN THE ENGLISH DRAMATIC PARATEXT

Printed editions of Italian playbooks often included self-conscious references to the editorial process leading to their publication. References to the origin of the printer's copy and the alleged accuracy of the impression are often advertised on the title page. Trissino's *La Sophonisba*, for example, whose status as a noteworthy literary endeavour is emphasized by its dedication to Pope Leo X, was reprinted several times throughout the sixteenth century, and each time the reader was reassured that an appropriate level of editorial attention had been bestowed on the improvement and correction of its text. Typically, the 1560 and the 1585 editions issued by Francesco Lorenzini in Turin and by Domenico Cavalcalupo in Venice claim to be 'newly corrected and reprinted'[8] and 'newly corrected and reprinted with great care'.[9] Similarly, the 1553 edition issued by the prestigious press of Gabriele Giolito in Venice characteristically claims to be 'newly reprinted and based on the first edition'.[10] Italian printed playbooks started to develop increasingly large paratextual apparatuses, within which editors explained the extent of their intervention and the rationale underlying their use of textual and commentary notes. One notable example is Girolamo Ruscelli's 1554 edition of contemporary Italian comedies. In the dedicatory epistle to Nicola Manuali, he describes his task in great detail:

Having decided to redeem from neglect many books, which have so far been poorly edited by their publishers, either through lack of care or to increase their profit, I have started by gathering in one volume our best writers of comedy. I have arranged their comedies in the order in which they were written, which can now be safely read even by our philologists. Purged from the many mistakes, which formerly abounded in their texts, these comedies will no longer offend the ears and judgment of those who hear them, nor the eyes of those who watch them. In order to please scholarly readers, I have added some short annotations to shed light on some obscure passages and to explain unfamiliar rules, which may be interpreted as errors and blamed on their authors. (A2v 26–37, A3r 1–2)[11]

The commentary notes reveal Ruscelli's familiarity with earlier editions, provide the etymology of unusual words and expressions, and explain why, on specific occasions, he has intervened or refrained from modifying the received text.[12] The notes on *La Mandragola* are introduced by an interesting account of the progressive degeneration of the text of this comedy and of the poor quality of posthumous editions of Machiavelli's works:

The poor quality of the texts of those works which were printed in Rome after his death is due to the inexperience of those who prepared them for the press, rather than to the author's ignorance of our language. New mistakes inevitably creep into the text, when it is carelessly transcribed or printed. Besides, those who published them were unfamiliar with the [Florentine] language and they emended what they thought were mistakes, thus forcing the text to speak their own language. (M3v 1–15)[13]

Even by Italian and Continental standards, Ruscelli's apparatus is highly professional and deservedly advertised on the title page of the collection.

When Italianate drama was at its most popular at Court and at Inns of Court, editions of English plays started to advertise editorial concerns, challenges and achievements, thus echoing the paratext of editions like Ruscelli's 1554 collection of Italian comedies. One example is the first edition of Thomas Norton and Thomas Sackville's *The Tragedy of Ferrex and Porrex (Gorboduc)*, printed by William Griffith in 1565 (STC 18684), which shows clear signs of Continental, and possibly Italian, influences. This edition is self-consciously literary: on its title page, for example, 'wrytten by' replaces 'compiled by' or 'made by', the conventional formulas used in interludes to signal attribution.[14] Italian influences must have been particularly strong on Sackville, who had started his literary career as a member of the Italianate school of poetry promoted by Richard Tottell, the publisher of the influential *Miscellany* of 1555.[15] Even more crucially, when John Day issued the second edition of *Gorboduc* in 1570 (STC 18685), he added an address to the reader, which raises interesting editorial concerns, by claiming that Norton and Sackville never intended their tragedy to be printed and that it was 'put ... forth excedingly corrupted' (Aiir lines 12–13). Day uses the startling image of a ravaged maid to describe the surreptitious edition of 1565:

euen as if by meanes of a broker for hire, he [the printer] should haue entised into his house a faire maide and done her villanie, and after all to bescratched her face, torne her apparell, berayed and disfigured her, and then thrust her out of dores dishonested. (Aiir lines 13–16)

Developing his simile further, Day announces that the authors, 'though they were very much displeased that she so ranne abroad without leaue, . . . haue for common honestie and shamefastnesse new apparelled, trimmed, and attired her in such forme as she was before' (Aiir lines 20–4). This passage suggests authorial annotation of the unauthorized version, which was then indeed used by Day as copy for his edition (Greg 1939–59: I 115; Cauthen 1962: 231–3). Although the differences between Griffith and Day's editions may not justify Day's attack on Griffith's edition,[16] the dramatic narrative provided by the printer's address to the reader foregrounds interesting editorial issues, including an ostensible anxiety about the origin of copy, which is personified and gendered by its vulnerability to corruption. Should his restored version of the text of *Gorboduc* receive a cold welcome, Day predicts that 'she poore gentlewomā wil surely play Lucreces part' (Aiir lines 35–6).[17]

Even more pronounced is the influence of Continental, and specifically Italian, editorial practices on *Supposes* and *Jocasta*, which Gascoigne translated and adapted from Ariosto's *I Suppositi* and Lodovico Dolce's *Giocasta*. *Supposes* and *Jocasta* were staged at Gray's Inn in 1566 and were first printed in Gascoigne's 1573 miscellaneous collection *A Hundreth Sundrie Flowers* (STC 11635). Italian influences are reflected not only in the choice of Italian sources, but also in the author's sustained editorial involvement, which is particularly prominent in *The Posies*, a revised version published in 1575 (STC 11636).

In *The Posies* Gascoigne added lengthy addresses 'To the reuerende Diuines', 'To al young Gentlemen' and 'To the Readers generally', in order to explain how he had reformed some of the shortest pieces included in the 1573 edition, which had caused offence, and how he had carefully edited his work:

[A]s [Theodore Beza] termed . . . [such Poemes as he vvrote in youth] . . . at last *Poëmata Castrata*, so shal your reuerend iudgements beholde in this seconde edition, my Poemes gelded from all filthie phrases, corrected in all erronious places, and beautified vvith addition of many moral examples. (¶.iv.r 18–23)

The Erasmian association between the 'correction of erronious places' and moral reform casts Gascoigne in the role of a *castigator*, the Latin term used by Erasmus and his collaborators to describe an editor, literally one who *castigates* words. A short note at the end of *Jocasta* draws attention to Gascoigne's most visible intervention in the text of this play:

NOte (Reader) that there vvere in *Thebes* fovvre principall gates, vvherof the chief and most commonly vsed vvere the gates called *Electrae* and the gates *Homoloydes*. Thys I haue thought good to explane: as also certē vvords vvhich are not cōmon in vse are noted and expounded in the margent. I did begin those notes at request of a gentlevvoman vvho vnderstode not poëtycall vvords or termes. I trust those and the rest of my notes throughout the booke, shall not be hurtfull to any Reader. (D3v 9–18)

Echoing Ruscelli, the author-editor-annotator of the 1575 edition advertises the commentary notes, which, along with the rest of the sprawling paratextual materials included in it, frame the dramatic text and turn it into a reading text.[18]

The influence of Italian editorial practices can be detected not only in the progressive emergence of explicit references to the editorial task in dramatic paratexts published during the 1570s, but also in the publishing careers of two prominent London stationers, John Wolfe and Richard Jones. Their profiles show distinctive similarities. Although they collaborated only occasionally,[19] they were both actively involved in the printers' rebellion against royal monopolies, which started in the late 1570s and culminated in the early 1580s under Wolfe's leadership.[20] Wolfe and Jones were the most adventurous of the London printers who took part in the rebellion in seeking alternative niche markets. Unlike the vast majority of their fellow stationers, Wolfe and Jones specialized in printing Italian and English literary books. Both printers targeted specific constituencies of literary-minded and affluent readers: while Wolfe catered for the Italian-speaking literary coteries in London and on the Continent, Jones developed a regular working relationship with the members of the Inns of Court, who supported his business both by working for him as authors, procurers of copy, editors and translators and by providing most of Jones's custom. Several of Jones's publications document his reliance on the students at the Inns of Court as collaborators and customers. *A Poore Knight his Pallace of Priuate Pleasures* (STC 4283), for example, was written, as the title page specifies, 'by a student in Cābridge' and 'published by I. C. Gent.', who signs the address to the reader as 'From my Chamber in Grayes Inne. I.C.' Another explicit reference to the extent to which Jones's business depended on the Inns of Court can be found in the address 'To the Gentlemen Readers' included in his collection, *The Arbor of Amorous Deuices* (1597, STC 3631). 'RIght courteous Gentlemen', Jones starts, 'your absence, this long time of vacation hindered my poore Presse from publishing any pleasing Pamphlet'. '[Y]et now', Jones continues on a more positive note, 'to giue you notice that your old Printer forgetteh not his best friendes, he hath thought it meet to remember his duetifull good wil he beareth to you all, publishing this pleasant [pamphlet]' (A2r 4–11). Jones also reprints books written by students of the Inns of Courts several years after their first edition: Edward Hake, for example, explains how he 'corrected' his collection of satires *Newes out of Powles Churchyarde* (STC 12606, 1579) 'in many places' (A4r 11–12) on behalf of Jones twelve years after it had first been published during his days as a student at the Inns of Chancery. Hake also points out that Jones has paid him no extra fee for 'writing altering or correcting of the same', though 'gaine', Hake adds, 'is not the onely, no nor the chiefest ende hee respecteth' (A3r 10–17).

Also remarkable is Wolfe's and Jones's recurrent use of paratextual materials, which introduce the reader not only to the subject matter, but also to the process whereby the copy was written, procured, brought to press and turned into print. Kirk Melnikoff has established that Jones 'penned a virtually unrivalled amount of prefatory material – sixteen extant dedications and addresses in all' and that 'only John Wolfe is comparable, having written approximately twenty prefaces . . . [and] published twice as many texts as Jones' (2001: 158 and 171, fn 31). The rest of this chapter is devoted to a detailed exploration of Wolfe's editorial practices and their influences on Jones, who, by turning to English commercial drama towards the end of his publishing career, provides a crucial link between the publication of Italian (and Italianate) drama and the publication of English plays written for the public stage.

'GIOVANNI VUOLFIO, INGLESE': THE PUBLICATIONS OF ITALIAN BOOKS IN LATE SIXTEENTH-CENTURY LONDON

Except for the Italian books printed by John Charlewood for Giordano Bruno during his visit to England in 1583–5,[21] and the small number of Italian books issued by other stationers,[22] Wolfe was solely responsible for printing the most influential books of the Italian Renaissance to be made available in London towards the end of the sixteenth century. Among these, particularly prominent are Aretino's *Ragionamenti* (1584) and his *Quattro Comedie* (1588), a tri-lingual edition of Castiglione's *The Courtier* (1588), Guarini's *Il Pastor Fido* (1590), and Machiavelli's *I Discorsi* (1584), *Il Principe* (1584), *Historie* (1587), *Arte della Guerra* (1587), and *L'Asino D'Oro*, in a collection which included *La Mandragola* (1588). The outstanding output of his press may be due to the fact that Wolfe seems to have completed his professional training in Italy. After serving seven years of his apprenticeship with John Day in London, Wolfe probably travelled to Europe and may have worked for the Giunti in Florence, as suggested by the imprints on two religious poems, published 'In Fiorenza, Ad Instanzia di Giovanni Vuolfio, Inglese, 1576'.[23] Further circumstantial evidence suggests that Wolfe worked and trained as a printer in Florence. As Mark Bland points out, Wolfe adopted the Giunti device on his return to England (1998: 102). Also significant is the fact that in his edition of Aconcio's *Vna Essortatione al Timor di Dio* (STC 92, 1579?), Giovanni Battista Castiglione explains that he was encouraged to publish this 'volumetto' by 'the timely arrival in this city of a young man, recently returned from Italy, where he diligently learned the art of printing'.[24] As late as 1593, Gabriel Harvey addressed his *A Nevv Letter of Notable Contents* (STC 12902) to 'My Loving Friend, Iohn Wolfe, Printer to the Cittie' and flattered Wolfe by praising his first-hand familiarity with Italian language and literature. '[H]e that hath read, and heard so many gallant Florentine Discourses as you haue done', Harvey remarks, 'may the better discerne, what is what' (A4r 23–5).

No documentary evidence has yet been found to confirm Wolfe's connection with the Giunti in Florence. However, there is no doubt that his decision to print Italian books in London was made possible by the close working relations which he established with prominent Italian émigrés once he settled back in London at the end of the 1570s. Wolfe conformed to the standard practice shared by the best printing houses on the Continent by enlisting the services of an impressive number of Italian authors and editors, including Giovan Battista Castiglione, Giacomo Castelvetro, Scipione Gentili, Giovan Battista Aurelio, Petruccio Ubaldini and John Florio. Castelvetro's role as an editor is particularly significant because, unlike the other authors and editors who worked for Wolfe, he devoted himself exclusively to the publication of other writers' works and never published his own. In this respect, Castelvetro represents one of the earliest instances of a 'professional' editor. Castelvetro left a scattering of elusive textual traces in Wolfe's books. Sheila Dimsey, for example, points out that Baocium Sultaceterum, the fictitious publisher of Thomas Lieber Erastus's *Explicatio* (1589), contains a cryptogram of Iacobum Casteluetrum (1928: 427). Similarly, Eleanor Rosenberg draws attention to an inscription in Castelvetro's hand on a copy of Wolfe's edition of Mendoza's *L'Historia della China* at the Library of Columbia University in New York (1943: 119–48). Building on the pioneering work by Dimsey and Rosenberg, Paola Ottolenghi demonstrates that although only seven volumes dating from 1584 to 1591 include signed dedications and addresses,[25] Castelvetro was also responsible for the prefatory material and the editorial work which went into Wolfe's editions of Machiavelli's and Aretino's works (Ottolenghi 1982).[26]

The extensive paratext included in Wolfe's books generally advertises the fact that the texts have suffered no editorial interference or tampering in the printing house, when the authors are still alive and directly involved in the publication process. A representative example is Robert Southwell's address to the reader in *Marie Magdalens Funeral Teares* (STC 22950, 1591). Southwell initially apologizes for the book's shortcomings but then he concludes that 'it seemed a lesse euill to let it flie to common viewe in the natiue plume . . . then . . . cast off from the fist of such a corrector, as might happily haue perished the sound, and imped in some sicke and sory fethers of his owne phansies' (A8r 13–21). Similarly, in his book, *Le vite delle donne illustri* (STC 24487.5, 1591), also published by Wolfe, Ubaldini refers to the risks involved by non-authorial interference with the printer's copy: 'as it happens, explanatory notes in the margins written by a different pen, often differ from the author's intentions'.[27] By contrast, references to editorial intervention proliferate in Wolfe's editions of eminent dead authors, including Aretino, Guarini and Machiavelli, who had already acquired the status of Italian classics and as such stimulated proprietary claims on the part of editors who felt obliged to explain to their readers how they had established their texts.

Editorial intervention is proudly advertised in Wolfe's 1584 edition of Machiavelli's *I Discorsi* (STC 17159), which, according to the fictitious imprint, was published by the heirs of Antoniello degli Antonielli in Palermo. This edition includes an address to the reader which was clearly written by a humanist scholar familiar with Machiavelli's classical sources. According to Ottolenghi, Castelvetro himself wrote this address to inform his readers that the author's holograph was regrettably unavailable and that two earlier editions published by the Aldine presses (1546) and by Giolito (1550) had served as copy-texts.[28] The reader is warned that orthographic inconsistencies, such as 'Prencipato, & Principato, Qualunque, & Qualunche, Condennare, & Condannare, Arezo, & Arezzo', stem from copy, and that the author himself is responsible for idiomatic and syntactically incorrect turns of phrase and for mistakenly quoting from Caesar instead of Livy. The 'discreet and knowing reader' is invited to emend the minor errors included in the list of errata at the end of the volume, and to forgive the compositors' mistakes, who, 'being Sicilian [read 'English'], [are] unfamiliar with the Tuscan language [read 'Italian']' (cc8v 31–4).[29] By far the most significant aspect of this address to the reader is the editor's confident appeal to those who have access to his copy-texts: 'should you care to collate them, you would find that my edition has removed errors, which . . . you wouldn't regard too lightly'.[30] Recurrent corrections in Wolfe's edition aim to replace the indicative with the more appropriate subjunctive tense,[31] and to ensure consistency between subject and verb in the same sentence.[32]

The prefatory materials attached to *La Prima Parte dei Ragionamenti di Pietro Aretino* (STC 19911.5, 1584) echo another familiar aspect of the Italian paratext, by conjuring learned disputes between competing printing houses and their editors. The address to the reader in Aretino's *Ragionamenti* is signed by 'Il Barbagrigia, Stampatore'. Only a learned man of letters, familiar with recent diatribes between humanist printers in Italy, could have known that Blado, the Roman publisher of the first edition of *Ragionamenti* (1539), used this pseudonym in order to 'enter into the spirit . . . of a sportive literary wrangle' (Lievsay 1969: 19). The fictitious place of publication chosen by Wolfe takes the literary joke further, 'Bengodi' being the utopian city which Boccaccio used as setting for the third story of the eighth day in his *Decameron*.[33] Under the guise of the fictitious printer Barbagrigia, the editor taunts his predecessors by claiming that his text restores authorial intentions by printing *Ragionamenti* as Aretino had wanted it to reach his readers and not as others had published it, full of errors and against his wishes.[34]

The new prefatory materials added to Machiavelli's *Historie* (STC 17161, 1587) conjure a similar controversy between Antoniello degli Antonielli, the fictitious publisher of Machiavelli's *I Discorsi* and *Il Prencipe* (1584), and the present publishers, 'gli heredi del Giolito', both parties being two of Wolfe's manifold incarnations. 'Gli heredi del Giolito' claim to have a much longer experience as printers and publishers of Machiavelli's works and have therefore contrived to pre-empt Antoniello's plan to publish the *Historie*, as announced in the address to the reader in Antoniello's 1584 edition of *I Discorsi*. 'Gli heredi' then proceed to reassure their readers that the present edition was 'emended in many places and diligently reprinted' (A5v 16–18)[35] from earlier versions issued by Giolito's presses. Wolfe's volume, like the earlier volumes issued by Giolito's presses, is a small sedicesimo, but the text is generally more attractively printed: a neat roman type replaces Giolito's italic and wider margins contribute to make Wolfe's page look less crowded. More importantly, the printer's copy must have been carefully annotated prior to being sent to press. Proper nouns are normalized,[36] archaisms are modernized,[37] abbreviations and contractions are correctly used,[38] grammar and punctuation are improved,[39] and roman numbers are consistently replaced by full alphabetical transcriptions. This last category of editorial interventions reveal a trained, expert eye, because a mistake which had eluded the Italian compositors and which was therefore even more likely to elude their English colleagues, is skilfully emended. As a result, 'MCCCXXXIIII' on A5v

10–11 (Giolito 1550) and on A5v 12 (Giolito 1554) becomes 'millequattro-cento trenta quattro' in Wolfe's edition (A5v lines 24–5), finally in keeping with its immediate context.[40] Also worth noticing, as in Machiavelli's *I Discorsi*, is the editor's peculiar effort to normalize verbs in the subjunctive tense.[41]

Wolfe's penchant for fictitious imprints is also worth considering in the light of his self-conscious efforts to emulate scholarly Continental printers. It is well known that Wolfe often forged his imprints and concealed his identity and place of publication by adopting the names of fictitious (or sometimes real) Italian, French or German printing publishers. As mentioned above, Wolfe published Machiavelli's *Il Principe* and *I Discorsi* as Antoniello degli Antonielli in Palermo, Machiavelli's *Historie* as 'gli heredi di Gabriel Giolito de Ferrari' in Piacenza, and *La Prima Parte dei Ragionamenti* by Pietro Aretino as 'Il Barbagrigia' in the fictitious town of Bengodi. As late as the end of the 1580s and the beginning of the 1590s, Wolfe published books as Giovanni Swartz in Munich, Marthurin Marchant in Verdun, Giovan Vincenzo del Pernetto in Turin, Giovan Battista Bofandino in Venice and Giovanni Maria Scoto in Naples. Wolfe's 'forgeries' were clearly motivated by profit, since Continental European imprints made books more desirable. However, the typographical and editorial quality of Wolfe's books was indeed comparable to contemporary books printed and published on the Continent. The fact that Wolfe's books were regularly bought and sold at the Frankfurt Book Fair (Hoppe 1933: 244) is a clear indication that he could compete with continental publishers and booksellers. Furthermore, as Mark Bland has also usefully pointed out, 'the typography of Wolfe's books must have suggested that the neo-classical elegance and decorum of the better Continental printers was also possible in London' (1998: 103). The prefatory materials attached to Wolfe's editions of Machiavelli and Aretino show that Wolfe's false imprints served a much more crucial function than just lucrative self-interest or an indomitable taste for real and mock confrontations with his fellow printers in London and abroad. As Huffman has noted, the prefatory materials in Wolfe's Italian books are clearly meant to construct a peculiarly Continental role for him as 'the humanist printer . . . [who] will find and choose texts and print them with great labor, exercising independence of spirit at every turn, and refusing to be silenced, or even to compromise' (1988: 11–12).

It is also worth stressing that the Italian plays published by Wolfe seem to have received as much editorial attention as any other of his literary publications. His edition of *Qvattro Comedie del Divino Aretino* (STC 19911, 1588), for example, includes a five-page list of errata. Wolfe remarks on its length by openly defying contemporary printers' reluctance to publish errata lists and by arguing that, instead of discrediting the printer's professionalism, those lists contribute to the progressive improvement of textual accuracy in subsequent editions: 'I have therefore decided to list [all the errors] despite the disingenuous opinion entertained by some, according to which listing errata jeopardises the sales of a book. On the contrary', the address continues, 'should others ever wish to re-print these Comedies, they will be able to do it perfectly'.[42] A short editorial note at the end of the volume accounts for the unusual length of the errata list. The copy-texts available at the time when the volume went to press, as the reader is duly informed, were much inferior to 'i testi perfetti', which the printer secured once the printing process was almost completed.[43] When Wolfe reprinted Machiavelli's *La Mandragola* as part of a collection of works by the same author in 1588 (STC 17158), he did not match the level of editorial attention invested by Ruscelli in this comedy in 1554, but he certainly surpassed some of the Italian printers and publishers who had in the meantime re-issued it. Wolfe's edition is an elegant volume, which includes a list of errata and an address to the reader where the quality of the earlier editions of Machiavelli's *Il Principe* and *I Discorsi* is invoked as a precedent of good editorial practice.[44]

The legacy of Wolfe's publishing ventures and his practice of enlisting the editorial services of scholarly assistants were not lost on native professional writers. Several young scholars, translators and men of letters became associated with Wolfe's printing shop in the 1590s, including, among others, John Thorius, John Eliot, Barnaby Barnes, Antony Chute and Anthony Munday. One scholar in particular, though, was going to replace Castelvetro in his editorial role, once Wolfe's troubles with the Stationers' Company came to an end and his commercial interest in Italian books waned. Contemporary allusions to their partnership suggest that Wolfe offered Gabriel Harvey board and lodging in his printing shop, directly opposite the great South Door at St Paul's in exchange for his editorial services.[45] Further evidence is provided by Harvey's biographer, Virginia Stern. In keeping with contemporary practice, most of Harvey's editorial work on contemporary authors was carried out anonymously. Paradoxically, however, as Stern points out, one of the few tangible traces which Harvey left behind in his role as Wolfe's new in-house editorial assistant can be found in a copy of the 1588 edition of *Perimedes* (1588) by his arch-enemy Robert Greene, which is now held in the Bodleian Library (Malone 575[4]). Stern identifies the proof-corrector's hand as Harvey's and believes that 'the book was probably proof-read for John Wolfe in anticipation of . . . a second edition' (Stern 1980: 102). Even more crucially, Wolfe set an important precedent for the publication of playbooks in London in the 1580s which was going to affect his fellow stationer and collaborator Richard Jones, when, after printing old-fashioned interludes, he turned to Italianate drama and then to English plays written for the commercial stage.

RICHARD JONES AND THE PUBLICATION
OF LATE TUDOR DRAMA

Like Wolfe, Richard Jones established working relations with professional writers, who belonged to the same circle of cultivated readers who bought his books. Among them, George Gascoigne seems particularly interesting, because of his connections with the Middle Temple, which he entered in 1548, and the Inner Temple, where *Supposes* and *Jocasta* were first performed. Gascoigne came from a wealthy family, but he squandered his fortunes and was disinherited while he was still young. He was therefore forced to earn a living. He went abroad as a soldier and he met George Whetstone and Thomas Churchyard while serving in an English regiment in the Low Countries in 1572. When they returned to London in 1575, the three friends were once again destitute and unemployed and found in professional writing a vital source of income.[46]

As mentioned above, the prefatory materials added by Gascoigne to the second edition of *A Hundredth Sundrie Flowres* reveal that he was actively involved in its extensive corrections and revisions. A book issued by Jones in 1576 shows that Gascoigne worked not only as an author but also as an editor and procurer of copy. In the address to the reader in Captain Humphrey Gilbert's *A Discouerie for a New Passage to Cataia* (STC 11881), Gascoigne specifies that this treatise is seven years old and that the author had no intention of publishing it. Gascoigne then mentions a visit he had recently paid to Captain Gilbert during which the latter 'tooke [him] vp to his Studie, and there shewed [him] sundrie profitable and verie cõmendable exercises, which he had perfected painefully with his owne penne' (¶¶.ii.r 4–9). The over-scrupulous Captain allowed Gascoigne to borrow *A Discouerie*, but only on condition that he would not take it to the printers. Probably pressed for money, Gascoigne ignored Gilbert's injunction and took it to Jones, who published it in 1576. Gascoigne rather disingenuously explains that he could not deny the public such a useful treatise, despite the Captain's reticence to publish it. He then entreats the reader's good will to excuse any mistake that escaped the author's attention, since the Captain, despite 'perfect[ing]' it 'with his owne penne', never meant it for the press:

[*A Discouerie*] was ment by th'autour, but as a priuate Letter vnto his Brother ... and therefore his imperfections therein (if any were) are to be pardoned, since it is very likely that if he had ment to publish the same, he would with greater heede haue obserued and perused the worke in euerie parte. (¶¶.iii.r 8–17)

Gascoigne also stresses that the Captain 'had neither warning nor time to examine' the proofs (¶¶.iii.v 1–2), since *A Discouerie* came out without his consent. Given the lack of authorial supervision, Gascoigne takes responsibility for 'set[ting] it in the sunshine' (¶¶.iiii.v 12–13).

    The origin of the printer's copy and the identity of the agents responsible for its publication also feature large in books where Jones himself wrote the prefatory materials. The address attached to *The Courte of Ciuill Courtesie* (STC 21134.5, 1577) foregrounds the publisher over the translator Simon Robson. Jones describes the text as 'the traueill of a Gentleman whom I know not, no not so mutch as by name, much lesse by person' (A2r 16–18). The key agent who vouches for the quality of this book is neither the unknown Italian author nor the translator, but the publisher himself, and on no other grounds than his critical judgement. Kirk Melnikoff remarks on Jones's proprietary attitude towards the books which he personally decides to publish as follows:

Unlike many of his peers in an age of censorship and burgeoning literary property, Jones becomes increasingly uninterested in establishing external accountability for his texts as his career proceeds; in fact, he is often forthright about his own personal agency in his choice of texts. (2001: 161)

In keeping with Jones's profile as a discerning publisher is his role as a compiler of literary collections.[47] In *Brittons Bowre of Delights* (STC 3633, 1591), Jones recommends this collection to his readers for 'the well penning' of its 'sundrie fine Deuices, and rare conceytes'. In his dedication 'To the Gentlemen Readers' in *Phillis and Flora* (STC 19880, 1598), Jones boasts about his 'accustomed maner ... to acquaint you with any Booke, or matter ..., that beareth some likelihood to be of worth' (A3r 6–9). This address ends with an interesting appeal, which is representative of Jones's tendency to cast himself as an arbiter of the literary qualities of the books he published: 'If the matter like you, thanke the Gentleman that translated it ... If otherwyse, ... I pray you to pardon mee the Printer, that procured the same from him to be published.' (A3r 23–7)

The prefatory materials included in his dramatic publications confirm Jones's role as procurer and annotator of copy. The two prefaces signed by Jones and already discussed in the Introduction reveal his commitment to fulfil both roles. The first one, 'The Printer to the Reader' in *The Princelye Pleasures, at the Courte at Kenelwoorth* (1576), paints a familiar picture of a publisher who is well aware of his readers' taste for fashionable literary entertainments and is prepared to procure what they most desire. Similarly, Jones's description of the editorial challenges presented by the publication of George Whetstone's *Promos and Cassandra* (1578) registers a combination of conventional modesty with a self-conscious stance towards the text which he, and not the author, prepared for the press: 'if I commit an error, without blaming the Auctor, amend my amisse' (A3v 9–11). Considering how much longer it would take before the name of the editor made its first appearance on the title page of a printed edition of an English play text, Jones's explicit reference to his role as annotator of an imperfect copy is particularly significant. Also telling is the fact that what prompts one of Jones's most detailed accounts of his editorial role is an Italianate comedy.

Jones's earlier dramatic publications lack the paratextual features and the explicit references to the preparation of copy which emerge in *Promos and Cassandra* (1578). The first play printed by Jones, William Wager's *The Longer Thou Livest, the More Fool Thou Art* (STC 24935, 1569?), is described on the title page as a 'mery and pithie commedie', but it is in fact, both in terms of subject-matter and typographical conventions, a humanist inter-lude. The Prologue, which explains to the audience how 'Holsom lessons now and than we shall enterlace, / Good for the ignorant, not hurtfull to the wise' (A2v 30–1), and which praises 'good education' as a 'noble thing . . . For all estates profitable' (A2r 16–17), could have been written by John Rastell. The play itself could have been prepared for Rastell's press. The play is not divided into acts and scenes and the sparse stage directions are either centred or crammed into the left margin. The text seems accurate and printed to very high standards. Mark Benbow, who edited the play in 1968, noticed that the 'quart[o] pose[s] no bibliographical problem' and that 'the manu-script . . . must have been clear, for the compositor had little difficulty with his copy' (1968: xx, xxi). Similarly, the next two plays published by Jones resemble earlier English interludes. Both *Damon and Pithias* (STC 7514, 1571) and *Apius and Virginia* (STC 1059, 1575) have no act and scene division, their speech prefixes are still centred, and paragraph signs are occasionally used to signal changes of speakers and stage directions. Even more cru-cially, neither *Apius and Virginia* nor *Damon and Pithias* registers any attempt to account for the origin of their copy or the identity of the agents involved in the process of their transmission into print. The publication of *Promos and Cassandra* therefore represents a significant turning point in the context of Jones's dramatic publications. Also worth mentioning is the fact that the publication of this play coincides with the beginning of Wolfe's publishing career in London.

When Jones published two more English plays in 1590, he interestingly decided to apply the same conventions introduced by *Promos and Cassandra* to Marlowe's *Tamburlaine* (STC 17425), but not to Robert Wilson's *The Three Lords and the Three Ladies of London* (STC 25783). The latter is advertised on the title page as a 'pleasant and Stately Morall', all its characters are allegorical, and it has no act and scene division. *Tamburlaine*, on the other hand, is, like *Promos and Cassandra*, divided in two parts and printed according to the conventions of Italianate drama. Marlowe's play, though written for the commercial stage, must have struck Jones as closer to the literary tragedies and comedies translated from their Italian originals than Wilson's allegorical play. Marlowe's immensely popular play, with its mighty lines and ambitious structure, must have seemed worthy of the complex presentation and conventions deployed in Jones's edition of *Promos and Cassandra*. As a result, these two plays look strikingly similar. Both title pages provide a brief abstract of the subject matter and then specify that the text is divided into two 'Discourses'. The only major difference between the two plays is that the name of the author in *Promos and Cassandra* has been replaced by the name of the theatrical company who performed *Tamburlaine* 'sundrie times . . . upon Stages in the Citie of London'. The similarities are even more striking once the reader moves beyond the title page. Both plays are divided into acts and scenes, speech prefixes have moved to the left margin and stage directions are centred. Even more importantly, both plays are introduced by paratextual materials detailing the circumstances of publication and the process through which their texts were established. *Tamburlaine*, whose title page omits to mention Marlowe's name, includes no address or dedication by the author, but, like *Promos and Cassandra*, offers an address signed 'Yours, most humble at commaundement, R. I. Printer'. Jones uses this address to explain the quality and purpose of his intervention as annotator of copy:

I haue (purposely) omitted and left out some fond and friuolous Iestures, digressing (and in my poore opinion) far vnmeet for the matter, which I thought, might seeme more tedious vnto the wise, than any way els to be regarded, though (happly) they haue bene of some vaine cōceited fondlings greatly gaped at, what times they were shewed vpon the stage in their graced deformities: neuertheles now, to be mixtured in print with such matter of worth, it wuld prooue a great disgrace to so honorable & stately a historie. (A2r 14–23, A2v 1–2)

Echoing some of the addresses prefaced to his earlier literary publications, Jones foregrounds his critical judgement by describing his intervention as a sustained attempt to distance the text of his edition from the commercial stage.

Internal evidence drawn from the three early editions of *Tamburlaine* printed by Jones suggests that his commitment to preparation of copy may have gone beyond the omission of 'fond and friuolous Iestures'. Recent editors have commented on the 'remarkably clean' quality of the text preserved in Jones's 1590 edition (O1) (Bevington and Rasmussen 1985: xxvi), which was then improved in both its second (1593, O2) and its third edition (1597, O3). Albrecht Wagner and Una Ellis-Fermor established that the second and the third editions derived independently from the first and that neither stems from consultation of a fresh and substantive authority (1885: xxii–xxxi; 1930: 281–2). Ethel Seaton was the first to question their conclusions:

[N]either [Wagner] nor Miss Eliis-Fermor explains how it is that O2, sometimes alone of all [the early editions], gives the correct reading or spelling in more than half a dozen instances ... Other changes from O1 in shades of expression or meaning seem to point to a desire for greater nicety, and thereby to suggest themselves as author's variants. (1932: 467–8)[48]

As explained in the Introduction, annotating readers and correcting authors might indeed introduce intriguingly similar corrections while preparing dramatic copy for the press. However, Seaton's theory of authorial involvement in the publication of O2 is undermined by the fact that O2 *and* O3 display similar variants and that by the time O3 was published Marlowe was dead and could not have been involved in the preparation of the printer's copy for this edition. O3 emends as many substantial mistakes as O2.[49] The type and number of variants introduced in O2 and O3 are also remarkably similar.[50] Both title pages and head-titles were not simply updated but carefully rewritten. In O2 the title page explains that the 'two Tragicall Discourses' were not only 'sundrie times shewed upon Stages in the Citie of London', as in O1, but 'sundrie times *most stately* shewed' etc. (my emphasis). In O3, Tamburlaine, who in O1 'from a Scythian Shephearde ... became a most puissant and mightye Monarque', rises more specifically 'from the *state* of a Shepheard in Scythia' etc. (my emphasis). The dialogue in O2 and O3 also shows a similar level of variation: both editions, for example, introduce seventy-eight verbal substitutions; O2 corrects nine proper nouns and O3 seven; O2 and O3 contain a mere seven interpolations each and fifteen and eight omissions respectively. It is also worth pointing out that O3, rather than O2, introduces six variants which suggest annotation of the printer's copy, rather than routine correction in the printing house. At A6r 10 and A6r 30, O3 adds two extra speech prefixes, so that the lines originally spoken by Ortygius are now assigned to 'All'. While this change seems perfectly appropriate, it is unnecessary. This change is therefore more likely to have originated during the preparation of the printer's copy for O3 than from consultation of the manuscript underlying O1. The omission of two exits at C4v 17 and C6r 28 and two speech prefixes at D4r 1 and F4v 19 indicates that editorial intervention may have been sporadically prompted by the influence of classical conventions. To sum up, the remarkable similarity in the type and number of variants in O2 and O3 challenges Seaton's hypothesis according to which O2 bears the marks of Marlowe's light annotation of the printer's copy. The similarity of variation between O1 and O2 and between O1 and O3 instead suggests accurate presswork and light, non-authorial annotation of copy. Overall, though, the fact that O2 was not used as copy for O3 and a failure to rectify the irregular act and scene division in both O2 and O3 rule out a systematic preparation of either edition for the press.

Further internal evidence suggests that Jones himself may have introduced sporadic changes into the printer's copy for O2 and O3. Jones re-issued Richard Edwards's *Damon and Pithias* in 1582. Both his first and his second editions were published respectively five and sixteen years after Edwards's death in 1566. The second edition of 1581 (Q2), like the second and third editions of *Tamburlaine*, seems to have been set from a lightly annotated copy of the first edition of 1571 (Q1). Most remarkable is the omission of nine exits, seven of which occur consecutively between C3v and F1r.[51] As in O3 *Tamburlaine* the omission of exits may reveal the influence of classical conventions. Another interesting variant in Q2 suggests light annotation of the printer's copy. At D4v 18, a verbal substitution replaces the final word 'pay' with 'yeelde'. Q2 also adds, 'speedely' at the end of this line, which is turned down because of lack of space. 'Yeelde' may represent memorial contamination, since the compositor had set 'to yeld my body here in this place' two lines earlier. However, 'speedely' can only have been added to the printer's copy, since 'speedely' is syntactically unnecessary and typographically awkward for the compositor to set. Overall, the internal evidence provided by Jones's editions of *Tamburlaine* and *Damon and Pithias* is fairly limited. However, Jones's profile as a publisher, his self-conscious intervention in the paratext of his dramatic and non-dramatic publications, and the type of variants which found their way into the multiple editions of these two plays suggest that if the printer's copy was indeed lightly annotated, Jones is the most likely agent responsible for it.

As mentioned earlier, the history of the development of English drama in print was discontinuous. Jones's edition of *A Knack to Know a Knave* (STC 15027, 1594) retains the typographical conventions introduced in *Promos and Cassandra* and *Tamburlaine*, but not the paratextual apparatus which made Jones's editions of these two plays resemble scholarly editions of dramatic texts published in Italy around the middle of the sixteenth century or by Wolfe in London in the 1580s. Furthermore, Jones's appraoch to the preparation of dramatic copy for the press was radically different from the principles which informed the editorial activities undertaken by Wolfe's team of eminent scholars and philologists. Jones's objective was to sporadically correct and improve his copy by distancing it from the commercial stage and not to recover authorial intentions. As with the Rastells, the influence of humanist editorial methods on Jones was qualified both by the status of commerical play texts, which was gradually improving but was still far from established, and by his disregard for authorial intentions. Jones's intervention was prompted by a wish to 'perfect' the text rather than by a programmatic attempt to restore the author's 'true reading'. Even so, Jones's *Promos and Cassandra* and *Tamburlaine*, furnished with paratextual materials which drew their readers' attention to the origin of their copies, their literary value, and the accuracy of their texts, must have had a considerable impact on the first commercial dramatists and their publishers, who managed to consolidate a reading market for printed playbooks during the last decade of the sixteenth century. More specifically, a playwright working for the public stage like Shakespeare, who used Whetstone's *Promos and Cassandra* as a source in *Measure for Measure*, must at the very least have become aware of the literary status granted to this play by its author and its publisher. By the early 1590s, the scene was set for Shakespeare's own debut in print.

PART II

The rise of Shakespeare in print

CHAPTER 3

The Wise Quartos (1597–1602)

Shakespeare the dramatist made his debut in print in 1594, but it was not until 1597 that a London stationer started to invest consistently in the publication of his dramatic works. Andrew Wise published as many as five Shakespearean quartos during his relatively short career (1593–1602), namely *Richard II* and *Richard III* in 1597 (STC 22314; STC 22307), *1 Henry IV* in 1598 (STC 22279a), and *2 Henry IV* (STC 22288) and *Much Ado About Nothing* (STC 22304) in 1600 with William Aspley. The first three quartos proved remarkably popular: Wise published the second and third quartos of *Richard II* in 1598, the second and third quartos of *Richard III* in 1598 and 1602, and the second and third quartos of *1 Henry IV* in 1598 and 1599. On the whole, no other London stationer invested in Shakespeare as assiduously as Wise did, at least while Shakespeare was still alive.[1] Besides, all five Shakespearean quartos published by Wise have traditionally been regarded as authoritative texts, with the possible exception of *Richard III*.[2] Given the authoritative quality of the texts of the Wise Quartos and Wise's consistent investment in Shakespeare during the crucial years while the latter was making a name for himself in print,[3] can we assume that Shakespeare himself corrected the texts of his popular history plays when Wise decided to, or was prompted to, reprint them? Or, are we to assume that he entrusted Wise with their transmission into print? The Wise Quartos, in other words, represent an ideal study case to test Pollard, McKerrow and Greg's optimistic assumption that a direct line of transmission connected authorial manuscripts to the so-called 'good' quarto editions of Shakespeare's works, without any significant 'intereference' from the non-authorial agents involved in their publication.

As Paul Werstine has explained, both R. B. McKerrow's category of 'the author's original draft' and Greg's category of 'foul papers' represent 'a purely ideal form of printer's copy of which there are no examples among extant dramatic manuscripts' (1990: 69). Both categories, still according to Werstine, are 'the product not of reason but of desire – our desire to possess in the "good" quartos Shakespeare's plays in the form in which he, as an individual agent, both began and finished them' (1990: 75). Scott McMillin has similarly pointed out that Pollard and Greg's efforts to establish the 'most economical line of transmission, from author (foul papers) to acting company (prompt book) to printing house' effectively erased non-authorial agents actively involved in the transmission of Shakespeare's texts (2001: 6). Relying on Andrew Gurr's theory that theatrical practice routinely generated variant scribal manuscripts, ranging from the play's 'maximal' version licensed by the Master of the Revels to 'minimal' versions reflecting different stages of theatrical abridgement and revision (1999: 68–87), McMillin argues that transcripts of performed versions of play texts were often presented to patrons or handed over to the printers (2001: 42). McMillin supports his views by referring to Humphrey Moseley's allusion to such manuscripts in the stationer's address to the reader in his edition of Beaumont and Fletcher's *Comedies and Tragedies* (Wing B1581, 1647):

VVhen these *Comedies* and *Tragedies* were presented on the Stage, the *Actours* omitted some *Scenes* and Passages (with the *Authour's* [sic] consent) as occasion led them; and when private friends desir'd a Copy, they then (and justly too) transcribed what they *Acted*. But now you have both All that was *Acted*, and all that was not; even the perfect full Originalls without the least mutilation; So that were the *Authours* living, (and sure they can never dye) they themselves would challenge neither more nor lesse then what is here published; this Volume being now so compleate and finish'd, that the Reader must expect no future Alterations. (A4r 29–37)

The closure of the theatres had prompted the sale of 'maximal' playbooks, which, under normal circumstances, the company would have retained as one of their key assets. Moseley can therefore boast about his copy being none other than 'the perfect full Originalls', as opposed to the minimal playbooks which, according to McMillin, had often served as printer's copy in the past. While McMillin identifies sources of textual proliferation within the working practices of early modern theatrical companies,[4] this chapter focuses on annotating readers as another potential source of textual proliferation within the process of transmission of the Wise Quartos into print.

The assumption that a direct line of transmission connected the authorial manuscripts with the acting company and the printing house lies at the heart of traditional compositorial studies, including Alan Craven's influential investigation of the textual variants in the Shakespeare Quartos set by Compositor A in Valentine Simmes's printing shop. In a typical New Bibliographical fashion Craven assumes that once dramatic manuscripts embarked on their journey to the printers, the quality of the text they preserved could only deteriorate. More specifically, by focusing on reprints set from earlier editions Craven claims to be able to establish the compositor's fidelity to his copy. Craven's method promises to 'strip the veil of print' when applied to texts like the second edition of *Richard II* (Q2), which was printed by Valentine Simmes (and entirely set by Compositor A) for Andrew Wise in 1598 from a copy of the first edition (Q1), and Q1, which had also been printed by Simmes (and mostly set by Compositor A) for Wise in 1597. Craven illustrates his methodology as follows:

Since Q2 was reprinted directly from Q1, a careful collation of the two will reveal the fidelity of Compositor A to copy-readings – the principle involved being that the alterations he made in setting Q2 from printed copy provide at least a rough index to both the number and kinds of changes ... he was likely to make when setting from the no longer extant manuscript (almost certainly Shakespeare's 'foul papers') which served as the copy for the first quarto. (1973: 50)

According to Craven, Compositor A was particularly prone to introducing verbal substitutions and other errors of a memorial nature, which are particularly difficult to spot because they contaminate the text without impairing the sense. Even more crucially, Craven attributes all 155 variants in Q2 to Compositor A,[5] including one single, isolated correction of a speech prefix at 13r 5, where 'yorke' is changed to 'King'. Craven's attribution rests on the assumption that Compositor A had worked out the degree of kinship and power relations among the four speakers in this exchange or that when he came to set the same line – 'Good aunt stand vp' – at 13r 24 he realized that the speech prefix he had set at line 5 was wrong and went back to correct it. Craven's attribution, in other words, relies on the problematic assumption that the compositor was alert to the dramatic consistency of the fictive world of the play, although, as explained in the Introduction, compositors were far more likely to focus their attention on the material and formal aspects of the printed copy, which they were expected to reproduce as closely as possible. A copy of Q1 held at the Huntington Library (69343) preserves one single manuscript annotation which emends the same speech prefix (fig. 20). This annotation is isolated and cannot be dated. However, it is more credibly attributed to an annotating reader than to a printing house agent, given that no other evidence suggests that Q2 was set from this copy of Q1 and that this type of annotation resembles the manuscript corrections added by early modern readers to the printed playbooks surveyed in the Introduction.[6]

More generally, Craven's attribution of all substantive changes which found their way into Q2 *Richard II* to Compositor A would seem to stem

His prayers are full of false hypocrisie,
Ours of true zeale and deepe integritie,
Our prayers do outpray his,then let them haue
. That mercy which true prayer ought to haue.
King ~~yorke~~ Good aunt stahd vp.
  Du. Nay,do not say, stand vp;
Say Pardon first,and afterwards, stand vp,
And if I were thy nurse thy tong to teach,
Pardon should be the first word of thy speach:
· I neuer longd to heare a word till now,
Say pardon King, let pitie teach thee how,
The word is short, but not so short as sweete,
No word like pardon for Kings mouthes so meete.
    yorke Speake it in French, King say, Pardonne moy.
    Du. Dost thou teach pardon pardon to destroy?
Ah my sower husband, my hard-hearted Lord!
That sets the word it selfe against the word :
Speake pardon as tis currant in our land,
The chopping French we do not vnderstand,
Thine eie begins to speake, set thy tongue there:
Or in thy piteous heart plant thou thine eare,
That hearing how our plaints and prayers do pierce,
Pitie may mooue thee pardon to rehearse.
    King H. Good aunt stand vp.
    Du. I do not sue to stand.
Pardon is all the sute I haue in hand.
    King I pardon him as God shall pardon me.
    Du. Oh happy vantage of a kneeling knee,
Yet am I sicke for feare, speake it againe,
Twice saying pardon doth not pardon twaine,
But makes one pardon strong.
    King H. I pardon him with al my heart.
    Du. A god on earth thou art.
    King H. But for our trusty brother in law and the Abbot,
With all the rest of that consorted crew,
Destruction strait shal dog them at the heeles,
Good vncle,help to order seuerall powers,
                I 3   To

20. *Richard II*, 1597

from a New Bibliographical desire to streamline the process of its transmission into print rather than from an accurate assessment of its textual variants and the network of agents, including its publisher, who may have been responsible for them. This chapter explores the possibility that an annotating reader, including Shakespeare or Andrew Wise himself, may have introduced substantive changes in the Wise Quartos, such as the correction of the wrong speech prefix in Q1 *Richard II*, or that Wise may have used copies sporadically emended by annotating readers, like the Huntington copy mentioned above. Andrew Wise was clearly not as enterprising, daring and ambitious as Richard Jones, as suggested by the fact that he wrote no addresses or dedications for his books. However, a closer look at his publishing career and a contrastive analysis of his Shakespearean editions with other playbooks printed in the 1590s show that he may indeed have invested in the perfection of his dramatic copies for the press.

PROFILING ANDREW WISE

Archival research has unearthed very little about Andrew Wise. We have records of his christening, which took place in the parish Church of Allerton (or Allerston) Mauleverer, in Yorkshire on 30 November 1563.[7] Wise then appears in *The Stationers' Register* when he was apprenticed to Henry Smith on 25 March 1580.[8] The following year Wise was transferred to Thomas Bradshaw, a well-established bookseller in Cambridge,[9] who was granted a lease by Trinity College to build a brand new shop at the west end of Great St Mary's on 1 October 1585 (Gray 1909: 235–49, esp. 238–41; Gray and Palmer 1915: 79–80). Wise was made free of the Stationers' Company on 26 May 1589.[10] From the first imprint featuring him as a retail seller,[11] we gather that Wise took over a shop at the sign of the Angel on the North side of Paul's Cross Churchyard[12] around 1593, which had previously belonged to John Perrin. Wise is last mentioned in *The Stationers' Register* when he transferred his copies of *Richard II*, *Richard III*, *1 Henry IV* and two of Thomas Playfere's English sermons to Matthew Law on 25 June 1603. While at the Angel, Wise financed the publication of twelve books (see table 3.1).

Wise's publishing career has so far received little sustained attention, which is rather surprising, given the significant number of Shakespearean Quartos which he published between 1597 and 1602. Peter Blayney has indeed remarked on the fact that such an obscure, small-scale publishing bookseller 'struck gold three times in a row in 1597–8 by picking what would become the three best-selling Shakespeare quartos as the first three plays of his short career' (1997: 389). Wise's exceptional 'good luck' has led Lukas Erne and Andrew Gurr to believe that the Chamberlain's Men must have established a regular professional relationship with him (Erne 2003: 87–8; Gurr 2003: 185). However, only Erne attempts to speculate on what must have encouraged the Chamberlain's Men to choose

Table 3.1. *Books published by Andrew Wise (1593–1602)*

STC 18366	Thomas Nashe	*Christs teares ouer Ierusalem* . . . Printed by Iames Roberts, and are to be solde by Andrewe Wise, at his shop in Paules Churchyard, at the signe of the Angel, 1593
STC 18367	Thomas Nashe	*Christs teares ouer Ierusalem* . . . Printed [by J. Roberts and R. Field] for Andrew VVise, and are to be sold at his shop in Pauls Church-yard, at the signe of the Angell, 1594
STC 20014	[Thomas Playfere]	*A most excellent and heauenly sermon* . . . At London: Printed [by J. Orwin], for Andrew Wise, 1595
STC 20014.3	[Thomas Playfere]	*A most excellent and heavenly* . . . London: Printed [by J. Danter] for Andrevv VVise, 1595
STC 20014.5	[Thomas Playfere]	*A most excellent and heavenly sermon* . . . London: Printed [by J. Danter] for Andrevv VVise, 1595
STC 20015	[Thomas Playfere]	*The meane in mourning. A sermon* . . . At London: Printed by the Widow Orwin for Andrew Wise, dwelling in Paules Church yeard, at the sign of the Angel, 1596
STC 20020	[Thomas Playfere]	*The pathway to perfection A sermon* . . . At London: Printed by Widow Orwin for Andrew VVise, dwelling in Paules church-yard, at the signe of the Angel, 1596
STC 20016	[Thomas Playfere]	*The meane in mourning A sermon* . . . At London: Printed by Iames Roberts for Andrew VVise, dwelling in Paules church-yard, at the signe of the Angel, 1597
STC 20021	[Thomas Playfere]	*The pathway to perfection A sermon* . . . At London: Printed by Iames Roberts for Andrew VVise, dwelling in Paules church-yard, at the signe of the Angel, 1597
STC 22307	[William Shakespeare]	*The tragedie of King Richard the second* . . . London: Printed by Valentine Simmes for Androw Wise, and are to be sold at his shop in Paules church yard at the signe of the Angel, 1597
STC 22314	[William Shakespeare]	*The tragedy of King Richard the third* . . . At London: Printed by Valentine Simmes [and Peter Short], for Andrew Wise, dwelling in Paules Chuch-yard [sic], at the signe of the Angell, 1597
STC 20601	John Racster	*William Alabasters seuen motuies* [sic] . . . At London: Printed by Peter Short for Andrew Wise dwelling in Paules Church-yard at the signe of the Angell, 1598
STC 20601.5	John Racster	*William Alabasters seuen moiuies* [sic] . . . At London: Printed by Peter Short for Andrew Wise dwelling in Paules Church-yard at the signe of the Angell, 1598
STC 22279a	[William Shakespeare]	*The hystorie of Henrie the fourth*, [London?: P. Short for A. Wise], 1598

Table 3.1. (*cont.*)

STC 22280	[William Shakespeare]	*The history of Henrie the Fourth* . . . At London: Printed by P[eter] S[hort] for Andrew Wise, dwelling in Paules Churchyard, at the signe of the Angell, 1598
STC 22308	[William Shakespeare]	*The tragedie of King Richard the second* London: Printed by Valentine Simmes for Andrew Wise, and are to be sold at his shop in Paules churchyard at the signe of the Angel, 1598
STC 22315	William Shakespeare	*The tragedie of King Richard the third* London: Printed by Thomas Creede, for Andrew Wise, dwelling in Paules Church-yard, at the signe of the Angell, 1598
STC 22281	William Shakespeare	*The history of Henrie the Fourth* . . . At London: Printed by S[imon] S[tafford] for Andrew VVise, dwelling in Paules Churchyard, at the signe of the Angell, 1599
STC 17671a	Anon.	*The battaile fovght betvveene Count Maurice of Nassaw, and Albertus arch-duke of Austria,* . . . Printed at London: [By P. Short] for Andrew Wise, 1600
STC 19154	Theophilus Field	*An Italians dead bodie,* London: Printee [sic] by Thomas Creede, for Andrew Wise, and are to be sold at his shop in Powles Church-yard, 1600
STC 19154.3	Theophilus Field	*An Italians dead bodie* . . . London: Printee [sic] by Thomas Creede, for Andrew Wise, and are to be sold at his shop in Powles Church-yard, 1600
STC 22288	William Shakespeare	*The second part of Henrie the fourth* . . . London: Printed by V[alentine] S[immes] for Andrew Wise, and William Aspley, 1600
STC 22288a	William Shakespeare	*The second part of Henrie the fourth* . . . London: Printed by V[alentine] S[immes] for Andrew Wise, and William Aspley, 1600
STC 22304	William Shakespeare	*Much adoe about nothing* . . . London: Printed by V[alentine] S[immes] for Andrew Wise, and William Aspley, 1600
STC 4543	Thomas Campion	*Obseruations in the art of English poesie* . . . Printed at London: By Richard Field for Andrew Wise, 1602
STC 22316	William Shakespeare	*The tragedie of King Richard the third* . . . London: Printed by Thomas Creede, for Andrew Wise, dwelling in Paules Church-yard, at the signe of the Angell, 1602

such an unlikely bookseller to publish their three most popular plays to appear in print during Shakespeare's lifetime. According to Erne it was James Roberts, the playbill printer who also entered three Shakespearean titles between 1598 and 1603 and had collaborated with Wise in 1593 and

1597,[13] who recommended Wise to the Chamberlain's Men (2003: 88). I believe that Wise's publishing career and his output suggest an even stronger connection between Wise and the Chamberlain's Men than the one posited by Erne.

Although the quick succession of dramatic best-sellers was certainly exceptionally fortunate, Wise's profile is far from unique when compared to the output of other late sixteenth-century stationers. In fact, the output of other publishers who, like Wise, had no strong connections with the Stationers' Company suggests that, as mentioned in my Introduction, their motivating impulse to invest in dramatic publication may have come from a connection with the world of the theatre and the professional writers who worked for it. Thomas Millington (1594–1603), for example, who, like Wise, was active for a period of about ten years from the early 1590s to the early 1600s, published four items of news,[14] two ballads (having entered five overall),[15] a report of James's entertainment from Edinburgh to London,[16] four plays, as well as entering and acting as a retail seller for two further plays. Millington's predominantly literary output included Henry Chettle's *England's Mourning Garment* (STC 5121, 1603), and although he never published them, he seems to have owned the copyright of Thomas Deloney's *Jack of Newbury* and *Thomas of Reading*. More crucially, Millington decided to invest in the publication and retailing of three Pembroke plays, *Titus Andronicus* (22328, 1594), *The first part of the contention betwixt the two famous houses of Yorke and Lancaster* (STC 26099, 1594), and *The true tragedie of Richard Duke of York* (STC 21006, 1595), soon after the company broke up in 1593. A similar pattern emerges from a survey of Richard Oliff's output. Oliff, who was also active for just over ten years between 1590 and 1601, published a few items of news,[17] Emanuel Ford's *Parismus* (STC 11171, 1598), *Greene's Groats-worth of Wit* (STC 12246, 1596), which was edited, or almost entirely written, by Chettle (Jowett 1993: 453–86), and four plays, all between 1600 and 1601, namely *The Wisdom of Doctor Dodypoll* (STC 6991, 1600), *The Maiden's Metamorphosis* (STC 17188, 1600), *The Weakest Goeth to the Wall* (STC 25144, 1600) and *Iack Drum's Entertainment* (STC 7243, 1601). Three of these plays had been written for the Children of Paul's. Both Millington's and Oliff's decision to invest in dramatic publication seems linked to their coming into contact with a specific company, or with an agent acting on the company's behalf.

At least one late sixteenth and early seventeenth-century London stationer acted both as publisher and as procurer of dramatic copy. John Busby senior (1590–1612), like Millington and Oliff, published predominantly literary texts written by professional authors, including Thomas

Lodge, Thomas Nashe, George Peele and Robert Greene. He also published the work of professional dramatists, including the first quarto of Shakespeare's *Henry V* with Millington in 1600, although he seems to have been rather more inclined to enter commercial plays in *The Stationers' Register* in order to transfer his rights to other publishers later on. Busby entered five plays between 1599 and 1608, none of which he went on to publish or to sell. Interestingly, the only time John Oxenbridge (1591–1600) invested in the publication of a play, *1 & 2 Edward IV*, he, like Wise, made a sound investment, because the first edition of 1599 was followed by a second edition in 1600. The link between Oxenbridge, who had until then published mostly religious books and sermons, and his decision to invest in a play which was to prove so popular as to require a second edition within a year, was clearly Busby, who entered the play in *The Register* with him on 28 August 1599.

The publishing careers of William Broome (1577–91) and his widow Joan (1591–1601) provide another striking example of a short-lived connection between publishers otherwise devoted to the more established market of religious publications and literary publishers with connections with the world of professional writers and the professional theatre, which prompted a bout of dramatic publications. Up to 1591, William Broome, like John Oxenbridge, had published mostly sermons and medical tracts, by sharing the risk with the successful publisher Thomas Man, whose output was almost exclusively made up of religious publications. Broome turned to dramatic publication in 1591 for the first time, when he issued the fourth edition of Lyly's *Campaspe* (STC 17049) and the third edition of *Sappho and Phao* (STC 17087). Both plays had been printed for Thomas Cadman in 1584. Although Cadman transferred the rights for both plays to Broome's widow in 1597, nothing suggests that William Broome acted without Cadman's blessing. In fact, Broome died in 1591 and the first item published by Joan in 1591 had also been published by Cadman.[18]

Widow Broome must have been keen to continue the partnership which her late husband William had started with Cadman because she also went on to publish Lyly's *Endymion* in 1591 and *Gallathea* and *Midas* in 1592. The connection with Cadman prompted a few other literary publications including the second and third editions of Greene's *Pandosto* in 1592 (STC 12286) and 1595 (STC 12287). Literary publications stopped when Joan, who, unlike other widows who married their husbands' ex-apprentices or business associates and devolved their business responsibilities to them, secured a lucrative agreement by acting as the London retail seller for Oxford printer and publisher Joseph Barnes. The spell of dramatic publications financed by William and Joan Broome in 1591 and 1592, which was clearly prompted by their association with literary publisher Thomas Cadman, struck Greg as being so well orchestrated as to suggest that a collection of Lyly's dramatic works was already on the cards as early as the beginning of the 1590s (Greg 1939–59: 177). William and Joan's plan was probably instigated by Cadman or by Lyly himself, who may have been keen to invest in the publication of his works after the Children of Paul's, the company for whom Lyly had been writing since 1584, was disbanded in 1590, following his involvement in the Martin Marprelate controversy (Gurr 1990: 33).

Like Thomas Millington, Richard Oliff, John Oxenbridge, and William and Joan Broome, Wise decided to invest in the publication of English commercial drama because he is likely to have had a strong personal connection with the world of the theatre. However, James Roberts may not be the most probable link between Wise and Shakespeare, as intimated by Erne. Wise's output is largely made up of works by three authors, namely Thomas Nashe, Thomas Playfere and Shakespeare (see table 3.1), who were all under the direct patronage of Sir George Carey.[19] Carey was the patron of Shakespeare's company, who were temporarily renamed the Lord Hunsdon's Men between 23 July 1596, when he inherited the company on the death of his father and former Lord Chamberlain Henry Carey, and 17 March 1597, when he took over the title of Lord Chamberlain after Lord Cobham's short-lived interregnum. Before he was appointed Lord Chamberlain, George Carey had paid for Thomas Playfere's university education at St John's College in Cambridge.[20] Carey had also bailed Thomas Nashe out of prison and offered him shelter at Carisbrooke Castle on the Isle of Wight, after Wise's edition of his *Christs Teares over Jerusalem* had got him into serious trouble with the City Fathers in the autumn of 1593. This work, which Nashe had dedicated to Carey's wife, Elizabeth, had incensed the Lord Mayor and the citizens of London against him and he may have revised the offensive passages for the second edition (also published by Wise in 1594) during his stay at Carisbrooke Castle earlier in the year.[21]

Wise is more likely to have had a personal connection with at least one of the three authors whose works he published,[22] and to have met the other two as a result of such a connection,[23] than to have had direct dealings with their powerful patron. In fact, no Lord Chamberlain seems to have had a role in an acting company's or a playwright's choice of publisher, although at least three of George Carey's successors intervened to support their companies' decision not to publish plays from their repertory, as explained in detail in the next chapter. The Chamberlain's Men's decision to sell some of their most popular plays for publication in 1596–7 may have been prompted by severe financial strictures.[24] If Blayney is right in confirming the common assumption that dramatic manuscripts would be sold 'at the cost of two pounds minus the cost of having the manuscript properly allowed by the authorities' (1997: 396), then it is hard to believe that the sale of a few manuscripts would have improved the company's cash-flow crisis. It seems safer to assume with Blayney that dramatic publication occurred when the actors wanted to generate new interest in their repertory (1997: 386). The timing of the publication of the first three Wise Quartos does indeed suggest that the company needed to generate further revenue, presumably to cover the cost of renting the Curtain after their lease on the Theatre expired. The King's Men's decision to sell at least three of their most popular plays to Andrew Wise at such a key time in the history of the company seems similarly far from accidental. However the connection between Wise and Carey's protégés may have started, the fact that Wise's output is almost entirely made up by authors under Carey's patronage seems remarkable.

Positing a Carey connection between Wise and the Chamberlain's Men ostensibly reinforces the optimistic assumption championed by Pollard and his followers, according to which a direct line of transmission linked the author's manuscripts with 'good' quarto editions of his works. However, if the printer's copies from which Wise's Shakespearean editions were set were indeed supplied directly by the author or by members of his company, does this also mean that Shakespeare should be held responsible for the substantive emendations which found their way into *Richard II*, *Richard III* and *1 Henry IV* as they were repeatedly published by Wise between 1597 and 1602? Even scholars who have recently argued that Shakespeare did take an active interest in the publication of his works believe that Shakespeare's intervention can best be described as a 'revision' rather than as a 'correction' of copy and can best be observed in the substantial differences between shorter and theatrical versus longer and literary versions of some plays, such as the first and the second quarto of *Romeo and Juliet* and *Hamlet* or the first quarto and the first folio edition of *Henry V* (Erne 2003: 220–44). But what are the chances that Shakespeare prepared the printer's copy for the early editions of plays like *Richard II, Richard III* and *1 Henry IV*? Can Shakespeare, in other words, be held responsible for good but sporadic emendations, like the correction of the misattributed speech prefix in Q2 *Richard II* mentioned above? Or, does a personal connection between Wise and the Chamberlain's Men suggest that he may have seen the plays on stage before he was entrusted with their transmission into print, or that he may have felt personally obliged to perfect their texts as and when they were repeatedly printed in the late 1590s and early 1600s? The final section of this chapter tackles these questions by closely examining the texts of the Wise Quartos.

PATTERNS OF TEXTUAL VARIATION IN THE WISE QUARTOS

Substantive variants in speech prefixes, stage directions and dialogue in the second and third quartos of *Richard II*, *Richard III* and *1 Henry IV* suggest that they were corrected as they were repeatedly reprinted between 1598 and 1602. Besides emending the speech prefix on 13r from 'yorke' to 'King', Q2 *Richard II* introduces at least one other substantive variant, which is often endorsed by modern editors, although it replaces a viable alternative in Q1. In Q1, the Queen speaks the following lines:

> It may be so; but yet my inward soule
> Perswades me it is otherwise: how ere it be.
> I cannot but be sad: so heauie sad,
> As thought on thinking on no thought I thinke,
> Makes me with heauy nothing faint and shrinke.   (D3v 21–5)

Q2 changes the first 'thought' in line 24 into 'though'. Modern editors have adopted either version,[25] thus showing how intervention in Q2 was not determined by an obvious misreading in Q1. The correction of a speech prefix and the modification of the sense of a complex line would not be as significant if other Wise Quartos did not provide comparable examples of textual variation which seem to stem from light annotation of the printer's copy, as opposed to the type of corruption routinely accrued, or the types of correction routinely carried out, in the printing house.

The first quarto of *1 Henry IV* (henceforth Q1)[26] lacks the entry direction which in modern editions marks the beginning of Act 4. Besides, Q1 also uses the variant speech prefix '*Per.*' ten times starting from G4v 27 instead of '*Hot.*', the usual prefix for Henry Percy, known as Hotspur. The second quarto (henceforth Q2) provides an exit direction at G4v 25, which clears the stage and shifts the action from Mistress Quickly's tavern to the rebel camp near Shrewsbury, adds a new direction at G4v 28 ('*Enter Hotspur, Worcester, and Douglas*'), and then changes all variant speech prefixes from '*Per.*' back to '*Hot.*'. These variants are generally attributed to a printing house agent.[27] I am however more inclined to believe that, like the emended speech prefix in the second quarto of *Richard II*, they require a level of

familiarity with the fictive world of the play, which, as I explained in my
Introduction, is more realistically associated with an annotating reader
than with a printing house agent. The same type of textual variation
emerges in the second (henceforth Q2) and the third quarto (henceforth Q3)
of *Richard III*. Q2 adds two lines at A3r 36, while Q3 adds five new stage
directions and modifies two, and by doing so it provides details of the
dramatic action which are not immediately obvious from the context.
Furthermore, as John Jowett points out, '[Q3] switches the order in
which the ghosts appear in 5.4 so that it more closely accords with the
order in which the figures die' (2000: 116).

Having described the extent of the changes in Q3 *Richard III*, Jowett then
turns to the vexed issue of attribution. In relation to the variant order in
which the ghosts appear in 5.4, Jowett advances the following hypothesis:

> The arrangement in Q1 probably reflects actual stage practice. It allows one of the
> boy actors who played the young princes to return as the ghost of Anne. The
> revision in Q3 could have arisen because, for example, the manuscript followed
> the Q3 arrangement whilst marking a transposition that was ambiguously indi-
> cated or optional; or because Wise became aware that the staging had been altered;
> or because Shakespeare himself demanded the change even though it was out of
> line with stage practice. (2000: 116–17)

According to Jowett, the author, the publisher and the compositor were all
potentially responsible for altering the order in which the ghosts appear in
5.4. Similarly, when Jowett discusses the emendations in Q2 *Richard III*, he
suggests that either Wise or Thomas Creede, the printer of Q1, Q2, and Q3
Richard III, should be credited with them. While in his textual introduction Jowett explains that the two extra lines added to Q2 'might indicate
that the printer's copy for Q1 was consulted here, presumably by Wise'
(2000: 115–16), his commentary note at 1.1.102 attributes them to Creede:

> An alteration of this order of a text with no self-evident flaw can scarcely have
> been made without some written or oral prompting. As the stationer Thomas
> Creede issued both Q1 and Q2 and would in the usual course of things have owned
> the manuscript, Q2 may, exceptionally, have been corrected here from the copy
> for Q1. (2000: 154)

Having regularly entered his copy of *Richard III* in *The Stationers' Register* on
20 October 1597 and having it then transferred to Matthew Law on 25 June
1603, Andrew Wise was in fact more likely than Creede to have owned the
manuscript. Furthermore, a contrastive analysis of the Wise Quartos with
other playbooks printed by Thomas Creede confirms that the latter would
not normally invest time and effort to perfect his dramatic copies.

Creede owned the copy of *A Looking Glass for London and England*, which he printed twice, in 1594 (STC 16679) and 1598 (STC 16680). No attempt was made to normalize or to add missing speech prefixes or to supplement the existing stage directions and dialogue.[28] Creede also printed the second edition of *Mother Bombie* for Cuthbert Burby in 1598 (STC 17085), which was set up from a copy of the first quarto printed by Thomas Scarlet in 1594, also for Burby (STC 17084). Once again, textual variation in these two editions rules out annotation of the printer's copy: instead of supplementing dialogue and stage directions, the second quarto accidentally omits five lines and one speech prefix. Since the second quarto fails to correct classical and Latin names, it seems fair to argue that not only was it set up from a copy of the first quarto which had not been annotated, but that, at least according to the standards described by Moxon in his tract on printing (1958: 246), it was also poorly printed.[29]

If Creede's intervention should be ruled out, then what are we to make of Jowett's theory that Shakespeare may have at least been responsible for instructing the printer to alter the order in which the ghosts appear in 5.4 in Q2 *Richard III*? And if Shakespeare is taken to be the source of this variant, should also all the other emendations in Q2 and Q3 *Richard II, Richard III* and *1 Henry IV* be attributed to him rather than to Wise as either annotator or procurer of annotated copy? Commenting on the title page in Q2 *1 Henry IV*, which adds 'Newly corrected by *W. Shake-speare*', A. R. Humphreys argues that it 'would be less misleading if "corrected" were followed by a full-stop' (1960: lxxi). However, other early modern playwrights did add sporadic corrections to the texts of their plays as they were preparing them for the press or for presentation volumes, as mentioned in the Introduction. Shakespeare's intervention cannot therefore be excluded. Similarly, though, Wise's intervention cannot be excluded either, since several of his Shakespearean editions include substantive emendations to their speech prefixes, stage directions and dialogue and not all publishers felt obliged to correct their dramatic copy or to seek annotated copy prior to reprinting the most popular plays in their possession. Cuthbert Burby, for example, used a fresh manuscript source for the second quarto of *Romeo and Juliet* which was printed by Simon Stafford for Burby in 1599. However, when no fresh copy was used, as in the case of Q1 and Q2 *The Taming of a Shrew*, which Peter Short printed for Burby in 1594 and 1596, or Q1 and Q2 *Mother Bombie*, which were discussed above, Burby seems to have made no effort to perfect his dramatic copies by introducing textual variants comparable to the ones which found their way into the Wise Quartos.

As I explained in my Introduction, preparation of copy was a function-rather than an agent-specific practice, and sporadic changes to stage directions, speech prefixes and dialogue cannot be definitively attributed to annotating readers or correcting authors, unless the paratext explicitly discusses the circumstances that led to publication and the agents involved in it. The range and types of corrections introduced in the Wise Quartos reveal the presence of one or more annotating hands, rather than their publisher's or their author's distinctive hands. In fact, author and publisher are as likely as each other to have introduced these corrections. Shakespeare may indeed have decided to check the texts of the Wise Quartos, as they were repeatedly committed to print at a time when his reputation as a published dramatist was peaking. However, if he did so, he intervened rather more like one of the early modern readers who introduced sporadic manuscript corrections in the printed playbooks surveyed in my Introduction than as the transcribing or the revising author envisaged by late twentieth- and early twenty-first-century scholars like E. A. J. Honigmann and Lukas Erne.

CHAPTER 4

The Pavier Quartos (1619)

Thomas Pavier was the main investor in Shakespeare the dramatist among London stationers in the 1610s.[1] Ironically, he is also the most reviled and notorious publisher connected with the rise of Shakespeare in print. W. W. Greg famously referred to the ten quarto editions of Shakespearean and apocryphal plays printed by William Jaggard and published by Pavier in 1619 as a 'mysterious', 'shady', and ultimately 'abortive scheme' (1955: 9). As shown in Table 4.1, six of the Pavier Quartos were indeed published with fake imprints, and five of them were wrongly dated. It is mostly because of these fake imprints that textual scholars are still unanimous in believing that in May 1619 a letter from the Lord Chamberlain prompted the Court of the Stationers' Company to issue an order to prevent the publication of 'playes that his Ma^{tyes} players do play' (Jackson 1957: 110), and that this order was directed at Pavier (Blayney 1991:3; Kastan 2001: 57; Erne 2003: 256; Murphy 2003: 40).[2] According to this popular narrative, the King's Men invoked the Lord Chamberlain's intercession against Pavier because they were already planning, or were inspired to plan, the First Folio of 1623 and thought that Pavier's projected collection repre-sented potentially damaging competition. Lukas Erne has recently pro-posed that Heminge and Condell's much debated attack against 'diuerse stolne, and surreptitious copies, maimed and deformed' prefaced to the First Folio refers to the Pavier Quartos, as opposed to the 'bad' quartos, as assumed by Pollard and his followers in the first half of the twentieth century. Erne thus reinforces the assumption that 'Pavier's venture was perceived by Heminge and Condell as an illegitimate threat to the pro-jected Folio edition' (2003: 257).

This chapter provides an alternative account of the circumstances that led to the publication of the Pavier Quartos in 1619. More specifically, this chapter challenges the common assumption that the Court order of 1619 was directed at Pavier and that this order forced him to forge at least some of their imprints and to sell his ten plays either individually or bound in

106

Table 4.1. *The 'Pavier Quartos': information included in the title pages and signatures*

Attribution	Title	Ownership of Copy	Imprint	Sigs.
William Shakespeare	*The Whole Contention*	Thomas Pavier	Printed at London, for T. P.	A–Q^4
William Shakespeare	*Pericles*	Derelict?	Printed for T. P., 1619	χ^1, R–Aa^4, Bb1
William Shakespeare	*A Yorkshire Tragedy*	Thomas Pavier	Printed for T. P., 1619	χ^1, A–C^4, D$^{1-3}$
William Shakespeare	*The Merchant of Venice*	Thomas Hayes?	Printed by J. Roberts, 1600	A–K^4
William Shakespeare	*The Merry Wives of Windsor*	Arthur Johnson	Printed for Arthur Johnson, 1619	A–G^4
William Shakespeare	*King Lear*	Nathaniel Butter	Printed for Nathaniel Butter, 1608	A–H^4
	Henry V	Thomas Pavier	Printed for T. P., 1608	A–G^4
William Shakespeare	*Sir John Oldcastle*	Thomas Pavier	London printed for T. P., 1600	A–K^4
William Shakespeare	*A Midsummer Night's Dream*	Thomas Fisher?	Printed by James Roberts, 1600	A–H^4

one volume, but not as a brand new collection, as he had originally planned. Pavier did change his mind, as suggested by the fact that only the first three plays issued by William Jaggard's press – *The Whole Contention* and *Pericles* – were printed with continuous signatures. However, I believe that Pavier's decision was prompted by an attractive business proposal rather than by the Court order of May 1619. Isaac Jaggard, who, along with his father William, printed the Pavier Quartos, went on to become one of the major agents involved in the publication of the First Folio. He, rather than the actors, was first inspired by Pavier's projected collection and persuaded the King's Men to invoke the Lord Chamberlain's support to prevent other stationers – and *not* Pavier – from securing previously unpublished plays from their repertory. Isaac also persuaded Pavier to issue his ten Quartos either individually or as a nonce collection, that is, as a volume gathering seemingly older and more recent editions, in order to whet, rather than satisfy, readers' demand for a new collection of Shakespeare's dramatic works. The benefits for Pavier were twofold: as well as minimizing the risks connected to his daring plan to publish the first collection of commercial plays in English by selling his ten Quartos *both* individually *and* as a nonce collection, Pavier secured further revenue from lending his rights to Isaac and to the other members of the Folio syndicate.[3]

Unfamiliar as it may sound, this alternative narrative accounts for many questions which the popular theory of literary piracy leaves unanswered. Why, for example, would the actors object to the publication of old plays which had already been printed at least once before and some of them as early as 1600? Why did Pavier make such a poor effort at covering his tracks, by issuing fraudulent title pages that did not even attempt to look like the title pages in the earlier editions he was assumedly attempting to copy? Why did the King's Men collaborate with Pavier's printers for the Folio project, if Pavier had successfully circumvented a court order issued to protect their financial interests? Why, if Pavier was the publisher of the 'diuerse stolne, and surreptitious copies, maimed and deformed', which the actors denounced in 1623, would they then use annotated copies of Pavier's *A Midsummer Night's Dream*[4] and, possibly, *King Lear*[5] for the Folio? Also problematic is the lack of retaliation on the part of Pavier's fellow stationers, if we are to assume that he contravened the Court order of 1619. Highly suggestive is the fact that the only recorded action taken by any stationer following the publication of the Pavier Quartos is Lawrence Hayes' belated decision to register his copy of *The Merchant of Venice*, once Pavier had reminded him that this play, originally published by his father in 1600, still had some commercial value worth protecting.

Besides addressing questions which the popular theory of literary piracy leaves unanswered, this chapter discusses previously overlooked evidence. The first section considers later interventions by the Lord Chamberlain's successors in 1637 and 1641 in order to establish whether the court injunction of 1619 can indeed be safely taken to represent a genuinely cautionary measure against Pavier. The second section reflects on the bizarre combination of genuine and fake imprints in the Pavier Quartos and what Pavier may have gained from it by discussing other Shakespearean editions published between 1619 and 1623. The third and final section demonstrates that the quality and frequency of textual variation in the Pavier Quartos are more in keeping with the effort that went toward the publication of other dramatic collections in the first half of the seventeenth century than with the shady and abortive scheme of a reckless fraudster.

THE PAVIER QUARTOS AND THE COURT
INJUNCTION OF 1619

Two letters written to the Stationers' Company by William Herbert's successors to protect the actors' interests from unauthorized publication in 1637 and 1641 challenge the popular assumption that the Court order of 1619 was directed at Pavier. All three Lords Chamberlain who held office before the closure of the theatres in 1642 – William Herbert, Earl of Pembroke (23 December 1615–3 August 1626), his brother Philip Herbert, Earl of Pembroke and Montgomery (3 August 1626–23 July 1641), and Robert Devereux, Earl of Essex (24 July 1641–12 April 1642) – intervened at least once in order to restrain the printing of plays in the repertory of companies directly patronized by the Court. While William Herbert's letter to the Stationers is lost, Philip Herbert's and Robert Devereux's letters, dated respectively 10 June 1637 and 7 August 1641, survive and provide useful insights into William Herbert's intervention of 1619, which is explicitly invoked as a precedent on both occasions.[6]

Philip Herbert's letter shows that the Masters and Wardens of the Stationers' Company had the power to prevent publication even after dramatic copy was entered in *The Stationers' Register* but not after plays had already been committed to print. In his letter of 1637, Herbert urges the stationers to ensure that

if any Playes bee allready entred, or shall heereafter bee brought vnto the Hall to bee entred for printing, that notice therof bee giuen to the Kinges & Queenes servants the Players, & an inquiery made of them to whome they doe belong, And that none bee suffered to bee printed vntill the assent of their Ma^ts sayd servants bee made appeare ... by some Certificate in writeing. (Chambers 1931: 384–5)

Herbert makes clear that his injunction applies both to plays 'already entred' and to plays which 'shall hereafter bee brought' to the Stationers' Company for registration, but nowhere in his letter does he suggest that printed editions of plays originally belonging to the King's or the Queen's Men should not be retailed or re-issued.

Further evidence to prove that actors could not impose their will on stationers who owned dramatic copy of plays which had already been committed to print comes from Robert Devereux's letter of 7 August 1641. None of the plays listed at the end of this letter had been printed before, although some of them were quite old. By contrast, as mentioned above, all the plays issued by Pavier in 1619, including the apocrypha, had been printed at least once before, some of them as early as 1600. Although

Greg argued that 'the [Court] order [of 1619] covered reprints as well as editions of hitherto unpublished plays' (1955), neither Philip Herbert's letter of 1637 nor Robert Devereux's letter of 1641 supports his assumption that leading theatrical companies regarded reprints of old plays as a financial liability or as a breach of their proprietary rights. In fact, the two letters written by William Herbert's successors in 1637 and 1641 suggest that the Lord Chamberlain's injunction to the stationers in 1619 may not have been prompted by the publication of the Pavier Quartos.

A contrastive analysis of the pattern of dramatic publication during the five-year periods preceding and following the Lord Chamberlains' letters of 1619 and 1637 confirms that the order issued by the Court of the Stationers' Company in 1619 was a *precautionary* rather than a *cautionary* measure.[7] The letter written by Philip Herbert in June 1637 is best understood as a genuine warning or deterrent, because it followed the publication of a relatively large number of new plays and had a tangible effect on the rate at which new plays belonging to the Queen's Men and to the King's Men found their way into print between 1633 and June 1637 and between June 1637 and 1641. Seven out of the thirteen Queen's Men plays published during the five years preceding Philip Herbert's letter of 1637 were new and may have been printed without the actors' permission. The seven Queen's Men plays published within a year from the date of their first performance[8] are: James Shirley's *The Bird in a Cage* and John Ford's *Love's Sacrifice* and *'Tis Pity She's a Whore* in 1633; John Ford's *Perkin Warbeck* and Thomas Heywood's *A Maidenhead Well Lost* in 1634; Joseph Rutter's *The Shepherds' Holiday* in 1635; and Thomas Heywood's *Love's Mistress* in 1636.[9] By contrast only two plays out of the twenty Queen's Men plays printed between 1637 and 1641, namely Lewis Sharpe's *The Noble Stranger* and Richard Brome's *The Antipodes*,[10] were new when they were published in 1640.[11] This sharp decline in the rate of publication of new Queen's Men plays after June 1637 matches a similar trend in the publication of new King's Men plays over the same period of time. Three out of the seven King's Men plays printed during the five years prior to Philip Herbert's letter to the Stationers were new, namely Richard Brome and Thomas Heywood's *The Late Lancashire Witches* in 1634, and William Davenant's *The Platonic Lovers* and Thomas Heywood's *A Challenge for Beauty* in 1636.[12] By stark contrast, only John Suckling's *Aglaura* out of the eight King's Men plays printed between June 1637 and 1641 was new, having being first staged in 1637 and then printed the following year.[13]

Interestingly, with the exception of Joseph Rutter, the three dramatists who wrote the six Queen's Men plays printed before Philip Herbert's letter of 1637 and shortly after their first performance were professional writers actively engaged in the publication of both their recent and their older plays in the 1630s. John Ford, Thomas Heywood and James Shirley may have personally sought a willing publisher against the wishes of the company who had staged their new plays. Thomas Heywood, who was no longer attached to a theatrical company, as he had been during his association with the Queen Anne's Men from their inception to their decline in the years preceding Anne's death in 1619, was also the author of two of the three King's Men plays which were printed before the Lord Chamberlain's injunction and shortly after their debut on stage. In fact, Thomas Heywood, who, in the address to the reader in his 1633 edition of *The English Traveller*, had blamed the actors for 'think[ing] it against their peculiar profit to have [his plays] come into Print', and had nevertheless published two new Queen's Men and two new King's Men plays in 1634 and 1636, may have been one of the main triggers of Philip Herbert's letter to the Stationers in 1637.[14] Whatever prompted Philip Herbert to intervene, the pattern of publication of new plays belonging to the Queen's and the King's Men after June 1637 suggests that his letter to the Stationers worked well as a cautionary measure. Suggestive in this respect is Herbert's invocation of royal authority and the combined influence of his fellow Privy Councillors to reinforce his injunction to the Stationers. In what sounds more like a warning than a genuine offer of support, Herbert reminds the Masters and Wardens of the Stationers' Company that 'if you shall haue need of any further Authority or power either from his Ma^{tye} or the councell table, the better to inable you in ye execution therof, vpon notice giuen to mee either by y^r selues or by the Players I will endeauor to apply that further remedye' (Chambers 1931: 385).

Unlike Philip Herbert's intervention of 1637, the Lord Chamberlain's letters of 1619 and 1641 can hardly be taken to represent a genuine warning against unauthorized publication of commercial play texts, because they follow a noticeable fall in the number of new plays committed to print in the mid-1610s and late 1630s. The list of mostly old and unpublished plays attached to Robert Devereux's letter of 1641 suggests that the actors were probably planning the publication of another large collection at a time when the future of the London theatres must have started to seem uncertain. Robert Devereux's letter may therefore have been intended to discourage other stationers from publishing any of the plays included in the list attached to it, until the actors had had a chance to make and finalize their own arrangements with a publisher or syndicate of publishers of their own choice. Robert Devereux's letter of 1641 lends interesting insights into what may have prompted the King's Men to seek Herbert's support in the late 1610s. In the five-year period prior to the Court Order of 1619 only two old plays belonging to the King's Men were printed for the first time.[15] It is therefore difficult to believe that William Herbert's letter of 1619 may have had a cautionary function similar to Philip Herbert's letter of 1637. The late 1610s were in fact characterized by a noticeable slump in the number of first editions of dramatic texts (Erne 2003: 251). It therefore seems more logical to assume that William Herbert's letter of 1619 had a precautionary function similar to Robert Devereux's letter of 1641 and that it may have included a list of plays which had never reached the press before, since on both occasions the company seems to have withheld them until publishers endowed with considerable literary clout and adequate financial means came along to publish them as collections.[16] If the evidence provided by the Lord Chamberlain's letters of 1637 and 1641 shows that the Court Injunction of 1619 is more likely to have fulfilled a precautionary rather than a cautionary function, one may then wonder why some of the Pavier Quartos bear a fake imprint on their title pages.

The fake imprints on the Pavier Quartos of *The Merchant of Venice*, *A Midsummer Night's Dream* and *Sir John Oldcastle* indicate that they were printed in 1600 and *King Lear* and *Henry V* in 1608. Similarly misleading are the imprints on *The Merchant of Venice* and *A Midsummer Night's Dream*, where James Roberts is identified as their printer and publisher, and on *The Merry Wives of Windsor* and *King Lear*, which appear to have been printed for Arthur Johnson and Nathaniel Butter. The investigative work that led to the correct dating of the Pavier Quartos represents one of the most spectacular achievements associated with the first generation of New Bibliographers at the beginning of the twentieth century. In a seminal article published in 1909, Greg demonstrated that the set of Shakespearean and non-Shakespearean quartos sometimes found bound together in a single volume were all printed on the same mixed stock of paper, and that they were therefore printed at the same time, despite the different dates recorded on their title pages (1908a: 113–31). Other typographical features led Greg to conclude that all ten plays had been printed for Thomas Pavier in 1619 and that the fake imprints were the result of Pavier's failure to pacify 'those who conceived their rights to have been invaded' (Greg 1909: 128). According to Greg, the injured parties were other stationers, and the fact that 'no trouble of a public nature ensued' (Greg 1909: 128) must mean that

Pavier's stratagem was successful. In 1934, Edwin Eliott Willoughby connected the Court injunction of 1619 to the Pavier Quartos and argued that the King's Men, rather than other stationers, were the injured party (1934: 3). Both Greg's and Willoughby's theories rest on the assumption that Pavier's fellow stationers and the actors were effectively misled by Pavier's fake imprints.

Greg's theory was first challenged as early as 1935, when William A. Jackson pointed out that Pavier's blatant failure to imitate the typographical features of the earlier editions published by their copyright-holders suggests that he may not have intended to deceive them in the first place. In 1992, Gerald Johnson argued that by 1619 Pavier was an established member of the Stationers' Company and that he was therefore unlikely to contravene a Court order by publishing unauthorized books. Johnson also stressed that Pavier owned the right to publish as many as five out of the ten plays he issued in 1619, namely *2* and *3 Henry VI*, which he published as a two-part play under the title *The Whole Contention between the two famous houses of York and Lancaster*, as well as *Henry V, A Yorkshire Tragedy*, and *The First Part of Sir John Oldcastle*. Besides, still according to Johnson, two of the other publishers whose names appear in the fake imprints probably collaborated with Pavier:

Among the copyright-holders was Nathaniel Butter, with whom Pavier had collaborated in the publication of *If You Know Not Me* in 1608 and 1610 ... In view of this and later connections between these two publishers, it appears likely that Butter agreed to the reprinting of *King Lear*. The records show only one tenuous association between Pavier and Arthur Johnson, who owned *The Merry Wives*. But the reprint of *The Merry Wives* is correctly dated, thus the intent cannot have been to pass it off as a remainder or twin edition of the 1602 first edition printed for Johnson. Since Johnson was still conducting business in London in 1619, he could clearly have protested if his copyright had been infringed. (1992: 37–8)

Similarly, at least one of the two former publishers of *Pericles*, Henry Gosson, belonged to the 'Ballad Stock', a syndicate of publishers which included Thomas Pavier as one of its founding members. Although the 'Ballad Stock' was formally established in 1624, its members, including Gosson and Pavier, had collaborated before then (Johnson 1992: 23–5). Furthermore, Edward Blount, who had originally entered *Pericles* on 20 May 1608 does not seem to have reclaimed his rights on this play when Henry Gosson and Simon Stafford published it in 1609 and 1611. Also problematic is the legal status of the last two plays re-issued by Pavier in 1619. *A Midsummer Night's Dream* and *The Merchant of Venice* had last been printed in 1600 by Thomas Fisher and Thomas Hayes. Nobody had formally reclaimed the rights to these two titles, although, as mentioned above, Pavier's venture spurred Thomas Hayes's son, Lawrence, to register *The Merchant of Venice* on 8 July 1619. Lawrence Hayes, like his father, was never particularly active as a publisher: having published one of the several rejoinders to Joseph Swetnam's *The Arraignment of Lewd, Idle, Froward, and Unconstant Women* in 1617,[17] he waited until 1637 to publish the third quarto of *Merchant of Venice*, the only other title he ever owned. It is therefore more likely that Lawrence Hayes was encouraged to register *The Merchant of Venice*, when he realized that the play had some market value thanks to Pavier's venture.[18]

To sum up, Greg's theory according to which Pavier successfully circumvented the Court order of 1619 and effectively defrauded his fellow stationers is undermined by the fact that Pavier owned the rights to five of them, that he probably collaborated with the stationers who held the rights to three further plays, and that the copy of the remaining two plays was derelict or had not been reclaimed since 1600. Equally significant is the fact that two of the plays whose rights Pavier *personally* owned bear the wrong date on their title pages. The imprints in *Henry V* and *Sir John Oldcastle* read 'Printed for T. P. 1608' and 'London Printed for T. P. 1600'. These two title pages present a real conundrum for those who believe that Pavier attempted to deceive other stationers by using fake imprints: overlooking the fact that Pavier owned the rights to *Henry V*, Greg, for example, rather preposterously argued that 'printing *Henry V* immediately after *King Lear* [which was first printed in 1608], he forgot to alter the date from 1608 to 1600 as he should have done' (1955: 16).[19] Greg's assumption that Pavier's intention was to deceive and that he nevertheless 'forgot' to alter the date on the title page of *Henry V* seems utterly perverse. According to Greg, rather than a crook, Pavier was a bumbling fool.

Willoughby's theory that the actors were the injured party who failed to see through Pavier's use of fake imprints is equally untenable. If the actors had indeed felt defrauded by Pavier's publishing venture, they would have monitored his activities and would probably have realized that at least some of the Pavier Quartos bearing his initials on their title pages were not unsold stock but new editions. Even more crucially, Willoughby's theory is invalidated by the fact that the actors would have had no means of legally challenging Pavier, since, as mentioned above, all the quartos he re-issued in 1619 had been printed before.

Attribution has recently been proposed as an alternative explanation for Pavier's decision to use fake imprints for at least one of his quarto reprints of 1619. John Jowett has interestingly argued that the fake date on the title-page of *Sir John Oldcastle* may have been prompted by an attempt to strengthen the other false claim made on its title page, according to which this play was 'Written by William Shakespeare':

Shakespeare's *1 Henry IV* as performed by the King's Men evidently continued to be known as *Oldcastle* as well as *1 Henry IV*, and Pavier therefore was able, or had the excuse, to generate a case of mistaken identity. He had not, however, perpetrated the error when he had published the original anonymous edition of 1600, and the new false ascription stands alongside the falsification in the imprint. He now gave his 1619 edition the date of 1600, as though the copies belonged to the original edition, and in so doing he generated the impression that the play had been attributed to Shakespeare during his lifetime. (2007: 45)

Jowett's theory applies neatly to *Sir John Oldcastle* but not to *A Yorkshire Tragedy*, which is published with a valid imprint,[20] nor to other Pavier Quartos with forged title pages. Pavier's 1619 edition of *Henry V*, for example, which was first printed by Creede for Thomas Millington and John Busby in 1600 and then by Creede for Pavier in 1602, is dated 1608, although no quarto edition (including Pavier's) attributes the play to Shakespeare.

An alternative explanation for Pavier's highly unusual decision to pre-date some *but not all* of his quarto editions of 1619 is that he meant to deceive neither his fellow stationers nor the actors but his readers into believing that what they were buying were either individual editions of plays printed and published by different stationers at different times or a nonce collection gathering seemingly older and newer editions. While theories resting on the assumption that Pavier was attempting to defraud either his fellow stationers or the King's Men, or both, fail to justify the fact that *A Yorkshire Tragedy* and *The Merry Wives of Windsor* are correctly dated, a contrastive analysis of the Pavier Quartos with other early modern dramatic nonce collections shows that the apparently bizarre use of genuine and fake imprints is perfectly understandable if Pavier was indeed planning to sell his quartos either individually or bound in what was meant to look like a nonce volume.

When dramatic collections in smaller formats than Jonson's or Shakespeare's Folio editions of 1616 and 1623 became popular and marketable in the mid-seventeenth century (Robinson 2002: 361–80), the plays in them were often freshly reprinted, as in Thomas Goffe's *Three Excellent Tragedies* (Wing G1005, 1656). By the middle of the seventeenth century even old printed playbooks were repackaged to look like new collections. Sir William Lower's *Three New Plays* (Wing L3319, 1661) was in fact a reissue of *The Enchanted Lovers*, *The Noble Ingratitude*, and *The Amorous Fantasm*, which had been printed at The Hague between 1658 and 1660

(Greg 1939–59: 893). The 1661 volume includes a new general title page and three individual cancel titles dated 1661 (Greg 1939–59: 1087). However, at the beginning of the seventeenth century, well before collections of English plays became marketable, no effort was made to hide the fact that nonce volumes gathered older as well as freshly printed (and sometimes previously unpublished) editions. The 1607 re-issue of Sir William Alexander's *The Monarchicke Tragedies* (STC 344) includes two additional plays, *The Alexandrean Tragedie* and *The Tragedie of Iulius Caesar*, both dated 1607, and two plays originally issued in the 1604 edition of *The Monarchick Tragedies* (STC 343). While one of these two plays has no individual title page, the other retains the original one and the date in the imprint is unchanged. As late as 1639, publishers made half-hearted attempts to present nonce collections as new collections to their readers. Thomas Nabbes's *Plays, Masks, Epigrams, Elegies, and Epithalamiums* (STC 18337), for example, has a new general title page dated 1639 and individual cancel titles for three plays, but no cancel titles for two further plays. Even the three plays for which cancel titles were printed retain their original title pages in some extant copies. Last, but not least, the fact that the general title page is dated 1639 did not stop the stationer who commissioned this nonce collection to add two further plays with individual titles dated 1640, which could presumably be added because the project was delayed (Greg 1939–59: 1098). To sum up, what even a quick survey of early modern nonce collections shows is that, rather than a poorly executed act of forgery, Pavier's use of genuine and false dates on the title pages of his 1619 quartos is a skilful imitation of their bibliographical make-up.

This hypothesis raises a fresh question: what could Pavier hope to gain from deceiving his readers into thinking that what they were buying was a nonce rather than a freshly printed collection? This question can best be addressed by considering the Pavier Quartos in the context of the dramatic output of two other London stationers, William and Isaac Jaggard. The Jaggards, printers of both the Pavier Quartos and Shakespeare's First Folio, provide a crucial link between the two undertakings, whose significance has often been downplayed or consciously overlooked as an embarrassment. How could the printers involved in Pavier's 'abortive scheme' then be allowed to play the same role in the later and larger project, which was ostensibly willed forward by Shakespeare's fellow actors, the custodians of the author's artistic legacy and preservers of 'True Originall Copies' of his works? My impression is that the Jaggards may have played a greater role than the one allowed by those critics and scholars who regard the two publishing ventures as ultimately antagonistic projects.

William Jaggard's literary output is scant and unassuming. As well as printing several plays for Thomas Pavier in the mid-1600s and in the late 1610s, he may have acted as the publisher of Thomas Dekker and John Webster's *Westward-Ho* (STC 6540, 1607) and two poetic works, a short occasional poem written to commemorate the death of the divine Hugh Broughton (STC 20393, 1612?) and *The Passionate Pilgrim* (STC 22341.5, 1599?). From the address to 'his approued good Friend, Nicholas Okes', which Thomas Heywood appended to his *Apology for Actors* (STC 13309, 1612), we learn that Jaggard included some poems taken from Heywood's *Troia Britannica* (STC 13366, 1608) to the third edition of *The Passionate Pilgrim* and that he inappropriately attributed the whole miscellany to Shakespeare. Although Heywood reports that Shakespeare was 'much offended with M. *Iaggard* (that altogether vnknowne to him) presumed to make so bold with his name' (G4v 2–4), Jaggard acquired the right to print playbills from James Roberts the following year, and is bound to have established working relations with the King's Men, despite having been the cause of their leading playwright's irritation a few months earlier.

The beginning of Isaac's career as a literary publisher seems to have been more auspicious than his father's, at least in its early stages. Although the publication of the First Folio effectively ends the list of literary works ascribed to Isaac, he seems to have acted as publisher of George Chapman's translation of *The Divine Poem of Musaeus* (STC 18304, 1616), of the third edition of Thomas Heywood's *A Woman Killed with Kindness* (STC 13372, 1617), and of an anonymous translation of Giovanni Boccaccio's *Decameron* (STC 3172, 1620). As Willoughby noted, 'the work had often been alluded to by English authors, and numerous versions and paraphrases of its tales had been incorporated into English books, but never until Jaggard issued this version by an unknown translator had a complete translation been available' (1934: 140). The book proved popular and plans were made to issue a second edition in 1625, although this time the project was forestalled by Puritan opposition (Willoughby 1934: 140).

The Jaggards' working relations with the King's Men and Isaac's penchant for literary publication may have alerted him to the potential importance of the venture, which his father had undertaken on Pavier's behalf in 1619. Textual scholars tend to attribute the merit of conceiving the grand plan for a collected edition of Shakespeare's dramatic works to the upmarket literary publisher Edward Blount, whose reputation has enjoyed a further boost thanks to recent reappraisals of his achievements as publisher and critic.[21] As early as the end of the nineteenth century, Sidney Lee ruled out the possibility that the Jaggards may have been responsible for initiating the long negotiations that eventually led to the publication of the First Folio in 1623. In his study of Edward Blount's career, Sidney Lee explained how '[i]t is reasonable to allow Blount the credit of first perceiving the advantage of collecting in a single folio Shakespeare's scattered plays' (1895: 491). Lee accounts for Blount's collaboration with the Jaggards in purely financial and logistical terms: since 'this great venture involved a larger expenditure than [Blount's] own capital would bear, [he] associated with himself, in the operation, one Isaac Jaggard' (1895: 489). Although Lee admits that the Jaggards' monopoly on the printing of the playbills and their familiarity with the main theatre companies 'gave the partners the opportunity of giving effect to their design', he ascribes the originating impulse behind the First Folio firmly to Blount (1895: 491).

Only recently have scholars started to remark on the fact that the upmarket Blount had never really paid much attention to play texts originally written for the commercial stage. As Peter Blayney has pointed out, Blount's high profile career as a literary publisher depended at least partly on the fact that 'most of his few . . . connections with dramatic texts [prior to his involvement with the First Folio] had been with masques, Latin plays, and closet drama rather than with the products of the public stage' (1996: xxviii). Blount did enter several commercial plays in *The Stationers' Register*, possibly because of his links with the world of the professional theatre,[22] but he then assigned his rights to other stationers,[23] or simply allowed his rights to become derelict.[24] Accordingly, Blayney is more inclined to believe that 'Isaac Jaggard was the one who first suggested the venture but that Blount was the principal investor' (1996: xxviii). Blayney also provides a further piece of circumstantial evidence to suggest that Blount joined the project at a fairly late stage, by pointing out that when the First Folio was advertised in the supplement of English titles attached to the Frankfurt Fair catalogue of 1622, the text of the advertisement mentions Isaac Jaggard's name, rather than Blount's (1991: 8).[25] The fact that, despite their joined *Stationers' Register* entry of 8 November 1623 (Arber 1875–94: IV 69), only Blount seems to have owned the copy of the sixteen plays first published in the First Folio[26] confirms Blayney's conclusion that Blount provided the clout and the money for a project that had probably been dreamt up much earlier by Isaac Jaggard.[27]

If Isaac first planned a larger collected edition of Shakespeare's dramatic works when he was inspired by Pavier's projected collection of 1619, he may also have played a part in Pavier's decision to sell his quartos either individually or bound in what would look like a nonce collection. Isaac's advantage in leading Pavier's prospective readers to believe that they were offered the scattered remains of a recently deceased playwright whose works had not been published since 1615 can probably best be described as a pre-publicity stunt. If Pavier had offered his ten plays as the first edition of Shakespeare's collected works, he may have pre-empted the demand for a larger collection later on. Pavier's marketing strategy was aimed at arousing rather than satisfying a specific demand for a product that was still relatively new to the English book market. Jonson's Folio of 1616 is often misleadingly regarded as a precedent for the Shakespeare Folio of 1623, but the latter is the very first collection of English plays written for the commercial stage. Earlier attempts to publish dramatic collections had floundered, even when the author was still alive and likely to have supported the publication of his own works. Instructive is William and Joan Broome's attempt to secure the rights to all but one of John Lyly's plays and probably to publish them as a collection, which failed to materialize until Blount's edition of 1632.[28] Isaac Jaggard may eventually have succeeded in finding an investor for his project because Pavier had paved the way for it in 1619 by significantly reviving the fortunes of Shakespeare in print.

If presenting the Pavier Quartos to contemporary readers either individually or as a nonce collection may have had marketing benefits for Isaac Jaggard, what would Pavier gain from it? As mentioned above, selling his quartos both individually and as a nonce collection would minimize Pavier's financial risk, given that his projected collection would have been unprecedented and its appeal with contemporary readers a genuine gamble. Besides, Pavier would gain additional revenue from lending the right to reprint his Shakespearean plays to other stationers, if Isaac were to prove successful in his attempt to drum up support for his plan to publish a considerably larger collection of Shakespeare's dramatic works.[29] Pavier may also have planned to be part of the syndicate of publishers who would eventually be involved in the publication of the First Folio in 1623, but was prevented to do so by having his capital tied up in other large projects, such as Joseph Hall's *Works* (STC 12635, 1624–5). Whether or not Pavier changed his plan to publish his quartos of 1619 as a new collection in order to collaborate with Isaac Jaggard in the Folio project or simply to minimize his risk and to gain further revenue from lending his rights on his Shakespearean plays to other stationers, he is unlikely to have regarded Isaac's larger collection as a rival venture, given that his Quartos and the First Folio would clearly appeal to different readers.

The publication of other Shakespearean quarto editions shortly before the First Folio reinforces my hypothesis that Pavier's marketing of his quartos of 1619 can best be understood as a pre-publicity strategy devised by Isaac Jaggard to boost his chances of getting the Folio project off the ground. If not on the same scale as 1619, 1622–3 marked another peak in the literary fortunes of Shakespeare in print, even before the First Folio was published at the end of 1623. The publication of some of these editions may have been an opportunistic move on the part of at least one stationer who was not involved in the Folio project and who probably realized that interest in Shakespeare would be stimulated by the First Folio but that few readers would be able to afford it. Matthew Law, who had acquired the copy of *Richard II, Richard III* and *1 Henry IV* on 25 June 1603, hired Thomas Purfoot to print the sixth and seventh quarto editions of *Richard III* and *1 Henry IV* in 1622. Law may indeed have tried to profit from the imminent publication of the First Folio both by re-issuing *Richard III* and *1 Henry IV* and by wrangling over copyright with the First Folio syndicate, as suggested by irregularities in the printing of *Richard II* and *1 Henry IV*. As Hinman explained, 'these irregularities, otherwise inexplicable, are almost certainly the result of difficulties raised by Law ... over the use of [his] plays in the Folio' (1963: 27–8). However, if Law's quartos were published to exploit the interest generated by the imminent publication of the First Folio, at least one other quarto edition was published around the same time by one of the members of the Folio syndicate to boost rather than to undermine its commercial success. R. Carter Hailey has recently established that the undated fourth quarto edition of *Romeo and Juliet* published by John Smethwick was printed in 1623 (forthcoming).[30] John Smethwick probably published this quarto edition undated because, like Thomas Pavier in 1619, he may have wanted to enhance the popularity of Shakespeare in print without giving potential buyers of the First Folio the impression that several *new* editions of his works were already available on the market, albeit in a different format.

The publication of Thomas Walkley's 1622 edition of *Othello* is also likely to have been encouraged rather than resented by the members of the Folio syndicate. A large portion of the titles ascribed to Thomas Walkley are commercial play texts; furthermore, all plays published by Walkley between 1619 and 1630 belonged to the King's Men.[31] Recent scholars have refuted E. A. J. Honigmann's theory that 'Walkley "pirated" his plays from the King's Men' (Lesser 2004: 215n). Walkley may in fact have had a working relation with the company or with one of their patrons, since the dedication to *A King and No King* identifies the printer's copy for this play as a private transcript rather than as a theatrical manuscript handed over to Walkley directly by the actors.[32] Even more to the point, Walkley may have had an agreement with the members of the Folio syndicate. It is hard to imagine how any stationer would have been able to regularly enter a previously unpublished play by Shakespeare in *The Stationers' Register*[33] after the Stationers' Court order of 1619 and shortly before the Folio went to press early in 1622 (Hinman 1963: 529) without at least the syndicate's tacit consent.

Although no documentary evidence is currently available to prove that the Pavier Quartos, Smethwick's fourth quarto edition of *Romeo and Juliet* and Walkley's *Othello* definitively functioned as pre-publicity for the First Folio, as well as commercial ventures in their own right, this chapter for the first time explains the combination of genuine and fake imprints on the title pages of the Pavier Quartos without relying on the discredited theory of literary piracy. The last section of this chapter reinforces the conclusions reached in its first two sections by showing how, far from being the product of a reckless and profit-driven literary pirate, the Pavier Quartos are more likely to have been the product of a carefully planned scheme, which included the correction of the printer's copy for the press.

TEXTUAL VARIATION IN THE PAVIER QUARTOS

Twentieth-century editors of the plays re-published by Pavier in 1619 agree that his editions show no evidence of consultation of fresh authoritative sources but that they were extensively, and in some cases, carefully 'edited'. However, editors generally focus on the play they are editing and pay little attention to the Pavier Quartos as a specific group of texts. As a result, views range from confident validations of the claim made on the title page of *The Whole Contention*, according to which the text that follows was 'newly corrected and enlarged' (Cox and Rasmussen 2001: 154), to despondent generalizations:

[T]he editing [in *The Merchant of Venice*] had little principle, and, as might be expected in a semi-underhand edition, no special authority; it could have been undertaken in the printing house without access to any secondary authority. The same is true of all Jaggard's reprints. (Brown 1955: xviii–xix)

The range of textual variants in the Pavier Quartos is indeed far from consistent. Interestingly, differences in the intrinsic quality of the texts of the ten quartos seem to have prompted varying degrees of correction. *A Midsummer Night's Dream*, for example, which according to one of its recent editors 'presents probably fewer textual problems than any other Shakespeare play published both as a quarto and as a part of the Folio of 1623' (Holland 1994: 112), was only lightly emended, whereas Pavier's edition of *Pericles* 'made the first serious effort' to improve on the notoriously bad text preserved in the first quarto and 'many of th[e] changes [first introduced in 1619] have been adopted by later editors' (Gossett 2004: 33). However, even allowing for varying levels of annotation, distinctive patterns of textual variants start to emerge when the Pavier Quartos are studied as a specific group of printed playbooks.

With the exception of *3 Henry VI*, the Pavier Quartos pay special attention to speech prefixes, ranging from *The Merry Wives of Windsor* and *A Midsummer Night's Dream*, which add and emend one speech prefix respectively,[34] to *Henry V, A Yorkshire Tragedy* and *Pericles*, which add and emend seven, ten and fifteen speech prefixes each.[35] As mentioned in earlier chapters, changes to speech prefixes are more likely to stem from annotation of copy prior to its submission to the printing house, where aspects of the texts which affect the internal logic and development of the fictive world of the play were least likely to be modified. The frequency with which missing speech prefixes are added and wrong ones emended suggests that, contrary to what is generally assumed, not all changes in the Pavier Quartos may have originated from compositorial tampering or from the involvement of a printing house corrector.

Even more extensive are the changes to the stage directions. All Pavier Quartos except *2 Henry VI* add missing entrances and exits.[36] This type of intervention is far from systematic, as many necessary entrances and exits are left unmarked. Also sporadic but worth noting is the addition of directions when the stage action is not immediately obvious from the dialogue. Pavier's *3 Henry VI*, for example, helps its readers visualize the violence implied by Edward's line 'Take that, thou likenesse of this railer here' by adding a new stage direction – '*Stabs him*' – at Q2r 17. *A Yorkshire Tragedy* expands the original direction in the first quarto of 1608 at B4r 21 '*Enters a seruant very hastily*' into '*Drawes his Dagger. Enter a seruant hastily*' at B3r 25, thus heightening the dramatic quality of the scene for its readers. Furthermore, Pavier's edition of *A Yorkshire Tragedy* introduces a good correction at C4r 11–2, by replacing a wrong speech prefix in the first quarto – '*Kni*. Heere, this waie, . . .' (D1r 2) – with a new stage direction – '*Cry within. /* Heere, this way, . . .' The speech prefix in the first quarto is clearly wrong, because the Knight first enters at D1v 1 and the new direction may have been inspired by a previous '*Crie within*' in the same scene. Pavier's edition of *King Lear* signals the timing of the death of the servant who mortally wounds Cornwall at G4v 3, by adding '*He dies*', while his edition of *Henry V* draws its readers' attention to one of the comic climaxes in the play, by adding a new direction for Fluellen at F4v 30 – '*He makes Ancient Pistoll bite of the Leeke*'. Pavier's *Merchant of Venice* adds '*Hee reads*' at E2r 16, possibly to highlight a change of speaker, since the message inside the silver casket is read out by Aragon, while the previous lines are spoken by Portia. *The Merchant of Venice* also omits a redundant direction at E3v 22 – '*Enter* Tuball' – which had been used twice in the first quarto of 1600.

While new stage directions are added to clarify the stage action or the dialogue, other directions signalling stage business, which, while useful to actors, may seem unnecessary for readers, are often removed. In *2 Henry VI*, the original direction '*Reade*' at line G1r 5 in the first quarto is omitted, possibly because in all editions the king speaks the following line: 'Yet stay, Ile reade the Letter once againe' (Q1, G1r 4; Q3, G1r 21). Similarly in *Pericles*, Pavier's edition omits the original direction in the third quarto – '*Enter all the Lord with Pericles*' (B1v 13) – because it replicates an earlier, almost identical direction – '*Enter Pericles with his Lords*' (Q3, B1r 13; Q4, R4r 17). This tendency to omit redundant directions is far more extensive in *Sir John Oldcastle* than in any of the other Pavier Quartos. Out of fourteen omitted directions, only one may safely be imputed to a compositorial oversight,[37] while all other omissions seem rather in keeping with an attempt to downplay references to stage business. For example, Pavier's *Sir John Oldcastle* systematically omits directions signalling the mode of delivery of specific lines – '*Both at / once al this*' (Q1, A4r 25–8) – specific gestures accompanying the action on stage – '*pointing / to the / beggars*' (Q1, B4r 17–9) – prompt-book-like calls for imminent entrances with props – '*one ready with pen / and incke*' (Q1, D3r 26–7) – or action which is already implicit in the dialogue, as at Q1, B4v 30, where the direction '*. . . and shrowde himselfe*' is possibly omitted because it replicates the invariant lines, 'as though he . . . / meant to shrow'd himselfe amongst the bushes' (Q1 and Q2, B4v 33–4).[38]

Some changes in the stage directions do represent necessary corrections. Pavier's *2 Henry VI* adds '*Edward*' to the original entrance direction in the first quarto at H3v 11–2 – '*Alarmes, and then flourish, and enter the Duke of Yorke and Richard*'. Similarly Pavier's *3 Henry VI* adds '*Gloster*' to '*Enter king Edward, Queene Elizabeth*, and a Nurse with the young prince and *Clarence*, and *Hastings*, and others' (O1, E7r 13–5), while *Merry Wives of Windsor* adds 'Page' to '*Enter Fenton and Anne*' (Q1 G4r 28). *King Lear* adds the highest number of characters missing from the stage directions in its source text: '*Kent, and Foole*' are added to '*Enter Lear*' (Q1, D2v 34); '*and a Knight*' is added to '*Enter King*' (Q1, E3r 35);[39] and '*Leicester*' is replaced by '*Glocester*' in '*Exeunt Lear, Leister, Kent, and Foole*' (Q1, F3r 5). Another emendation in the stage directions of Pavier's *Pericles* falls into the same category: Q3's '*Enter Pericles, Atharsus, with Cleon and Dioniza*' (E4v 8) becomes '*Enter Pericles at Tharsus, with Cleon and Dionizia*' in Q4 (X3r 27).

Other corrections in the stage directions in the Pavier Quartos fulfil a similarly practical function: directions in *3 Henry VI*, *The Merchant of Venice*, *Pericles* and *Sir John Oldcastle* are re-positioned to improve their timing in relation to lines which obviously serve as their cues within the dialogue.[40] However, another specific category of changes in the Pavier Quartos reveals a tendency to rewrite, rather than to correct, the stage directions in their source texts and to emphasize their literary qualities.

Similarities in the rephrasing of stage directions in eight out of ten plays suggest that the printer's copies used to set the Pavier Quartos may have been annotated by a single hand. Some plays regularize syntax in long directions. Some examples from *2 Henry VI*, *3 Henry VI*, and *Sir John Oldcastle* are listed below:

Alarums for the battaile, and sir *Humphrey Stafford* and his brother is slaine. Then enter Iacke Cade againe and the rest. (*2H6* Q1, F4v 26–8)

Alarmes to the battell, where sir Humfrey Stafford and his brother are both slaine. Then enters Iacke Cade againe, and the rest. (*2H6* Q3, G1r 4–6)

the *Queene* is taken, & the prince, & Oxf. & *Sum.* (*3H6* O1, E4r 30)

the Queene, Prince, Oxford, and Somerset are taken (*3H6* Q3, Q1v 21–2)

In this fight the Lord Herbert is wounded, and fals to the ground, the Maior and his company goe away crying clubbes, Powesse runnes away, Gough and other of Herberts faction busie themselues about Herbert; enters the two Iudges in their roabes, the Sheriffe and his Bailiffes afore them, &c. (*Oldcastle* Q1, A3v 33–6, A4r 1)

In this fight the Lord Herbert is wounded, and fals to the ground, the Maior and his company cry for clubs: Powesse runs away, Gough and Herberts faction are busie about him. Enter the 2. Iudges, the Sheriffe, and his Bayliffes afore them, &c. (*Oldcastle* Q2, A3v 33–6)

Here as they are ready to strike, enter Butler and drawes his weapon and steps betwixt them. (*Oldcastle* Q1, G1r 23–4)

As they proffer, enter Butler, and drawes his sword to part them. (*Oldcastle* Q2, G1r 23–4)

enter the Irish man with his master slaine. . . . The Irish man falls to rifle his master. (*Oldcastle* Q1, I3r 25, 28)

Enter the Irishman with his dead master, and rifles him. (*Oldcastle* Q2, I3r 11)

Sometimes the rephrasing is even lighter, but no less distinctive, as in the following examples from *3 Henry VI*, *Sir John Oldcastle* and *A Midsummer Night's Dream*, which show a tendency to omit the redundant conjunctive 'and':

Enter king *Edward*, the *Queene* and *Clarence*, and *Gloster*, and *Montague* and *Hastings*, and *Penbrooke*, with souldiers (3H6 O1, D3r 27–9)

Enter King Edward, the Queene, Clarence, Gloster, Montague, Hastings, and Penbrooke, with Soldiers (3H6 Q3, O1v 33–4)

Enter Quince, *the Carpenter; and* Snugge, *the Ioyner; and* Bottom, *the Weauer; and* Flute, *the Bellowes mender;* & Snout, *the Tinker; and* Starueling *the Tayler.* (MSND Q1, B1v 25–7)

Enter Quince the Carpenter, Snug the Ioyner, Bottome the Weauer, Flute the Bellows-mender, Snout the Tinker, & Starueling the Taylor (MSND Q2, B1v 25–7)

As they are lifting their weapons, enter the Maior of Hereford, and his Officers and Townes-men with clubbes (Oldcastle Q1, A3v 8–9)

As they are fighting, enter the Maior of Hereford, his Officers and Townesmen with Clubs (Oldcastle Q2, A3v 8–9)

On several occasions, minimal syntactical adjustments normalize even the shortest of directions, as shown in the following examples from *A Yorkshire Tragedy*, *The Merchant of Venice*, and *King Lear*.

spurns her; Teares his haire; Striues with her for the child; Throws her down; W. wakes catches up the yongest; ouer comes him (Yorkshire Q1, B1r 8–9; C2r 20; C3r 11–12; C3r 15; C3r 19–20; C3v 19)

He spurns her; He teares his haire; he striues with her for the childe; He throwes her downe; His wife awakes, and catcheth up the youngest; Husband ouercomes him (Yorkshire Q2 A4r 8; C1r 20; C2r 11; C2r 16; C2r 20; C2v 22)

open the letter; play Musique (MV Q1, F2v 27; I2v 20)

He opens the Letter; Musicke playes (MV Q2, F3v 33; I4v 7)

Enter Gonerill and Gentleman (KLR Q1, C3r 11)

Enter Gonorill and a Gentleman (KLR Q2, B4r 23)

The literary quality of the light rephrasing undergone by some directions in the Pavier Quartos is also reflected in their layout and format, which make the page look less crammed. When stage directions are already arranged on a separate line in the source text, the Pavier Quartos allow for an extra line of blanks above and below them. Directions are quite often arranged at the end of one or more lines of dialogue, flush right, in the earlier editions from which the Pavier Quartos were set. These directions are commonly re-arranged on a separate line and centred. As many as fourteen directions in the first quarto of *King Lear* are re-set in this fashion in the Pavier edition.[41] This typographical feature may account for some of the local cuts to the dialogue in *Sir John Oldcastle*. Editors of this play tend to explain the recurrent omission of lines of dialogue in pragmatic terms. Commenting, for example, on the fact that '[e]xcisions in both prose and verse become more pronounced in the later sheets, Hɪr-K4v', Jonathan Rittenhouse comes to the conclusion that '[t]he Q2 compositor seems intent on saving time and space, and so from Hɪr he "edits" the remaining twenty-four pages of his copy into twenty-two and a half pages' (1984: 4). Rittenhouse's argument seems flawed for two reasons: first of all the cuts in the final section of the play would not have a dramatic impact on the cost of the paper, since the space saved amounts to the last one and a half pages on sheet K; and secondly, it is worth wondering whether the cuts, which are cleverly executed because they hardly ever impair the sense, would be a time-effective alternative to setting up an extra one and a half pages of type.[42] Alternatively, at least some of the cuts in *Sir John Oldcastle* seem to be closely related to the new convention of centring and spacing stage directions. On four occasions between Hɪr and K4v the omission of dispensable lines is followed by the elegant re-setting of directions originally crammed in the right margin. Furthermore, this strategy is not confined to sheets H and K: there are three similar examples in sheet C alone. Careful pruning of the original dialogue in Pavier's edition of *Sir John Oldcastle* therefore seems to stem from a wish to retain a similar overall number of lines so as to avoid using an extra sheet of paper, while allowing for the additional space required by the new layout.[43]

   The sustained attention paid to speech prefixes and stage directions in the Pavier Quartos often extends to the dialogue. Lines are rewritten to rectify factual mistakes, to introduce or record changes in the dramatic structure of the play, or to make sense of mangled passages in the source texts. Pavier's edition of *2 Henry VI*, for example, corrects the genealogy of York, which in the first quarto erroneously identifies York's ancestor, Edmund of Langley, with the second son of Edward III, thus invalidating York's claim to the throne on the grounds of his father's marriage to one of the daughters of Lyonell Duke of Clarence, the third son of Edward III. This passage in Pavier's edition of *2 Henry VI* was extensively emended and it seems reasonable to assume that all the corrections were added before the printer's copy reached Jaggard's printing house. Bold type in the emended version highlights the corrections introduced in Pavier's edition:

Yorke.   My Lords our simple supper ended, thus,
          Let me reueale vnto your honours here,
          The right and title of the house of Yorke,
          To Englands Crovvne by liniall desent.

VVar.   Then Yorke begin, and if thy claime be good,
        The Neuils are thy subiects to command.
Yorke. Then thus my Lords.
        Edward the third had seuen sonnes,
        The first vvas Edvvard the blacke Prince,
        Prince of Wales.
        The second vvas Edmund of Langly,
        Duke of Yorke.
        The third vvas Lyonell Duke of Clarence.
        The fourth vvas Iohn of Gaunt,
        The Duke of Lancaster.
        The fifth vvas Roger Mortemor, Earle of March.
        The sixt vvas sir Thomas of Woodstocke.
        William of Winsore vvas the seuenth and last.
        Novv, Edvvard the blacke Prince he died before his father, and left
        behinde him Richard, that aftervvards vvas King, Crovvnde by the
        name of Richard the second, and he died vvithout an heire.
        Edmund of Langly Duke of Yorke died, and left behind him tvvo
        daughters, Anne and Elinor.
        Lyonell Duke of Clarence died, and left behinde Alice, Anne, and Elinor,
        that vvas after married to my father, and by her I claime the Crovvne, as
        the true heire to Lyonell Duke of Clarence, the third sonne to Edward the
        third. (Q1, C4r 11–36, C4v 1)

Yorke. My Lords, our simple supper ended thus,
        Let me reueale vnto your honors heere,
        The right and title of the house of Yorke
        To Englands Crowne by lineall desent.
War.   Then Yorke begin, and if thy claime be good,
        The Neuils are thy subiects to command.
Yorke. Then thus my Lords.
        Edward the third had seuen sonnes,
        The first was *Edward* the blacke Prince,
        Prince of *Wales*.
        The second was **William of Hatfield**,
        Who dyed young.
        The third was *Lyonell*, Duke of Clarence.
        The fourth was *Iohn of Gaunt*,
        The Duke of *Lancaster*.
        The fift was *Edmund of Langley*,
        Duke of Yorke.
        The sixt was *William of Windsore*,
        Who dyed young.
        The seauenth and last was Sir *Thomas of Woodstocke*, **Duke of**
        Yorke.

Now, *Edward* the blacke Prince dyed before his Father, **leauing** behinde
him **two sonnes,** *Edward* borne at *Angolesme,* **who died young, and**
Richard **that was after crowned King,** by the name of *Richard* the
second, **who** dyed without an heyre.
Lyonell Duke of Clarence dyed, and left him one only daughter,
named *Phillip,* **who was married to Edmund Mortimer earle of**
March and Vlster: and so by her I claime the Crowne, as the true
heire to Lyonell Duke of Clarence, the third sonne to Edward the third.

(Q3, C4r 11–35, C4v 1–5)

Although the Pavier Quartos contain no other example of factual correction on a comparable scale to the York genealogy in *2 Henry VI,* there is
another group of corrections which require familiarity with the fictive
world of the play, and, therefore, are more likely to have been introduced
by an annotating reader rather than by a printing house agent. The first
quarto of *Sir John Oldcastle* mistakenly refers to 'Rochester' as 'Winchester'
on three occasions at I4r 19, K4r 8, and K4v 2. All three factual mistakes are
rectified in the second quarto at I3v 31, K3v 5, and K3v 30.

Other lines in the Pavier Quartos are rewritten to accommodate minor
changes in the dramatic structure of the plays. In *2 Henry VI,* for example, a
change of speaker involves the rewriting of half a line and the substitution
of the speech prefix that follows it: 'Vnckle of *Winchester* I pray you reade
on. / *Cardinal.*' at A3r 3–4 in the first quarto is turned into 'My Lord of
Yorke, I pray do you reade on. / *Yorke.*' at A3r 1–2 in Pavier's Quarto. Since
the version preserved in the first quarto is perfectly viable, this correction is
more likely to stem from annotation of copy prior to its submission to the
printers than from the intervention of a compositor or a proof-reader in the
printing house. Similarly, a change of addressee in Pavier's *Merchant of*
Venice effects a local revision, rather than a correction, of the whole speech:
while in the source text Antonio addresses Bassanio while referring to
Shylock as if the latter could not hear him – 'is hee yet possest / How
much you would?' (Q1, B3r 4–5) – in Pavier's edition Antonio addresses
Shylock directly, turning Bassanio into the referent of the third-person
pronoun 'he' – 'are you resolu'd, / How much he would haue?' (Q2, B3r
23–4). Once again, the combination of changes to the phrasing of
Antonio's question and to the deictic pronouns in it suggests a concerted
effort on the part of an annotator, rather than the outcome of impromptu
compositorial tampering.

A far greater number of changes in the dialogue of the Pavier Quartos
stems from an attempt to make sense of mangled lines in the source
texts. Local emendations in plays, such as *A Yorkshire Tragedy, The Merry*

Wives of Windsor, and *A Midsummer Night's Dream*, may well have been the result of a willing compositor, who made a genuine effort to improve some obvious shortcomings in the lines he was setting. An alert compositor or alert reader scanning through his copy of *A Yorkshire Tragedy* is equally likely to have been responsible for changing 'On her your posterity' (Q1, B2v 24) into 'On her and your posterity' (Q2, B1v 27), and 'To plead for pardon my deare husbands life' (Q1, D3r 29) into 'To plead for pardon for my deare husbands life' (Q2, D2v 9). The same can be said of two local corrections in the dialogue of *A Midsummer Night's Dream*: 'waues' (Q1, A2r 9) is replaced by the far more appropriate 'wanes' (Q2, A2r 9), and a slight syntactical irregularity in 'where we might / Without the perill of the *Athenian* lawe' (Q1, G1r 8–9) is smoothed out in Pavier's edition, which reads 'where we might be / Without the perill of the *Athenian* Law' (Q2, G1r 8–9). Local changes in the dialogue of *The Merry Wives of Windsor* seem to fall into the same category: 'Tis great pittie we should leaue him' (Q1, E1v 25) becomes 'Tis great pitty we should leaue him so' (Q2, E1r 17), and the nonsensical 'old numbers' (Q1, G1v 33) becomes 'odde numbers' (Q2, G1v 19).

The more problematic the source-text, the greater the frequency with which either a careful annotating reader or an alert compositor turned their attention to local errors. It is therefore hardly surprising that this category of changes is far more frequent in *Pericles* than any of the other Pavier Quartos. While the majority of local interventions in the dialogue of this text might equally be attributed to either an annotator or a compositor,[44] other local attempts to improve badly mangled lines in the first quarto of 1608 are more likely to derive from an annotating reader because they offer economical and effective solutions, which require sustained commitment and effort on the annotator's part. According to a recent editor, one such attempt – 'VVhat need we leaue our grounds the lowest' in the third quarto (B4v 19) becomes 'VVhat need we feare, the ground's the lowest' in Pavier's edition (s3v 7) – represents 'the least radical way to make sense of this passage' (Gossett 2004: 215) and is therefore widely adopted in modern editions of the play. Another variant introduced in Pavier's edition of *Pericles* shows, once again, a good mind at work: 'Contend not sir, for we are Gentlemen, / Haue neither in our hearts, nor outward eyes, / Enuies the great nor shall the low despise' (Q3, D1r 25–7) is skilfully normalized to read 'Contend not sir, for we are gentlemen, / That neither in our hearts, nor outward eyes, / Enuie the great, nor do the low despise' (Q4, T4r 11–13). Another local correction consists of a single but ingenious verbal substitution, which clarifies a rather elliptical remark in the third quarto – 'my ship-wracke now's no ill / Since I haue here my father gaue in his well' (Q3, C3v 14–15) – by replacing 'gaue' with 'gift' – 'my shipwrack now's no ill, / Since I haue here my fathers gift in's will' (Q4, T2r 35–6).

Collectively, the corrections to the dialogue in the Pavier Quartos, along with the frequent intervention to correct or add missing speech prefixes, and the extensive rewriting, re-formatting and correction of the stage directions, signal the intervention of an annotating reader. It is also worth stressing that further changes in the Pavier Quartos have more to do with stylistic preferences than with the need to emend their source texts. Except for extensively rewritten passages in *2 Henry VI*, which 'clearly indicate reference to some source other than Q1' (Montgomery 1985: II, xxxiii), other variant passages in the Pavier Quartos stem from the annotator's tendency to normalize syntactically unusual lines. The rephrasing of two passages in *3 Henry VI* and *Henry V*, for example, suggests a penchant for regular syntactical structures:

Edward.   *Clarence* and *Gloster*, loue my louelie Queene,
             And kisse your princely nephew brothers both. (*3H6* O1, E7v 14–16)

Edw.   Brothers of Clarence and of Gloster,
             Pray loue my louely Queene,
             And kisse your Princely Nephew, both. (*3H6* Q3, Q4r 31–3)

King. . . . yet keepe the French the field (*H5* Q1, E4r 1)

King. . . . the French keepes still the field (*H5* Q3, E4r 5)

Stylistic sophistication may provide an alternative explanation for what several scholars take to be mere 'padding' caused by the inaccurate casting-off of copy in the final sections of *3 Henry VI*. Eric Rasmussen and John Cox have already brilliantly demonstrated that '[a]lthough Q3 . . . includes a few words not found in O, the number of lines of text does not change; so, in this instance [in Q4r], the expansion can have nothing to do with problems of casting off' (Cox and Rasmussen 2001: 156).

Although the evidence provided by the Pavier Quartos is too limited to posit light stylistic revision as an alternative theory to account for *all* variant passages which are not obvious corrections of their source-texts, two further examples show another pattern of intervention which may explain *some* otherwise puzzling variants in *Henry V* and *Sir John Oldcastle*. The two following passages, for example, were apparently rewritten to avoid repetition:

Host. . . . honest gētlewomē
         That liue honestly (*H5* Q1, B1v 19–20)

Host.	. . . gentlewomen
	That liue honestly (*H5* Q3, BIV 19–20)

Lady cobh.	Why seeme ye so disquiet in your lookes?
	What hath befalne you that disquiets your minde?
	(*Oldcastle* QI, E3r 28–9)

L. Cobh.	Why seeme ye so disquiet in your lookes?
	What hath befalne you that disturbes your minde?
	(*Oldcastle* Q2, E3r 29–30)

Although these are two isolated examples, if considered alongside the number of stage directions and unusual lines which were syntactically normalized, they suggest that the same hand may also have been responsible for the editing of repetition, which is itself a form of stylistic irregularity.

The level of preparation of copy in the Pavier Quartos seems even more remarkable if the latter are compared *as a group* to other quarto editions of play texts which were first printed at the beginning of the seventeenth century and then republished in the mid- to late-1610s. Two such play texts are *The Weakest Goeth to the Wall*, first published in 1600 (STC 25144, henceforth QI) and then re-issued in 1618 (STC 25145, henceforth Q2), and *Jack Drum's Entertainment*, first published in 1601 (STC 7243) and then reprinted by Stansby in 1616 (STC 7244). The textual variants in Q2 *The Weakest Goeth to the Wall* are clearly compositorial in origin: they are the product of local memorial contamination and are limited to verbal substitutions,[45] transpositions,[46] and an unnecessary change of tense.[47] Unlike the Pavier Quartos, Q2 fails to change or improve speech prefixes. In fact, speech prefixes become visibly worse on two occasions: one is accidentally dropped at I4r 12 and another is erroneously added at E3v 17. The unnecessary addition of a wrong speech prefix at E3v 17 was probably due to the fact that the Q2 compositor mistook the opening of line E3v 17 in QI – '*Jacob*' – for a speech prefix, wrongly assumed that the prefix was a mistake because the following line is spoken by Jacob, and replaced it with '*Bunch.*', thus introducing another anomaly, since Bunch already speaks lines E3v 14–16 in both editions. This variant is particularly instructive because it shows what changes are likely to be introduced by a solicitous compositor, as opposed to an annotating reader familiar with the fictive world of the play. The only correction introduced in Q2 is the obvious omission of a word that had been set twice in QI.[48] Also worth noting is the fact that the page layout is, if anything, more crammed in Q2 than in QI. Similarly, the second edition of *Jack Drum's Entertainment* (henceforth Q2) represents an accurate reprint of the first edition (henceforth QI) but shows no sign of the type of editorial intervention observed in the Pavier Quartos. Stansby's compositor(s) introduced hardly any variants, one possible exception being the transposition of two half-lines.[49] The high quality of Stansby's presswork is also reflected in the frequent re-arrangement of turned lines, which is also a recurrent feature in several Pavier Quartos. Q2 however differs substantially from the Pavier Quartos, primarily because the claim made on its title page, according to which the text had been 'Newly corrected', is supported only by the correction of two obvious mistakes in Q1.[50]

More generally, despite the difference in the quality of the presswork, the second editions of *The Weakest Goeth to the Wall* and *Jack Drum's Entertainment* show what level of textual variation is to be expected when the text of a play was simply reset from an earlier, un-annotated printed edition. When compared to these two quartos, the Pavier Quartos look less like contemporary reprints and more like the text of plays included in later dramatic collections, which clearly elicited a similar level of intervention in the preparation of the printer's copy for the press. Tellingly, the same type of variants introduced in the Pavier Quartos can be found in the text of *The Dutch Courtesan* in William Sheares's 1633 edition of *The Workes of Mr. Iohn Marston* (STC 17471). Sheares's edition improves its source text published in 1605 (STC 17475) by adding two speech prefixes at Aa4r 4 and Dd2r 8, by correcting one at Cc5v 29, and by regularizing and correcting another two at Bb6v 2 and Bb7r 4. Sheares's edition also modifies one stage direction[51] and corrects the dialogue on at least one occasion.[52]

Overall, the variants in the Pavier Quartos seem hardly in keeping with a traditional understanding of this publishing venture as a 'shady' and 'abortive' affair. Considering that no collection of exclusively commercial play texts in English had yet been published, Pavier was in fact breaking new ground. If Pavier had the vision to at least plan the first collection of English plays originally written and performed for the public stage, may he have also been responsible for the several corrections, changes, additions and local abridgements in his quarto editions of 1619? Could Pavier, in other words, have invested not only his capital in a new, and therefore, financially risky type of book, but also his time to perfect the texts of his ten plays for the press?

THOMAS PAVIER: FROM RECKLESS FRAUDSTER
TO ANNOTATING READER?

Establishing the identity of the annotator(s) who prepared the printer's copy for the Pavier Quartos from internal evidence only is virtually impossible.

However, some patterns in Pavier's earlier output as a publisher suggest that he is at least a likely candidate. One of the plays which Pavier published at the beginning of his career provides a suggestive parallel to the editorial intervention observed in the Pavier Quartos of 1619. *A Looking Glass for London and for England* was first printed by Thomas Creede and sold by Pavier's old master, the draper William Barley, in 1594 (STC 16679, henceforth Q1) and then again in 1598 (STC 16680, henceforth Q2). This play, along with *Jack Straw*, *Henry V* and *The Spanish Tragedy*, was transferred to Pavier on 14 August 1600 (Arber 1875–94: III 63), shortly after he was freed as a member of the Drapers' Company on 9 April and then admitted to the Stationers' Company on 22 May (Johnson 1992: 15). Pavier published the third edition in 1602 (STC 16681, henceforth Q3). While Q2 offers no evidence of being set from annotated copy, Q3 shows a familiar pattern of intervention, by adding one stage direction[53] and nine new speech prefixes,[54] and by emending the dialogue on at least one occasion.[55] What is even more striking about Q3 *A Looking Glass for London and England* is the way in which some of its directions are normalized and slightly rephrased:

Embrace him; Embrace his necke; Kisse.; *K*isse him.; Faints. Point; Embrace him (*Looking Glass* Q2 G1r 10, G1r 14, G1r 16, G1r 20, G1r 26, G1v 2)

She imbraceth him; She embraceth his necke; She kisseth him; She kisseth him againe; She faints, and points; She embraceth him (*Looking Glass* Q3 F3v 10, F3v 14, F3v 16, F3v 20, F3v 26, F4r 2)

This type of rewriting is suggestively close to the way in which stage directions were rephrased in at least two of the Pavier Quartos:

spurns her; Teares his haire; Striues with her for the child; Throws her down; W. wakes catches up the yongest; ouer comes him (*Yorkshire* Q1, B1r 8–9; C2r 20; C3r 11–12; C3r 15; C3r 19–20; C3v 19)

He spurns her; He teares his haire; he striues with her for the childe; He throwes her downe; His wife awakes, and catcheth up the youngest; Husband ouercomes him (*Yorkshire* Q2 A4r 8; C1r 20; C2r 11; C2r 16; C2r 20; C2v 22)

open the letter; play Musique (MV Q1, F2v 27; I2v 20)

He opens the Letter; Musicke playes (MV Q2, F3v 33; I4v 7)

What the textual variants in Q3 collectively show is not only that the printer's copy for this edition had been annotated but also that the annotating hand may be the same as the one responsible for the preparation of the Pavier Quartos for the press in 1619. Since Pavier is the only agent involved in both publishing ventures he should at least be regarded as a possible candidate for the role of annotator of the printer's copy underlying his quarto editions of 1619.

Further evidence to argue that Pavier was the annotator who prepared copy for press in 1602 and 1619 can be found in the second quarto of *Henry V*, which Thomas Creede printed for Pavier, also in 1602. Strangely, Pavier used a copy of the first quarto of 1600 (STC 22289, henceforth Q1) as a source-text for his edition of 1619 (STC 22291, henceforth Q3), instead of relying on his own edition of 1602 (STC 22290, henceforth Q2). What is worth stressing, though, is the fact that Q2 introduced several of the textual variants which then re-emerge in the text of 1619. One of the most notable features of Q3 *Henry V* is the amount of attention devoted to the correction of wrong speech prefixes, the omission of redundant ones, and the addition of new ones. All instances of intervention to correct, omit, and add speech prefixes in Q3 are anticipated by Q2. More specifically, both editions introduce the speech prefix '*Bish.*' at A2v 1; omit the redundant speech prefix '*Pist.*' at D3r 23 and D3v 21; correct two speech prefixes from '*3. Lord.*' to '*3. Soul.*'at D4r 35 and D4v 35 and from '*2. L.*' to '*2. Soul.*' at D4v 5 and E1r 4; and add the speech prefixes '*King.*' at F3r 10 and F3v 30, '*Exe.*' at F3r 12 and F3v 32, and '*King.*' at F3r 14 and F3v 35.

A closer look at Pavier's entire output as a publisher shows that he was also eager to secure freshly annotated copy, when the text had been extensively revised or when he had reasons to believe that any of his earlier publications needed to be corrected or updated. His edition of *The Spanish Tragedy* (STC 15089), for example, which rightfully boasts to be 'Newly corrected, amended, and enlarged with new Additions of the *Painters* part, and others, as it hath of late been diuers times acted', adds over 300 lines and five additional passages to the text of the previous edition. The New Mermaids editor, J. R. Mulryne, identifies Pavier as the agent potentially responsible for securing and adding the supplementary lines and passages to his source text: 'Pavier ... may have received from the theatre, or from some intermediary, authorised or not, portions of the new copy; he would then incorporate them as best he could into an example of 1592' (1989: xxxiv). Circumstantial evidence provided by a very different type of publication, Pavier's 1613 edition of *The Path-Way to Knowledge; Containing the Whole Art of Arithmeticke* (STC 23677), confirms that Pavier was indeed renowned for taking an active interest in the quality of the texts of his books. The first edition of *The Path-Way to Knowledge* was published by William Barley in 1596 (STC 19799). The second edition published by Pavier in 1613 is radically different from the first one. As the reviser explains in the address to the reader, it was Pavier who approached him to secure his collaboration in revising this text:

> by the translators ouersight, or the Printers negligence I know not, [the first edition] was published in many places, not onely obscure and difficult for a learners apprehension, but also somewhat confused . . . and the whole impression beeing dispersed and gone, my said friend to whome the interest of the sayd Coppy did belong, willing to reprint the same, and withall very desirous to haue it perused and put into a more plainer and easy method . . . importuning such as hee could heare of to effect the same . . . onely I . . ., beeing much pressed, began the methode in the plainest manner that possible I could. (A4r 12–27)

The profile of the committed and scrupulous publisher outlined in this address to the reader clashes with traditional assessments of Pavier's professional integrity and his publishing venture of 1619. Far from being a shady fraudster Pavier is more likely to have been a conscientious, if not a fussy, publisher, who took an active interest in the quality of the texts he published. Pavier may in fact be one of those early annotating readers, the first 'editors' of Shakespeare, whose legacy represents an integral part of the editorial tradition and of Shakespeare's texts, as we still know them today.

CHAPTER 5

The making of the First Folio (1623)

The publication of the First Folio edition of Shakespeare's collected dramatic works in 1623 (henceforth FI) is the most important event in the history of Shakespeare's fortunes in print prior to the official rise of the editorial tradition at the beginning of the eighteenth century. FI included thirty-six plays, eighteen of which had never been published before. The manuscript copies of these plays were provided by the King's Men, as attested by the dedicatory epistle and the address to the reader prefaced to FI, which are signed by two share-holding members of Shakespeare's company, John Heminge and Henry Condell. Their claim that *all* Folio plays were set from the 'true and originall copies' (AIr 6) of Shakespeare's works and replaced the 'stolne, and surreptitious copies' (A3r 25) underlying quarto editions printed before 1623 has caused much controversy, mostly because some of the other eighteen plays were set fairly closely from the very editions Heminge and Condell seem to disparage. This chapter focuses specifically on a selection of Folio plays set from printed copy in order to reassess current theories about the origin of substantive departures from their source texts.

The debate over the origin of the printer's copies used to set FI has shifted since the late nineteenth century from widespread scepticism to a more optimistic, if conditional, endorsement of Heminge and Condell's assessment of the qualities of the quarto editions printed prior to 1623. Having established that some Folio plays were set from earlier quartos, the editors of the Cambridge edition of 1863–6 voiced their disappointment at the seemingly cavalier and self-interested attitude displayed by the executors of Shakespeare's artistic legacy: '[a]s the "setters forth" are thus convicted of a *suggestio falsi* in one point, it is not improbable that they may have been guilty of the like in another' (Clark and Glover 1863: 24–5). At the beginning of the twentieth century, as mentioned earlier, Pollard advanced his influential theory that only some of the earlier quarto editions had been set from 'stolne and surreptitious copies' and that they should be distinguished from other quarto editions which were clearly set from authoritative sources and were presumably passed over to their publishers with the blessing of the author and his company. Pollard's distinction between 'good' and 'bad' quartos was hailed as one of the most significant advancements in Shakespeare textual studies, mostly because, as John Dover Wilson pointed out, it exonerated Heminge and Condell from reproach:

[I]f I were asked to say how the new criticism chiefly differs from the old, I should not think first of bibliographical methods, or of the way in which our accumulated knowledge of the Elizabethan theatre has been brought to bear upon textual problems; I should single out something much simpler and more fundamental. It is that belief in the essential integrity of ordinary human nature which, like the English law, regards a man innocent until he has been proved guilty. Acting on this faith, Mr. Pollard has refused to believe ... that Heminge and Condell were either knaves in league with Jaggard to hoodwink a gullible public, or else fools who did not know how to pen a preface. (1924: 76–7)

More recently, increased attention to the sixteenth and seventeenth-century usage of the term 'orginall' has further contributed to the rehabilitation of Heminge and Condell's reputation. Margreta de Grazia, for example, has usefully pointed out that the theatrical origin of some Folio plays which had been previously published in fuller, authoritative versions did not contradict Heminge and Condell's claim, given that the term 'originall' and its variant forms associated to 'regenall' (from the Latin *regere*) 'denoted proximity to the script regulating performance' rather than fidelity to 'what Shakespeare originally wrote, his authentic manuscript' (1991: 88–9).

The paradigmatic shift from late nineteenth-century views according to which not all, if any, of the Folio plays were set from Shakespeare's own manuscripts, to a late twentieth-century understanding of the Folio as a collection of authoritative texts, used and endorsed by Shakespeare's company, has affected scholarly opinion so deeply that even Folio plays set from printed copy are now largely believed to have been prepared for press through occasional consultation of theatrical manuscripts. Such confidence in the existence of a direct link between some Folio texts and the official theatrical manuscripts owned by the King's Men is relatively new. In his *The Shakespeare First Folio: Its Bibliographical and Textual History*, W. W. Greg concluded that some Folio plays, including *Love's Labour's Lost*, *Romeo and Juliet* and *1 Henry IV*, were set from printed copy without reference to any playhouse authority (Greg 1955: 223, 232, 264). Greg did point out that some reference was made to theatrical manuscripts in preparing the printed copy of other Folio plays, but he also stressed that, as with the Folio text of *Much Ado About Nothing*, the consultation of the theatrical authority 'can have been no more than superficial' (Greg 1955: 281). Less than twenty years later, J. K. Walton revisited Greg's conclusions in his own investigation of *The Quarto Copy for the First Folio of Shakespeare*. While Walton confirmed that 'the quarto copy . . . [of *Romeo and Juliet*] cannot have been altered with reference to a manuscript', he detected 'very casual reference . . . to the prompt-book in preparing the quarto copy [of *Love's Labour's Lost*]', and 'desultory collation' of the quarto copy of *1 Henry IV* with a play-house manuscript or 'editorial tinkering based partly on a remembrance of the play's performance' (1971: 237). By the mid-1980s, the team of editors who prepared the Oxford edition of *The Complete Works* had come to believe that 'reference to a theatrical manuscript [was in fact] . . . consistent with the usual treatment of printed copy for Folio plays' (Wells and Taylor 1987: 289).

This chapter shows that the current confidence in the theatrical origin of sporadic variants in Folio plays set from printed copy may be primarily due to the increasing desire to value 'the text closer to the prompt-book of Shakespeare's company' (Wells and Taylor 1987: 15) over the author's manuscript drafts. As much as Pollard's narrative about the origin of the copy underlying the 'good' quartos, the current belief in the annotation of printed copy through sporadic consultation of theatrical manuscripts may also prove 'the product not of reason but of desire' (Werstine 1990: 75). While new scenes added to earlier printed versions of the same play, such as the abdication scene in *Richard II* or the fly-killing scene in *Titus Andronicus*, were probably transcribed from a theatrical manuscript, the assumption that the busy environment of an early modern commercial theatre or printing house would allow any of their agents the leisure to collate two texts, known *not* to differ from each other radically, in order to recover a handful of variant readings, seems highly doubtful, especially when such readings are not strictly remedial.

Also instructive is the fact that those playwrights who saw their own plays into print often focused on making the texts of their plays less, rather than more, explicitly theatrical. John Lyly, for example, is believed to have omitted the songs and dumb show from the printer's copy for the first edition of *Endymion*, which were then re-introduced by Edward Blount in his edition of 1632, in order to make his play seem more literary. As David Bevington explains in the introduction to his Revels edition of 1996:

The omission in [the first quarto] of the dumb show . . . seems especially to underscore the literary nature of this text. Rather than upstage Endymion's own account of his dream in v.i with a purely theatrical description of stage action, Lyly omits the dumb show from his text. The dumb show is not necessary for sense in reading the play, and clearly Lyly does not intend his text as a record of theatrical performance. (1996: 4)

The desire to remove the printed play text from the world of the theatre was not confined to early modern dramatists intent on fashioning their literary personae in print. As shown in chapter 2, the stationer Richard Jones advertised his efforts to 'correct' and 'reform' those aspects of Marlowe's *Tamburlaine* which seemed suited to the stage but inappropriate for his readers. Why should we then assume that time and resources would be invested by the Folio syndicate to ensure that texts already in their possession, known not to differ radically from the stage versions preserved by the King's Men, were lightly edited in order to bring them closer to a theatrical authority? Although two actors identify themselves as the executors of Shakespeare's artistic legacy, other aspects of the Folio, including the fashioning of Shakespeare's authorial persona in its preliminaries (Marcus 1988: 2–25; de Grazia 1991: 14–48), the arrangement of the plays into well-established generic categories, its size and format, and consequently its price, suggest the extent to which the Folio was conceived as an up-market, literary enterprise, and not as a record of the plays as they were acted on stage.

Textual variants seemingly derived from the sporadic consultation of theatrical manuscripts are sometimes alternatively explained as the product of annotation for performance. Dover Wilson, for example, believed that the quarto copy used to set the Folio text of *Love's Labour's Lost* had served as a prompt-book (1923: 187–8). Dover Wilson's hypothesis was rejected by other scholars, including Greg, who regarded the variants in the Folio text of *Love's Labour's Lost* as too limited and inconsistent to suggest theatrical origin (1942: 128). Theatre historians since Dover Wilson and Greg have established that the very term 'prompt-book' is an anachronism, since the early modern 'play-book', or simply 'the book', was not used to ensure the accurate delivery of individual lines but was instead kept at the back of the stage to regulate the timing of key entrances, exits and special effects, as well as the use of large and unwieldy properties which required the intervention of stage-hands. The book-keeper therefore had no reason to annotate his book in order to ensure that all its speech prefixes were consistent or his stage action systematically regulated by timely and full directions.[1] However, the range of variants in some of the Folio plays set from printed copy is still at odds even with what theatre historians now believe was the type of intervention prompted by annotation for performance, which, as I explained in my Introduction, is even more limited to pragmatic concerns related to the staging of a play when a theatrical agent annotated a printed edition, as opposed to a dramatic manuscript.

Extant printed playbooks annotated for performance show that theatrical annotators were largely unconcerned by inconsistencies in the dialogue. Leslie Thomson, for example, who has studied the manuscript annotations in the quarto edition of the *The Two Merry Milke-maids; or, The Best Words Wear the Garland* (STC 4281, 1620) held at the Folger Shakespeare Library, has established that the alterations to the dialogue were made by a different hand (Hand C) from the two other hands, which she identifies as Bookkeeper A and B (1996: 176–210). Charles Read Baskerville is even more explicit in stressing how the early seventeenth-century theatrical functionaries who annotated the undated quarto edition of *A Looking Glass for London and England* (STC 16681.5), currently in the holdings of the University Library in Chicago, left the text of this play virtually unaltered:

> Perhaps some principle of disturbing the printed form as little as possible is responsible also for the state of the [speech prefixes] and of the text proper ... Except for the changes described earlier, which attempt to correct the text only by supplying a missing line, the text of the play has not been altered. Yet it is exceptionally corrupt. The prompt-book completely ignores all errors and misprints, including meaningless words and phrases and even one meaningless line resulting from the printer's having set parts of two lines as one in addition to printing both lines ... correctly. (Baskerville 1932–3: 50–1)

Assuming that the printed playbooks studied by Baskerville and Thomson are representative examples of how early seventeenth-century theatrical agents would annotate a printed text for performance, the range of variants in some Folio plays set from printed copy can hardly be attributed to the same category of agents. Even Folio texts where the majority of variants affect stage directions and speech prefixes include changes to the text of the dialogue which seem to fall outside the remit of a seventeenth-century theatrical annotator. By using *Romeo and Juliet* and *Love's Labour's Lost* as my main examples, I will instead argue that the Folio variants in these plays are more likely to derive from the idiosyncratic and sporadic manuscript corrections added by annotating readers than from annotation for performance or from sporadic consultation of a theatrical manuscript. While I do not wish to downplay the impact of theatrical agents on the preparation of the manuscripts supplied by the King's Men for those plays which had never been printed before or had been substantially revised since they had first appeared in print, I propose that at least some of the Folio plays set from printed copies were annotated by a category of agents associated with the publishers who owned those copies.

THE FOLIO TEXT OF *ROMEO AND JULIET*

Textual scholars generally agree that the copy for the Folio text of *Romeo and Juliet* received less editorial attention than any of the other Folio plays set from printed copy. Nevertheless, recent editors have argued that the printer's copy may have been lightly annotated with reference to a theatrical manuscript or by somebody who had some recollection of the play as staged by the King's Men (Reid 1982: 66; Wells and Taylor 1987: 289). It is certainly true that stage directions and speech prefixes received some attention. The Folio adds eleven stage directions,[2] edits and regularizes another eleven,[3] and attempts to correct two.[4] The Folio also corrects one wrongly assigned prefix and removes a redundant one.[5] As S. W. Reid pointed out in 1982, it would be unreasonable to ascribe this type of intervention to a compositor or to a printing house agent, as assumed by those textual scholars who used to believe that the Folio text of *Romeo and Juliet* was simply a reprint of the third quarto of 1609 (Duthie 1951: 3–29; Wilson 1955: 81–9; Greg 1955: 231–2; Walton 1971: 232–3). However, the alternative hypothesis involving consultation of a theatrical authority or the annotator's familiarity with the play as staged seems equally unjustified, since all the changes to stage directions and speech prefixes add no extra information beside what is implied by their immediate context, and are therefore not beyond the grasp of an alert reader. Furthermore, some of the stage directions in the Folio, although edited and expanded, are less accurate than their counterpart in the printer's copy.

'*Exit*' at E4v 23 in the third quarto (STC 22324, 1609, henceforth Q3) is, for example, replaced by '*Exit Nurse and Peter*' at TLN 1309 in the Folio.[6] Since there are other speaking characters on stage beside the Nurse and Peter by the time this direction is used to clear the stage, the ostensibly improved direction in the Folio is more misleading than its equivalent in the third quarto, since 'Exit' and 'Exeunt' are often used interchangeably to mark the end of a scene. Although consultation of a theatrical authority is assumed to have been sporadic and annotation for performance unsystematic, it seems counterintuitive that even desultory reference to a theatrical authority should increase, rather than reduce, ambiguity in the stage action. Even more significant are two sets of variant stage directions later on in the play:

Exeunt: manet.
Musi.   Faith we may put vp our pipes and be gone.
Nur.   Honest goodfellowes, ah put vp, put vp,
      For well you know, this is a pitifull case.
Fid.   I by my troath, the case may be amended.
     Exeunt omnes.   *Enter* (K3r 32–7)

Exeunt
Mu.   Faith we may put vp our Pipes and be gone.
Nur. Honest goodfellowes: Ah put vp, put vp,
        For well you know, this is a pitifull case.
Mu.   I by my troth, the case may be amended. (TLN 2675–9)

Once again, the first entry direction is less accurate in the Folio than in the third quarto, from which the Folio was set, since at least the Nurse stays on stage from the previous sequence, where Juliet is presumed dead and her death lamented by members of the Capulet household, including the Nurse who discovers the body. The next exit direction in the third quarto fails to signal that the musicians stay on stage and take part in the next exchange with the servant Peter. While the Folio omits the misleading exit direction, it fails to indicate that at least the Nurse leaves the stage after her brief exchange with the musicians. It is therefore worth stressing that on at least two occasions the Folio provides less accurate entry and exit directions when compared to its source text. Collectively, these Folio variants challenge the current view, according to which the copy for Folio *Romeo and Juliet* was annotated by reference to a playbook used in the theatre, or through memories of the play as staged, given that they remove, rather than increase, the number of clues about the stage action.

Another variant in the exchange quoted above reinforces my impression that, despite focusing on stage directions and speech prefixes, intervention in the printer's copy from which the Folio text of *Romeo and Juliet* was set was not influenced by consultation of a theatrical authority or by the annotator's recollection of the play as staged. The change in the speech prefix '*Fid.*' at K3r 36 in Q3 to '*Mu.*' at TLN 2679 in the Folio is part of a more general attempt to regularize speech prefixes in the Folio. In the ensuing exchange between Peter and the musicians, the different speech prefixes used to identify the musicians in the third quarto – '*Fidler*' (K3v 4), '*Minstrels.*' (K3v 7), and '*Min.*' (K3v 9, 11, 14, 18, 27 and K4r 1) – are replaced by the invariant prefix '*Mu.*' (TLN 2684–719). The attempt to normalize speech prefixes is not limited to this exchange and is not always as straightforward. In fact, on other occasions the annotator makes telling mistakes, which discredit, once again, the related theories of consultation of a theatrical manuscript, where speech prefixes, though not systematic, would have been more rather than less consistent than in the third quarto, and of memorial recollection of the play as staged, which would have improved the annotator's chances of remembering the identity of secondary characters. One such mistake occurs in the concluding scene where the Folio's use of the prefix '*Boy.*' (TLN 3036 and TLN 3146) conflates Paris's page – wrongly identified as '*Watch boy.*' in the third quarto at L4r 21 – with Romeo's man – correctly prefixed in the third quarto as '*Balth.*' at MIV 18. Further changes in the speech prefixes as they appear in the Folio confirm the annotator's willingness to tamper with his copy even when not strictly necessary, thus ruling out the intervention of a compositor or a theatrical agent, as at TLN 3052, where the new prefix '*Con.*' [i.e. Constable] replaces '*Chiefe watch.*' in the third quarto at L4r 34. The annotator's willingness to tamper with his copy for stylistic, rather than for strictly remedial purposes, is not matched by a satisfactory level of familiarity with the fictive world of the play. As observed above, the annotator's ability to identify secondary characters is often poor. A line of dialogue, erroneously set in italic type and centred like a stage direction in the third quarto – '*O Lord they fight, I will go call the Watch*' (L2v 21) – is rightly reset in roman type and aligned with other lines of dialogue in the Folio, but it is wrongly assigned to '*Pet.*' (TLN 2924) rather than to Paris's page.

Variants in the dialogue of the Folio text of *Romeo and Juliet* confirm that the printer's copy had been sporadically emended by a solicitous, but not always consistently inspired, annotating reader. Textual scholars now believe that the Folio text of *Romeo and Juliet* was mostly set by an apprentice in Jaggard's printing shop, who is normally referred to as Compositor E (Hinman 1963: 200–6; Howard-Hill 1980: 156–78). This partly explains the high number of new errors introduced in the Folio.[7] However, at least three variants in the dialogue as it appears in the Folio attempt to improve the text of the play as preserved in the third quarto. The first variant is as puzzling as it is strictly speaking unnecessary. The Friar's appeal for Romeo to be 'plaine . . . and homely' in his account of his first encounter with Juliet is slightly rephrased in the Folio:

Fri.   Be plaine good sonne and homely in thy drift, (Q3 EIV 5)

Fri.   Be plaine good Son, rest homely in thy drift, (F TLN 1062)

As the Oxford editors argue, '[the Folio]'s more unusual reading is difficult to explain if it has no authority'. Ultimately, though, and rightly so, the Oxford editors regard this reading as non-authorial, because, as they continue, 'there is not a class of comparable variants where [the Folio] possibly improves on common quarto readings' (Wells and Taylor 1987: 295). In other words, this reading represents an uncommon and isolated occurrence and can hardly be associated with authorial or substantial revisions recovered by an agent intent on registering variant readings from a fresh witness, as it may indeed have been the case with the quarto copy used to set Folio plays,

such as *The Tragedie of King Lear.* A more likely explanation for this type of
variant is that an annotating reader, fastidious enough to change the speech
prefix '*Chiefe watch.*' (Q3 L4r 34) to '*Con.*' (F TLN 3052), may also have crossed
out the prosaic 'and' in the Friar's line as it appears in the third quarto to
replace it with 'rest'. Equally intriguing is the use of '*Capulets*' instead of the
variant '*Capels*' in the following line:

The day is hot, the *Capels* abroad: (Q3 F2v 3)

The day is hot, the *Capulets* abroad: (F TLN 1433)

Besides normalizing the Capulets' family name, this Folio variant improves
the metre. Also worth noting is the attempt to restore the metre in another
line, where the final word had either been accidentally dropped or was
never included in the versions preserved in the second and third quartos,
since 'his' functions both as an adjective or as a pronoun:

And hide me with a dead man in his, (Q3 I3v 1)

And hide me with a dead man in his graue, (F TLN 2380)

By adding 'graue', the annotator successfully restored the metre. However,
as mentioned above, the quality of the annotator's corrections often failed
to match his willingness to intervene. On this occasion, he simply repeated
the final word in the previous line, which is invariant in both editions – 'Or
bid me go into a new made graue,' (Q3 I3r 36; F TLN 2379).

 The Folio variants analysed above show that the annotator who prepared
the printer's copy for the Folio text of *Romeo and Juliet* was familiar with
the fictive world of the play and that he was willing to correct what he
perceived as shortcomings in his text, although his corrections often fail to
improve it. In other words, like recent scholars, including Reid, I believe
that the annotator cannot have been a printing house agent intent on
reproducing his copy as closely as possible (Reid 1982: 45). However, unlike
the majority of scholars since Reid, I find no evidence in the Folio text of
Romeo and Juliet to support the theory according to which the annotator
sporadically consulted a theatrical manuscript or relied on personal memories of the play as staged.

THE FOLIO TEXT OF *LOVE'S LABOUR'S LOST*

The first twentieth-century scholar to carry out a systematic investigation
of the early textual transmission of *Love's Labour's Lost* was Dover Wilson.

Dover Wilson argued that the copy of the first quarto of 1598 used to set the Folio text of 1623 must have been annotated by a playhouse agent, because, in his view, some Folio variants were 'clearly beyond the scope of a compositor' (1923: 187–8). For example, he regarded the addition of the sound cue 'Song' at TLN 771 as 'a sign-post insertion by prompter or stage-manager' and the final half-line 'You that way; we this way' at TLN 2899 as 'virtually a fresh stage-direction'. Dover Wilson therefore concluded that the quarto copy used to set the Folio text had been annotated to serve as a prompt-book. Greg rejected Dover Wilson's conclusions by arguing that 'the addition of "Song" at III.i.1 follows indications in the text' and that the half-line added at the very end of the play is a 'desperate attempt to fit the final words of Q into the structure of the play' (Greg 1955: 223). Greg found Dover Wilson's theory that the Folio text of *Love's Labour's Lost* 'was printed from a copy of [the first quarto] that had been used as a prompt-book . . . inconceivable' (1955: 223n) because he believed that for the printer's copy of the text of *Love's Labour's Lost* as it appears in the Folio to have served as a prompt-book 'there would have had to be far more tidying up' of the overall text (1942: 128).

Greg's views were still prevalent when Stanley Wells surveyed a counter-tradition of dissenting opinions in the early 1980s, starting with Peter Alexander in 1939, who believed that 'Heminge and Condell . . . had [the quarto copy] checked . . . with a stage version in their possession', and ending with Walton in 1971, who concluded that 'some very casual reference was made to the prompt-book in preparing the quarto copy for [the Folio]' (quoted in Wells 1982: 281). Although they provided a salutary alternative to Greg's scepticism, Wells lamented the fact that these dissenting opinions were voiced by scholars who, instead of re-examining the whole range of quarto and Folio variants, simply aimed 'to discover whether any of the Folio's readings could be judged so superior to the Quarto's as to be beyond the capacity of an annotator without access to a manuscript' (1982: 282). Wells's commitment to a full-scale analysis of quarto and Folio variants produced remarkable results. He, for example, provided the most convincing explanation for the Folio's addition of the apparently redundant speech prefix '*Prin.*' in a speech already assigned to '*Queen.*' in both editions, when the Princess of France makes her first appearance (QI, B4r 21; F, TLN 504):

The scene's first twenty lines are made up of recapitulation and compliments. The line . . . before which the otherwise redundant prefix is added – 'You are not ignorant all telling fame . . .' – would make a strong opening to the scene; and I suggest that the annotator derived his prefix from a manuscript in which the opening lines had been marked for omission. (1982: 285)

More generally, Wells's study provided new evidence to support the theory according to which the printer's copy of *Love's Labour's Lost* was annotated by reference to a fresh manuscript source. Wells was however forced to admit that the manuscript consulted by the annotator was not 'conspicuously superior' to the printer's copy underlying the first quarto:

> The evidence lies primarily in the fact that many of the alterations to the Quarto seem not necessarily improvements but totally inexplicable except on the hypothesis that someone has had access to a document which he believed to be of superior authority to the Quarto, and which he followed, at times, without concerning himself about the reason of its variants. (1982: 282)

If the manuscript envisaged by Wells was indeed what he describes as 'immediately post-foul-papers', as opposed to the company's official prompt-book or what Andrew Gurr calls a 'minimal playbook' (1999: 68–87), then one wonders, along with John Kerrigan, why Shakespeare himself or a playhouse scribe would 'writ[e] out a manuscript only marginally fairer' than that which was already available (1982: 337). Kerrigan, who agrees with Wells in regarding the Folio text as reflecting a further stage of revision than the text preserved in the first quarto, does not believe that its variants derived from sporadic consultation of a theatrical manuscript: 'my own view', Kerrigan explains, 'is that the annotator, certainly usually and perhaps always, worked from his memory of the play in performance' (1982: 337). Like Wells, Kerrigan regards Folio variants as authoritative: 'I do not myself believe that any Q–F variants fall into the category of performed but not Shakespearean text' (1982: 337–8). However, like Wells, he believes that the Folio text fails to provide an accurate account of Shakespeare's revisions: while Wells blames the quality of the manuscript sporadically consulted by the annotator of the quarto copy used to set up the Folio text, Kerrigan blames the reporter, whose patchy memory or low level of engagement with his task led him to annotate only some of Shakespeare's changes (1982: 338).

Wells's and Kerrigan's desire to identify and preserve authorial revisions is hindered by obvious shortcomings in the text of the Folio. Its uneven quality forces Wells to admit that the manuscript consulted by the annotator was not consistently better than the printer's copy underlying the first quarto and to make a selective use of Folio variants. For example, the Folio notoriously fails to straighten out the Rosaline-Katherine tangle in Act 2 scene 1. The annotator correctly amended two speech prefixes used in the opening sequence in Act 2. In the first quarto the lady who met Longueville 'at a marriage feast' (B4v 13) and will later be wooed by him, that is Maria, is designated as '*I. Lad.*'. When the Princess seeks confirmation that her opinion of Longueville is correct – 'Some merrie mocking Lord belike, ist so?' (B4v 25) – a generic '*Lad.*' replies 'They say so most, that most his humors know' (B4v 26). In the Folio the generic '*Lad.*' is correctly turned into '*Lad. I*', that is Maria. In the same sequence, '*2. Lad.*' (B4v 29) and '*3. Lad.*' (B4v 37), that is Katherine and Rosaline, disparage Dumaine and Biron, with whom they will be paired off later on in the play. In the Folio the last speech prefix, '*3. Lad.*', is correctly changed into '*Rossa.*' (TLN 556). The Folio also corrects the first exchange between Biron and Rosaline: in the quarto, the lady who outwits Biron is identified by the speech prefix '*Kather.*' or '*Kath.*' (C1v 13–25); in the Folio, all seven speech prefixes are changed into '*Rosa.*' (TLN 610–22). By the second exchange Shakespeare had already started to think of Biron's match as Rosaline, as shown by the speech prefixes '*Ros.*' in the quarto (C2v 5–16), which are normalized in the Folio into '*La. Ros.*' (TLN 678–89). The Folio also changes all the speech prefixes in this exchange except the last from '*Ber.*' [Biron] to '*Boy.*' [Boyet]. This change can hardly be attributed to the same annotator who successfully identifies '*3. Lad.*' with '*Rossa.*' a few lines earlier, and it is therefore more likely to stem from compositorial misreading.[8] However, the annotator did fail to rectify the next exchange, where Shakespeare went back to thinking of Rosaline as Katherine and vice versa, as suggested by the fact that Dumaine asks after Rosaline and Biron after Katherine.

The final sequence in 2.1 is even more problematic, because the pairings which helped the annotator and still help editors tackle the Rosaline-Katherine tangle in the first half of 2.1 are not so useful in the second half, where the ladies' remarks do not seem to be directly addressed to the lords with whom they will pair off later on in the play. The Oxford editors, who believe that the annotator consulted a theatrical manuscript, follow the speech prefixes as they appear in the final sequence of the Folio: while the quarto identifies the ladies as '*Lad.*' (C3v 6), '*Lad. 2*' (C3v 7), '*Lad. 3*' (C3v 9), '*Lad.*' (C3v 12), and '*Lad.*' (C3v 14), the Folio opts for '*Lad. Ro.*' (TLN 758), '*Lad. Ma.*' (TLN 760), '*Lad. 2*' (TLN 762), '*La. 1*' (TLN 765), and '*Lad. 2.*' (TLN 767). Following the identification of '*Lad.1*' with Maria and '*Lad. 2*' with Katherine in the opening sequence of 2.1, the Oxford editors trust the annotator and identify the speakers accordingly. However, the Oxford editors do not trust the annotator, when a few lines earlier in the final sequence in 2.1 he changed the speech prefix '*Lady Ka.*' in the quarto at C3r 6 to '*La. Ma.*' at TLN 720, possibly because the Folio erroneously assigns the next line to '*La. Ma.*', which is spoken by Boyet in the Quarto. The wrong assignment of TLN 721, however, must be a local compositorial oversight, since it spoils the repartee between Boyet and the witty lady, alternatively identified as Katherine in the quarto and as Maria in the Folio. One may therefore wonder on what grounds the annotator is trusted at TLN 758–67 and not at TLN 720.

The Oxford editors decide not to trust the annotator on another occasion, even though, according to Wells, the variant version provided by the Folio makes theatrical sense. In the Folio, Dull's 'Fare you well' at TLN 435 is followed by the new direction '*Exit.*'. Here's how Wells explains his decision to ignore the alternative stage action preserved by the Folio:

> Editors usually reject [this direction], and certainly it could easily be an independent, mistaken deduction from the dialogue. Yet it could be right if we interpret the words "Come, Jaquenetta, away," spoken by Costard in Q and F but attributed by Theobald and later editors to Dull, as Costard's instruction to Jaquenetta to leave, not a request for her company. (Wells 1982: 286–7)

Although this Folio direction is perfectly in keeping with the dialogue, the Oxford editors cannot confidently identify it as authorial and therefore reject it. Overall, their selection of Folio variants seems to stem from a local evaluation of their theatrical and dramatic desirability.

Kerrigan's approach to the Folio text of this play is similarly divided: while he identifies the source of its variants as authoritative, he often regards them as an inaccurate report of Shakespeare's intentions. Both Kerrigan and the Oxford editors are, for example, openly critical of Folio variants which affect the dialogue of this play. A puzzling reading in the quarto – 'A man of soueraigne peerelsle he is esteemd' (B4v 17) – is changed in the Folio to read 'A man of soueraigne parts he is esteem'd' (TLN 536). The solution offered by the Folio is ingenious but the Oxford editors, like most modern editors, reject it. According to the Oxford editors,

> [t]he Folio reading may reflect annotated copy, or may be a guess (it is not certainly correct). As 'peerless' is appropriate to the context, it is also possible that the compositor, misled by the words' similar openings, accidentally omitted 'parts', and that the annotator, seeing it inserted, mistook it for a substitution. This assumes a hexameter. [Richard] Proudfoot conjectures 'peerless parts'. (Wells and Taylor 1987: 272)

Similarly, Kerrigan regards the Folio's attempt to rectify another quarto reading – 'Hence herrite then my hart, is in thy breast' (I4v 38) becomes 'Hence euer then, my heart, is in thy brest' in the Folio (TLN 2776) – as spurious and 'irresponsibly speculative' (1982: 337).

Wells's and Kerrigan's narratives about the origin of the printer's copy underlying the Folio text of *Love's Labour's Lost* seem unnecessarily complicated because they both imply a link with an authoritative source only to then posit the annotator's failure to represent Shakespeare's intentions accurately. The Folio variants in *Love's Labour's Lost* seem more simply in keeping with the pattern of intervention associated with annotating readers who corrected their text by drawing on no other source than their own judgement. The addition of the apparently redundant prefix '*Prin.*' in the first speech already assigned to the Princess of France in 2.1 is the only Folio variant which would indeed seem to indicate consultation of a different textual witness where the beginning of this speech was marked for omission, as argued by Wells. However, no other Folio variants seem beyond the grasp of an alert annotating reader. The *willingness* to rectify speech prefixes, to add or modify stage directions, and to tamper with obscure readings in the dialogue is typical of editions set up from annotated copy, as shown in earlier chapters in this book. The *failure* to rectify speech prefixes, to effectively modify existing stage directions, and to restore maimed readings is even more clearly associated with annotation of copy *without* the support of a fresh manuscript or first-hand knowledge of the play as staged. Conversely, the addition of a redundant speech prefix provides too little evidence in itself to support theories which link the Folio text *as a whole* to a fresh authoritative source.

The alternative hypothesis of annotation of copy without the support of an authoritative source may also account for similarities in the Folio texts of both *Love's Labour's Lost* and *Romeo and Juliet*. Both Folio texts are only partially successful at rectifying speech prefixes, supplying missing stage directions, and providing viable, if not satisfactory, alternatives to obscure readings in their source texts. Besides, both plays belonged to the same stationer, John Smethwick, who was also one of the four members of the Folio syndicate. Could Smethwick have acted as an annotator of copy or as a procurer of annotated copy, as Andrew Wise and Thomas Pavier may have done before him? Could the publisher, in other words, rather than the author or a reporter of the play in performance, have functioned as the source or catalyst of the changes introduced in the Folio texts of these two plays?

'PLAYING THE MIDWIFE'S PART': THE FIRST FOLIO
AND ITS PUBLISHERS

The agents responsible for Folio variants which cannot reasonably be ascribed to compositorial tampering or authorial second thoughts are generally referred to as the 'Folio editors'. The use of the word 'editor' is an anachronism, which highlights the prevalent inability to identify these agents and to understand their approach to the preparation of dramatic copy for the press. Textual scholars seldom agree on what category of agents may have fulfilled this role. According to Sidney Lee, 'one or other of [the publishers] prepared and arranged the plays for press, and corrected the proofs', while Pollard believed that Edward Blount, 'probably possessed of more literary feeling than the other partners, ... [was] not impossibly the editor of the volume' (quoted in Greg 1942: 78). Greg suggested that Isaac Jaggard was also a likely candidate: '[t]hat he may, for anything we know, have had the ability and inclination for the task need not be denied, and he would seem to have been a man of some literary interests'. Greg however admitted that Isaac 'must have been kept fairly busy superintending the printing of the Folio and other works', and that 'his activities would necessarily have been limited to such material as Heminge and Condell chose to hand over' (Greg 1942: 79). Following Greg's reasoning, later textual scholars have tended to identify the actors, rather than the publishers, as the most likely party to have fulfilled the editorial tasks involved in the preparation of copy for the Folio, because, as Greg himself put it, 'it was they who had access to the material and were in a position to estimate its value' (Greg 1942: 78). Those who subscribe to Greg's theory tend to exclude Heminge and Condell on the ground of their age or their involvement in the day-to-day management of a large theatrical company. As Greg explains, the 'Address to the great Variety of Readers' subscribed by Heminge and Condell says nothing 'to make us believe that they personally performed the arduous duty of detailed supervision; and it is unlikely that two busy actors, with the management of a large company and two theatres on their hands, would have found leisure for their task' (Greg 1942: 77). Similarly, the Oxford editors ruled out Heminge and Condell: 'it seems unlikely that all the work was shouldered by Heminge and Condell – old men, with many other responsibilities, and with more experience of the theatre than of publishing' (Wells and Taylor 1987: 36). The Oxford editors also echoed Greg in assuming instead that 'in so far as the King's Men did oversee the volume, the detailed work was probably delegated to their book-keeper (Knight?) and any other scribes who (like Crane) regularly worked for the company' (Wells and Taylor 1987: 36).[9]

The lack of general consensus about the identity of the 'Folio editors' has not stopped textual scholars from assuming that one single category of agents was specifically appointed to fulfil the editorial tasks involved in such a large publishing venture and that such agent(s) had a clear sense of what principles should inform their intervention. The Oxford editors, for example, describe the cumulative effect of the changes introduced in the First Folio as a consistent progression towards ideological, as well as textual, uniformity:

From [the Folio] emerges a Shakespeare less profane, and less political, than the original. A choppier Shakespeare too: his *œuvre* divided into three genres, his scripts divided into five acts, his syntax divided into innumerable clauses and parentheses and modifiers by the heavy punctuation of the Folio compositors and of the scribal transcripts from which they usually worked. And a modernized Shakespeare, his texts beginning already to be subtly reshaped to reflect changing theatrical conditions, changing legal restraints, changing standards of spelling and punctuation and grammar. (Wells and Taylor 1987: 39)

If uniformity in presentation may indeed reveal the concerted efforts of the printing house agents who worked under the close supervision of their masters, William and Isaac Jaggard, the range of Folio variants in some of the plays set from printed copy highlights interesting differences, rather than similarities, in the preparation of printed copy for the press.

The Folio variants in plays set from printed copy show that their preparation for the press was not informed by a uniform set of principles or general rationale. The Folio texts of *1 Henry IV* and *Much Ado About Nothing* for example introduce familiar patterns of variants, which affect speech prefixes, stage directions and dialogue, while being noticeably different from the Folio variants in *Romeo and Juliet* and *Love's Labour's Lost*. A closer look at the Folio texts of *1 Henry IV* and *Much Ado About Nothing* shows that while their variants suggest the presence of an annotating hand, as opposed to the sporadic consultation of a theatrical authority, the corrector may not have been the same agent who annotated the printer's copy of *Romeo and Juliet* and *Love's Labour's Lost*.

The Folio text of *1 Henry IV* adds two missing speech prefixes – '*Peto.*' and '*Prince.*' – at TLN 1503 and TLN 1508, in a speech which is erroneously marked as continuing to the Prince in the source text (STC 22284, 1613, henceforth Q5). The Folio text of *1 Henry IV* also modifies, omits, and adds several stage directions. More specifically, the Folio omits the quarto entry direction for Poins at A4v 25 and wrongly adds Poins to the entry direction at the beginning of this scene. This change probably stemmed from the annotator's assumption that Poins speaks the second half of Fastaff's speech, given that Poins's name at the beginning of A4v 26 is italicized and indented, and therefore looks like a speech prefix. As a result, the quarto direction '*Enter Prince of Wales and Sir Iohn Falstaffe*' at A3v 7 reads '*Enter Henry Prince of Wales, Sir Iohn Falstaffe and Pointz*' in the Folio at TLN

113–4. Three new stage directions in the Folio mark very obvious scene breaks at TLN 733, TLN 2585, and TLN 2955. Another direction added to the Folio at TLN 451 – '*Enter Worcester*' – implies a level of familiarity with the play which can be more easily associated with an annotator than a compositor, since the agent responsible for this direction successfully identified Hotspur's uncle, who is mentioned in the line immediately preceding his entrance – 'Here comes your vncle' (Q5, B3v 25); 'Heere comes your Vnckle' (F, TLN 451) – as Worcester. An exit direction added to the Folio at TLN 1466 is also suggested by Falstaff's invariant 'Ile hide me' (Q5, E3v 27, F, TLN 1466). Douglas's entrance and Worcester and Vernon's exit, first marked in the Folio at TLN 2983 and TLN 3152, can also be inferred from the context, since Douglas speaks at TLN 2984 and the king orders that the two traitors be escorted off stage at TLN 3150.

While the variants which affect speech prefixes and stage directions in the Folio text of *1 Henry IV* are in keeping with the type and range of changes introduced in the Folio texts of *Romeo and Juliet* and *Love's Labour's Lost*, the level and quality of attention devoted to the dialogue are significantly different. Particularly noteworthy are the addition of several new part-lines and the high number of slightly rephrased lines. The frequency of substantive changes to the dialogue of the Folio text of *1 Henry IV* has led some recent scholars to conjecture the influence of a literary transcript, which the annotator assumedly consulted while preparing the printer's copy (Wells and Taylor 1987: 332). The Oxford editors also believe that this transcript preserved authorial second thoughts, which were recovered by the annotator and transferred to the Folio text via the printer's copy. Although the frequency of variants in the dialogue of the Folio text of *1 Henry IV* is unusual, the types of variants are not uncommon in other editions where textual scholars detect neither the influence of a literary transcript nor of authorial second thoughts.

One good example of Folio variants in the dialogue of *1 Henry IV* is a part-line, which the Oxford editors regard as authorial:

[*Wor.*]   Good Coosen giue me audience for a while.
Hot.   I cry you mercy. (Q5, B4v 33–4)

[*Wor.*]   Good Cousin giue me audience for a-while,
      And list to me.
Hot.   I cry you mercy. (F, TLN 535–7)

According to the Oxford editors, 'F's part-line is not convincingly explained except as an authorial addition incorporated from a [manuscript]' (Wells and Taylor 1987: 333). Similar part-lines were added to other Folio texts, including *2 Henry IV*, which was set from a literary transcript. Eleanor Prosser has refuted the conventional belief that since the eight substantial additions to the Folio text of *2 Henry IV* must come from a fresh authoritative source, all other Folio variants must also be authorial (Prosser 1981: 3). More specifically, Prosser has challenged the traditional attribution of ten part-lines in the Folio text of *2 Henry IV* to the consultation of the manuscript from which the eight additional passages were recovered. Six of these part-lines were added to unusually short lines, two create new short lines, one disrupts the metre of a regular line, while the last one is added at the end of a prose passage. The two part-lines that create new irregularly short lines resemble very closely the half-line added in the Folio text of *1 Henry IV*:

King   God put in thy mind to take it hence, (Q1, I2r 3)

King.   O my Sonne!
             Heauen put it in thy minde to take it hence, (F, TLN 2712–13)

Prince   You won it, wore it, kept it, gaue it me, (Q1, I2v 9)

Prince.   My gracious Liege:
             You wonne it, wore it: kept it, gaue it me, (F, TLN 2757–8)

These new half-lines in *1* and *2 Henry IV* add emphasis that leaves the substance of the original speech unaffected. As much as the other part-lines studied by Prosser, they seem to 'range from flat repetition to pedestrian amplification' (Prosser 1981: 3).

   If Prosser's study shows that part-lines added to the Folio text of *2 Henry IV* are more likely to be scribal than authorial, the addition of similar part-lines to editions which were set from printed copy with no reference to a fresh manuscript source shows that this type of variants is as likely to be introduced by a scribe as by an annotating reader. Pavier's edition of *Henry V* provides particularly instructive parallels to the half-line added in the Folio text of *1 Henry IV*:

I had made no offence. (Q1, F3r 12)

I had made no offence, my gracious Lord, (Q3, F3r 32)

Inough Captaine, you haue astonisht him. (Q1 F4r 30)

Enough Captaine,
You haue astonisht him, it is enough. (Q3, F4v 21–2)

There is a shilling (Q1, F4v 5)

Looke you now, there is a silling for you (Q3, G1r 2)

Harry.   No faith *Kate* not I. But *K*ate,
            In plaine termes, do you loue me? (Q1, G2r 3–4)

Harry.   No faith Kate not I.
            But Kate prethee tell me in plaine tearmes,
            Dost thou loue me? (Q3, G2v 6–8)

While these examples show that annotating readers were as likely as scribes to add part-lines which 'range from flat repetition to pedestrian amplification', why they would do so is less clear.

The slight rephrasing of a few lines in the Folio text of *1 Henry IV* has also led recent editors to posit scribal, or even, authorial influence. The Oxford editors, once again, regard the following Folio variants as authorial:

I answered indirectly (as I sayd) (Q5, B2v 38)

Made me to answer indirectly (as I said.) (F, TLN 388)

Albeit I make a hazard of my head. (Q5, B3v 23)

Although it be with hazard of my head. (F, TLN 449)

Commenting on the first of these two Folio variants, David Scott Kastan questions the authorial attribution proposed by the Oxford editors: '[This Folio reading] is indeed unlikely to be compositorial, but why it might not be scribal or editorial is unclear to me' (Kastan 2002: 114). Similar rephrasings in editions set up from literary transcripts or from annotated printed copy confirm that this type of variant can indeed be associated with literary scribes or annotating readers. The rephrasing of five passages in the Pavier quarto of *2 Henry VI* is, for example, attributed to the influence of a different scribal report from the one used to set the first quarto of 1594 (Montgomery 1985: II, xxxiii). The rephrasing in the Pavier Quarto of *2 Henry VI* is even more radical and extensive than in the Folio text of *1 Henry IV*, as shown in the following exchange:

[*Suff.*]   My Lord Protectors Hawke done towre so well,
            He knowes his maister loues to be aloft.
Hum.   Faith my Lord, it is but a base minde
            That can sore no higher then a Falkons pitch. (Q1, C1v 26–9)

[*Suff.*]   My Lord Protectors hawkes do towre so well,
            They know their master sores a Faulcons pitch.
Hum.   Faith my Lord, it's but a base minde,
            That sores no higher then a bird can sore. (Q3, C1v 20–23)

Substantive rephrasings are not unknown in editions set up from annotated printed copy either. In Pavier's 1619 edition of *Pericles*, for example, the dialogue is often corrected and occasionally rephrased. A section of Gower's speech connecting the brothel scenes with Pericles' arrival in Mytilene is rewritten as follows:

Gower   And to hir Father turne our thoughts againe,
        Where wee left him on the Sea, wee there him left,
        Where driuen before the windes, hee is arriu'de. (Q3, H2r 26–8)

Gower   And to her Father turne our thoughts againe,
        Where we left him at sea, tumbled and tost,
        And driuen before the winde, he is arriude. (Q4, z4r 19–21)

As Suzanne Gossett has recently pointed out, 'the corrector of Q4 [the Pavier Quarto of 1619] worked from Q3, and there is no reason to believe he had anything but his own wits to aid him' (2004: 33). We can therefore assume that 'tumbled and tost' was introduced by the annotator in order to avoid a repetition in his source text.

Overall, the extensive changes in the dialogue of *1 Henry IV* as it appears in the First Folio of 1623 are not unlike the changes introduced by annotating readers. As David Scott Kastan has noted, 'the Folio's alterations of Q5 need not have resulted from anything more than an aggressive hand and do not clearly imply access to an alternative authority for the text itself' (2002: 115). When compared to the changes introduced in the dialogue of the Folio texts of *Romeo and Juliet* and *Love's Labour's Lost*, the Folio variants in the dialogue of *1 Henry IV* seem exceptional both in terms of their type and frequency. However, when compared to other editions set from annotated printed copy, they seem exceptional only quantitatively rather than qualitatively. The aggressive hand detected by David Scott Kastan may indeed have belonged to an annotating reader who, like the corrector of the Pavier Quarto of *Pericles*, 'had [no]thing but his own wits to aid him'. What seems worth stressing is that this aggressive hand is unlikely to have been responsible both for the annotation of the printer's copy of the Folio text of *1 Henry IV* and for the annotation of the printer's copies of the Folio texts of *Romeo and Juliet* and *Love's Labour Lost*. Although, as mentioned earlier, the annotation of the printer's copy for the press is best understood as function- rather than agent-specific, because several agents, ranging from a correcting author or scribe to an annotating reader routinely performed it, the different level of attention paid to the dialogue in the Folio text of *1 Henry IV* and in the Folio texts of *Romeo and Juliet* and *Love's Labour's Lost* suggests the presence of different annotating hands.

The Folio text of *Much Ado About Nothing*, which was also set from printed copy (STC 22304, 1600, henceforth Q1), provides a good example of what seems to be yet another annotating hand. The sparse substantive variants in the Folio text of this play affect mostly its speech prefixes and stage directions, and, only occasionally, its dialogue. Changes to its stage directions would seem to support the current theory that the printer's copy for this Folio text was sporadically annotated with reference to a theatrical manuscript. The new direction at TLN 494 – '*Maskers with a drum*' – and a variant direction at TLN 868 – '*Enter prince, Leonato, Claudio, Musicke*' (Q1, D1r 3) and '*Enter Balthaser with musicke*' (Q1, D1r 10) are replaced by '*Enter Prince, Leonato, Claudio, and Iacke Wilson*' in the Folio – do suggest a link between the Folio text of *Much Ado About Nothing* and a prompter's book.[10] However, even the substitution of the name of a fictional character with the name of the actor who performed that role, which would seem to provide incontrovertible evidence of its theatrical provenance, is complicated by the fact that at least on one other occasion the Folio text replaces the name of an actor used as a speech prefix ('*Couley*' in the first quarto at G4v 14) with the name of a fictional character ('*Sex.*' in the Folio at TLN 2059). Besides, at least one variant in the dialogue[11] is certainly more in keeping with the pattern of intervention associated with annotating readers than with sporadic consultation of a manuscript annotated for performance. In Q1 Claudio's epitaph reads as follows:

> Done to death by slauderous tongues,
> Was the Hero that heere lies:
> Death in guerdon of her wronges,
> Giues her fame which neuer dies:
> So the life that dyed with shame,
> Liues in death with glorious fame.
>   Hang thou there vpon the toomb,
>   Praising hir when I am dead. (I2v 4–11)

The last line in Claudio's epitaph in F1 replaces 'dead' with '*dombe*'. The last two lines are thus turned into a couplet (TLN 2530–1), which matches the rhyming pattern of the previous two lines ending in '*shame*' and '*fame*' (TLN 2528–9). This type of intervention can hardly be attributed to a compositor, whose main task was to reproduce his copy as accurately as possible, except for obvious typographical mistakes, or to a theatrical annotator, whose main concern was to prepare a text to regulate performance. It seems equally unreasonable to attribute this isolated stylistic improvement to authorial revision, since nothing else in the Folio text of *Much Ado About Nothing* suggests that this play underwent substantial alteration. All in all, the variants in the Folio text of this play seem more likely to derive from an annotating reader who was familiar with the play in performance but was at best guided by intermittent memories of what he had seen on stage.

Generally speaking, variants in the speech prefixes used in the Folio text of *Much Ado About Nothing* suggest inaccurate recollection of the play as staged and a fussy literary sensitivity on the annotator's part. As mentioned above, the Folio replaces the name of an actor used as a speech prefix in the quarto – '*Couley*' (G4v 14) – with the name of a character – '*Sex.*' (TLN 2059). This variant shows that the annotator's recollection of the play in performance must have been rather poor, since the prefix '*Couley*' is generally used to identify Verges, Dogberry's partner, and not the sexton. Other changes in FI show a literary tendency to increase variation in the prefixes used to identify Leonato's brother, who is alternatively referred to as a type, 'Old Man.', as a relative, 'Brother', and, occasionally, by his proper name, 'Anthony'. Similarly, other changes in the stage directions may stem from a misguided attempt to reduce the theatrical apparatus, which as Prosser observes in relation to the Folio text of *2 Henry IV*, involves eliminating all mutes, 'even when they are referred to and thus indisputably required in a given scene' (1981: 19). One good example is the stage direction '*Enter Leonato, his brother, and the Sexton*' at H4r 22 in the quarto, which is cut down to '*Enter Leonato*' in the Folio at TLN 2341. The sexton has indeed no lines, although his entrance is announced in the invariant line immediately before this stage direction – '*Con. 2* Here, here comes master Signior Leonato, and the sexton too' (QI, H4r 21); '*Con. 2* Here, here comes master *Signior Leonato*, and the *Sexton* too.' (F,TLN 2339–40). However, the annotator must have overlooked the fact that Leonato's brother does speak later on in this scene in both editions – '*Brot.* Farewell my lords, we looke for you to morrow.' (QI, III 20); '*Brot.* Farewell my Lords, vve looke for you to morrow.' (F, TLN 2416–17). Similarly, the annotator may have omitted '*Iohn and Borachio, and Conrade*' from the quarto direction at CIV 23–4, because, although they must be on stage to hear about Claudio and Hero's engagement, they have no lines. The annotator's literary taste was however as desultory as his recollection of the play, since he overlooked the fact that Leonato's wife, who is only mentioned once in the opening stage direction in both editions, is a ghost character.

Overall, the Folio variants in *Much Ado About Nothing* are more likely to have originated from the annotator's patchy recollection of the play in performance than from the annotator's sporadic consultation of a theatrical manuscript. While early modern playbooks are now believed to have retained inconsistencies in aspects of the texts which regulated performance, such as speech prefixes and stage directions, the assumption that alterations derived from a playbook used in the theatre would make the stage action *less* clear seems counterintuitive. More to the point, the different level of attention paid to the three main areas of interventions associated with annotating readers, i.e. speech prefixes, stage directions, and dialogue, in the four Folio texts considered so far suggests that more than one corrector prepared the printer's copies of these four Folio plays. While the annotator of the printer's copy of the Folio text of *1 Henry IV* focused consistently on the dialogue of this play and only occasionally on its speech prefixes and stage directions, the annotator of the printer's copy of the Folio text of *Much Ado About Nothing* seems mainly to have used what he remembered of the play in performance to clarify the stage action. Also suggestive is the fact that one profanity systematically removed from the Folio text of *1 Henry IV* – 'O Iesu' (Q5, E1r 23; Q5, E2v 3; Q5, E2v 8; Q5, G3r 29) – is allowed to stand in the Folio text of *Romeo and Juliet* – 'by Iesu' (Q3, E2v 4); 'Iesu' (F, TLN 1133).

The similarities between the Folio variants in *Romeo and Juliet* and *Love's Labour's Lost* seem therefore all the more significant, especially if, as mentioned above, one bears in mind that the copies of these plays belonged to the same stationer, John Smethwick. While the first half of this chapter has highlighted the relative similarity of intervention in *Romeo and Juliet* and *Love's Labour's Lost*, the second half will consider the four members of the Folio syndicate, including John Smethwick, in order to shed light on the extent to which the latter may have been personally involved in the preparation of his Shakespearean plays for the press.

JOHN SMETHWICK'S ROLE IN THE MAKING OF THE FIRST FOLIO

John Smethwick, who acquired the rights of *Romeo and Juliet* and *Love's Labour's Lost*, along with *Hamlet* and *The Taming of a Shrew*, on 19 November 1607 (Arber 1875–94: III 161), has traditionally been regarded as a minor member of the Folio syndicate, which included Edward Blount, William and Isaac Jaggard, and William Aspley. According to Charlton Hinman, for example, 'the connexion of Smethwick and Aspley with the First Folio . . . is known exclusively . . . from the appearance of their names in the colophon' (1963: 26n). Similarly, Leah Scragg believes that of the four members in the syndicate, 'Smethwick and Aspley appear to have played a relatively minor role in the undertaking', and that since they '[b]oth possessed rights in plays previously published . . . [they] may have been incorporated into the group for this reason alone' (Scragg 1997: 118). As copyright holders of a large share of the Folio plays set from printed copy, Smethwick and Aspley may in fact have played a crucial role in preparing them for the press and their profiles are worth investigating in detail, especially in relation to the publishing careers of the other, and better-known, members of the Folio syndicate.

The best-known member of the Folio syndicate is Edward Blount, a prominent London stationer, whose entire career was informed by a distinctive interest in literary works. Blount received a solid humanist education at the Merchant Taylors' School and established long-term personal and working relations with some of the most influential writers of his time. John Lyly, John Florio, Christopher Marlowe, Ben Jonson, Montaigne and Cervantes are some of the authors whose works he published, thus showing, as his most recent biographer has put it, 'an unparalleled gift for recognizing new works that would eventually become classics'.[12] Besides revealing critical acumen, Blount's publications document the extent to which he became involved in their transmission into print. Blount signed nine dedications, and the recurrence of a peculiar set of imagery and literary tropes in them has led some scholars to suspect that, although signed by Heminge and Condell, the dedication to the Earls of Pembroke and Montgomery in the Shakespeare First Folio was also penned by Blount. While earlier scholars, including George Steevens, E. K. Chambers, and Greg, believed that both the dedicatory epistle and the address 'To the Great Variety of Readers' were written by Jonson, Leah Scragg has persuasively argued that, 'while Jonson was responsible for commending the work to the reading public, it was Blount who shouldered the task of recommending the volume to its patrons' (1997: 126). Scragg's analysis, which relies mostly on internal evidence and on the fact that Blount had already dedicated one of his books to the same patrons, was anticipated at the end of the nineteenth century by Sidney Lee, who believed that Blount's involvement with the publication of the First Folio exceeded his roles as major investor and most likely author of the dedication. According to Lee, Blount's interest in the books he published went as far as overseeing at least some of them through the press (1895: 493).

The address to the reader in John Earl's *Micro-cosmographie: Or, a Peece of the World Discouered in Essays and Characters* (STC 7440.2, 1628) would certainly seem to support Lee's theory. In this address, Blount explains that the author, who had initially disowned his work, was alarmed by the fact that its manuscript circulation ('in loose Sheets', A2v 3) resulted in the proliferation of 'so many sundry dispersed Transcripts, some very imperfect and surreptitious' (A3r 1–5), which threatened to reach the press.

The author was therefore forced to reclaim his work and had become 'vnwillingly willing to let them passe as now they appeare to the World' (A3r 12–5). Despite the author's change of heart, Blount claims responsibility for the quality of the text:

If any faults haue escap'd the Presse, (as few Bookes can bee printed without) impose them not on the Author I intreat Thee; but rather impute them to mine and the Printers ouersight, who seriously promise on the re-impression hereof by greater care and diligence, for this our former default, to make Thee ample satisfaction. (A3r 15–17, A3v 1–13)

If this short address suggests that Blount may have fulfilled a similar role when the First Folio went through William and Isaac Jaggard's press, other dedications signed by Blount show that he was more often inclined to act as a procurer and presenter of copy. Both roles involved a high degree of critical discernment. Earlier in the same address prefaced to Earl's *Micro-cosmographie*, Blount compares himself to a literary midwife: 'I Haue (for once) aduentur'd to playe the Mid-wifes part, helping to bring forth these Infants into the World, which the Father would haue smoothered' (A2r 5–13, A2v 1). Similarly, in his address to the reader in Grey Brydges' *Horae Subseciuae* (STC 3957, 1620), Blount specifies that his appreciation of this collection of observations and discourses is shared by other literary-minded readers:

The Author of this Booke I know not; but by chance hearing that a friend of mine had some such papers in his hand; and hauing heard them commended, I was curious to see and reade them ouer; and in my opinion (which was also confirmed by others, iudicious and learned) supposed if I could get the Copie, they would be welcome abroad. My friends courtesie bestowed it freely vpon me, and my endeuour to giue you contentment, caused mee to put it in print. (A2v 3–15)

The better-known epistle prefaced to Blount's edition of Lyly's *Six Court Comedies* has also been interpreted as a self-conscious critical assessment of Lyly's role in fashioning current literary taste. As Leah Scragg has observed, 'the emphasis of the epistle falls not on the biography of the writer, but on his literary significance' (1995: 7). Gary Taylor has similarly highlighted the 'epistemic authority' which Blount enjoyed among his fellow stationers and contemporary literary circles both as a good 'reader' and 'critic' of contemporary English and European literature (forthcoming).

While useful in establishing Blount's potential role as supervisor of the press and presenter of FI to its prestigious patrons, the extensive paratext signed by Blount sheds little light on his willingness to engage with the preparation of the printer's copies for the press. In fact, the body of works he published both before and after 1623 shows that he had never regarded dramatic publication *per se* as one of his priorities. Although his name is associated with some of the major dramatic collections of his time – William Alexander's *The Monarchick Tragedies* (STC 343, 1604), Samuel Daniel's *The Tragedie of Philotas* (with *A Panegyrike Congratulatorie* and *A Defence of Ryme*, STC 6263, 1607), Shakespeare's First Folio (STC 22273, 1623), and John Lyly's *Six Court Comedies* (STC 17088, 1632) – he hardly ever took an interest in commercial drama.[13] Possibly thanks to his close relation to the world of the theatre, both as self-styled friend and literary 'executor' of Christopher Marlowe[14] and, possibly, as the 'friendly stationer' who had dealings with the King's Men as early as 1608 (Kirschbaum, quoted in Scragg 1997: 118), Blount entered several plays in *The Stationers' Register*, but then transferred them to other fellow stationers.[15] As mentioned earlier, scholars now believe that Blount only became involved in the Folio project as late as 1622, and that the driving force behind it, at least initially, was the vision of another literary-minded young stationer, Isaac Jaggard.[16] Blount is likely to have been attracted by the literary quality of Isaac's projected collection and by the proposed size and format of the volume, which dignified Shakespeare's plays with a higher status than they had been granted by the quarto format in which they had appeared until then. The fact that Blount had never, except once, undertaken the publication of single editions of commercial plays and that the sixteen plays which he entered on 8 November 1623 had never been printed before, provides no precedent to establish whether he would regard preparation of dramatic copy as a priority.

The only item in Blount's entire output, which could shed light on his involvement with the annotation of dramatic copy for the press, is his 1632 collection of Lyly's *Six Court Comedies* (STC 17088, 1632), because they were all re-set from earlier quarto editions. However, a contrastive analysis of the texts of these six comedies as they appear in Blount's collection and in their source-texts shows no sign of the presence of an annotating reader. The only major intervention is the addition of twenty-one songs and one dumb show. As G. K. Hunter and David Bevington explain, the origin of the songs added to Blount's collection is ultimately uncertain:

The songs were not printed in Lyly's lifetime ... The possibility that Blount derived the song texts from sources that were not authentic is thus opened up as an intriguing hypothesis. It is a hypothesis impossible to disprove; but the evidence that has been adduced to support it is equally without force. (Hunter and Bevington 1991: 301)

What seems bibliographically significant is that, whether or not the songs are authentic, the texts of these six comedies introduce none of the changes and emendations so far associated with the intervention of an annotating reader. In fact, as Leah Scragg puts it, 'though important in terms of authorship, the history of Lylian criticism, and the inclusion of the songs, Blount's collection is not textually significant' (2002: xv). More specifically, Blount's edition emends only obvious typographical mistakes in the dialogue and introduces new ones: while Blount's edition of *Endymion* rightly replaces 'maine' with 'maime' at E7v 24, in Blount's *Gallathea* Diana is no longer described by Venus as a 'goddess of hate', but as a 'Goddesse of hare' at S5r 1–2. Omissions are clearly accidental, as at X3v 4–5 in *Midas*, where 'shake' is dropped from 'which makes beasts shake for feare' in its source text. Changes to speech prefixes and stage directions are also limited to accidental variation and omissions, a rare isolated exception being the addition of an 'Exit' direction in *Gallathea* at P9v 26. Given that the vast majority of changes introduced in the 1632 edition seems to derive from compositorial tampering, it would seem reasonable to assume that Blount, who endeavoured to offer his readers an 'enlarged' version of Lyly's comedies, did not prepare the printer's copy for the press. However, although internal evidence would certainly seem to support this hypothesis, the exceptionally good quality of the quarto editions of Lyly's plays from which Blount's collection was set[17] makes it impossible to come to any definitive conclusion.

The second best-known member of the Folio syndicate is Isaac Jaggard, who, as explained above, may well have been responsible for planning F1 as early as 1619. The other books published by Isaac before 1623 show that, like Blount, he had a strong interest in literary publications. Isaac's first publishing venture was *The divine poem of Musaeus . . . Translated According to the Originall, by Geo: Chapman* (STC 18304, 1616), and was followed in 1620 by the first complete English edition of Giovanni Boccaccio's *Decameron* (STC 3172). As well as classical poetry and Italian novellas, Isaac published Thomas Heywood's *A Woman Killed with Kindness* (STC 13372, 1617), a commercial play previously printed and published by his father William (STC 13371, 1607).

Isaac's edition of *A Woman Killed with Kindness* is advertised on its title page as 'The third edition', which may equally suggest an error on Isaac's part or that no copies of a second edition have survived. Isaac's edition (henceforth Q2) introduces changes in the first edition of 1607 (henceforth Q1), which resemble the pattern of variants associated with the intervention of annotating readers. A closer look at Q2 variants provides interesting evidence to establish whether either Isaac or Thomas Heywood can be held responsible for introducing such changes. Assessing Isaac's potential involvement with the publication of Q2 provides no direct evidence to argue that he fulfilled a similar role in the publication of FI. However, establishing the level of his involvement in earlier dramatic publications does at least suggest whether he would or could personally undertake such a task.

The most interesting variants in Q2 affect speech prefixes and stage directions and fall into five main clusters. The first alteration in a stage direction – '*killing one of Sir Francis his huntsmen*' (QI B3r 22–3); '*killing both of Sir Francis his men*' (Q2, B2v 18–19) – is followed by a related emendation in the dialogue, where QI's 'poore Innocent' at B3r 26 becomes 'poore innocents' in Q2 at B3r 22. The second cluster of variants involves the systematic alteration of the name of Sir Charles Mountford's sister from Jane to Susan in one stage direction, in subsequent speech prefixes and dialogue.[18] In another related cluster of variants both the name 'Iane' and the preferred alternative 'Susan' are replaced by the generic 'Sister'.[19] If the systematic replacement of 'Jane' with 'Susan' involves detecting an inconsistency in the identification of this character within the fictive world of the play, thus involving a type of intervention which falls beyond the remit of a printing house corrector or compositor, the replacement of the perfectly viable 'Susan' at GIv 33 in QI with 'Sister' is unnecessary and, as such, it definitively rules out the involvement of a printing house agent.

Another group of variants occurs in related stage directions later on in the play. In QI the direction '*Exeunt*' at D2r 26 would seem to clear the stage after Sir Charles's arrest, which is instigated by the opportunistic Shafton. However, having witnessed her brother's arrest, Susan is still on stage to lament his misfortunes when Acton and Malby enter at D2r 27:

Shaf.   Come Irons, Irons away,
     Ile see thee log'd far from the sight of day.   *Exeunt.*
     Enter Acton and Malby.
Susan.   My harts so hardned with the frost of griefe,
     Death connot pierce it through, Tyrant too fel,
     So lead the Fiends condemned soules to hel. (QI, D2r 25–30)

In Q2, the exit direction is removed, possibly because the annotator realized that at least Susan stays on stage to speak the following three lines. However the annotator overlooked the fact that the other characters involved in the episode of Sir Charles's arrest do leave the stage at this

point. The removal of the exit direction from Q1 is not accidental, as
suggested by the fact that Acton and Malby's entrance is delayed:

Shaf.   Come, irons, irons; come away,
         Ile see thee lodg'd farre from the sight of day.
Sus.   My heart's so hardned with the frost of greefe,
         Death cannot pierce it through; Tyrant too fell:
         So leade the fiends condemned soules to hell.
         Enter Acton and Malby. (Q2, D3r 13–18)

Although not entirely accurate, the alternative directions in Q2 change the
sequence of events presented in Q1. Similarly, the last cluster of variants
resolves the misidentification of two speakers and one character mentioned
in the dialogue. In the final scene in Q1, Anne Frankford has a short exchange
with Sir Charles Mountford and with her brother, Sir Francis Acton:

Anne.   You halfe reuiude me with those pleasing newes,
          Raise me a little higher in my bed.
          Blush I not maister Frankford? blush I not sir Charles?
          Can you not read my fault writ in my cheeke?
          Is not my cryme there? tell me gentlemen?
Charles. Alasse good mistris, sicknesse hath not left you
          Bloud in your face enough to make you blush:
          Then sicknesse like a friend my fault would hide,
Anne.   Is my husband come? My soule but tarries
          His ariue and I am fit for heauen.
Charles. I came to chide you, but my wordes of hate,
          Are turnd to pitty and compassionate griefe:
          I came to rate you, but my bralles you see,
          Melt into teares, and I must weepe by thee. (Q1, H3r 7–20)

Master Frankford enters only a few lines after this exchange in both
editions and Q2 rectifies Anne's first speech accordingly, by replacing
'maister Frankford' in line H3r 9 with 'Brother Acton' (I2v 31). Q2 also
re-assigns line H3r 14 to Anne and lines H3r 17–20 to Sir Francis, because the
intent to reproach Mistress Frankford for her adultery is more likely to
come from her brother than from a character who had spoken to her only
once before in the opening scene.

   Overall, the quality and the range of the variants introduced in Q2
suggest annotation of the printer's copy before it reached the printing
house, but they provide too little evidence to establish whether Thomas
Heywood or Isaac Jaggard were responsible for them. However, a
re-assessment of Heywood's attitude to dramatic publication and additional
textual evidence drawn from Q2 offer further insights into their origin.

Some textual scholars believe that Thomas Heywood never regarded publication as a viable outlet for his dramatic works. This popular opinion rests at least partly on Heywood's well-known disclaimer prefaced to *The Rape of Lucrece*, where he explains that 'for though some haue used a double sale of their labours, first to the Stage, and after to the presse, For my owne part I heere proclaime my selfe euer faithfull in the first, and neuer guiltie of the last' (STC 13360, 1608, A2r 8–11). Douglas Brooks, for example, believes that 'at the very moment that print publication was transforming a bricklayer's son into "self-creating Ben Jonson", or a committed company playwright like Shakespeare into … the "Starre of Poets" … Heywood found the journey from stage to page either formidable or unappealing' (2000: 196). By contrast, Benedict Scott Robinson has argued that, once Heywood stopped writing for the theatre and eventually devoted himself to dramatic publication in the 1630s, he no longer had reservations towards print culture. In fact, Robinson specifies that there is no contradiction between Heywood's announcement of the imminent publication of 'an handsome Volumne' gathering all his *Age* plays in 1632 (STC 13340, A2r 17–18), and Heywood's well-known attack, only a year later, against dramatists like Jonson, who 'exposed' their dramatic works 'unto the world in Volumes' (STC 13315, A3r 10–11). Heywood's admission that 'it neuer was any great ambition in me, to bee in this kind Volumniously read' (STC 13315, A3r 16–17) had generally been interpreted as symptomatic of Heywood's bitter disappointment that his volume was never published. Rather than accusing Heywood of protesting too much, Robinson points out that he never planned to emulate Jonson and that his projected volume in fact anticipated a different type of publication, closer to the smaller dramatic collections published by Moseley in the 1640s and 1650s than to Jonson's monumental edition:

Heywood's own hope [was] that the printing of these plays would bridge the gap between his Red Bull audience and an elite readership for published drama. The question remains whether such a social divide could be negotiated in the bibliographic space of a dramatic collection. It seems reasonable to suggest that Heywood's collection foundered on the contradictions of its own position in the early seventeenth-century book market. Heywood was attempting to adapt a mode of presentation designed for elevating the status of a text for a book designed to mediate culture in the opposite direction. (Robinson 2002: 374)

While Robinson offers a useful reassessment of Heywood's attitude to dramatic publication in the 1630s, he still underestimates the extent to which Heywood was already committed to the transmission of his dramatic works into print in the late 1600s and the early 1610s. Even during this early stage of his career, when he had regular working relations with the

Queen's Men, Heywood engaged fruitfully and systematically with the press.

The traditional opinion according to which Heywood was averse to dramatic publication is mainly due to the fact that two addresses to the reader regularly quoted by Heywood scholars were also used as a prime source of documentary evidence by the founders of the New Bibliography. To question how these addresses have been interpreted means not only to upset familiar assumptions about Heywood's attitudes towards the press, but also, and more crucially, familiar textual categories introduced by the New Bibliography at the beginning of the twentieth century on the back of Heywood's vocal complaints against literary piracy. For example, Heywood's address to the reader in *The Rape of Lucrece* (STC 13360, 1608) would seem to provide prime evidence to support the theory of memorial reconstruction:

some of my plaies haue (vnknown to me, and without any of my direction) accidentally come into the Printers handes, and therfore so corrupt and mangled, (coppied onely by the eare) that I haue bene as vnable to know them, as ashamde to chalenge them. (A2r 11–15)

The prologue added to the 1639 quarto edition of the ever popular *If You Know Not Me, You Know Nobody, Part I* (STC 13335) similarly suggests that this notoriously 'corrupt and mangled' text was set from a surreptitious copy:

Ill Nurst,
Yet well receiv'd, and well perform'd at first:
Grac'd, and frequented; and the Cradle age
Did throng the Seates, the Boxes, and the Stage
So much, that some by Stenography, drew
The Plot: put it in print, scarce one word true:

(A2r 8–13)

Although, as explained earlier, recent scholars have effectively questioned the distinction between 'good' and 'bad' quartos, which these addresses seemingly support (Blayney 1997: 383–422; Maguire 1996; Werstine 1990: 65–86 and 1999: 310–33), opinions about Heywood's attitude towards dramatic publications have endured. And yet the early printed editions of Heywood's dramatic works indicate that an unusual amount of effort went into their transmission into print.

The recurrence of Heywood's name on the title page or in the paratext of his editions starting from around 1607–8 is remarkably frequent when compared to explicit authorial attribution in contemporary English drama in print.[20] The frequency with which paratextual materials started to be included in Heywood's dramatic and non-dramatic works also from around 1607–8 is equally above average.[21] The years 1607–8 clearly marked an important turning point in Heywood's relation to the press. Heywood's famous addresses prefaced to *1 If You Know not Me, You Know Nobody* and *The Rape of Lucrece* might well refer to those plays which were published anonymously and without paratextual materials before 1607–8, namely *1 & 2 Edward IV, How a Man May Choose a Good Wife from a Bad, 1 & 2 If You Know Not Me*, and *The Fair Maid of the Exchange*.

Another interesting pattern in Heywood's publishing career is his long-standing collaboration with Nicholas and John Okes.[22] Their partnership represents a crucial element of continuity, which bridges the gap in Heywood's investment in literary and dramatic publication between the mid-1610s and the early 1630s. This partnership would be difficult to explain, if past and recent textual scholars were right in claiming that Heywood was largely indifferent to publication and that his isolated bout of enthusiasm for the projected collection of 1632 was soon curbed by Nicholas or John Okes' failure to publish it. Heywood went on publishing with them after 1632–3, thus fostering a professional partnership, which had started twenty years earlier. In fact, for somebody supposedly indifferent to publication, Heywood was exceptional among contemporary commercial playwrights for establishing such a close working relationship with a publisher. Similarly remarkable is the tribute that Heywood paid to Nicholas Okes in his *Apology for Actors* (1612). Heywood refers to his printer as 'his approued good Friend' and praises him for being 'careful', 'industrious', 'serious' and 'laborious'. Heywood's praise seems prompted by his disappointing experience with another printer, William Jaggard, who printed Heywood's *Troia Britanica* in 1609. In the opening section of this address Heywood explains why he fell out with Jaggard:

THE infinite faults escaped in my booke of *Britaines Troy*, by the negligence of the Printer, as the misquotations, mistaking of sillables, misplacing halfe lines, coining of strãge and neuer heard of words. These being without number, when I would haue taken a particular account of the *Errata*, the Printer answered me, hee would not publish his owne disworkemanship, but rather let his owne fault lye vpon the necke of the Author. (G4r 3–13)

Troia Britanica was not a play but an important book, which Heywood dedicated to the Earl of Worcester. However Heywood must have found Jaggard's lack of professional standards generally unacceptable, because Nicholas Okes and then his son John went on printing and publishing Heywood's work until the end of his career, whereas Jaggard never worked with Heywood again. Since Heywood had expressed such negative views on William Jaggard's professional standards five years earlier, and had not since sought his services, he may have had no part in Isaac's publication of Q2. However, interesting patterns of variants in other early editions of Heywood's plays printed more than once during his lifetime suggest that Heywood may have prepared his plays for the press.

The Four Prentices of London, for example, was first printed in 1615 (STC 13321, henceforth Q1) and then reprinted in 1632 (STC 13322, henceforth Q2). Both editions were printed by Nicholas Okes.[23] The title page in Q1 – '*Written by* THOMAS HEYWOOD' – is modified in Q2 to suggest Heywood's direct involvement – '*Written and newly reuised by* THOMAS HEYWOOD'. Q2 is quite literally strewn with verbal substitutions. Although a substantial number of such changes simply remove profanities, many other variants seem perfectly indifferent. While some are likely to derive from compositorial corruption, some reveal local attempts to re-phrase, tinker and revise. The dedication alone offers a few examples: 'To you' in Q1 at A2r 3 becomes 'None but to you' in Q2 at A2r 4; and 'the City' in Q1 at A2v 7 becomes 'this Renowned Citty' in Q2 at A2v 11. A compositor may be responsible for the following verbal substitutions: 'the earths *vaste* wombe' in Q1 (B1v 25, my emphasis) becomes 'cold' in Q2 (B1v 25); '*much* profites' in Q1 (B2r 31, my emphasis) become 'great' in Q2 (B2r 31); the nonsensical 'and then *preferre* my vow' in Q1 (B3r 16, my emphasis) is improved in Q2 and reads 'performe' (B3r 16); at B4v 4-5 in Q1, Godfrey suggests 'let vs in one ship/ Lanch all together', but in Q2 'ship' becomes 'Fleete' (B4v 4); the 'stormy tempests, that disturbe the sea' in Q1 at C1r 8, disturb the 'Maine' in Q2 (C1r 8). Other changes are even more arbitrary and extensive: lines C2r 15–17 in Q1 – 'the selfe same winde and fortune/ That parted them, may bring them altogether./ Their sister followes them with zealous feete' – are altered in Q2, where 'once to meete' replaces 'altogether' and 'loue' replaces 'feete' (C2r 16–18). Equally gratuitous is the substitution of '*Canwicke-streete*' in Q1 (D4v 15) with '*Gracious-streete*' in Q2 (D4v 14). Several changes in Q2 are so arbitrary that one may well suspect authorial second thoughts.

A short address added to the 1630 and 1638 editions of *The Rape of Lucrece* also suggests authorial involvement in their publication:

> Because we would not that any mans expectation should be deceiued in the ample printing of this booke. Lo (Gentle Reader) we haue inserted these few songs, which were added by the stranger that lately acted *Valerius* his part in forme following. (STC 13362, 1630, K3v 2–6)

Far from being indifferent to what happened to his plays once they reached the press, Heywood seems to have been anxious to provide his readers with a complete text of this play but also to specify exactly what parts should not be regarded as his own work. If only for a brief moment, Heywood seems to indulge in proprietary foibles which scholars tend to ascribe to literary dramatists like Ben Jonson, who used publication as an opportunity to purge his work from any trace of theatrical collaboration.

The frequency of signed paratextual materials and substantive variants in Heywood's early dramatic editions provide suggestive evidence to argue that he may have personally prepared the printer's copy for Q2 *A Woman Killed with Kindness* for the press. However, further textual evidence drawn from Q2 makes the hypothesis of authorial involvement less certain.[24] When Master Frankford and Nick exchange a copy of the house keys and a fake letter, which will give Master Frankford the pretext to leave his house later on in the evening, Q1 assigns two consecutive speeches to Nick:

Frank.   This is the night, and I must play the tuch,
            To try two seeming Angels, whers my keies?
Nick.   They are made according to your mold in wax,
            I bad the Smith be secret, gaue him mony,
            And there they are.
Nick.   The Letter sir.
Frank.   True take it, there it is,
            And when thou seest me in my pleasantst vaine
            Ready to sit to supper, bring it me. (E4v 36–7, F1r 1–7)

A half-line, possibly a half-line reply by Frankford between F1r 3 and F1r 4, would seem to be missing from the version of this exchange preserved in Q1. Q2 tackles the anomaly of the two consecutive speech prefixes as follows:

Fran.   This is the night, that I must play my part,
            To try two seeming Angels: where's my keyes?
Nick.   They are made according to your mold in wax,
            I bad the smith be secret, gaue him money,
            And heere they are. The Letter sir.
Fran.   True, take it, there it is;
            And when thou seest me in my pleasants vaine
            Ready to sit to supper, bring it me. (F3r 1–8)

Q2 runs together the two half-lines at F1r 3 and F1r 4 and removes the second speech prefix marked 'Nick.' at F1r 4, thus transforming a metrically regular shared verse line ('The Letter . . . there it is;') into a four-foot line for Nick, and a three-foot line for Frankford. Two consecutive speeches assigned to the same character may have caught the eye of a solicitous compositor and running F1r 3 and F1r 4 together is the most efficient way to remedy this anomaly. However, other changes in the version of this exchange in Q2 – 'and I must play the tuch' at E4v 36 in Q1 is replaced by 'that I must play my part' at F3r 1 in Q2 – are not remedial and suggest a sustained attempt to clarify and rephrase this exchange as a whole. The intervention of a corrector seems therefore more likely than the improvisation of a solicitous compositor.

Could the corrector have been Heywood himself? Why, if the corrector was indeed Heywood, would he have opted for an efficient, but metrically awkward, solution in order to resolve the anomaly of two consecutive speech prefixes assigned to Nick in Q1? Although this exchange in Q2 would seem to rule out authorial intervention, Heywood may conceivably have forgotten a half-line, if a half-line is indeed missing, given the time-lag which intervened between the publication of Q1 and Q2. Besides, Heywood's lines are often metrically irregular. In other words, the evidence provided by a single variant exchange in Q2 seems too limited to offset the considerable amount of paratextual and textual evidence in Heywood's printed playbooks, which indicates Heywood's likely invoelment in their transmission into print. On the other hand, the type and range of sub-stantive variants in the early editions of *A Woman Killed with Kindness* and *The Four Prentices of London* have little in common and may have been added by different annotators. To sum up, a close analysis of Isaac Jaggard's literary output and of Heywood's attitude to dramatic publica-tion provides no definitive evidence to establish whether either of them may have been directly responsible for preparing Q2 *A Woman Killed with Kindness* for the press. Ultimately, and regrettably, as with Edward Blount, there seems to be insufficient evidence to argue that Isaac Jaggard would have regarded the annotation of the printer's copies as a crucial stage in the preparation of F1 for the press.

While Edward Blount and Isaac Jaggard acquired the copy of sixteen previously unpublished plays as late as 8 November 1623 (Arber 1875–94: IV 69),[25] William Aspley and John Smethwick had owned most of the Folio plays which were set from printed copy for several years and had already issued some of them more than once. As explained above, some of the plays they owned accrued local changes, corrections and re-phrasings, as well as new typographical mistakes, as they were re-issued in the First Folio, and, in some cases, several times prior to it. Although less well-known than Blount and Jaggard, Aspley and Smethwick are therefore more likely to have had a direct impact on the textual make-up of the First Folio and their profiles are consequently worth investigating in detail.

William Aspley had a long and prosperous career. Like Thomas Pavier, he invested in dramatic publication mostly before he became an established stationer. His first books included *Celestina* (1598), which is now lost, *A Warning for Fair Women* (STC 25089, 1599), *Old Fortunatus* (STC 6517, 1600), and the first quarto editions of *Much Ado About Nothing* (STC 22304, 1600) and *2 Henry IV* (STC 22288, 1600), which he published with Andrew Wise. The other commercial plays he published also belong to the early stages of his career, namely the three editions of *The Malcontent* in 1604 (STC 17479–81), the two issues of *Eastward-Ho* in 1605 (STC 4970–1), and *Bussy D'Ambois* in 1607 (STC 4966). Like Pavier, Aspley moved to religious, political and travel literature in the 1610s and to larger projects in the 1620s and 1630s, which, like the First Folio, involved working in close collaboration with several other stationers. Aspley does not seem to have had strong literary interests, because the few literary titles he published were joint ventures in partnership with Edward Blount, including, for example, Thommaso Buoni, *Problems of Beauty* (STC 4103.5, 1618). Aspley must have been an enterprising stationer, because he secured the rights over successful titles, such as the third part of John Norden's *A Pensive mans practice* (STC 18626a.5–8, 1609–33). Even more remarkable is the fact that a few authors chose Aspley as their main, or their only, publisher. Aspley, for example, published John Boys' entire canon, including eleven books of postils on the church's prescribed lectionary, which proved so popular as to require as many as twelve editions between 1610 and 1616 (Knafla 2004: 121). Similarly Roger Fenton, preacher at Gray's Inn, entrusted Aspley with the publication of five out of his seven extant religious treatises and sermons. The 'Preface to the Christian Reader' in his *Treatise of Vsurie* (STC 10806, 1611) shows how highly Fenton regarded the authority and accuracy of the printed text over circulation in manuscript. Unlike many of his contemporaries, who felt obliged to justify their decision to go to press by blaming their friends for insisting that their work should be published or unscrupulous publishers for threatening to print their work from unauthorized and maimed copies, Roger Fenton explains why he consciously decided to commit his work to print:

GEntle Reader; thy gentlenesse and patience is much exercised in these times, with the multitude of bookes; which men say they bee commonly forced to put vpon thee by the importunity of their friends. This to mee is no reason at all, for the publishing of this Treatise . . . Yet three motiues I haue which may make sufficient apologie for me . . . [The] second motiue hath been the mistakings of some which haue occasioned misreports; as if in the end I concluded nothing, or defended some kind of Vsurie. Which censures I may impute vnto two causes. The first is ordinarie . . . for part of that which is only spoken, must needs vanish in the aire, before it can bee fully fastned in the mind, and fitted to the whole frame and current of speech ... But howsoeuer it was either not so exactly deliuered, or distinctly taken, as it should: the onely remedie which now remaineth, is to exhibit the effect of that in writing which then was said; that such as make scruple, may at their pleasure, and best leisure, pause vpon it. (B1r 4–15; B1v 9–13, 16–19, 32; B2r 1–5)

The register and the stress on the progressive reliability of the spoken, the written, and the printed medium are reminiscent of Thomas More's preface to *A dyalogue* (STC 18085, 1530) discussed in chapter 1. The problem of being misinterpreted, or of having one's opinions misrepresented, so deeply felt by More in the early 1530s, but equally crucial to Fenton's religious and moral credentials in the 1610s, led these two public figures to praise the ability of the printed text to preserve authorial intentions more effectively than either the spoken word, or, as More insisted, manuscript copy, which could be annotated (and maimed) by hostile or simply unintelligent readers. In another dedicatory epistle prefaced to his *Sermon Preached on the 8. day of May 1615 ...*; (STC 10802, 1615), Fenton even specified that, although many preachers rewrote and expanded the text of their sermons when they decided to have them printed, he intended to use the printed text as an exact record of his sermon as he had delivered it to the congregation, so as to avoid any accusation of moral or intellectual inconsistency:

And albeit this subiect deserueth to bee amplified much more then my leasure in the throng of other businesse would at this time permit: yet vnderstanding of a rumour spread, as if vpon conference with some, I should beginne to alter my minde; I haue chosen rather to set it downe word for word as it was at that time vttered, then to enlarge any branch of it. (A4r 6–16; A4v 1–7)

Fenton's desire to have the text of his sermon set 'word for word' as he had preached it, and presumably 'word for word' as it appeared in the copy he entrusted to Aspley, obviously depended on Fenton's trust in the latter's professional competence and in his ability to find a reliable printer. Aspley hired different printers to set Fenton's manuscript copies into print. We can therefore safely assume that Aspley was the agent repeatedly approached and trusted by such a self-conscious author as Fenton.

Frustratingly enough, though, we only have Fenton's word to argue that Aspley would not interfere with the printer's copy in order not to tamper with authorial intentions. As well as the first quartos of *Much Ado About Nothing* and *2 Henry IV*, which were re-issued in 1623, Aspley's dramatic output includes plays which were only printed once or plays whose copy was prepared by their authors or revised because of official censorship.

Authorial preparation of copy is for example likely to have occurred between the first and the second edition of *The Malcontent*, while extensive revision took place in the third, where the addition of a new induction was occasioned by the exceptional change of acting company and venue. Alternatively, substantive changes in the second issue of the first edition of *Eastward-Ho* were prompted by the anti-Scottish jibes which upset King James and caused its authors to be arrested. Unfortunately, as with Edward Blount and Isaac Jaggard, none of Aspley's dramatic publications provide a viable precedent to determine whether he would routinely prepare dramatic copy for the press or whether he would seek annotated copy prior to reprinting the Shakespearean plays he owned in FI.

By contrast, a larger body of evidence is available to establish John Smethwick's attitude to dramatic publication. Smethwick, the fourth and last member of the Folio syndicate, started his publishing career by issuing mostly religious and occasional literature, including several prose works by Nicholas Breton. Then in 1607, he registered sixteen titles which had previously belonged to the recently deceased fellow stationer Nicholas Ling. The 1607 entry includes *A booke called Hamlett, The taminge of A Shrewe, Romeo and Julett* and *Loues Labour Lost*, as well as several other popular titles, which Smethwick kept re-issuing for the rest of his professional life (Arber 1875–94: III 365).

The paratext in the books published by Smethwick sheds little light on his willingness to invest in the preparation of the printer's copy for the press. The only exception may be a brief address to the reader prefaced to William Burton's translation of Erasmus's *Seauen Dialogues* (STC 10458a, 1624), if 'printer' means, as it often did in the early modern period, the agent who arranged and paid for the book to be printed:

The Printer to the Reader.
Courteous Reader, there haue in this impression some faults escaped, whereof I must acquite the Author [re: translator], and pleade thy pardon for my selfe, he being both absent, and vnacquainted with the sodaine publication of his booke; and I, sometimes mis-led by doubt and difficulty of the copie. The number and moment of them is not so great, but I hope thy kindenesse will be greater, in giuing what thy selfe (as being a man) doost somtimes neede, excuse of errors. (A4v 1–11)

A passing reference to the 'difficulty of the copie' would seem to suggest that this address was indeed written by the printer, who is the most likely agent to have had troubles deciphering the copy. However, this edition was re-set from printed copy and the 'printer' mentions the circumstances of its publication, including the whereabouts of the translator and his lack of involvement with this venture. Overall, the 'printer' is therefore more likely to have been the publisher, i.e. John Smethwick, and the printer's reference to the 'difficulty of copie' may signal the publisher's attempt to correct a difficult text in the absence of its translator.

While the paratext in Smethwick's books offers only limited circumstantial evidence, the patterns of textual variation in *Romeo and Juliet*, which he re-issued three times in quarto editions[26] and twice in the Folios of 1623 and 1632, show that he was actively committed to the preparation of dramatic copy for the press. Recent scholars have remarked on the significance of textual variation in the early quarto editions of *Romeo and Juliet*. Lynette Hunter, for example, believes that 'all the early quartos . . . [were] intelligently edited' (2001b: 9). Hunter also argues that the number of instances when the fourth quarto follows readings first introduced in the third quarto (STC 22325, henceforth Q4, and STC 22324, henceforth Q3) indicates that the annotator who prepared these two editions for the press may have been the same person (2001b: 11). The imprints on Q3 and Q4 fail to specify the name of their printers. However, the ornaments on the title-page of Q3, which was printed in 1609, have allowed textual scholars to identify John Windet as the stationer responsible for its impression (Greg 1939–59: 235), while the presswork in Q4 is generally attributed to William Stansby. Since Stansby was apprenticed to Windet and started printing books on Windet's behalf in the first decade of the seventeenth century (Bland and Bracken, quoted in Hunter 2001b: 12), Stansby may actually have printed both editions. Even so, John Smethwick is the most prominent and obvious link between Q3 and Q4, as confirmed by the absence of similar textual variation in other books printed by Windet while Stansby was working for him in 1608–9 (Hunter 2001b: 12). It is therefore worth considering whether Smethwick may have annotated or sought annotated copy for Q3 and Q4 *Romeo and Juliet*, and whether, in turn, he may have done the same when *Romeo and Juliet* and *Love's Labour's Lost* were re-issued in the First Folio in 1623.

A re-examination of the textual variants in Q3 and Q4 *Romeo and Juliet* shows that while Hunter is right in detecting an intelligent agent at work in the text of both editions, the annotators of Q3 and Q4 are highly unlikely to have been the same person. Preparation of copy for Q3 was mostly limited to sporadic corrections in the dialogue. Some of these corrections are straightforward emendations of typographical errors in the second quarto (STC 22323, henceforth Q2), and were probably rectified by a printing house agent.[27] Other corrections are subtler, and may indicate the intervention of an annotator, although none of them stems from an attempt to change any aspect of the dialogue other than obvious inconsistencies in it.[28] Q3 introduces no changes in stage directions and adds only one new speech prefix. The new speech prefix is added to an exchange where Q2 had produced a new anomaly by adding another speech prefix to the version preserved in the first quarto (STC 22322, henceforth Q1), as shown below:

> *Iul*:   Sweet so would I,
>   Yet I should kill thee with much cherrishing thee.
>   Good night, good night, parting is such sweet sorrow,
>   That I shall say good night till it be morrow.
> *Rom*:   Sleepe dwell vpon thine eyes, peace on thy breast,
>   I would that I were sleep . . .   (Q1, D3v 13–18)
>
> *Iu.*   Sweete so would I,
>   Yet I should kill thee with much cherishing:
>   Good night, good night,
>   Parting is such sweete sorrow,
>   That I shall say good night, till it be morrow.
> *Iu.*   Sleep dwel vpon thine eyes, peace in thy breast.
> *Ro.*   Would I were sleepe   (Q2, D4v 6–12)
>
> *Iu.*   Sweet so would I,
>   Yet I should kill thee with much cherishing:
>   Good night, good night.
> *Ro.*   Parting is such sweete sorrow,
>   That I shall say goodnight, till it be morrow.
> *Iu.*   Sleepe dwell vpon thine eyes, peace in thy breast.
> *Rom.*   Would I were sleepe . . .   (Q3, D4v 6–12)

The addition of a further speech prefix for Romeo in Q3 is clearly remedial, and although the version of this exchange preserved in Q3 was carried over to the First Folio, which was set from Q3, modern editors tend to prefer the version preserved in Q1.

Hunter's main reason for arguing that the agents responsible for the annotation of Q3 and Q4 *Romeo and Juliet* may have been the same person is that, in her own words, Q4 'hardly ever changes the text where Q3 has already changed it, even where Q1 has a different solution'. Q4 certainly adopts the straightforward corrections introduced in Q3 to emend typographical errors in Q2, but does not necessarily follow Q3 every time Q3 changes Q2. A few of Q4's departures from Q3 may be due to the fact that Q3 changes its source-text for the worse, as at A4v 5, where it replaces Q2's 'farther' in 'To know our farther pleasure in this case' with 'Fathers'. This line is spoken by the Prince, who nowhere else in the play, and in none of the extant early editions, seeks the advice of his father, or indeed mentions him. This variant is more likely to be the result of compositorial error, rather than annotation of the printer's copy, and Q4 departs from Q3 because the annotator must have realized that this reading is wrong. Similarly, and on the same page, Q3 changes Q2's 'humor' to 'honour' in Benvolio's lines 'Being one too many by my wearie selfe, / Pursued my humor, not pursuing his' (A4v 33–4), thus offering a less satisfactory alternative which Q4 rejects. Another example of the same kind of discretionary attitude on the part of the annotator of the printer's copy for Q4 occurs at D1v 3, where Q3 introduces another unsatisfactory verbal variant – 'striueth' for 'stirreth' in Mercutio's line 'He heareth not, he striueth not, he moueth not' (D1v 3). Once again, Q4 rejects the reading preserved in Q3. While on all three occasions Q4 opts not to reproduce Q3 variants because they are self-evidently poor word choices, on at least one occasion Q4 does not trust the genuinely remedial alternative offered by Q3. The same exchange between Romeo and Juliet quoted above provides a telling piece of evidence to argue that the annotator of the printer's copy for Q4 was unsatisfied with the solution offered by the annotator of Q3, who resolved the problem created by Q2's addition of an extra speech prefix for Juliet at D4v 11 by adding a further prefix for Romeo at D4v 9. Instead of following Q3, the annotator of Q4 either referred back to Q1 or independently emended this exchange to read as in Q1:

> *Iu.*   Sweet so would I,
>   Yet I should kill thee with much cherishing:
>   Good night, good night.
>   Parting is such sweet sorrow,
>   That I shall say good-night, till it be morrow.
> *Ro.*   Sleepe dwell vpon thine eyes, peace in thy brest.
>   Would I were sleepe . . .   (Q4, D3r 17–23)

Even more significant is the different quality of intervention in Q3 and Q4 *Romeo and Juliet*, which make it difficult to imagine why the same annotator would have missed so many opportunities to improve not only the dialogue, but also stage directions and speech prefixes in the earlier edition, which were then duly rectified in the later one. The dialogue in Q4, for example, reveals the intervention of a shrewder annotator than the dialogue in Q3. Besides following the straightforward corrections and rejecting the doubtful alternatives provided by Q3, Q4 introduced variant readings which were neither anticipated by the earlier quarto editions nor adopted by the Folio.[29] For the first time Q4 emends Romeo's nonsensical reference to Juliet as 'My Neece' at the end of the balcony scene (D4r 25 in

Q2 and Q3, and TLN 974 in F) by changing it into 'My Deere' (D2v 36). Also unprecedented is Q4's improvement of Juliet's lines, after she learns from the Nurse that Romeo has slain her cousin Tybald, by turning the slightly incongruous 'dimne saint' (G2v 11 in Q2 and Q3, and TLN 1731 in F) into 'damned saint' (F4v 28). The annotator of Q4 also shows some initiative where previous editions had left a metrically irregular line unaltered or had offered some unimaginative remedial alternatives. While, as mentioned above, the annotator of the printer's copy for F adds 'graue' at the end of Juliet's line as it appears in Q3 – 'And hide me with a dead man in his,' (I3v 1) – thus replicating the ending of the previous line (TLN 2379), Q4 offers a genuine alternative by adding 'shroud' to IIr 36. Similarly, Q4 expanded another imperfect line, which reads 'my hart is full' in all other early editions (K3v 4–5 in Q2 and Q3, and TLN 2686 in F) into 'my hart is full of woe' (KIv 3–4). Other emendations first introduced in Q4 are now generally rejected, but they still show an alert agent intent on perfecting his source-text. When Juliet impatiently waits to be joined by Romeo after their secret wedding, she invokes the 'gentle night' in Q2–3 and F as follows: 'Give me my *Romeo*, and when I shall die, / Take him and cut him out in little starres' (GIv 20–1, TLN 1665–6). Q4 normalizes the logic of Juliet's appeal by replacing 'when I shall die' with 'when hee shall die' (F4r 4). Similarly, Q4 attempts to improve the Friar's line 'The Roses in thy lips and cheekes shall fade / Too many ashes' in Q2–3 and F (I3v 15, TLN 2395) by replacing 'Too many ashes' to 'Too paly ashes' (IIv 14).

Besides showing more initiative in perfecting the dialogue, the annotator of Q4 also demonstrates a more developed sense of the text as a theatrical script than his predecessor in Q3. Once again, Q4 introduces stage directions where the other editions, including F, provide none and corrects speech prefixes which were either missing or wrong in the other editions. At H4r 14, for example, Q4 adds an explicit exit direction for the Nurse, and, at KIv 18, it adds the prefix '*Peter.*', when all the previous quarto editions and F continue the speech which includes this line to '*2 M.*'. Besides, at K4v 20, Q4 adds the right prefix '*Page*', where even F had made the wrong guess, by attributing the line 'O Lord they fight, I will go call the Watch' to Peter (TLN 2924). Another interesting cluster of variants in Q4 shows the annotator's willingness to intervene even when the other editions offer an acceptable, but imprecise, alternative, as at LIV 1–19, when five speech prefixes designating a generic '*Man.*' in QI–3 and F are replaced by '*Balt.*'. Overall, even allowing for the temporal gap that intervened between the publication of Q3 in 1609 and the publication of Q4,[30] the quality of the intervention in the two editions suggests that they were indeed annotated prior to being re-printed, but not by the same hand. Also worth noting is the fact that, albeit sensitive to theatrical aspects of his copy-text, the annotator of Q4 paid more attention to the dialogue than to stage directions and speech prefixes. On a few occasions, Q4 added and emended the same directions and prefixes that were altered in F.[31] On several other occasions, though, Q4 failed to intervene to supply stage directions, which, as observed earlier on in this chapter, are the main area of editorial intervention in F.[32] Overall, the patterns of variants in Q3, Q4 and F *Romeo and Juliet* reveal three different annotating styles, or hands. Consequently, Smethwick seems more likely to have regularly sought annotated copy, rather than to have prepared the printer's copy for each of these editions himself, as was probably the case with other publishers, including Richard Jones and Thomas Pavier.

Scholars interested in the textual transmission of *Romeo and Juliet* have often wondered why, given the amount of editorial effort that went into the preparation of copy in Q3, and especially, in Q4, the latter was not used as printer's copy for F. Q4, as mentioned above, is undated, and the simplest explanation is that Q4 postdates F. However, in 1965 George Walton Williams advanced the influential theory according to which the progressive deterioration of the tailpiece used by William Stansby at the end of Q4 and in many other books produced in his printing house 'make it reasonably definite that the quarto was printed in 1622' (Williams 1965: 253). Lynette Hunter queries Williams's theory, by arguing that the breaks in the tailpiece 'are not uniform in appearance . . ., nor are the printings of the endpiece in different copies of other books consistent'. Hunter therefore believes that 'it is impossible to date Q4 accurately on this basis, and that from the evidence of the tailpiece alone Q4 may have been printed any time from 1616 to around 1628' (Hunter 2001a: 282). However useful Hunter's proviso, her analysis does not exclude 1622 as a possible date of publication of Q4, nor, more generally, does it exclude the hypothesis that Q4 may predate F. Hunter then advances her own hypothesis as to why Smethwick may have failed to capitalize on the corrections accrued by his quarto editions by using the latest as copy for F:

If Q4 had been printed but was not accessible to Jaggard's printing house, then it may indicate that while individual printers like Stansby seem in this case to have had a policy of retaining old marked-up copy, there was little exchange between establishments. (2001a: 285)

Hunter's explanation rests on the problematic assumption that annotated copy would be retained by the printer, when in fact annotated copy, as much as un-annotated copy, ultimately belonged to the publisher, who had an interest in retaining it because he also had the right to decide whether and when to reprint it and what printer he should hire for the job. An alternative explanation is that Smethwick did not use Q4 when he contributed to the Folio venture of 1623 because Q4 was not available, either because it was printed after the Folio, or because the two ventures overlapped.[33] The flurry of Shakespearean editions published immediately before the Folio would indeed suggest that Smethwick regarded his roles as one of the members of the Folio syndicate and as publisher of Q4 as distinct but compatible. As Hunter points out, the relationship between Q4 and F remains 'radically uncertain' (2001a: 281). However, what seems less doubtful is that Smethwick regularly sought annotated copy prior to re-issuing this popular play, and that he may even have duplicated the editorial effort when he planned a re-issue in quarto format either immediately before, or at the same time as, the Folio was going through Jaggard's press. More generally, if Smethwick regularly invested in the preparation of dramatic copy for the press, he is even more likely to have done so by seeking an annotator for his copies of *Romeo and Juliet* and *Love's Labour's Lost* for the prestigious Folio venture of 1623.

Although I fully endorse Charlton Hinman's warning that 'the copy for Folio plays must be established on a case-by-case basis' (1963: 5), I am inclined to believe that at least the four plays discussed above provide no consistent evidence to support the theory of consultation of a theatrical authority as 'the usual treatment of printed copy for Folio plays' (Wells and Taylor 1987: 289). The Folio variants in some of the plays set from printed copy and in some of the playbooks published by Smethwick in fact reinforce my impression that, while consultation of theatrical manuscripts for plays which had not been altered in the theatre and were already available in print must have been costly and impractical, annotation of copy was a common and welcome practice. This chapter has also confirmed that, rather than seeking to recover authorial or theatrical intentions, early modern publishers like Smethwick valued the progressive improvement of their texts and relied on the collaboration of annotating readers, who, like the 'worthy Gentleman' mentioned in the address to the reader in Beaumont and Fletcher's *Comedies and Tragedies* (1679), '[took] the pains (or rather the pleasure)' to correct their dramatic copies for the press.

CHAPTER 6

Perfecting Shakespeare in the Fourth Folio (1685)

The transmission of Shakespeare's works following the printing and publication of the first substantive quarto and folio editions in the late
sixteenth and early seventeenth centuries and prior to the official rise of
the editorial tradition at the beginning of the eighteenth century is still
widely regarded as a process of progressive textual degeneration. While
Nicholas Rowe's 1709 *The works of Mr. William Shakespear* is generally
hailed as the forefather of all subsequent *editions*, the seventeenth-century
texts of plays which were printed more than once from their earliest
substantive versions are dismissed as derivative *reprints*. Significant steps
have already been taken towards a better understanding of the evolution of
the Shakespearean text from the mid to the late-seventeenth century. Ann
Thompson, for example, has recently argued that at least one alteration in
the 1683 quarto edition of *Hamlet* 'seems . . . to suggest that someone had
finally turned to the folio tradition' (1999: 141). Thompson therefore calls
into question the traditional assumption that the 'Players' Quartos' 'run
on, heedless except very rarely of the Folios, and then almost invariably
with every appearance of casual coincidence' (Spencer 1927: 175). Similarly,
at the beginning of the last century, Pollard made a strong case in favour of
the hypothesis of editorial intervention in the Second Folio of 1632 (henceforth F2). According to Pollard,

[t]he Second Folio did not merely alter the First in order now and again to make
the colloquial syntax more regular, . . . but in a real sense began the work of lawful
and necessary emendation . . . [I]t was in 1632 that a start was made in re-editing
the First Folio, and thus no survey of the history of Shakespeare's text can be
complete which does not take into account the work of these anonymous compositors and correctors. (1909: 157)

Pollard's views were endorsed and reinforced by A. Nicoll in the 1920s
(1924: 157–78) and by M. W. Black and M. A. Shaaber in the 1930s (1937).
Also significant is the amount of attention devoted to the transmission of

Shakespeare's text immediately before Nicholas Rowe's edition of 1709. In 1951, Giles E. Dawson demonstrated that a batch of seventy unruled pages in some copies of the Fourth Folio, now generally referred to as the Fifth Folio, had been re-set and reprinted around 1700 (1951: 93–104). As Eric Rasmussen has usefully noted, 'renewed attention to the reprinted Fifth Folio pages reveals that the person responsible for the text behaved very much like an eighteenth-century editor' (1998: 318–22).

The Fourth Folio (WING S2916, henceforth F4) has so far received little attention, despite the fact that Rowe used it as the basis for his edition of 1709 and that later eighteenth-century editors followed their immediate predecessors, until Dr Johnson started to champion the textual superiority of the First Folio over the other seventeenth-century Folio editions. Although Rowe was responsible for the introduction of conventions which affected the structuring and presentation of Shakespeare's plays until the early 1980s (Mowat 1994: 314–22), the text of Rowe's influential edition often left its source text fundamentally unaltered. Although Rowe did occasionally conflate variant versions of the same play,[1] it is also clear that whenever he dealt with texts which had appeared only in one substantive version, his intervention was predominantly cosmetic. Rowe silently adopted most F4 corrections, which then, in turn, were inherited by his successors.

This chapter shows that some F4 variants are not accidental changes or compositorial tampering accrued by this edition during the printing process but rather corrections, which earlier chapters in this book associate with the preparation of the printer's copy for the press. By focusing on the F4 text of *Coriolanus*, this chapter will also attempt to identify the annotating hand who corrected it. Definitive identification of early modern annotating readers is hardly ever possible, except when their intervention is explicitly discussed in signed paratextual materials or when the provenance of an annotated volume can be safely established, as with King Charles I's annotations in his copy of Beaumont and Fletcher's *The Maid's Tragedy*, which was briefly mentioned in the Introduction. Although no firm conclusion can be reached in relation to the identity of the annotator of the printer's copy underlying F4 *Coriolanus*, a close investigation of the pattern of intervention in this text sheds light on how the practice of preparing dramatic copy for the press evolved from the rise of English drama in print at the beginning of the sixteenth century to the last quarter of the seventeenth century. Changes in the approach to the preparation of dramatic copy for the press during the sixteenth and seventeenth centuries will then be compared to the intervention of named editors belonging to the 'official' editorial tradition of Shakespeare ushered in by Rowe's edition in 1709.

THE FOURTH FOLIO TEXT OF *CORIOLANUS*

Current perceptions of F4 as a mere reprint of the Third Folio (henceforth F3) derive mainly from Black and Shaaber's *Shakespeare's Seventeenth-Century Editors, 1632–1685*. In this influential study, Black and Shaaber argue that, because the printing of F4 was shared by three different printers, 'some or all of the changes found in F4 may be the work of three different correctors of the press, each regularly employed in one of the three printing offices involved' (1937: 29). Although they consider the alternative that an agent 'probably unconnected with the printing trade ... superseded the regular correctors of the three printing houses' (1937: 29), they ultimately believe that textual variation in F4 stems from the idiosyncratic intervention of three different press-correctors. Black and Shaaber's conclusions are questionable. Their analysis of F4 relies on the collations provided by the Furness-Variorum edition (1871–1928), and, for those plays which were yet to appear in this series, on the second edition of the Cambridge Shakespeare (1891–3). Black and Shaaber themselves admit that 'the Cambridge editors collated [F4] somewhat negligently', and that they 'doubt that [their] own data do it full justice' (1937: 65). A fresh collation of the text of *Coriolanus* as it appears in F3 and F4 shows that, at least so far as this play is concerned, the alternative theory that an annotating reader 'probably unconnected with the printing trade ... superseded the regular correctors of the three printing houses', should not be too hastily dismissed.

Some of the most noteworthy corrections in F4 *Coriolanus* affect the dialogue. In F1, the eponymous Roman leader, who is forced to seek shelter among his former enemies, reflects on the fickleness of allegiance:

> Oh World, thy slippery turnes! Friends now fast sworn,
> Whose double bosomes seemes to weare one heart,
>   ... shall within this houre,
> On a dissention of a Doit, breake out
> To bitterest Enmity.   (TLN 2638–44)

The F2 compositor mangles TLN 2639, which reads 'Whose double bosomes seene weare on heart'. F3 leaves F2 unaltered, whereas F4 shrewdly restores F1, modernizing the number of the verb: 'Whose double bosoms seem to wear one Heart'. This line in F4 is more likely to be the result of speculative intervention rather than consultation of FI, as shown by another variant reading later in the same speech. FI is clearly corrupt when Coriolanus argues:

> So with me,
> My Birth-place haue I, and my loues vpon
> This Enemie Towne: Ile enter, if he slay me
> He does faire Iustice: (TLN 2648–51)

F2 makes things worse by dropping the first letter in 'place' and turning 'loues' into 'lover'. F3 reprints the nonsensical version provided by F2. F4 offers the best alternative by restoring 'Birth-place', by adding 'left' after 'Lover', and by revising the punctuation, which now establishes a link between the preposition 'upon' and the verb 'enter', so that TLN 2649 reads as follows: 'My Birth-place have I, and my Lover left; upon / This Enemy's Town I'le enter, if ... '. Modern editions follow Capell and emend FI's 'haue' to 'hate' – 'my birthplace hate I' – and the unusual plural 'loves' to 'and my love is upon / This Enemie Town'. The solution provided by F4 is clearly speculative and not as satisfactory as Capell's. F4's emendation must have been regarded as perfectly acceptable, however, since it was endorsed by all eighteenth-century editors up to Capell, including Nicholas Rowe.

Another example of sophisticated intervention in F4 *Coriolanus* occurs in Act 5. After Coriolanus has granted Volumnia's request to spare Rome, it is Aufidius's turn to reflect on the fickleness of allegiance. In FI, Aufidius's lines read as follows:

> ...   I tooke him [Coriolanus],
> Made him ioynt-seruant with me: Gaue him way
> In all his owne desires: Nay, let him choose
> Out of my Files, his proiects, to accomplish
> My best and freshest men, seru'd his designements
> In mine owne person: holpe to reape the Fame
> Which he did end all his; and tooke some pride
> To do my selfe this wrong: (TLN 3684–91)

Irregular punctuation probably led to tampering in F2 and F3, where 'holpe', a form occasionally used as the past tense or past participle of the verb to 'help', is replaced by 'hope'. F4 could not restore 'holpe' from 'hope', but nevertheless normalized the tense of the verb by turning 'hope' into 'hop'd' and made sense of this sentence by replacing 'end' with 'make'. As a result, F4 reads 'hop'd to reap the Fame / Which he did make all his'. If judged in relation to their distance from the version preserved in FI, the alternative readings in F2–4 can be regarded as increasingly corrupt.

However, while not attempting to restore F1, F4, unlike F2–3, 'perfects' its source-text, by making this sentence syntactically and logically viable. Once again, the solution provided by F4, though speculative and far from satisfactory, was obviously good enough for Rowe and his successors, who silently endorsed it.

Sophisticated corrections in the text of the dialogue in F4 *Coriolanus* are matched by similarly ingenious alterations to speech prefixes and stage directions, the two other main categories of intervention associated with the intervention of early modern annotating readers in the earlier chapters of this book. In F4 *Coriolanus*, Titus Lartius, one of the two generals in the wars against the Volscies, is renamed Titus Lucius. As Philip Brockbank points out, the name 'Titus Lucius' is a mistake, while 'Titus Lartius' is, historically and bibliographically, the correct alternative (1976: 21–2). What is significant, though, is that the decision to replace the name 'Titus Lartius' with the name 'Titus Lucius' must have been taken before the F4 compositor began to set his text. The spurious alternative 'Titus Lucius' was probably prompted by TLN 262 in F1–3, where Titus Lartius is mistakenly addressed as Titus Lucius. It seems unlikely that a compositor should have decided to emend all the other fifteen occasions where Titus's second name is Lartius, including speech prefixes and stage directions. It seems even more unlikely that a compositor would have chosen to adopt the one spurious occurrence of the name Titus Lucius in his source-text and emend all the other occurrences of the name Titus Lartius not only after TLN 262, but also retrospectively, at TLN 245. It seems more likely that the compositor was setting his text from an annotated copy of F3 where the name Lartius had consistently been crossed out from dialogue, speech prefixes, and stage directions and replaced by Lucius.

Even more significant is the attention devoted to making sure that proper names in the stage directions and speech prefixes are consistent with their counterparts in the dialogue. The stage direction which prompts the first entrance of the generals and the Tribunes of the people in Act 1 – '*Enter Sicinius Velutus, Annius Brutus Cominisu* [sic], *Titus Lartius, with other Senatours*' – is emended in F4, where '*Annius Brutus*' is replaced by 'Junius Brutus'. F4 therefore ensures consistency between this stage direction and an earlier speech in the same scene, where Coriolanus mentions that Sicinius Velutus and Junius Brutus are two of the five tribunes granted to the people of Rome in order 'to defend', as Coriolanus puts it, 'their vulgar wisdoms'. In F4, this stage direction is in keeping with the dialogue for the first time.

Further evidence that the corrections of F4 *Coriolanus* derive from annotation of the printer's copy rather than from the intervention of a printing house agent stems from the fact that, as mentioned above, the printing of F4 was shared by three printers.[2] A comparison between F4 *Coriolanus* and at least one other play set up and corrected in the same printing house shows that not all plays printed by the same printer introduce the same level of substantive changes. If, as Black and Shaaber suggest, F4 variants were 'the work of three different correctors of the press, each regularly employed in one of the three printing offices involved' (1937: 29), one would expect a consistent pattern of corrections in all the texts included in the same division. The texts of *Coriolanus* and *Richard II* belong to the same division. Yet the number of corrections introduced in these two texts varies considerably. Six corrections in F4 *Richard II* hardly compare to the frequent and sophisticated emendations introduced in F4 *Coriolanus*.[3] The sporadic distribution of substantive emendations in the second division of F4 can best be explained in terms of the unsystematic annotation of the printer's copy underlying it.

As Hinman pointed out in relation to F1, 'the copy for Folio plays must be established on a case-by-case basis' (1963: 5). While a full collation of the texts of Shakespeare's plays as they appear in F4 would be necessary to draw general conclusions about the level of annotation undergone by the copy of F3 from which F4 was set, a contrastive analysis between the changes introduced in two plays included in the same division shows that preparation of copy was not systematic and that it may have been prompted by the annotator's familiarity with a specific play or by the intrinsic quality of his source text. While more general conclusions about the origin of F4 variants cannot be drawn until a comprehensive collation of the entire edition becomes available, the rest of this chapter attempts to identify the annotating reader who prepared F4 *Coriolanus* for the press in order to then compare his corrections to the intervention of earlier anonymous readers and later named editors.

THE ANNOTATOR OF THE FOURTH FOLIO TEXT
OF *CORIOLANUS*

Circumstantial evidence shows that the London stationer Henry Herringman, the main publisher of F4,[4] regularly sought John Dryden's editorial services. In *The Medall of John Bayes* (Wing S2860, 1682), for example, Thomas Shadwell insinuated that Dryden had 'turn'd a Journeyman t'a Bookseller; / Writ Prefaces to Books for Meat and Drink, / And as he paid, he would both write and think' (quoted in Winn 1987: 95). As early as 1660, the address 'To the Reader' in the edition of Robert Howard's collection of *Poems* published by Herringman suggests that Dryden's duties extended beyond those of a journey-man or a literary hack. In this address, Howard acknowledges 'having prevailed with a worthy Friend to take so much view of my blotted Copies, as to free me from grosse Errors'. According to James Winn, Dryden's biographer, 'Dryden is the likeliest person to have performed such editorial services' for his publisher (1987: 99). James Osborn anticipated Winn's theory by arguing that Dryden was 'one of the bookseller's staff' (1940: 175). Although Shadwell's claim that Dryden lodged with Herringman cannot be verified (Winn 1987: 95), the arrangement between Dryden and his publisher would seem to be in keeping with the established tradition of authors who received board and lodging in exchange for their editorial services.

Given his professional association with Herringman, John Dryden is at least one potential candidate for the role of annotator of F4 *Coriolanus*. By 1685, Dryden had adapted *The Tempest* with William Davenant (1670) and *Troilus and Cressida* (1679), and had written his own play inspired by *Antony and Cleopatra* (1678). More crucially, the 1683 edition of *Hamlet*, which inherited extensive theatrical cuts and several verbal changes from the 1676 Quarto, was probably annotated and emended by Dryden (Paul 1934: 369–75). Both the 1676 and the 1683 editions of *Hamlet* were published by Herringman.

Herringman himself may have acted as annotator of F4 *Coriolanus*, as other literary publishers had done before him. In 1684, Herringman sold his bookshop, a popular rendezvous for cultivated Londoners on the Strand often mentioned by Samuel Pepys in his *Diary*, to the retailers Joseph Knight and Francis Saunders. From 1684 Herringman devoted himself to the publication of elegant and expensive Folio collections of literary works,[5] and thus became, as Edward Arber puts it, 'the first London Wholesale Publisher, in the modern sense of those words' (1903–6: II 642). Only three years after Herringman's publication of Shakespeare's F4, Jacob Tonson played a crucial role in the editing of the 1688 Folio edition of Milton's *Paradise Lost*, as recorded in his letters published in the *Grub Street Journal* in January 1732. According to Stuart Bennet, the external evidence provided by the 1732 letters is substantiated by a contrastive analysis of Tonson's edition and earlier editions of *Paradise Lost*, which reveals 'how incisive his insights into the problems of editorship were' and 'how intimate his involvement was in this and, doubtless, many of his other important publishing projects' (1988: 251, 250). After turning the retailing side of his business to Knight and Saunders, Herringman, like Tonson, might have had the leisure to devote more time and energy to the preparation of his copies for the press. Unfortunately archival evidence concerning Herringman's management of his business is limited to a number of deeds held at the Westminster Archives and records of court cases with which Herringman was implicated.[6] No private correspondence survives. It is therefore difficult to speculate about Herringman's involvement in the publication of his Folio collections of literary and dramatic works after 1684. However, the internal evidence provided by one Folio edition published by Herringman in 1693 suggests that, rather than carrying out the preparation of the printer's copy for the press himself, he continued to employ professional correctors even after 1684.

The third part of the eighth edition of Abraham Cowley's *Works* (Wing c6659), which Herringman published in 1693, includes *Six Books of Plants*, which had been 'made in English by several Hands', including Nahum Tate's. It is interesting that Tate, rather than the other translators, should write the dedication and a short prefatory essay on the Classical influences in Cowley's Latin works. It is even more significant that the errata listed at the end of the preliminary matters should include only corrections in Books IV and V, the two books translated by Tate. The text of Cowley's *The Cutter of Cole-man Street*, which was re-set from a 1663 quarto edition prior to its inclusion in Herringman's 1693 collection, is also noteworthy for the frequency and quality of its substantive corrections. As in the text of *Coriolanus* in F4, the annotator of *The Cutter of Cole-man Street* pays particular attention to improving stage directions and speech prefixes. Herringman's edition, for example, adds the prefix 'Truman Jun.' at B1r 3, which was missing in the 1663 edition. At B2v 11, the attribute 'jun.' is added to the original speech prefix 'Truman' in order to avoid confusion. Nahum Tate's potential involvement with the publication of Cowley's *Works* suggests that Herringman valued annotated copy but that he was more likely to employ somebody else to prepare the printer's copy for press even after he turned wholesale publisher in the mid-1680s, when he published F4.

The internal evidence discussed so far is too limited to support a definitive conclusion as regards the identity of the annotator of F4 *Coriolanus*, but Nahum Tate, rather than Dryden, seems to have been the main editorial agent regularly employed by Herringman in the mid-1680s. It is suggestive, for example, that by the time Herringman published F4 in 1685, Dryden was already working for other publishers, including Tonson, who would become Dryden's exclusive publisher for the rest of his literary career. It is also significant that Dryden had started delegating unwanted work to Tate from around 1682 and that Tate continued to work for London publishers throughout his working life. In the prefatory material to *A Memorial for the Learned* (Wing D38, 1686), Tate explains that, 'being sent [this treatise] from a conceal'd Author, with permission to make it publick, . . . [he] found a double Care incumbent upon [him], both to secure it from errors of the Press, and procure its Recommendation to the World, by the Patronage of some Honourable Person' (A2r 8–10, A2v 1–7). Tate makes a similar remark in the preface to *The Four Epistles of A. G. Busbequius*, published by J. Taylor and J. Wyat in 1694 (Wing B6219): '[t]he Translator of this ingenious and most useful Piece not surviving to see it publish'd, upon Perusal of the Copy, I found the excellent Performance and Merit of the Work did not only deserve just Care of the Impression, but also some Eminent Person to Recommend its Appearance in the World.' (A2r 7–15, A2v 1–2). Given Tate's involvement with these publishing ventures and with the publication of Cowley's *Works* in 1693, an earlier collaboration with Herringman in the mid-1680s should not be ruled out.

Internal evidence confirms that Tate might have replaced Dryden as Herringman's corrector and assistant and that he might have annotated F4 *Coriolanus* for the press. Tate's 1682 adaptation, *The Ingratitude of a Common-Wealth* (WING T190), anticipates some of the substantive emendations subsequently introduced in F4 *Coriolanus*. For example, the belly in Menenius's parable, which replies 'taintingly' in F1 and 'tantingly' in F2 and F3, is finally allowed to reply 'tauntingly' to the 'discontented members, the mutinous parts' of the body politic in F4 (TLN 112). This reading follows Tate's emendation in *The Ingratitude* at B2r 21–2. The same belly is reported to answer in the past tense only in Tate's adaptation at B2r 17 and in F4 at TLN 107. The variant F4 version of the first Senator's defiant warning to the Romans during the siege of Corioles – 'our Gates,/ Which yet seem shut, we have but pinn'd with Rushes' (TLN 506–7) – is anticipated by Tate at C2r 3, which emends the alternative 'pin'd' preserved in the earlier Folios. Other F4 variants are gratuitous changes and are therefore even more significant in singling out Tate as a potential candidate for the role of annotator of the printer's copy of F4 *Coriolanus*. Tate added two references to 'the Commons' in his 1681 adaptation of *King Lear* (WING S2918) at E1v 16 and H4v 30, where his Shakespearean originals contain none.[7] As Richard Strier points out, '[Tate] says "the Commons" here, not the crowd, the multitude, or the rabble, [because] he conceives of this group politically and respectfully' (1995: 223). When he adapted *Coriolanus* in 1682, Tate chose the more topical title, *The Ingratitude of a Common-Wealth*, which, still according to Strier, suggests a 'different view of politics, . . . [once] both the parliamentary and the popular movement had been defeated' (1995: 206). Independently of whether Tate's attitude to the Exclusion Crisis changed between 1680–1 and 1682, the term 'Commons', as opposed to 'crowd', 'multitude' or 'rabble', retains its highly topical and political connotations. Besides the title, Tate also changed the Shakespearean original twice by turning 'the People' at TLN 1380 into 'the Commons' at D2r 25 and 'the Common' at TLN 1709 into 'the Commons' at E1r 23. The staggered entrances at the beginning of Act 2 in Shakespeare, including the 'two Tribunes of the People' at TLN 896, are replaced by two entrances at C4r 8–9 and C4r 13, where the Tribunes of the People are not mentioned individually but as part of the 'Commons of Rome'. It is interesting that F4 should similarly emend 'Commoners' at TLN 3735 in order to introduce an extra reference to the 'Commons' in a play where the people of Rome have such a crucial role and yet are referred to as 'the commons' only three times.

Although unusually suggestive, internal evidence alone cannot provide a definitive identification of the annotator of F4 *Coriolanus*. Only a few years later Nicholas Rowe was to include his name on the title-page of his edition of Shakespeare's *Works*. However, as late as 1685 and in keeping with the early modern practice of annotating dramatic copy anonymously, the identity of the annotator of F4 *Coriolanus* remained undisclosed. Also in keeping with earlier annotating readers, the annotator of F4 *Coriolanus* perfected the text of this play without consulting earlier editions. The primary objective of the annotation of dramatic copy for the press was still to 'improve' the text, not to 'restore' authorial or theatrical intentions. Despite these strong elements of continuity in the preparation of dramatic copy for the press between the early sixteenth and the late seventeenth century, important differences started to emerge. While focusing on such differences, the last section of this chapter will also highlight the survival of some of the defining features of the early modern practice of perfecting dramatic texts for the press well beyond the rise of the official editorial tradition of Shakespeare in 1709.

ANNOTATION OF DRAMATIC COPY IN THE LATE
SEVENTEENTH CENTURY AND BEYOND

Like the other early modern annotators of dramatic copy discussed in this book, the annotator of F4 *Coriolanus* emended speech prefixes, stage directions and nonsensical readings in the dialogue sporadically, anonymously and irrespective of the readings preserved in earlier textual witnesses. However, unlike his predecessors, the annotator of F4 was more likely to be a professional literary agent than the publisher himself. The role of the professional annotator of dramatic copy for the press was not entirely unprecedented. Henry Chettle is a good example of an early modern professional writer who regularly offered his editorial services to John Danter and may have been involved in the preparation of the first quarto edition of *Romeo and Juliet*, which Danter published in 1597 (Jowett 1993: 452–86 and 1998: 53–74). However the role of the literary publisher, who, like Richard Jones and Thomas Pavier, would annotate his own dramatic copies for the press, was gradually disappearing. Jacob Tonson's preparation of Milton's *Paradise Lost* for his 1688 edition harked back to an older model of the scholarly publisher, who would simultaneously fulfil several roles, as investor in and sometimes chief retailer of his books, but also as a critically alert reader and critic, who shrewdly selected the books he published and often prepared them for the press. More in keeping with the evolution of the practice of preparing dramatic copy for the press was Tonson's decision to hire some of the most prominent literary figures of his time to prepare his editions of Shakespeare's works once he secured their their copyright a few years later. In this respect, Herringman's reliance on Dryden and Tate as annotators and correctors of his books anticipated the metamorphosis of the anonymous early modern annotators of dramatic copy into the fully fledged professional editors of Shakespeare at the beginning of the eighteenth century.

Towards the end of the seventeenth century, English drama in general, and Shakespearean drama in particular, were about to be granted the same level of editorial attention accorded to the tragedies and comedies written by Ariosto, Trissino, Machiavelli, Aretino and Cinthio during the first half of the *Cinquecento* in Italy. However, while the involvement of classically trained professional editors in the publication of contemporary Italian drama was prompted by the progressive application of editorial methods devised to prepare new editions of classical texts to vernacular literature, the beginning of the official editorial tradition of Shakespeare coincided with the legal recognition of intellectual property and the advent of copyright legislation. Both the Statute of Anne and Nicholas Rowe's edition of Shakespeare's *Works* were issued in 1709. The trigger for the rise of the professional editor of Shakespeare, in other words, was not only the increasing literary status enjoyed by his works, but also a wider legal impulse towards the definition of intellectual property, including editorial activities.

The rise of proprietary editorship represented a genuinely radical break from the tradition of anonymous annotation of dramatic copy in the sixteenth and seventeenth centuries. While before 1709 the 'perfecting' of a dramatic text was seen as a collective ongoing process, the 'editing' of Shakespeare after 1709 turned specific emendations, and, ultimately, specific versions of his texts into the intellectual property of his editors. Samuel Johnson openly denounced editors who, like Thomas Hanmer, had failed to acknowledge the proprietary rights of his predecessors. In his highly critical assessment of Hanmer's edition of 1743–4 Johnson observed that 'by inserting his emendations, whether invented or borrowed, into the page, without any notice of varying copies, he . . . appropriated the labour of his predecessors, and made his own edition of little authority' (Johnson 1765: 1 D2v 8–12). Johnson is also cautious not to make the same mistake in his own edition of 1765. In his preface, he scrupulously explains that he is willing to forfeit his proprietary claim over any of his emendations, should they, even unwittingly, replicate the work of others:

Whatever I have taken from [my predecessors] it was my intention to refer to its original authour, and it is certain, that what I have not given to another, I believed when I wrote it to be my own. In some perhaps I have been anticipated; but if I am ever found to encroach upon the remarks of any other commentator, I am willing that the honour, be it more or less, should be transferred to the first claimant, for his right, and his alone, stands above dispute; the second can prove his pretentions only to himself, nor can himself always distinguish invention, with sufficient certainty, from recollection. (1765: 1 D5r 5–17)

Johnson's concerned realization that even what seems original can in fact be an unwitting repetition or a recollection suggests the extent to which proprietary editorship had become rooted in eighteenth-century literary culture.

The rise of proprietary editorship went hand in hand with the programmatic desire to restore 'the Exactness of the Author's Original manuscripts' (Rowe 1709: 1 A2r). While the anonymous annotator of dramatic copy in the sixteenth and seventeenth century aimed to correct the text in order to achieve the best possible reading, the first named editors of Shakespeare aimed to correct the text in order to recover the true reading as intended by its author. The recognition of editorial labour as intellectual property implied the recognition of the primacy of authorial intentions in the interpretation of a literary work. Also new was the relevance accorded to the author's biography as a key point of entry into his work. Nicholas Rowe furnished the first edition of Shakespeare's work to bear the name of its editor on the title page with an 'Account of the Life & c. of Mr. William

Shakespear', which was then regularly reproduced in later eighteenth-century editions, because, as he puts it, 'the knowledge of an Author may sometimes conduce to the better understanding of his Book' (1709: 1). By the time Lewis Theobald edited Shakespeare's work in 1733, Rowe's interest in Shakespeare's biography as a relevant context for the accurate interpretation and emendation of his works had transferred to several other areas of inquiry:

Besides a faithful Collation of all the printed Copies, . . . let it suffice to say, that, to clear up several Errors in the Historical Plays, I purposely read over *Hall* and *Holingshead's* Chronicles in the Reigns concern'd; all the Novels in *Italian*, from which our Author had borrow'd any of his Plots; such Parts of *Plutarch*, from which he had deriv'd any Parts of his *Greek* and *Roman* Story: *Chaucer* and *Spenser's* Works; all the Plays of *B. Jonson*, *Beaumont* and *Fletcher*, and above 800 old *English* Plays, to ascertain the obsolete and uncommon Phrases in him: Not to mention some Labour and Pains unpleasantly spent in the dry Task of consulting Etymological *Glossaries*. (1733: 1 lxvii–lxviii)

Within the space of a couple of decades from the debut of the first named editor of Shakespeare, the effort to rid the author's text of spurious readings had extended from a brief account of the author's life and experience to a systematic investigation of what the author may have read and of the evolution of the English language since his plays were first written.

Despite the staggering speed at which the principles and the methods informing the preparation of dramatic copy for the press changed at the beginning of the eighteenth century, the influence and the legacy of the anonymous annotators of Shakespeare on their eighteenth-century successors should not be underestimated. At least according to Edmond Malone's point of view, Rowe's edition marked no clear progression from the dubious practices of the anonymous annotators before 1709 to some of his predecessors' approach to the editing of Shakespeare's text in the early eighteenth century. Taking his distance from Johnson's belief that the three folio editions published after Shakespeare's First Folio only deviate from it 'by accident or negligence', Malone argues that

the second folio does indeed very frequently differ from the first by negligence or chance; but much more frequently by the editor's profound ignorance of our poet's phraseology and metre, in consequence of which there is scarce a page of the book which is not disfigured by the capricious alterations introduced by the person to whom the care of that impression was entrusted. (1790: 1 xix)

Unlike Johnson, Malone did not deny the intervention of an annotator in the preparation of the printer's copy underlying the Second Folio for the press, but concluded that the annotator's efforts were misguided and ultimately deleterious. What is worth stressing is that Malone's criticism against the annotator of the Second Folio is then directed at Alexander Pope:

This person in fact, whoever he was [re: the annotator of the Second Folio], and Mr. Pope, were the two great corrupters of our poet's text; and I have no doubt that if the arbitrary alterations introduced by these two editors were numbered, in the plays of which no quarto copies are extant, they would greatly exceed all the corruptions and errours of the press in the original and only authentick copy of those plays. (1790: I xix–xx)

Not only does Malone call both the annotator of the Second Folio and Pope 'editors', thus showing that he perceived no need to use different terminology to underscore crucial differences in their approaches to Shakespeare's text, but he also accused both agents of making 'arbitrary alterations'. Ironically, Pope had laid the same accusation at his predecessors' door: 'how many faults may have been unjustly laid to [Shakespeare's] account from arbitrary additions, expunctions, ... corruptions of innumerable passages by the ignorance, and wrong corrections of 'em again by the impertinence, of his first editors?' (1725: I xix) It is however worth stressing that, although Pope vouched to have 'discharg'd the dull duty of an editor ... with a religious abhorrence of all innovation, and without any indulgence to my private sense or conjecture', his edition has indeed become notorious for its 'arbitrary alterations'. Although Pope cast himself as an editor intent on restoring Shakespeare's text to its original integrity, he often emended without collating, or even consulting, the early editions. The rhetoric of Pope's preface is in keeping with the new model of proprietary editorship, but his approach to the preparation of Shakespeare's text for the press is, at least in this respect, still closer to the *modus operandi* associated with his anonymous predecessors.

Similarly, the editors of the first Cambridge edition of 1863–6 criticized Hanmer's edition for introducing changes in the text of Shakespeare on the basis of personal taste and judgement. Hanmer's description of his approach to the editing of Shakespeare would indeed apply to the annotating practices observed in F4 *Coriolanus* and the other early editions discussed in this book. Speaking of his role as editor in the third person, Hanmer explains that he 'hath made it the amusement of his leisure hours for many years past to look over [Shakespeare's] writings with a careful eye, to note the obscurities and absurdities introduced into the text, and according to the best of his judgement to restore the genuine sense and purity of it' (quoted in Clarks, Glover and Wright 1863–6: xxxii). Even the

terminology used by Hanmer smacks of a pre- rather than a post-1709
attitude towards the annotating of dramatic copy for the press: in the
restoration of the genuine sense and purity of Shakespeare's text 'he
proposed nothing to himself but his private satisfaction in making his
own copy as perfect as he could' (quoted in Clarks, Glover and Wright
1863–6: xxxii). Hanmer, as much as the anonymous annotators of
Shakespeare and early modern drama before 1709, used only 'his judgement' to make his copy as perfect as he could whenever a reading seemed
corrupt. His objective was to prepare a 'good' rather than a 'genuine'
edition of Shakespeare. When the Cambridge editors outlined Hanmer's
role as an editor of Shakespeare – 'a country gentleman of great ingenuity
and lively fancy, but with no knowledge of older literature, no taste for
research, and no ear for the rhythm of earlier English verse, amused his
leisure hours by scribbling down his own and his friends' guesses in Pope's
Shakespeare' (quoted in Clarks, Glover and Wright 1863–6: xxxii) – they
may well have been describing the 'ingenious and worthy Gentleman
[who] had taken the pains (or rather the pleasure) to read over' and to
annotate the first edition of Beaumont and Fletcher's *Comedies and
Tragedies*.

The criticism levelled against Pope and Hanmer by Malone and the
Cambridge editors signals a later point of departure from the conjectural
annotation of dramatic copy discussed in this book. Editors like Edward
Capell, George Steevens and especially Edmond Malone certainly did spell
out the need for editors to support their intervention by carrying out a full
investigation of the early editions. Recent scholars have disagreed as to
whether any of these editors actually managed to break away from the past
(de Grazia 1991; Jarvis 1995). However, their editions did mark a progression from a predominantly conjectural to a systematic and bibliographical
approach to the editing of Shakespeare. According to the Oxford editors,
the anonymity of seventeenth-century annotators of dramatic copy has
prevented a systematic survey of their contributions to the official editorial
tradition. 'Literary historians', they explain, 'usually regard Nicholas Rowe
as Shakespeare's first editor, because he is the first we can confidently name'
(Wells and Taylor 1987: 53). The similarities, rather than the differences, in
the approach to the early editions of Shakespeare's texts both before and
after 1709 may also be responsible for the silence surrounding the role of
early modern annotators of dramatic copy. The marginalization of editions
like F4, which are all too often dismissed as derivative, and therefore devoid
of any textual interest or value, may be due to the fact that they blur the line
between the nebulous pre-history and the official history of the editorial

tradition of Shakespeare. The impact that anonymous annotators had on the 'official' editorial tradition until at least as late as the 1790s does not only force us to admit, as Greg put it, that 'it is impossible to exclude judgement from editorial procedure' (1950–1: 26). Even more crucially, the practice of conjectural and anonymous preparation of dramatic copy for the press, including the printer's copies used to set up Shakespeare's early quartos and folios, forces us to reconsider what we mean when we refer to these editions as 'Shakespeare's texts'.

Conclusion

This book has established that the preparation of dramatic copy for the press prior to the rise of the 'official' editorial tradition of Shakespeare in 1709 involved the sporadic annotation of the source-text and was often carried out by non-authorial agents without reference to other textual witnesses. Some literary dramatists, including Samuel Daniel, Ben Jonson, John Marston and Philip Massinger, did tidy up their own plays for the press (Peters 2000: 29, 325n). However, as each chapter in this book has demonstrated, dramatic annotators of printed copy were often publishers or professional writers and gentlemen readers who supplied annotated copies to them. What earlier chapters have not emphasized enough is the fact that the process of 'perfecting' a play text did not stop with its transmission into print but extended to its readers.

Several addresses to the reader prefaced to early modern dramatic and non-dramatic books are genuine appeals to perfect the text. Sometimes authors themselves invite readers to correct not only printing house inaccuracies, but also their own mistakes. One good example is the address to the reader in the second edition of Thomas Lodge's translation of Seneca's works (STC 22214, 1620):

> GEntle Reader, I present thee once more with *Senecaes* Translation, if not so fully and exactly clensed from his former misprisions and errours, as I wish; yet I hope, in such sort examined and perused, that the iudicious Reader shall find lesse matter to except against; and the indifferent, better light to vnderstand him. My businesse being great, and my distractions many; the Authour being seriously succinct, and full of *Laconisme*; no wonder if in somthings my omissions may seeme such, as some whose iudgement is mounted aboue the Epicycle of Mercurie, will find matter enough to carpe at, though not to condemne ... If thou wilt Correct, bee considerate before thou attempt, lest in pretending to roote out one, thou commit many errors. (b1r 2–15, 22–4)

Despite the final note of caution, Lodge is happy for the reader to continue a process of revision and correction, which he had no time to complete before his copy went to press. Although early modern authors and their publishers are generally far readier to blame their printers than to take responsibility for 'literall' (or, typographical) and 'materiall' (or, conceptual) faults,[1] Lodge's example is far from unique. Nicholas Breton also devolved the correction of *The Mothers Blessing*, his 'little tract of morall discipline', to his judicious reader (STC 3669, 1602). Breton is however careful, like Lodge, to elicit his readers' collaboration as opposed to their harsh censure: 'yet if it please you to peruse it, I hope you will not vtterly disdaine it: such as it is, I leaue it to your discreete censures, and kinde corrections' (A4r 15–17).

Similar appeals are also common in dramatic publications from the period. Possibly ironic is the address in Samuel Harding's *Sicily and Naples* (STC 12757, 1640). The author of this address, identified only by the initials 'P. P.', apologizes to readers for submitting a fair copy to the printer, which leaves them little opportunity to display their skills as correctors: '[t]hou shalt pardon mee this onely fault, that I have hereby dull'd that praise, which thy selfe might'st have receiv'd in making a good play, since I have layd before thee so faire a copy to write by' (*2r 21–4). Although the register of this address is probably ironic, it does suggest that early modern readers often (and perhaps too often) corrected the printed text, and that they understood their intervention as an integral part of the collective effort of 'making a good play', 'good' meaning here textually correct, rather than generically more attractive or attuned to the readers' own theatrical and literary taste. The address 'To the Knowing Reader' in Robert Davenport's *King John and Matilda* (Wing D370, 1655A) probably makes a similar allusion to the readers' role as correctors, when it claims that 'A Good Reader, helps to make a Book' (A2r 2). Although the phrasing is generic enough to suggest different ways in which a reader can 'make (or unmake) a Book' – by granting it a fair response, by recommending it to other readers, or simply by buying it – it does not exclude the sense suggested by 'P. P.' in the earlier address, where readers share the editorial responsibility of ridding the text of 'literall' and 'material' mistakes with the other agents involved in its transmission into print. Far more explicit is the analogy drawn by Richard Hawkins, the publisher of the third quarto edition of Francis Beaumont and John Fletcher's *Philaster: Or, Love Lies a Bleeding* (STC 1683, 1628), between the readers' intervention as correctors of the text of this play and the craft of the goldsmith, who refines and improves the quality of the raw mineral: 'the best Poems of this kind', Hawkins observes, 'in the first presentation, resemble that

all-tempting Minerall newly digged up, the Actors being onely the labour-
ing Miners, but you [the readers] the skilfull Triers and Refiners' (A2v 3–7).
Thanks to the intervention of annotating readers, Hawkins adds, 'the first
Impression[, which] swarm'd with Errors, proou[ed] it selfe like pure
Gold, which the more it hath beene tried and refined, the better is
esteemed' (A2r 15, A2v 1–3).

　　Not all addresses invoking editorial intervention grant the reader such a
prominent role. In fact, readers of printed playbooks are often expected
to correct only typographical mistakes of little consequence, which may
easily be amended or even ignored. Indeed, according to Humphrey
Moseley '[f]or *literall Errours* committed by the Printer, 'tis the fashion to
aske pardon, and as much in fashion to take no notice of him that asks it'
(Beaumont and Fletcher, *Comedies and Tragedies*, WING B1581, 1647, A4v 1–2).
Similarly, John Marston refers to typographical mistakes as 'slight errors in
orthography [that] may bee as slightly or'epassed' (*The Malcontent*, STC 17479,
1604, A4r 17–19) and urges readers not to 'let some easily amended errors in the
Printing afflict thee since thy owne discourse will easily setvprightany [sic]
such vneuenness' (*Sophonisba*, STC 17488, 1606, G3v 37–9), 'setvprightany'
being either a genuine typographical accident or a premeditated instance of
typographical wit.

　　Good-humoured wit and ingenious invention are also the dominant
features in the short address prefaced to Thomas Dekker's *Satiromastix*
(STC 6521, 1602), where readers are invited to be tolerant and to gracefully
emend the typographical mistakes included in the errata list: '*Ad Lectorem*.
IN steed of the Trumpets sounding thrice, before the Play begin: it shall not
be amisse (for him that will read) first to beholde this short Comedy of
Errors, and where the greatest enter, to giue them in stead of a hisse, a
gentle correction' (A4v 1–5). Quite often, though, even typographical
errors leave early modern dramatic authors and their publishers feeling
nervous and at least potentially exposed to criticism. The note included
at the end of James Shirley's *The Bird in a Cage* (STC 22436, 1633), for
example, lists three substantive errors and then goes on to stress that 'many
other Errors, (though for the most part literall,)' the reader cannot 'with
safetie of [his] owne, interpret a defect in the Authors Iudgment' (K4r
8–10). Both the author and the reader are at fault, this address nervously
suggests, if they attach too much importance to typographical errors,
especially when readers blame them on the author. Similarly, John Ford
hopes that readers who think of themselves as being cultivated enough to
penetrate the meaning of his 'Sence' will also have the basic literary skills to

correct typographical mistakes in his edition of *'Tis Pity She's a Whore* (STC 11165, 1633):

The generall Commendation deserued by the Actors, in their Presentment of this Tragedy, may easily excuse such few faults, as are escaped in the Printing: A common charity may allow him the ability of spelling, whom a secure confidence assures that hee cannot ignorantly erre in the Application of Sence. (K4r 24–9)

Also instructive is the note appended to the errata list in Samuel Holland's *Don Zara del Fogo: A Mock-Romance* (Wing H2437, 1656), which includes a masque called *Venus and Adonis* in the third chapter of the third book. In this note to the reader, the author admits that faults escaped in the printing of his work threaten to impair the sense of his words: 'COurteous Reader I desire thee to mend severall litterall faults and points misplaced which doth sometime make the sence harsh' (P4r 2–4). Considering that the errata list highlights only one of the 'severall litterall faults' mentioned in the note, readers are presumably expected not only to emend what has already been detected and brought to their attention, but also to identify mistakes scattered across the volume.

What these addresses collectively show is that the early modern printed text was understood and treated as perfectible, and therefore never definitive. Readers were accordingly invited to contribute to its perfection by acting as graceful and patient correctors. Even recent scholars who regard the early modern printed text as fluid and unstable normally stop short of grasping the extent to which such instability was due to the fact that its perfection was regarded as an open-ended process. Stephen Orgel, for example, has interpreted specific printing practices as symptomatic of a *structural* instability in the early modern printed text:

The [Renaissance] book was a fluid text, not the final correct authorized version of the work. Renaissance printers incorporated proof corrections in the text while printing was in progress, and both corrected and uncorrected sheets were used in the final bound books. There was nothing in print technology requiring this (to us) odd system; had the printers wished to avoid it, it would only have been necessary to stop the press for the ten minutes or so it took to read through the proof sheet, make the corrections and then continue. But clearly the idea of a book embodying the final, perfected text was not a Renaissance one. (1999: 117)

While Orgel is right in stressing that 'the idea of a . . . *perfected* text was not a Renaissance one' (my emphasis), he overlooks the fact that instability stemmed primarily from a Renaissance understanding of the printed text as endlessly *perfectible*. Instability was not simply a side-effect of a peculiar printing practice which affected only one stage in the process of the text's transmission through the press. Instability also stemmed from the assumption that the author's working manuscript could and should be *perfected* for press and that each time the text was reprinted it could be and should be 'newly corrected and amended'. Peters comes closer to defining the type of instability that informs the early modern printed text when she describes it as 'ongoingly corrigible' (2000: 134). More specifically, I would add that the early modern period regarded printed playbooks not only as *perfectible* but also as the material repositories of collective rather than individual (or authorial) intentions, at least partly because the process of perfection extended to non-authorial agents *and* to the reading public.[2]

As E. A. J. Honigmann reminds us, 'every theory of transmission . . . has its own implications for editorial policy' (1997: 354). I would therefore like to conclude by pointing out how my findings about anonymous annotators of printed dramatic copy in the sixteenth and seventeenth centuries impact on current editorial pratices and on how contemporary editors think they should re-present early modern printed playbooks to the modern reader.

'WHAT'S IN A TEXT?': OR, 'EDITING AFTER THE END OF EDITING'

This final section of my book is named after an article by Paul Werstine (1996: 47–54). This article has helped me establish how my work on early modern annotators of dramatic copy for the press contributes to a wider poststructuralist movement, aimed at 'exposing and deconstructing the author Shakespeare, the word, and the work(s) – complete or otherwise – as metaphysical categories' (1996: 51). As Werstine explains, Pollard's optimistic assumption that 'for many of Shakespeare's plays, only the book's manufacture stood between the authorial manuscript and the present-day editor and reader' (1996: 50) led many mid- to late-twentieth-century textual scholars to carry out bibliographical work in order to identify and remove the influence of printing house agents. This work was in turn seen 'as preparatory to . . . an edition [which would] end all editions' because 'definitive and entirely objective' (1996: 50). Still according to Werstine, the revisionist movement initiated by a new generation of textual scholars in the 1980s did not depart from, but rather intensified, the New Bibliographical tendency to privilege the author function over the other agents involved in the process of transmission of an early modern text into print. In Werstine's own words, when the Oxford editors, Wells and Taylor, opted for versioning as their method of editing *King Lear*, they did so because they interpreted all but a handful of the variants between the 1608 and 1623 *Lear* texts as Shakespeare's; that is, they apparently believed that, out of a whole culture, only the author could make a difference in the play. (1996: 50–1)[3]

My theory that some textual variants in early modern printed playbooks may derive from an overlooked category of non-authorial agents could be regarded as an offshoot of the New Bibliographical programmatic desire to isolate and remove any spurious tampering accrued by the text during the process of its transmission into print. My analysis of variant editions of early modern printed playbooks certainly owes a great deal to the methods devised by the New Bibliography to identify the nature of the printer's copy underlying a printed text. However, I do not share the same degree of confidence displayed by earlier textual scholars in firmly ascribing textual variants to the intentions of a specific agent, or category of agents. As I explained in my Introduction, preparation of dramatic copy during the sixteenth and the seventeenth centuries seems to have been function- rather than agent-specific: several agents, in other words, including correcting authors and annotating readers, perfected the dramatic text as it was repeatedly committed to print. Some early modern annotators, mostly literary publishers and professional writers, can be identified either from signed paratextual materials, or, more tentatively, from distinctive patterns of textual variation in some early modern printed playbooks. However, the ultimate objective of this study is not to tease these elusive textual agents out of anonymity, but to reflect on the principles which informed the annotation of dramatic copy as a practice and the implications of such practice for contemporary editors.

In this respect, my work complements Honigmann's commitment to exploring the similarities in readings produced by another category of agents, namely scribal and authorial agents, when they transcribed a working manuscript into a fair copy to be used for theatrical, presentational or publication purposes. A suggestive change in Honigmann's attitude towards the indeterminacy of attribution of indifferent variants even in 'good' editions of Shakespeare's plays emerges over time, from the publication of *The Stability of Shakespeare's Text* in 1965 to his 1997 Arden edition of *Othello* (and its companion, *The Texts of 'Othello' and Shakespearian Revision*). Honigmann's increasingly pessimistic response to the indeterminacy of textual agency in early modern printed playbooks is symptomatic of wider changes in the field of Shakespeare textual studies and is therefore worth considering in detail.

Faced by the realization that local authorial revisions, or second thoughts, cannot always, if ever, be distinguished from scribal or even compositorial tampering, Honigmann displays a radically divided attitude to the editorial task, even when he writes about it as a textual scholar in *The Stability of Shakespeare's Text*. Only a few pages separate positive and encouraging mission statements – 'the editor must screw his courage to the sticking place and choose between each pair of variants' (1965: 168) – from despondent cautionary warnings – 'the editor will tamper as little as possible with his substantive texts, preferring to retain a doubtful reading rather than to emend, and recognising his inevitable limitation in finalising a play based on two arch texts' (1965: 170). The problematic issue of 'finalising a play based on two arch texts' leads to pragmatically (and syntactically) awkward compromises:

[Editors] must recognis[e] . . . that to attempt a feat left undone by Shakespeare, to finalise an unfinalised text, will create a version that never existed in the author's hand. At first this will seem a wrong-headed ambition. Reflect, *however*, that an editorial tradition of long standing (proceeding, *however*, from different assumptions) lends its authority to our search for the best possible synthetic text, and the suggestion loses most of its daring. (1965: 168, my emphasis)

There may be safety in numbers, as this passage suggests, but the lack of consensus within 'an editorial tradition of long standing' provides little reassurance to an editor intent on completing 'a feat left undone by Shakespeare' himself. It is hardly surprising that even editorial 'enterprises of great pitch', such as finalizing a play like Shakespeare's *Othello*, 'lose the name of action', when editors realize that hundreds of indifferent variants cannot be safely attributed to any of the individual agents involved in its transmission. The editorial despondency brought about by textual indeterminacy is however still relatively contained and the overall register of Honigmann's conclusions in *The Stability of Shakespeare's Text* is predominantly constructive:

It seems to me more realistic to grant the presence of an unknowable than to deny its existence because it happens to be inconvenient. How, then, can editors come to terms with the unknowable? A critical edition offering notes and collations ought, I think, to cite all variants in substantive texts that are not manifest misprints or nonsense . . . If *some* of the variants in a play derive from Shakespeare, *all* the variants in that play spring to life – in the sense that all of them deserve pondering as possible first or second shots . . . There is no end to the 'good' variants which then require open-minded reconsideration. (1965: 152, 110)

When Honigmann moved from textual scholarship to the front-line of copy-text editing, his willingness to 'screw his courage to the sticking point' waned, despite the growing amount of work that had in the meantime been carried out to identify scribal hands and their idiosyncrasies.[4] The exciting multiplicity of 'first' and 'second' thoughts which Honigmann had glimpsed at in 1965 gave way to the troubling challenge of sifting through the indifferent substantive variants preserved in the quarto and folio texts of *Othello*, what Honigmann tellingly refers to as 'an editorial witching brew' (1996: 144). Hence his admission that 'Arden 3, though far less committed to F as "copy-text" than previous editions, still prints scores – or perhaps hundreds – of F variants that are scribal or compositorial substitutions, not the words written by Shakespeare' (1997: 359). Honigmann's candid evaluation of the problems he faced while editing *Othello* is a testament to a widespread uneasiness towards copy-text editing among editors of Shakespeare and early modern drama at the turn of the twenty-first century.

Some editors have responded to the increasing realization of the inde-terminancy of textual agency and intentions in early modern printed playbooks by arguing that the contribution of authorial and non-authorial agents cannot, *and* should not, be disentangled. As David Scott Kastan has observed, the sociological approach championed, among others, by Don McKenzie and Jerome McGann, 'radically complicates, if not thoroughly undermines, the traditional basis of editing'. Still according to Kastan, 'the sociological focus . . . point[s] away from editing, toward the abandonment of edited texts in favor of facsimiles of the early printed editions, which supply a richer field of signifying material offering evidence of the histor-ical contingencies of their production' (1996: 35). Facsimile editions and the technology of hypertext have often been hailed as an alternative to copy-text editing because they 'reliev[e] an editor of the necessity to choose and reliev[e] the reader from having editorial choice imposed on her' (Werstine 1996: 52).

My work on early annotators of dramatic copy has identified a textual practice which was often carried out anonymously by a variety of agents and which therefore sharpens our sense of the indeterminacy of attribution of substantive readings instrinsic to the bibliographical make-up of early modern printed playbooks. The further realization that the perfection of dramatic copy was regarded as an ongoing process upsets the conflicting assumptions of what constitutes an authoritative text on both sides of the current theoretical divide between those who support and practice copy-text editing and the so called 'un-editors'. Both editorial practices rest on a fundamentally anachronistic understanding of the very nature of early modern printed playbooks. While copy-text editors value and strive to recover the author's first or second thoughts imperfectly reproduced by the printed text, the un-editors idealize the material integrity of the early playbooks by arguing in favour of their presentation to the modern reader in photographic facsimiles or digital images. Neither approach considers the possibility that the early modern printed text was understood as a process, as opposed to a finite and definitive state *anterior* or *immanent* to the material witness itself. Paradoxically, both copy-editors and un-editors understand early modern printed playbooks as static entities, either as imperfect manifestations of essential and unchanging lost originals, which can be recovered through an exercise in archeological bibliography, or as specific stages in the process of their transmission, frozen and abstracted by the seemingly unmediated nature of photographic facsimiles of specific material witnesses. The emphasis placed on authorial *and* non-authorial preparation of dramatic copy for the press and the projection of the perfecting task onto the text's very recipients, its readers, show that the text preserved in early modern printed playbooks was in fact regarded as positively fluid and always in the process of being perfected.

The realization that two of the main current editorial approaches to Shakespeare – copy-text editing and un-editing, or, author and text-centred fundamentalism[5] – run against an early modern understanding of printed playbooks as endlessly perfectible does not make these approaches ineffective. Given that the early modern agents involved in the transmission of dramatic texts regarded them as perfectible, it seems inappropriate to send them to their 'account, with all [their] imperfections on [their] head', as the un-editors do. However, members of the scholarly community who have no access to the early editions will benefit from the wider availability of facsimiles and digital images. Conversely, the fact that the agents involved in the early stages of Shakespeare's transmission into print valued a perfected text over an imperfect one, even when the latter happened to be closer to the author's working manuscript and the former had been emended by non-authorial annotators, does not mean that twenty-first century editors should do the same.

Like any other textual practice, editing is embedded within wider cultural and literary contexts, which affect the way in which editors feel they should re-present early modern printed playbooks to their readers.

However editors decide to carry out this task, a better understanding of how early modern printed playbooks were produced seems vitally important to ensure that readers are not misled into thinking that what they are offered are texts which reflect stable authorial or theatrical intentions. This book has accordingly focused on 'historicizing editorial method and terminology', one task, which according to Werstine, 'clamor[s] for attention from future Shakespeare editors' (1996: 53).

Notes

INTRODUCTION

1 *M. William Shak-speare: his true chronicle historie of the life and death of King Lear and his three daughters* (STC 22292: 1608), B2r 18.

2 The title of this opening section was inspired by Paul Werstine's 1996 article 'Editing After the End of Editing'; this article will be discussed in further detail in the conclusion.

3 The legacy of Jacob Tonson as the founder of a powerful publishing monopoly of Shakespeare's works was investigated by a group of scholars at the end of the 1960s and beginning of the 1970s (see, more specifically, Papali 1968, Geduld 1969, and Lynch 1971). More recently, scholarly efforts have focused on Jacob Tonson's own editorial activities (Bennett 1988 and Walsh 1997) and on the tradition established by the eighteenth-century literary editors who worked for the Tonson cartel (Mowat 1994, Seary 1990 and Jarvis 1995).

4 For an alternative account of the origin of the printer's copy underlying the First and the Second Quartos of *Romeo and Juliet*, see, most recently, Erne 2003: 220–30.

5 Extant examples of non-dramatic printer's copies are also discussed in Percy Simpson 1935: 46–109.

6 The first recorded use of the term 'publisher' to indicate 'one who puts a book into the world' dates back to 1654 (*OED* 2a). However, this term can reasonably be applied retrospectively to those sixteenth and seventeenth-century members of the Stationers' Company who acquired a text, often entered it in *The Stationers' Register* to secure their exclusive right to publish it, hired a printer, and then sold copies of the printed text wholesale to retailing booksellers. The three main roles played by early modern stationers – printer, publisher and bookseller – often overlapped: some publishers owned their own printing press and their printing houses sometimes included a shop. However, the decision to invest capital in acquiring a text and to arrange for its transmission into print was conceptually distinct from manufacturing a book and retailing it.

7 This edition is only known from a reprint included in *Kenilworth Illustrated* (1821). For further details, see Greg 1939–59, 168.

8 A similar phrase – 'the first originall' – is used in 'An aduertisement to the Reader' prefaced to *Of Ghostes and Spirites*, translated by R. H. (STC 15320, 1572) to describe a copy that 'was somewhat obscurely written' (quoted in Simpson 1935: 34).

9 Allusions to the circumstances under which copy for this play was secured suggest that the term 'printer' in this address refers to the publisher, that is, to the stationer who purchased the manuscript copy which would then be passed on to the printer. For further details on the early modern use of the term 'printer' to describe the stationer who was responsible for getting a manuscript printed, i.e. the 'publisher', see note 6 above.

10 For recent editors' views on the textual accuracy of the first quarto edition of Lyly's *Endymion*, see chapter 5, page 162.

11 As chapter 5 will make clear, the authorship of this dedicatory epistle is a matter of contention (for further details see page 159); however, uncertainty about the authorship of this epistle does not affect my reading of the allusion to the perfection of the printer's copy included in it.

12 This second address to the reader ('To the Reader' A2r–A3v), which refers explicitly to *The Sad One: A Tragedy* as 'this Dramatick Piece of Sir *John Suckling*', often precedes the general address with which Moseley obviously intended to introduce the whole collection ('The Stationer to the Reader', A2r–A3v).

13 Jeffrey Masten is one of the scholars who have charted the rise of singular authorship during the early modern period. Interestingly, Masten regards notable publishing ventures, including Jonson's and Shakespeare's Folios, as symptomatic of a new desire for singular authorship, while stressing that 'it is important not to see the construction of dramatic authorship in the early seventeenth century as anything resembling a *fait accompli*' (1997: 120). Similarly, Julie Stone Peters has pointed out that 'even while title pages continued to represent multiple authorship and multiple authority ... the imperatives of print (the authorial authentication readers seemed to demand and the authorial proprietorship the needs of commerce seemed to require) created a pressure towards individuating authorship' (2000: 137). Peters agrees with Masten in specifying that 'the representation of singular authorship and theatrical collaboration in print continued to be in flux throughout the seventeenth century' (2000: 138).

14 The assumption that the early Quarto and Folio editions of Shakespeare simply deteriorated as they were re-set from their immediate predecessor dates at least as far back as the eighteenth-century editor, Lewis Theobald. In the preface to his edition of 1733, Theobald claimed that 'for nearly a century, his Works were republish'd from the faulty Copies without the assistance of an intelligent Editor' (I xxxix). Samuel Johnson similarly remarked that 'whoever has any of the folios has all, excepting those diversities which mere reiteration of editions will produce' (1765: I DIV 8–12). This negative assessment of the quality of the texts preserved in the early editions of Shakespeare was perpetuated by the Cambridge Shakespeare editors in the nineteenth century: 'when the First Folio is corrupt', they explain, 'we have allowed some authority to the emendation of F2 above subsequent conjecture, and secondarily to F3 and F4; but a reference to our notes will show that the authority even of F2 in correcting is very small' (Clark, Glover and Wright 1863–6: I xi). Divergent views started to emerge at the beginning of the twentieth century. For further details, see chapter 6, pp. 180–1.

15 The addition and the alteration of stage directions in this section of the play
   seem connected to the omission of what Robert Kean Turner regards as 'signs
   of revision during composition' in the First Folio text of 1647 (Bowers 1966–96:
   VI, 360). In the First Folio text Valerio speaks the same line twice ('And when
   you please, and how, allay my miseries'), Frederick enters eight lines before he
   speaks, and there is no entry direction for Sorano, the addressee of Frederick's
   opening question ('Hast thou been with him?'). According to Turner, 'Fletcher
   at first intended to conclude III.ii with the initial occurrence of the [repeated]
   line, and to begin III.iii with Frederick alone. This proving unsatisfactory for
   some reason, Fletcher decided to bring Sorano as well into the opening of III.iii.
   As Sorano, however, had exited from III.ii only at line 118, the new scheme
   required that Valerio's speech should be lengthened.' (Bowers 1966–96: VI, 362)
   Turner suggests one possible solution: 'the first occurrence of III.ii.127 and *Enter
   Frederick* should have never been cancelled' (Bowers 1966–96: VI, 362). The
   alternative offered by the text of the Second Folio may not be as acceptable, but
   it shows that the annotator was aware of a local anomaly and that he introduced
   a coherent group of changes in order to resolve it, by directing Sorano to exit at
   III.ii.118 (this direction is endorsed by Turner), by allowing Valerio to speak
   only the first line of his speech as it appears in the First Folio text and to exit at
   III.ii.119, and by having Frederick and Sorano enter together at III.iii.o.I.

16 Even when Moxon suggests that a printing house corrector should restore the
   author's meaning, he does so in relation to misspellings due to the author's
   poor knowledge of foreign languages: 'A *Correcter* should (besides the *English*
   tongue) be well skilled in Languages, because sometimes authors have perhaps
   no more skills than the bare knowledge of the Words and Pronunciations, so
   that the Orthography (if the *Correcter* haue no knowledge of the Language)
   may not only be false to its Native Pronunciation, but the Words altered into
   other words by a little wrong Spelling, and consequently the sense made
   ridiculous, the purpose of it controvertible, and the meaning of the Author
   irretrievably lost to all that shall read it in After times' (1958: 246–7).

17 The manuscript corrections on the outer forme of sheet B are also discussed in
   Simpson 1935: 79–80, Ferguson 1968: 84–5, and Craven 1974: 368–9. Simpson
   (1935) provides several other examples of extant proof-sheets preserving printer's
   corrections of mis-spellings, punctuation and turned letters. For an annotated
   list of extant proof-sheets, see also Moore 1992: 65–86.

18 Baskerville and Thomson are also discussed in chapter 5, p. 140.

19 'Lis: to him selfe | For all this laughter | I lyke not this' (H4v, left margin, opposite
   lines 32–5); 'Lis: to the King | sʳ, as you loue goodness | or your selfe, let me | haue
   halfe an hours free | & priuat discourse with | you, before you goe to Bed. Kin:
   I will.' (11r, right margin, opposite lines 6–11). Percy Simpson rightly interpreted
   these two additional speeches as a critical response to two pivotal scenes, where the
   'low level of intelligence in Court circles . . ., when the issue involved was something
   so serious as the murder of a king', clearly alarmed the royal reader (1935–7: 261).

20 By 'correcting authors' I mean early modern playwrights who emended an
   existing (printed or manuscript) copy of a play text, rather than 'transcribing

authors', whose habits were closely studied, among others, by Honigmann 1965.

21 See, for example, *The Bondman*, L4r 36, *The Renegado*, K4v 2 and L2v 9, and *The Roman Actor*, B4r 36. For full lists of corrections in these plays see Greg 1924–25: 65–8.

22 *The Roman Actor*, B3v 11, listed in Greg 1924–25: 68.

23 For a full list of Massinger's corrections in the dialogue, see Greg 1923–24: 207–18 and Greg 1924–25: 59–91.

24 For a fuller discussion of the changes introduced by Middleton as he transcribed the text of *A Game at Chess*, see Honigmann 1965: 51–2, 59–62, and 64.

25 See also Howard-Hill 1990b: ix. It is also worth stressing that when Middleton prepared the printer's copy for the first quarto edition of *A Game at Chess*, which was printed the following year, he seems to have paid more attention to its accuracy: still according to Trevor Howard-Hill, 'the text shows 646 readings which are found in no other witness' and although 'close analysis might show that some of them could be assigned to the compositors ..., there is a substantial residue which any editor would hesitate to relegate to compositorial inefficiency or highhandedness' (1987: 314).

26 Dr Johnson, for example, believed that Shakespeare's works were 'printed ... without the concurrence of the author, without the consent of the proprietor, from compilations made by chance or by stealth out of the separate parts written for the theatre' (1923: 3).

27 See, for example, Patterson 1968 and Rose 1993. A classic and often quoted example of the strained negotiations between authors and publishers in the early modern period is George Sandys' 1635 petition for a patent to publish his *Paraphrase Upon the Psalmes*, where he accuses stationers who 'ingrosse to themselves the whole profit of other mens Labours' (Bodleian MS Bankes 11/62 dated 1635, printed in Greg 1967: 321). Also well known is George Wither's *The Schollers Purgatory, Discovered in the Stationers Common-wealth* (STC 25919, 1624), an outspoken appeal to protect his patent for *The Hymnes and Songs of the Church* (STC 25908 1623), where Wither pitches the rules and regulations of the Stationers' Company against the authority of 'the lawes of nature', according to which an author should be entitled to enjoy 'the benefit' of his own labour (A3r 14–15).

28 Pollard himself revisited the views he had expressed in 1909, when he focused specifically on the issue of literary piracy in his *Shakespeare's Fight with the Pirates* (1917). Instead of arguing that early modern English publishers would not infringe the natural right of authors to benefit from the publication of their own work, Pollard now claimed that they could not, given the protection afforded to playwrights like Shakespeare by his royal patrons: 'That a company with the Lord Chamberlain or the Lord High Admiral as its protector should have submitted to any systematic robbery is in the highest degree unlikely. On the other hand, the hostility of the City and occasional trouble at Court rendered the position of the players always more or less precarious, and to trouble a great

lord over a small matter when they might need his help in a much more important one would not have been wise. Hence we need not be surprised if we find a company submitting to occasional loss rather than trouble their protector, as long as the loss does not become too frequent' (37–8). Pollard ultimately proposed what he describes as a 'more realistic picture than that which represents men like Burby, Roberts, and Blount as playing the pirates' game, and the servants of the Lord Chamberlain and of the King Majesty himself as sitting down tamely under their attacks' (54), by arguing that the occasional collaboration between early modern theatrical companies and the publishers who were approached to publish plays from their repertoires co-existed alongside occasionally successful acts of literary piracy.

29　Peter Blayney responded to Farmer and Lesser's article in the same issue of *Shakespeare Quarterly* (2005: 33–50). In turn, Farmer and Lesser's rejoinder was published in the following issue of *Shakespeare Quarterly* (2005a: 206–13).

30　See, for example, Patterson 1984.

31　Both Margreta de Grazia and Leah Marcus identify bibliographical strategies that led to the gradual effacement of the various agents involved in the making of the First Folio. According to de Grazia, for example, '[t]he 1623 preliminaries work to assign the plays a common lineage: a common origin in a single parent and a shared history of production that includes patrons, readers, printers, theatrical company, audiences, and praising poets ... "Shakespeare" was the name that guaranteed the consanguinity and therefore the coherence of what might otherwise have been no more than a miscellany ... The preliminaries translated the personal patronymic into a bibliographical rubric under which the heterogeneous printed and scripted textual pieces gathered by Heminge and Condell coalesced. The diverse functions that led to the production of the Folio ... collapsed into that one name. As a bibliographical rubric rather than a proper name, "Shakespeare" functioned synecdochally, the authorial part standing for the collective whole of production'. For further details see de Grazia 1991: 39. Similarly, Marcus has noted how 'the First Folio suppresses particular data about the plays that might undermine the appeal to universality. The quarto editions had regularly included information about staging on the title page, as though to assure buyers that the play text they were about to read would bring them as close as possible to the experience of attending a performance ... This reticence can be understood in terms of the First Folio's elevation of Shakespeare and his work' (1988: 25).

1 ENGLISH HUMANISM AND THE PUBLICATION OF EARLY TUDOR DRAMA

1　'The early Tudor Group of Playwrights', the first chapter in Boas 1933, is a rare exception. Although Boas points out that 'Tudor drama begins as almost a family affair, with the genial, finely-tempered spirit of More presiding over it' (1933: 3), he does not explore the implications of the Rastells' association with

More's humanist circle in relation to the printing and publication of early English interludes.

2 As Rudolf Hirsch reminds us, 'humanism did not remain the monopoly of an elite. In the vernacular it reached a broad spectrum of readers, a development which Erich Auerbach aptly called "vulgär-humanismus"' (1978: 58). The phrase 'vulgär-humanismus' coined by Auerbach is particularly useful because it suggests that there were important parallelisms between classical textual scholarship and the humanist movement which originated and developed on the Continent, on the one hand, and English humanism and print culture, on the other. Conversely, the opposite view according to which humanism was strictly limited to the re-discovery of the classics ignores such parallelism. See, for example, Wilson 1969.

3 Alan Nelson usefully reports that 'our discovery that Medwall was with Morton by 1490 makes it a virtual certainty that Medwall would have become acquainted with Thomas More in 1491–2, when at the age of fourteen, More lived as a page in Morton's household' (1980: 17). The *Oxford Dictionary of National Biography* dates More's admission to Morton's household even earlier, around 1489.

4 Some textual scholars believe that *Andria* was in fact printed in Paris. See, for example, Axton 1979: 16.

5 See, for example, Mowat 1997 and Erne 2003.

6 For more details, see Hirsch 1978.

7 For more details, see, for example, Weiss 1964: 23–7 and 43–44.

8 See, for example, Trapp 1991: 6, 52, and 54, and Surtz and Hexter 1965: lxxi.

9 See also, Allen 1913–15: 297–321.

10 For more details on the analogy between the textual challenges faced by an editor and Hercules's labours, see Jardine 1993: 72–3.

11 In the address 'To the Reader' in *Novum instrumentum* (1515), Erasmus, for example, explains that 'if differences between the copies or alternative punctuations or simply the ambiguity of the language give rise to several meanings, I laid them open in such a way as to show which seemed to me more acceptable, leaving the final decision to the reader' (Mynors and Thomson 1976: 200, lines 58–62).

12 The five faults are listed as follows: 76, I, vii: the fault, 'spyrituall man/ but'; the correction, 'spyrytuall man to my knowelege/ but'. 76, I, xv: the fault, 'this of'; the correction, 'this daye of'. 95, I, xiii: the fault, 'after holy'; the correction, 'after this holy'. 162, I, xviii: the fault, 'teache'; the correction, 'do and teache'. 219, II, iii: the fault, 'many wyll'; the correction, 'many a man wyll' (Gg3r 19–22, Gg3r 26, Gg3r 27, Gg3v 5).

13 See, for example, his 'Introduction' in Johnson 1765 and Johnson 1923: esp. 3–4.

14 Howard B. Norland, among others, establishes such a link, by pointing out that 'Erasmus made ancient Greek and Roman playwrights the cornerstone of his program of study, which he sent to Colet for his newly established St Paul's School' (1995: 90). Similarly Greg Walker observes that '[a]s humanist teaching methods found their way into the curricula of the English Universities and

schools, the plays of Plautus, Seneca, and particularly Terence began to find favour as set texts. Terence was taught at Cambridge from 1502 and at Oxford from some point after 1505' (1998: 10).

15 See, for example, Bevington 1968, and, more recently, Westfall 1990: esp. 180–99, Norlan 1995: esp. 111–60, and Johnston 2004: 430–47.

16 Two other early owners sign this copy of *Fulgens and Lucrece*: 'P.D.' underneath the woodcut on the title page and 'Mr. Ashborne' on the final page after the colophon.

17 Unusually the annotator introduces superfluous speech prefixes on B1v, but they may have been added by a different hand.

18 There are a few notable exceptions. One of these is a direction in *The Play of the Weather* which prompts the entrance of a boy, 'the lest that can play' (Robinson 1987: line 1024; see also list of actors on the title page).

19 In *The Play of the Weather* Jupiter speaks in rhyme royal stanzas, whereas the human characters speak mostly in loose couplets. In *The Play of Love*, the main characters – 'A man a lover not beloved', 'A woman beloued not louyng' and 'A man a louer not beloued' – also use regular verse, until the vice – 'nother louer not beloued' – comes in and disrupts it.

20 See, for example, Erne 2003 and Loewenstein 2002.

21 Earlier scholars who anticipated Norland's views include, among others, Baldwin 1944: 1 116 and Jones 1977: 13.

2 ENGLISH HUMANISM AND THE PUBLICATION OF LATE TUDOR DRAMA

1 Alexandra F. Johnston has traced the decline of native dramatic traditions back to the 1520s and 1530s, when 'Cromwell and Bale took the dramatic discourse out of the Court and into the public domain, deliberately using the popular forms of civic and parish drama to attack the hierarchy of the Roman Church' (2004: 435). By the 1540s, even official Protestant drama was substantially curbed. David Bevington, for example, reports that 'after ... 1540, Henry saw no more Protestant drama. In fact, he saw little drama at all, turning instead to sumptuous reveling as a respite from official cares and poor health. From 1540 to 1546, the court enjoyed sixteen masques and perhaps one or two plays.' Bevington adds that 'the sole extant morality fragment of the period, dramatizing *The Four Cardinal Virtues and Vices Contrary to Them* (printed ca. 1541–1547), pointedly warns against those who climb too high ... [and] religious arguments are notably absent'. Overall, during the last few years of Henry's reign, still in Bevington's words, 'the government suppressed reformed polemicism as it had Catholic cycles' (1968: 105–6).

2 Focusing on civic and parish drama, Johnston points out that 'with the accession of the boy Edward VI and his Protestant uncles the established pattern of drama and ceremony began to crumble as the traditions of religious drama and ritual were attacked for their Catholicism'. Johnston also observes that

although 'with the accession of Mary, in July 1553, many of the annual community celebrations were revived with enthusiasm ... much of [the] accustomed activity in the countryside ... was irretrievably lost and continued to be lost under her sister' (2004: 436–7). Dramatic activities more generally continued to be strictly monitored under Edward VI. As Bevington explains, 'the new government repealed the Act of 1543 regulating "interpretation of Scriptures" ... [and] the result was predictably explosive. Ultimate return of control was necessary for public peace: in 1549 all plays were banned for a period of two months, and in 1551 a government proclamation required licensing of all professional troupes of actors, even in the house of their patron' (1968: 106). Although Catholic cycles were revived under Mary, her government issued legislation against seditious and factional drama soon after her accession and continued to tighten the strict control ushered in during the last years of Henry's reign and reinforced under Edward (Bevington 1968: 114–15).

3   *The Chief Promises of God* (STC 1305, 1547?), *The Temptation of Christ* (STC 1279, 1547?) and *The Three Laws* (STC 1278, 1548?) were probably printed at Wesel by Dirik van der Straten (Greg 1939–59: 98–9).

4   While Tottell and Berthelet focused on classical drama by issuing translations of *Troas* (STC 22227) and *Thyestes* (STC 22226) respectively in 1559 and 1560, William Copland printed most of the English interludes which survive from the early Elizabethan period. See, for example, *Jack Juggler* (STC 14837, 1562?) and the second edition of *Impatient Poverty* (STC 14113, 1561?).

5   David Bevington, among others, believes that 'Queen Elizabeth handled the political drama of her early reign with a finesse that baffled both critics and admirers' (1968: 127).

6   For more details, see Richardson 1999: 96. Among the most well known mid-sixteenth-century editions of Italian drama edited by Dolce and by Ruscelli, see *Il Negromante comedia di m. Lodouico Ariosto, tratta dallo esemplare di man propria dell'Autore. In Vinegia: appresso Gabriel Giolito de Ferrari, e fratelli, 1551* [dedicatory epistle signed by Lodovico Dolce, A2r–A2v]; *La mandragola comedia di Niccolo Macchiavelli fiorentino. Nuouamente riueduta, & ricorretta per Girolamo Ruscelli* (Venetia: Plinio Pietrasanta, 1554); *Delle comedie elette nuouamente raccolte insieme, con le correttioni, et annotationi di Girolamo Ruscelli, libro primo. Nel quale si contengono l'infrascritte comedie, La Calandra del cardinal Bibiena. La Mandragola del Machiavello. Il Sacrificio, et gli inganni degl'Intronati, L'Alessandro, et L'Amor costante del Piccolomini* (Venetia: Gabriele Giolito, 1553).

7   The male gendering of the text in Webbe's dedication to Wilmot is peculiar and worth pointing out, since, as Wendy Wall has observed, early modern writers generally 'figured books as unruly women (malcontented, painted, and beautified) who necessarily relied on the care and supervision of their publishing authors' (1993: 67). Webbe's reference to the text of *Tancred and Gismund* as male is especially remarkable since, as Wall herself reports, Wilmot's address to 'the Gentlemen Students of the Inner Temple' opts for the more familiar association of the printed text with 'his beloved mistress whom he

reluctantly displays in her wanton (painted) form to the print audience "abroad"' (1993: 66).

8 'corretta di nuovo et ristampata'

9 'di nvovo con somma diligenza corretta, e ristampata'

10 'di nvovo ristampata e tratta dal svo primo esemplare'

11 'Et così uolendomi far da un capo à cauar come delle tenebre molti libri, che per poca cura ò troppa auidità del guadagno sono fin qui stati pessimamēte trattati da molti di coloro che gli sono uenuti dando fuori, ho tolto da principio à ridurre in volume i Comici, et son uenuto scegliēdo i buoni; et nel metterlè prima ò poi, ho seruato l'ordine de' tempi ne' quali essi hanno scritto. Onde potranno hora esser sicuramente letti dagli studiosi della nostra Lingua, & con le tante scorrettioni, nelle quali erano immerse dall'un capo all'altro, non offenderanno il giudicio & l'orecchie, ò gli occhi di chi l'ode ò legge. Et per maggior sodisfattione de gli studiosi vi ho fatte in fine alcune mie brieui annotationi, per dichiaratione di qualche luogo che n'ha bisogno, & per auuertimento d'alcune regole per quei che potesser prenderui errore, ò volessero cauillarui sopra, & riprenderne gli Autori.'

12 Representative of the scholarly standards of Ruscelli's annotations is a note added to elucidate the following verse – '*Ancorche faccia Esergiere à colui, / Che può portar miglior mantel di lui*' – in Machiavelli's *La Mandragola*: 'This verse reads the same, that is "Esergiere" as one word with capital "E", in our edition as in earlier ones printed in Rome, Venice, and Florence. In the last edition printed in Florence "Esergiere" is spelt "è sergiere", starting with a small and stressed "è". Since neither solution seems right, I have decided to leave it unaltered and to add this note to explain what the verse means. "To act like Sir Geri" is a vulgar proverb which in Florence means, as we would put it in the rest of Italy, "to attend, to serve, to follow as a servant does to his master"' (M4v 17–28, M5r 1–7). 'Questo luogo in tutti gli stampati così in Roma, come in Venetia & in Fiorenza da già molti anni, sta così come noi l'habbiamo lasciato, cioè Esergiere tutto una parola & con la E grande in principio. In quella che ultimamēte è stāpata in Fiorenza stà è sergiere, con la è picciola, & separata, & con l'accento graue sopra. Che ueramente niuno de' detti modi non sta bene, ma à me è paruto di lasciarla secondo che hanno i più, perche in ambedue i modi sta male, & farui sopra questa poca annotatione, per dichiarare che il luogo ueramente ha da dire Ancorche faccia il ser Geri à colui &c. perciocbe fare il ser Geri in quell di Fiorenza quantunque non sia però molto trito prouerbio, uuol dire quello che più communemēte in Italia diciamo corteggiare, ò più tosto fare il seruitore, & andare appresso ò dietro, come seruitore al patrone'.

13 '& per questo uedendosi che i suoi discorsi, & molte di quell'altre cose che furono stampate in Roma doppo la morte sua, sono in moltissime cose scorrette di lingua, non diremo che fusse perche egli non la sapesse, ma perche quegli che le fecero stampare & corressero, le guastassero, & scorreggessero in quella guisa; ò perche il trascriuere porta sempre errori, quando non ui si ha molta cura, & così lo stampare; ò ancor più tosto perche quei che n'hebber cura, non sapēdo essi la lingua, et trouando in quel libro alcune uoci & modi

diuersi dalla lingua che essi hauean per buona, li tenessero per corrotti, & li facessero parlare nel lenguaggio loro, poi che l'haueuā sotto, & poteuano senza gabbia farli apparare; ò proferire à lor modo'.

14 Thomas L. Berger, in conversation.

15 For more details, see Baker (1939: 24–5).

16 There is little agreement among editors and textual scholars about the significance of the corrections introduced in Day's edition of 1571. Greg, for example, downplays it: 'the obvious errors [in the first edition] are few, and the textual differences between the two editions neither frequent nor important, the only notable change in [the second edition] being the omission, possibly on political grounds, of eight lines in V.i' (1939–59: 115). Irby B. Cauthen, on the other hand, regards the variants between the first [Q1] and the second [Q2] edition as symptomatic of careful and painstaking preparation of copy: 'There are some one hundred and eighty substantive changes made in Q1 readings for Q2. But Q2 retains at least five of Q1's errors and introduces some nine manifest errors of its own. Moreover, Q2 omits an eight-line passage, perhaps for political reasons. . . . The scribe that prepared the copy-text for John Day, even though he was correcting the corrupt Q1, moved slowly and carefully in his duties. He restored omitted words and corrected evident misreadings; he regularized the meter and substituted words and phrases that, in context, seem to be superior to the Q1 readings' (1970: xxix–xxx).

17 For a discussion of the gendering of the first edition of *Gorboduc* in the paratext prefaced to John Day's reprint, see Wall 1993: 182–4.

18 For further details about Gascoigne's commitment to carrying out a thorough revision and correction of *A Hundreth Sundrie Flowers* (STC 11635) when he personally prepared the printer's copy for *The Posies of George Gascoigne esquire. Corrected, and augmented* (STC 11636), see Kerrigan 2001: 119–25.

19 George Whetstone's *A Remembraunce of . . . Thomas Late Erle of Sussex* was printed by Wolfe and Jones in 1583 (STC 25344); R[ichard] R[obinson]'s *The Auncient Order . . . of Prince Arthure* was printed by Jones for Wolfe also in 1583 (STC 800). From 1583 to 1586–7, Wolfe printed most of the books he published. Their last collaboration took place in 1588, when Wolfe printed a ballad for Jones (STC 14067).

20 See, for example, Hoppe 1933: 241–89, Huffman 1988, and Melnikoff 2001: 153–84.

21 Bruno's books are: *La Cena delle Ceneri* (STC 3935, 1584); *De la Causa, Principio et Uno* (STC 3936, 1584); *De l'Infinito Vniverso et Mondi* (STC 3938, 1584); *Spaccio della Bestia Trionfante* (STC 3940, 1584); *De gl'Heroici Furori* (STC 3937, 1585); and *Cabala del Cauallo Pegaseo* (STC 3934, 1585). For more details, see Bassi 1997: 437–58 and Ciliberto and Mann 1997.

22 For a full list, see Lievsay 1969: 24–8.

23 *La historia e oratione di Santo Stefano Promartire* and *Historia et vita di Santo Bernardino* were first published separately in 1576 and then included in *Il terzo libro di feste, rappresentazioni, et comedie spirituali*, a collection published by the Giunti in Florence in 1578.

24 'l'occasione d'vn giouane di questa Città venuto di nuouo d'Italia, ou'ha con molta industria appreso l'arte de lo Stampare' (A2v 17–20).

25 These books include three Italian works gathered into two volumes – the translation of Mendoza, *Dell'Historia della China* (1587: STC 12004) and Guarini's *Il Pastor Fido* and Tasso's *Aminta* (1591: 12414) – four Latin works – Giambattista della Porta, *De furtivis litterarum notis, vulgo de ziferis* (1591: STC 20118), Giulio Cesare Stella, *Columbeidos* (1585: STC 23246), Scipione Gentili's translation of Torquato Tasso's first book of his *Gerusalemme Liberata* (1584: STC 23700) and a second, augmented edition (1584: STC 23701) – and one English work – William Cecil, First Lord of Burleigh, *Execution of Justice in England* (1584: STC 4907).

26 Earlier scholars identified Petruccio Ubaldini as Wolfe's in-house editorial assistant. See, for example, Giordano-Orsini 1937. Huffman endorses this earlier theory (1988: 17), but fails to consider Ottolenghi's alternative hypothesis, which is by now more widely accepted.

27 'auuenendo spesso, che le cose interpretate, & notate da diuersa penna, sono anche diuersamente intese dalla intention del primo loro autore' (A4r 12–15).

28 '[P]er ver dirti, con tutta la mia sollecitudine, & spesa nő mi pare d'hauere del tutto ottenuto l'honesto mio desiderio, nő hauendo io potuto (auenga che ci habbia impiegato l'opera di molti amici miei) trouare il testo composto & scritto di mano dell'autore: ma ben trouai quello stampato in ottauo da figliuoli d'Aldo in Vinegia nel 1546, & quello duodecimo del Giolito nel 1550' (A3v 3–11).

29 'L'aueduto, & discreto lettore ammendera da se gli altri minori errori, e questi ancora, perdonandogli a compositori, i quali per essere eglino Siciliani, & per non saper la fauella toscana, con tutta la loro diligenza non gli hanno potuti euitare.'

30 '[M]a ben ti dico, . . . che tu ti volessi prendere la fatica di conferirgli insieme, che trouaresti il mio liberato d'alcuni altri errori, che . . . perauentura non ti parerebbono cosi leggeri' (A4r 3–8).

31 On B1v, for example, the verb 'contengono' in Giolito's 1550 edition (A1v 26) is replaced by 'contengano' (B1v 9); two further verbs in the subjunctive in Giolito's 1550 edition – 'ricorrino' (A1v 16) and 'possino' (A2r 2) – are normalized into 'ricorrano' (B1v 2) and 'possano' (B1v 19).

32 Giolito's 'COloro, che leggeranno . . . non si meruiglierà, che tanta uirtu si sia per piu secoli mantenuta in quella città . . .' (A2r lines 13–17) is emended in Wolfe's edition to read 'Coloro, che leggeranno . . . non si marauiglieranno, che tanta virtu si sia/ per piu secoli mantentuta in quella città . . .' (B1v 28–31).

33 For more details, see Huffman 1988: 4.

34 '[H]oggi vi presento di loro una buona parte . . . da me ridotte ne la maniera, ch'egli le compose, e ne la medesima maniera, ch'egli haueua determinato di farle la prima volta stampare, s'altri (contra sua voglia) non l'hauessero prima di lui date per mezzo de la stampa in luce assai male acconcie' (A2r 14–21).

35 '[C]osi hoggi incominciamo a darti la presente in molti luoghi ammendata, & da noi con ogni diligenza ristampata'.

36 Giolito 1550: 'Ruffo' (A1v 38); Giolito 1554: 'Ruffo' (A1v 39); Wolfe 1587: 'Ruffino' (A8r 14).

37 Giolito 1550: 'ruine' (A2v 6); Giolito 1554: 'ruine' (A2r 26); Wolfe 1587: 'rouine' (A2v 2). Also, Giolito 1550: 'ruina' (A4v 18); Giolito 1554: 'ruina' (A4v 18); Wolfe 1587: 'rouina' (A4v 25).

38 Not only does Wolfe 1587 introduce conventional contractions correctly, such as, Giolito 1550: 'spen/ti' (C1ov 12–3); Giolito 1554: 'spen/ti' (C1ov 13–14); Wolfe 1587: 'spêti' (D3r 16), but it also deploys less conventional and grammatically correct contractions, such as Giolito 1550: 'male uso' (C11r 2); Giolito 1554: 'male uso' (C11r 2); Wolfe 1587: 'mal'vso' (D3v 10).

39 Punctuation is normalized throughout. Besides, if the following variant is likely to indicate an oversight on the compositor's part – Giolito 1550: 'è posta' (C11v 7); Giolito 1554: 'è posta' (C11v 7); Wolfe 1587: 'e posta' (D3v 16) – an earlier variant – Giolito 1550: 'e diuidersi' (A6r 19); Giolito 1554: 'e diuidersi' (A1r 17–18); Wolfe 1587: 'è diuidersi' (A7r 23) – can only be a conscious correction, presumably introduced by the annotator of the printer's copy, as opposed to the English compositor.

40 The right date in Roman numbers, 'MCCCCXXXIIII', occurs no fewer than four times in the same paragraph (Giolito 1550: A5v line 14, line 23, line 27, line 28; Giolito 1554: A5v lines 15–16, line 25, line 29, line 31; Wolfe A5v line 28, A6r lines 4–5, line 9, line 11).

41 See, for example, Giolito 1550: 'vedessi, ch'io fusse' (A2v 18); Giolito 1554: 'vedessi, ch'io fusse' (A2v 12); Wolfe 1587: 'vedesse, ch'io fussi' (A2v 17).

42 'Il Correttore al benigno Lettore': 'Laonde mi son determinato di raccogliergli qui tutti, non riguardando alla vana opinione, che alcuni hanno, che lo stampare gli errori, impedisca la vendita de libri accioche se ad altri venisse voglia di far ristampare queste Comedie, lo passa [sic] perfettamente fare.' ([Pp4v] 19–23)

43 'L'essermi (Benigno lettore) auenuto, nella fine della stampa di queste belle Comedie, quello, che se cosi nel principio fosse auenuto m'hauerebbe portato grandissimo giouamento, e stata la principale cagione, che ci sieno scorsi tanti errori, cioe, se hauessi allhora hauuti i testi perfetti, come dal principio del terzo atto di questa ultima in qua ho hauuti . . .' ([Pp4v] 1–6).

44 In this address Wolfe explains that he decided to publish Machiavelli's *Lasino doro . . . con tutte le sue altre operette* when he heard that 'the good printer Antoniello de gli Antonielli from Palermo [Wolfe himself] had died without fulfilling the promise he had made to [his readers] in the prefatory matter included in his editions of *I Discorsi* and *Il Principe*, which had been printed with great care, to furnish [them] with a new edition of such works' (A2r 5–16). 'LHauere io inteso, come il buon Stampatore Antoniello de gli Antonielli di Palermo haueua fornito il corso di questa misera vita, senza hauerti pero attenuta la cortese promessa, che ti fece ne la sua pistola, quando ti presentò i Discorsi, e'l Prencipe di questo rado huomo, da lui, con non poca cura, stampati, m'ha mosso a darti hora quel, che in detta pistola ti promise, che furono le presenti operette.'

45 Most evidence comes from Thomas Nashe's vituperative attacks against
   Harvey. In *Have with You to Saffron Walden* (STC 18369, 1596), Nashe reports
   that Harvey lived 'in the ragingest furie of the last Plague ... at VValfes in
   Powles Church-yard' (N4r 19–22) and that 'for seauen and thirtie weekes space
   together he did, while he lay at VVolfes coppying against mee, neuer stir[ed]
   out of dores' (P1r 21–3).

46 Unlike Churchyard, who contributed only one commendatory epistle to
   books printed by Jones (see, *The Auncient Order ... of Prince Arthure*, STC
   800, 1583), Whetstone, like Gascoigne, published a substantial number of his
   literary works with Jones between 1578 and 1587, which is possibly the year of
   his death.

47 Jones's anthologies include *A Handful of Pleasant Delites* (first edition STC
   21104.5, 1575?; second edition STC 21105, 1584), *A Gorgious Gallery of Gallant
   Inuentions* (STC 20402, 1578), *The Bookes of Honor and Armes* (STC 22163, 1590),
   Brittons Bowre of Delights (first edition STC 3633, 1591; second edition STC 3634,
   1597) and *The Arbor of Amourous Deuices* (STC 3631, 1597).

48 The emendations identified by Seaton as potentially authorial are: 'Treading'
   O1, 'Trading' O2, at I:I.i.38; 'pitch' O1, 'pitcht' O2, at I:II.ii.15; 'Harpyr' O1,
   'Harper' O2, at I:II.vii.50; 'Bassoe, maister' O1, 'Bassoe-maister' O2, at I:III.iii.173;
   'Clymeus' O1, 'Clymenes' O2, at I:IV.ii.49 and II:V.iii.231; 'Caldonian' O1,
   'Calidonian' O2, at I:IV.iii.3; and 'treshes' O1, 'tresses' O2, at I:V.ii.78. The
   second category of seemingly authorial variants identified by Seaton includes:
   'are' O1, 'be' O2, at I:II.ii.28; 'breath and rest' O1, 'rest or breath' O2, at I:III.iii.51;
   'heart' O1, 'soule' O2, at I:IV.ii.17; 'glories' O1, 'bodies' O2, at II:IV.I.77; 'gaspe' O1,
   'gape' O2, at II:V.I.208.

49 Corrections first introduced in O3 include 'The Lord' O1, 'The Lords' O3, at
   I:I.I.182; 'and' O1, 'aimd' O3, at I:2.5.32; 'apace' O1, 'apeece' O3, at I:2.5.86;
   'hower' O1, 'bower' O3, at I:4.4.132; 'ay' O1, 'ayre' O3, at I:5.1.300; 'this' O1, 'these'
   O3, at II:1.3.144; 'make' O1, 'makes' O3, at II:2.4.51; 'stature' O1, 'statute' O3, at
   II:2.4.140; 'march' O1, 'martcht' O3, at II:3.2.111; 'friend' O1, 'friendes' O3, at
   Two 3.3.13; 'holds' O1, 'hold' O3, at II:3.3.63. For further details, see, Fuller 1998,
   esp. xlvii–liii.

50 A full list of O2 and O3 variants can be found in Fredson Bowers (ed.),
   Christopher Marlowe: The Complete Works, 2 vols. (Cambridge: Cambridge
   University Press, 1973), vol. I, 239–2.

51 Other substantial emendations include: 'graue' Q1, 'great' Q2 at (7a); 'patron'
   Q1, 'pattern' Q2 at (10b); 'too' Q1, 'two' Q2 at (33d); 'each' Q1, 'such' Q2 at (37b);
   'where opinion simplenesse have' Q1, 'who in opinion of simplenesse have' at
   (38a); 'injurie' Q1, 'inquiry' Q2 at (39d); 'pay' Q1, 'yeelde speedily' Q2 at (40a);
   'Master' Q1, 'Father' Q2 at (54d); 'Well' Q1, 'Will' Q2 at (55d); 'were' Q1, 'was' Q2
   at (57a); 'very' Q1, 'merie' Q2 at (59b); 'Boulon' Q1, 'Bolton' Q2 at (60a); 'finely'
   Q1, 'trimly' Q2 at (64d); 'painted' Q1, 'vaunted' Q2 at (69d); 'stream' Q1,
   'streams' Q2 at (70a), 'within' Q1, 'who in' Q2 at (79d). The 1582 edition
   occasionally emends Latin words and phrases as at (9b) where the correct but
   nonsensical 'consultat' in Q1 is replaced by 'consuit' in 'Morum similitudo

consuit amicitias', that is, 'similar customs cement friendships'. For more details, see Farmer 1906: 161–6.

3 THE WISE QUARTOS

1 Thomas Millington (1594–1603) and Cuthbert Burby (1592–1607) published four Shakespearean plays each, albeit some of them are now regarded as collaborative works. Millington published *Titus Andronicus* (STC 22328) and *2 Henry VI* (STC 26099) in 1594 and *3 Henry VI* (STC 21006) in 1595. A five-year period intervened before Millington turned to Shakespeare again in 1600, when he published the first quarto of *Henry V* (STC 22289), along with the second quarto editions of *2* and *3 Henry VI*. Burby published *The Taming of a Shrew* (STC 23667), which is only tenuously associated with Shakespeare, in 1594, *Edward III* (STC 7501), which has only recently been at least partly attributed to Shakespeare, in 1596, along with the second quarto edition of *A Shrew*, and *Love's Labour's Lost* (STC 22294) in 1598. The fourth Shakespearean play associated with Burby, the second quarto of *Romeo and Juliet* (STC 22323), which had been published before, albeit in a radically different version, was also published in 1598.

2 John Jowett has refuted the 'usual diagnosis', according to which the printer's copy underlying the first quarto edition of *Richard III* was based on 'a reconstruction of the play put together by the actors of the Lord Chamberlain's Men . . . when they found themselves on tour without their playbook' (2000: 123). Jowett argues that 'although precise diagnosis of the origin of [this edition] may prove impossible, . . . the text is more plausibly designated as "theatrical" than "memorial"', or, more specifically, that 'it was given its distinct form by an adapting theatrical scribe, with some contribution at some point by Shakespeare as reviser' (2000: 127).

3 Lukas Erne believes that Shakespeare first established his dramatic reputation in print in the late 1590s: 'If we consider the suddenness and the frequency with which Shakespeare's name appears on the title pages of printed playbooks from 1598 to 1600, it is no exaggeration to say that in one sense, "Shakespeare," the author of dramatic texts, was born in the space of two or three years at the end of the sixteenth century' (2003: 63).

4 See also Long 1999: 414–33, and, more recently, Ioppolo 2006.

5 Craven's methodology was first challenged by Peter Davison, who pointed out that Compositor A may have been 'setting Q2 from a copy of Q1 which had more uncorrected sheets than have come down to us in the four extant copies of Q1' (1977: 130). Davison's objection is sound but reductive, because in establishing what types of alternative substantive readings the copy from which Compositor A set Q2 may have included he focused solely on press variants.

6 The absence of other substantive emendations to speech prefixes, stage directions and dialogue in this copy of Q1 *Richard II* rules out another alternative

scenario, namely that this manuscript correction postdates Q2 and that it stems from a collation of Q1 with Q2, rather than from the isolated intervention of an annotating reader.

7 Besides McKerrow 1910: 296, see also *The International Genealogical Index* (available online at www.familysearch.org; last accessed on 01.06.06).

8 'xi° die Aprilis ... Andrewe Wythes sonne of Henry Wythes of Ollerton Mallyveries in the county of York y[e]oman hathe putt him self Apprentice to henry Smithe Staconer for Eight yeres from our Lady day Last past [25 March 1580] ... ii^s vj^{d}' (Arber 1875–94: II, 96).

9 A note added to the entry dated 11 April 1580 quoted in footnote 8 above (Arber 1875–94: II, 96) specifies that 'Henry Smythe put [Wise] to Thomas bradshawe of Cambridge and newly bound to him x° aprilis 1581' (Arber 1875–94: II, 96). However, the actual entry dated 10 April 1581 identifies Thomas Bradshaw as 'Cytizen and Staconar of London' (Arber 1875–94: II, 104). R. B. McKerrow lists only one Thomas Bradshaw, 'stationer at Cambridge, 1573–1610' (1910: 47).

10 '26 maij [1589] ... Andrewe wythes, Sworne and admitted A freeman of this Companye' (Arber 1875–94: II, 705).

11 *Christs teares ouer Ierusalem Wherunto is annexed, a comparatiue admonition to London. By Tho. Nashe*, At London: Printed by Iames Roberts, and are to be solde by Andrewe Wise, at his shop in Paules Churchyard, at the signe of the Angel, 1593 (STC 18366).

12 For further details about the location of Wise's shop, see Blayney 1990: 23.

13 Wise acted as the retailing bookseller and publisher for three books printed by James Roberts in 1593 – the first edition of Thomas Nashe's *Christs teares ouer Ierusalem* (STC 18366) – and 1597 – the fifth and second edition of two sermons by Thomas Playfere (STC 20016, STC 20021).

14 STC 18654 in 1594; STC 5066, STC 13119 and STC 18895.5 in 1595.

15 STC 14032 in 1598 and STC 5631.3 in 1600; the three entries are STC 18644 in 1595, STC 10611.7 in 1596, and STC 13852 in 1598.

16 STC 17153 in 1603.

17 STC 1313 in 1590, STC 3059.2 in 1591, and STC 20595.5 in 1598.

18 *A prooued practise for all young chirurgians, concerning burnings with gunpowder, and woundes made with gunshot, sword, halbard, pike, launce, or such other ... by William Clowes, maister in chirurgery. Newly corrected and augmented. Seene, and allowed, according to the order appoynted.*, [London]: Printed by Thomas Orwyn, for Wydow Broome, 1591 (STC 5445) had previously been printed by Thomas Orwyn for Thomas Cadman in 1588 (STC 5444).

19 Wise also published *Obseruations in the art of English poesie* (1602 STC 4543) by Thomas Campion, who may have 'served under Sir Robert Carey in Essex's expedition to aid Henry IV against the Catholic League in 1591–2'; in David Lindley's entry in *The Oxford Dictionary of National Biography (ODNB)* 9 (2004), 880.

20 For further details, see P. E. McCullough's entry in *ODNB* 44 (2004), 567.

21 For further details, see Charles Nicholl's entry in *ODNB* 40 (2004), 242.

22 Wise may have met Thomas Nashe when they were both in Cambridge in the early 1580s – Nashe as sizar scholar at St John's College and Wise as an apprentice with the bookseller Thomas Bradshaw.

23 Thomas Playfere's claim in the epistle dedicatory addressed to Lady Elizabeth Carey in the 1596 edition of *The meane in mourning* (STC 20015) that he never authorized the earlier editions published by Andrew Wise in 1595 ostensibly contradicts my theory that Wise had a long-standing working relation with the authors whose works he published. However, Playfere's claim seems disingenuous. Although Wise published this sermon under a different title (*A most excellent and heauenly sermon*, STC 20014, 20014.3 and 20014.5) and he failed to include the name of the author on its title page, Playfere's address to Elizabeth Carey suggests rhetorical disavowal rather than genuine outrage. 'For this sermon', he begins, 'hath been twise printed already without my procurement or priuitie any manner of way. Yea to my very great griefe and trouble. Nevertheles', he seamlessly continues, 'I have / thought good to complaine of no man' (A2r 18–22, A2v 1). One further clue suggests that Playfere, like most early modern preachers, felt anxious about going to press, as publication could be taken to denote ambition or the wish to pursue financial gain, both of which were regarded as irreconcilable with their religious calling. Playfere explains that his decision not to report those responsible for taking down his sermon and printing it without his permission is due to the fact that he does not know the culprits. However, the 1595 editions consistently advertise Andrew Wise as their publisher, making it hard to justify the fact that the authorized editions of 1595 and 1596 (STC 20015 and STC 20016) were also published by Wise.

24 See, among others, Gurr 1996: 284.

25 Forker 1998 opts for Q1 'As thought, on thinking on no thought I think' (2.2.31), while Ure 1966 and Wells 1969 prefer Q2 'As, though on thinking on no thought I think' (2.2.31).

26 Although STC 22280 is usually referred to as the *first* quarto edition of *1 Henry IV*, there is another earlier quarto edition, which was also printed by Peter Short for Andrew Wise in 1598 (STC 22279a), and which is known as Q0 from the only extant fragment (quire C) now in the holdings of the Folger Shakespeare Library in Washington DC. For further details, see, for example, Kastan 2002: 108–9. Kastan's edition includes a facsimile of the fragment in Appendix 5 (357–65).

27 See, for example, Humphreys 1960: lxxi, who argues that 'Q2's changes are mostly printing-house variations' and Kastan 2002: 111, who similarly claims that 'Q2 is closely based on Q1; what differences exist are not the result of the author's corrections or revisions but of the normal procedures of a printing house'.

28 For further details on textual variation in the dramatic texts printed by Thomas Creede, see Yamada 1994, esp. 215–37. For textual variation in *A Looking Glass for London and England*, see the Greg 1932 and Hayashi 1969.

29 For further details on textual variants in the first and second quarto of *Mother Bombie*, see Lea 1939 and Andreadis 1970.

4 THE PAVIER QUARTOS

1 Excluding two apocryphal plays, Pavier published eight Shakespearean quartos in 1619 (see table 4.1, p. 107). The other stationers who published Shakespeare's dramatic works in the 1610s did so much more infrequently: Matthew Law (1595–1629) published quarto editions of *Richard III* (STC 22318, 1612), *1 Henry IV* (STC 22284, 1613), and *Richard II* (STC 22312, 1615), while John Smethwick (1597–1641), Edward White (1577–1613?), and Simon Stafford (1596–1633?) published one quarto edition each, namely *Titus Andronicus* (STC 22330), *Hamlet* (STC 22277), and *Pericles* (STC 22336), all in 1611.

2 Gerald D. Johnson, who argues that Pavier's reputation as a literary pirate is hardly deserved (1992: 12–50), and E. A. J. Honigmann, who wonders 'whether the Lord Chamberlain's letter of 1619 pointed to the Pavier Quartos, or, in the first instance, to the Beaumont and Fletcher's plays published in 1619' (1996: 26), are rare exceptions. Also, Andrew Gurr, in conversation.

3 Pavier seems to have retained ownership of his Shakespearean plays until they were transferred to Edward Brewster on 4 August 1626, as attested by the following entry in *The Stationers' Register*: 'More to Edward Brewster / Master Paviers right in SHAKESPERES plaies or any of them' (Arber 1875–94: IV 165).

4 See, for example, Hinman 1963: 415–26.

5 Some scholars believe that the Folio text of *King Lear* was set from an annotated copy of Pavier's Quarto. See, among others, Taylor 1985: 17–74, 70. Others believe that the Folio text was set from manuscript copy with reference to Pavier's Quarto. See, for example, Howard-Hill 1982: 1–24 and Peter Blayney, quoted in Halio 1992: 67.

6 Philip Herbert starts his letter by stressing that 'complaint was heretofore presented to my Deare brother & p^rdecessor by his Ma^ts servants the Players, that some of the Company of Printers & Stationers had procured, published & printed diuerse of their books of Comædyes. Tragedyes Cronicle Historyes' (Chambers 1931: 384). Similarly, Robert Devereux reminds the Masters and Wardens of the Stationers' Company that 'The players which are his Ma^ts servants haue addressed them selues vnto mee as formerly to my p^rdecessors in Office, complaining that some Printers are about to Print & publish some of their Playes which hitherto they haue beene vsually restrained from by the Authority of the Lord Chamberlain' (Chambers 1931: 398).

7 The closure of the theatres in 1642 invalidates a similar comparison between the rate at which new King's Men plays were published during the five-year period before and after Robert Devereux's letter of 1641.

8 My source for the dating of the first performance of plays mentioned in this section of chapter 4 is Harbage 1989.

9 The other six Queen's Men plays first published between 1633 and June 1637 are Philip Massinger's *A New Way to Pay Old Debts*, Christopher Marlowe's *The Jew of Malta*, James Shirley's *The Witty Fair One* and Thomas Heywood's *The English Traveller* in 1633; James Shirley's *The Traitor* in 1635; Philip Massinger's

The Great Duke of Florence in 1636; and Thomas Heywood's *The Royal King and the Loyal Subject* and James Shirley's *Hyde Park, The Lady of Pleasure* and *The Young Admiral* in 1637.

10 It is well known that *The Antipodes* was published in contravention of the contract which Richard Brome renegotiated with the Salisbury Court in August 1638. For further details, see Dutton 1997: 153–78, 159–60.

11 The other eighteen Queen's Men plays first published between June 1637 and 1641 are James Shirley's *The Example* and *The Gamester* and Thomas Nabbes' *Hannibal and Scipio* in 1637; John Ford's *The Fancies*, Henry Shirley's *The Martyred Soldier*, James Shirley's *The Duke's Mistress*, and Thomas Nabbes' *Tottenham Court* and *Covent Garden* in 1638; James Shirley [and George Chapman?]'s *The Ball* and George Chapman [and James Shirley's?] *Chabot Admiral of France*, James Shirley's *The Maid's Revenge* and Beaumont and Fletcher's *Wit Without Money* in 1639; James Shirley's *The Coronation, Love's Cruelty, The Opportunity* and *The Arcadia*, John Fletcher's *The Night Walker*, and Shakerly Marmion's *The Antiquary* in 1641.

12 The other four King's Men plays first published between 1633 and June 1637 are: John Ford's *The Broken Heart* in 1633; William Shakespeare and John Fletcher's *The Two Noble Kinsmen* in 1634; Willim Davenant's *The Wits* in 1636; and John Fletcher's *The Elder Brother*, which was entered in *The Stationers' Register* in March 1637.

13 The other seven King's Men plays first published between June 1637 and 1641 are: Lodowick Carlell's *1 and 2 Arviragus and Philicia*, John Fletcher's *Monsieur Thomas*, Philip Massinger's *The Unnatural Combat*, Fletcher and Massinger's *Rollo Duke of Normandy* and Jasper Mayne's *The City Match* in 1639; and John Fletcher's *Rule a Wife and Have a Wife* in 1640.

14 Andrew Gurr believes that the Lord Chamberlain's letter of 1637 was in fact prompted by a protracted bout of the plague, which forced London theatres to close for sixteen months between summer 1636 and early autumn 1637. According to Gurr, 'the usual royal bounty came to the company for the long lay-off they suffered' both as 'a weekly fee of £1, payable for so long as the king allowed' and as 'a letter from the new Lord Chamberlain ordering the Stationers' Company to check on its authority to print certain playbooks'. Still according to Gurr, the letter was meant to forestall 'the old practice in times of long closure where unemployed players made money by putting together texts from memory to sell to printers' (Gurr 1996: 382). Gurr's theory relies on assumptions which are no longer widely endorsed, including the related narratives of literary piracy and memorial reconstruction, which were once believed to increase at times of crisis, including periods of inactivity due to the protracted closure of the theatres. Recent scholars tend to believe not only that theatre companies were not adverse to publication *per se*, but merely cautious about the timing of release to the press (Erne 2003: 122), but also that companies used publication as a means of pre-publicity when they hoped that their theatres would re-open as a means to revive public interest in their repertory (Blayney 1997: 386).

15 The two King's Men plays which were entered in *The Stationers' Register* before May 1619 are Beaumont and Fletcher's *The Maid's Tragedy* and *A King and No King.*

16 Philip Herbert's letter of 1637 may in fact have functioned both as a cautionary measure against self-promoting authors like Thomas Heywood and as a precautionary measure, because it did not only have a direct impact on the number of new plays belonging to the Queen's Men that reached the press after 1637, but it also ushered in a distinctive stage in the publication of plays by their leading dramatist James Shirley, at a time when the theatres were closed due to a long bout of plague (May 1636–October 1637) and shortly after Shirley moved to Dublin. Up to 1637, Shirley had found in the London stationer William Cooke a regular and trusty collaborator. While John Grove and Francis Constable had published *The Wedding, The Grateful Servant* and *The School of Compliments,* Shirley's first three plays to appear in print between 1629 and 1631, William Cooke published the entire body of Shirley's works to reach the press between 1631 and 1637, namely two masques and four plays. The timing of Herbert's letter to the Stationers interestingly coincides with the beginning of a lasting collaboration between William Cooke and Andrew Crooke, who was going to become a leading publisher of dramatic literature in the mid-seventeenth century. Both stationers registered Shirley's *Hyde Park, The Lady of Pleasure,* and *The Young Admiral* on 13 April 1637, just a few months before Philip Herbert wrote to the Masters and Wardens of the Stationers' Company. The steady release of Shirley's plays to the press under the auspices of the Cooke–Crooke partnership and Shirley's absence from London may suggest an agreement, if not an active collaboration, between the Stationers and the Queen's Men, who may have had a vested interest in fostering Shirley's reputation now that he was living and working in Dublin. Between them, Cooke and Crooke published as many as twelve pre-1636 plays by Shirley between 1637 and 1640. More specifically, they published the whole of Shirley's dramatic output in print with the exception of *The Royal Master,* which was staged in Dublin in 1637, and *The Arcadia,* which was unusually published in the same year as its debut on stage in 1640. *The Arcadia* was also unusually published by John Williams and Francis Eglesfield and clearly brought an end to a distinctive stage in the publication of Shirley's dramatic works. Shirley's return to London in 1640 may have prompted Williams and Eglesfield to defy the virtually unchallenged monopoly that Cooke and Crooke had enjoyed over his pre-1636 plays since 1637.

17 Constantia Munda (pseud.), *The Worming of a Mad Dog: Or, a Soppe for Cerberus* (1617, STC 18275)

18 Incidentally, Lawrence Hayes' entrance of 8 July 1619 reinforces my theory that the order issued by the Court of the Stationers' Company, contrary to what Greg assumed in 1955, did not apply to plays which had already been committed to print before that date.

19 In Greg 1939–1959: 1108, the correct dating of *The Merry Wives of Windsor* is also described as an 'oversight'. This time, though, Greg implies that the

printer rather than Pavier was responsible for failing to alter the date on the title page of *Henry V*, and, presumably, *The Merry Wives of Windsor*.

20 John Jowett, in conversation.

21 See, for example, Gary Taylor's entry on 'Edward Blount' in *The Oxford Dictionary of National Biography* 6 (2004), 297–8, his McKenzie Lectures delivered at the University of Oxford in late January and late February 2006, as well as Scragg 1995: 1–10.

22 Taylor 2004: 297–8 and Scragg 1995: 1–10.

23 Commercial plays entered by Blount in *The Stationers' Register* include Jonson's *Sejanus* (entered on 7 November 1604, and then assigned the following year to Blount's friend, Thomas Thorpe); Daniel's *Philotas*, which was printed for Simon Waterson in 1605, and *A King and No King* (entered on 17 August 1611, and first printed for Thomas Walkley in 1619). Blount also entered a play by Cyril Tourneur, called *Play Booke*, which was apparently destroyed by John Warburton's cook in 1754.

24 See my discussion of the legal status of the copy of *Pericles* earlier on in this chapter (p. 113).

25 See also Kastan 2001: 61.

26 The First Folio actually included eighteen previously unpublished plays, namely *The Tempest*, *The Two Gentlemen of Verona*, *Measure for Measure*, *The Comedy of Errors*, *As You Like It*, *All's Well That Ends Well*, *Twelfth Night*, *The Winter's Tale*, *1 Henry VI*, *Henry VIII*, *Coriolanus*, *Timon of Athens*, *Julius Caesar*, *Macbeth*, *Antony and Cleopatra* and *Cymbeline*, as well as *King John* and *The Taming of the Shrew*, which are now regarded as separate plays from *The Troublesome Reign of King John* (STC 14644, 1591) and *The Taming of a Shrew* (STC 23667, 1594).

27 It is worth stressing that the imprint on the title page of the First Folio – 'Printed by Isaac Iaggard, and Ed. Blount' – is generally regarded as inaccurate because Blount acted as one of the publishers, and not as the printer. However, the imprint may be accurate at least in implying that Isaac acted as *both* printer *and* publisher, if, as is often the case in early modern imprints, the lack of the name of a stationer, or stationers, *for whom* a book was printed meant that the printer(s) also acted as publisher(s), i.e. as primary investor(s). That the Jaggards, if not Isaac alone, had invested part of the capital required for the publication of the First Folio is confirmed by the colophon, which reads 'Printed at the Charges of W. Jaggard, Ed. Blount, I. Smithweeke, and W. Aspley, 1623'.

28 For further details on William and Joan Broome's Lylian publications, see chapter 3 (pp. 99–100).

29 Normally stationers who granted permission to other members of the Company to re-issue their books would get a share of the copies of the new edition as opposed to monetary compensation.

30 For further details on the dating of the fourth quarto of *Romeo and Juliet*, see chapter 5 (pp. 178–9); R. Carter Hailey refutes other recent studies, which argue that another undated quarto of *Hamlet* issued by John Smethwick also pre-dates the First Folio (see, for example, Rasmussen 2001: 21–9).

31 These plays are: Beaumont and Fletcher's *A King and No King* (STC 1670, 1619; STC 1671, 1625) and *Philaster* (STC 1681-1.5, 1620; STC 1682, 1622); Fletcher and Massinger's *Thierry and Theodoret* (STC 11074, 1621); William Shakespeare's *Othello* (STC 22305, 1622); and Philip Massinger's *The Picture* (STC 17640, 1630).

32 Zachary Lesser endorses Scott McMillin's view that 'all of Walkley's early plays may have been printed from [private] transcripts' (2004: 215) and that such practice was far from unusual or improper.

33 Walkley entered *Othello* in *The Stationers' Register* on 6 October 1621 (Arber 1875–94: IV 59).

34 *MWW* F2r 2; *MSND* D2r 4.

35 *H5* A2v 1, D3v 21, D4v 35, E1r 4, F3v 30, F3v 32, F3v 35; *Yorkshire Tragedy* A1r 22, A2r 26, B1v 3, B4v 5, C2r 21, C3v 19, C4v 12, C4v 17, C4v 26, D2r 18; *PER* R4r 15, S2r 28, S3v 4, T1r 22, V1r 26, X3v 35, X4r 9, X4v 12, Z1v 9, Z1v 11, Z1v 13, Z4v 27, Z4v 27–8, A2[2]v 13, A2[4]v 3.

36 *Yorkshire Tragedy, MWW*, and *H5* add one direction each at A4v 23, F4r 9, and D3r 12; *3H6* and *Oldcastle* add two each at K4v 27 and O1v 7, and C3v 20 and E3r 17, respectively; *MV* adds three at C3r 23, C4v 19, and G2v 14; *KLR* adds six at C2v 34, D1r 6, D4v 2, H2v 2, K3v 32 and K4r 25; *MSND* adds seven at C2v 12, E1r 34, F1r 6, F2v 9, G1V 7, G1V 23, and G2r 5; and *PER* adds thirteen at R3r 35, V2r 20, Y3r 27, Y4v 19, Y4v 20, Z2r 15, Z2r 37, Z3v 3, A2[1] 13, A2[3]v 12, A2[3]v 32, A2[3]v 33, A2[4]v 33.

37 At G1V 34, Pavier's edition of *Sir John Oldcastle* omits the original exit direction in its source-text, the first quarto of 1600.

38 Other omissions in this category of directions include: '*they trippe*' (Q1, F3v 34); '*they play at dice*' (Q1, F3v 36); '*they fight*' (Q1, H3v 11); '*Roch. within*' (Q1, H3v 22); '*they leade / them away*' (Q1, H4v 34–5); and '*giues them / a purse*' (Q1, K4v, 14–15). On at least two occasions, omissions of directions seem harder to justify on the ground that the dialogue supplies the same information: see '*They rise from the table*' at Q1 H4v 6 and '*all kneeling*' a few lines later in the same scene in Q1, H4v 32. A similar cluster of omissions in stage directions occurs in one scene in *A Yorkshire Tragedy*: Pavier's edition omits '*Wif. alone*' (Q1, B4v 1), '*Exit seruant / for wine*' (Q1, C1V 3–4), and '*Drink both*' (Q1, C1V 11).

39 In this case Pavier's edition still fails to add the Fool, the other speaking character in this scene.

40 Such re-positioning occurs in *3H6* at I3v 21, in *PER* at V3r 25 and V3r 29, in *MV* at D1r 1, and in *Sir John Oldcastle* at D3r 29.

41 A recurrent attempt to foreground the literary quality of the dramatic text is also evident in the minor adjustments undergone by overlong and unusually short lines (see, for example, *Yorkshire* A4v 20, A3v 20; *H5* F3r 12, F3r 32, F4v 5 and G1r 2) and by the systematic avoidance of turned lines (see, for example, *2H6* E2v 10, *MWW* B3r 13, B3r 21 and B3r 26, and *KLR* F1r 13 and F1r 34).

42 Although printers tended to leave the verso side of the last page blank in order to protect the printed text while the book was unbound, the recurrent cuts in Pavier's edition of *Sir John Oldcastle* seem rather aimed at saving space throughout the text of the play and not only towards the end.

43 Incidentally, it is worth noting that although the skilful abridgements of the dialogue suggest the premeditated effort of an annotator rather than the improvisation of a compositor, the annotator overlooked the fact that scenes 16–20 are out of sequence. While mindful not to impair the local economy of single lines and short exchanges the annotator must have lost sight of the overall structure of the rather convoluted plot of this play.

44 Compare, for example, 'spake' (Q3, B1v 21) and 'sparke' (Q4, R4v 24); 'from' (Q3, B2r 2) and 'from thee' (Q4, S1r 3); 'now message' (Q3, B3v 4) and 'my message' (Q4, S2r 31); 'Which tels in that glory once he was' (Q3, D1v 4) and 'VVhich tels me in that glory once he was' (Q4, T4r 26); 'cast one the shore' (D2r 16) and 'cast on the shore' (V1r 1); 'as the earth did quake' (Q3, E3r 18) and 'as if the earth did quake' (Q4, X1v 33); 'as we' (Q3, F4r 16) and 'as well as we' (Q4, Y2v 11); 'men stir you vp' (Q3, G1r 3) and 'men must stir you vp' (Q4, Y3r 25); 'That dignities the renowne of a Bawde' (Q3, G4r 9) and 'That dignifies the renowne of a Baud' (Q4, Z2r 13).

45 'accents' at B4v 4 in Q1 is replaced by 'actions' at B4v 4 in Q2; 'turne' at H4v 10 in Q1 becomes 'runne' at H4v 10 in Q2.

46 'dare *I*' at G3r 15 in Q1 reads 'I dare' at G3r 16 in Q2; 'that haue *I* tried' at I4r 1 in Q1 is rearranged into 'that I haue tride' at I4r 2 in Q2.

47 'The weakest still did go vnto the walles' at I3v 37 in Q1 is normalized to read 'The weakest still doe goe vnto the walles' at I4r 1 in Q2.

48 'that that I may' at H3v 32 in Q1 is emended to read 'that I may' at H3v 32 in Q2.

49 '*Puff.* And I know that . . . / *Page.* I see that . . .' at C2v 1, 3 in Q1 becomes '*Puff.* I see that . . . / *Page.* And I know that . . .' at C2v 1, 3 in Q2.

50 The head-title on the first page of the text in Q1, 'IOHN DRVMS' (A2r 1), is emended to read 'JACKE DRVMS' in Q2 (A2r 1); a misspelling in Q1, '*Forunes*' (E3v 14), is changed into '*Fortunes*' in Q2 (E4r 4).

51 The original direction '*He sings, she sounds*' (H1r 16) is re-arranged to read '*Freevile* sings' at Dd1v 12 and 'She swounds.' at Dd1v 20.

52 Sheares's edition rephrases 'as our much care hath bin' (H4r 36) to read 'as our much care be seene' (Dd5v 13), thus avoiding a repetition of the ending of the previous line, '*If* with content our hurtlesse mirth hath bin' (H4r 35).

53 Q2 I3v 8 – ; Q3 I3r 10 Exeunt.

54 Q2: A3r 6 – ; B2r 22 – ; B2r 32 – ; B2v 2 – ; B2v 6 – ; B2v 21 – ; B2v 26 – ; B3r 4 – ; B3r 8 – ; Q3 A2r 6 Rasni; B1r 12 Smtih; B1r 23 Smith; B1r 28 Smith; B1r 32 Smith; B1v 11 Smith; B1v 16 Smith; B1v 30 Smith; B1v 34 Clowne.

55 Q2 I1r 22 tent; Q3 H3v 22 teat.

5 THE MAKING OF THE FIRST FOLIO

1 As William B. Long explains, 'manuscript plays are by no means invariably neat and orderly; authorial stage-directions are very seldom changed in the theater; speech-heads are not regularized; copious markings do not appear to handle properties, entrances and music. Regularization and completeness simply were

not factors in theatrical marking of an author's papers' (1985: 125). Tiffany Stern also observes that performance annotations were unsystematic and highly idiosyncratic, since they were meant for the prompter's eyes only: 'the prompter ... did not expect anyone else to have dealings with his book ..., so he wrote in a form he understood – he was under no obligation to have a system that an outsider could comprehend' (2004: 144).

2 '*Fight*' (TLN 70); '*Exit*' (TLN 450); '*Cals within*' (TLN 938); '*Within*' (TLN 952); '*Within*' (TLN 954); '*Exit*' (TLN 959); '*Enter Tybalt*' (TLN 1556); '*Enter Mother*' (TLN 2592); '*Enter Appothecarie*' (TLN 2785); '*Kils herselfe*' (TLN 3035), '*Exeunt omnes*' (TLN 3185).

3 '*... with clubs or partysons*' (Q3, A4r 9) is shortened to '*... with Clubs*' (F TLN 71); '*Away Tibalt*' (Q3 F3v 17) is normalized to read '*Exit Tybalt*' (F TLN 1522); '*Exit*' (Q3 G1r 34 and I2r 21) is changed to '*Exeunt*' (F TLN 1643 and TLN 2292); and '*Enter Capels*' (Q3 L4v 7) is expanded into '*Enter Capulet and his Wife*' (F TLN 3061). A further six directions are similarly expanded to specify what characters are involved in specific entrances and exits: '*Exeunt*' in Q3 at E3v 27 becomes '*Exit. Mercutio, Benuolio*' in F at TLN 1242; '*Exit*' in Q3 at E4v 23 becomes '*Exit Nurse and Peter*' in F at TLN 1309; '*Exit*' in Q3 at I2v 31 becomes '*Exit Paris*' in F at TLN 2338; '*Exeunt*' in Q3 at I4v 8 becomes '*Exeunt Iuliet and Nurse*' in F at TLN 2465; '*Exit*' in Q3 at I4v 20 becomes '*Exeunt Father and Mother*' in F at TLN 2477; and '*Exit*' in Q3 at K4v 3 becomes '*Exit Man*' in F at TLN 2758.

4 The wrong direction '*Enter Romeo*' in Q3 at C2v 28 is replaced by a redundant '*Enter Seruant*' in F (TLN 568), while the redundant direction '*Enter Capulet and his Wife*' in Q3 (L4v 20) is omitted from F.

5 '*Rom.*' at E2r 30 in Q3 is replaced by '*Ben.*' at TLN 1123 in F, and the redundant prefix '*M.*' at F1r 3 in Q3 is omitted.

6 Line references to the Folio are based on the through-line-numbering of Hinman 1968.

7 New mistakes in the text of the dialogue in the Folio include: omissions ('Tis true' at A3r 21 in Q3, 'True' at TLN 19 in F; 'are here writ' at B3r 14 in Q3, 'are writ' at TLN 289 in F; 'his minum rests' at E2r 33 in Q3, 'his minum' at TLN 1127 in F; 'it is well said' at E3v 7 in Q3, 'it is said' at TLN 1217 in F; 'as gentle as a Lamme' at F1r 31 in Q3, 'as gentle a Lambe' at TLN 1355 in F; 'this bloudy fray?' at F4v 22 in Q3, 'this Fray?' at TLN 1595 in F; 'as I' at G4v 3 in Q3, 'as' at TLN 1868 in F; 'it is so very late' at H2v 14 in Q3, 'it is so late' at TLN 2030 in F; 'the Larke' at H3r 2 in Q3, 'Larke' at TLN 2053; the Folio also drops five quarto lines, i.e. G4r 16–17, H4v 32, I3v 32–3, and K3v 6, which may represent accidental omissions); verbal substitutions ('I will cut' at A3r 26 in Q3, 'and cut' at TLN 26 in F; 'But with a rereward' at G3r 18 in Q3, 'But which a rere-ward' at TLN 1775 in F; '*Iuliet* thy loue' at G4v 3, '*Iuliet* my Loue' at TLN 1868 in F; 'mishaued' at H1v 17 in Q3, 'mishaped' at TLN 1960 in F; 'we must' at I2v 28 in Q3, 'you must' at TLN 2335 in F); repetitions ('the' at E2v 18 in Q3, 'the the' at TLN 1149 in F; 'all this did I' at F1r 33 in Q3, 'all this this did I' at TLN 1357 in F; 'such excesse' at F2r 30 in Q3, 'such such excesse' at TLN 1426 in F); interpolations ('*napkins*' at C2v 27 in Q3, '*their napkins*' at TLN 567 in F; 'stay good Nurse' at E4r 30 in Q3, 'stay thou good

Nurse' at TLN 1281 in F; 'all this day' at K4r 8 in Q3, 'all this an day' at TLN 2726 in F); transpositions ('And she shall scant shew well' at B3v 35 in Q3, 'And she shew scant shell, well' at TLN 348 in F; 'light it growes' at H3r 16 in Q3, 'it light growes' at TLN 2067 in F; 'is in this?' at L4v 34, 'in is this?' at TLN 3089 in F); and typos ('and so bound' at C1v 9 in Q3, 'and to bound' at TLN 473 in F; 'in delay' at C1v 34 in Q3, 'I delay' at TLN 498 in F; 'deadly' at H1r 12 in Q3, 'dead' at TLN 1919 in F; 'starue' at I1v 7 in Q3, 'straue' at TLN 2239 in F; 'Being' at I2v 16 in Q3, 'Benig' at TLN 2323 in F; 'As rich shall *Romeos*' at M2r 13 in Q3, 'As rich shall *Romeo*' at TLN 3178 in F).

8 Stanley Wells alternatively attributes this variant speech prefix to *scribal* mis-reading: 'a playhouse scribe might have misread "*Ber.*" as an abbreviation of Boyet (who speaks shortly before and after this exchange), and the annotator of the Quarto could have unthinkingly, if incompletely, "corrected" his copy' (Wells 1982: 284).

9 William B. Hunter represents an interesting, if isolated, exception among recent textual scholars for holding Heminge and Condell personally respon-sible for the textual variants which found their way into those Folio plays, which had previously appeared in print in a substantially invariant version. According to Hunter, Heminge and Condell's intervention focused on 'stage and speech directions, activities of performances in which the actor/editor had participated rather than emendations of individual speeches, their words not so clearly remembered' (Hunter 2002: 11). Hunter also specifies that the sparse and unsystematic intervention that can be detected in the preparation of printed copy for the press can best be explained by the fact that the two actors would remember only those scenes in which they had acted. Hence their 'failure to make similar changes in those in which [they] did not appear'. Hunter's theory is attractive because it identifies a link between some Folio plays and the staging practices associated with two senior members of Shakespeare's own acting company. However, the main strength of Hunter's theory – it provides an *ad hoc* explanation for a specific class of variants in a specific group of Folio plays – is also its main weakness, in that it relies on the assumption that we can establish which roles Heminge and Condell played, including the parts they doubled, and that they had the leisure, as well as the philological sensitivity, to 'improve' a printed playbook by bringing it closer to their memories of the original performance.

10 Other stage directions added to the Folio text of *Much Ado About Nothing* are prompted either by breaks in the stage action or by explicit cues in the dialogue, as at TLN 1043, TLN 1197, TLN 1329, TLN 1655, TLN 2415.

11 The other alterations to the dialogue of the Folio text of *Much Ado About Nothing* stem from new typographical mistakes, as the text was re-set in Jaggard's printing shop, and the correction of a few obvious typographical mistakes in the first quarto. Among these, 'bothers' in Q1 at B2v 30 is emended to read 'brothers' in F1 at TLN 388; similarly 'and oy- / ster' in Q1 at C4v 29–30 and 'one / the sensible Benedicks head?' in Q1 at H3r 26–7 become 'an oyster' in F1 at TLN 857 and 'on the sensible *Benedicks* head?' in F1 at TLN 2267.

12 Gary Taylor's entry in *The Oxford Dictionary of National Biography* 6 (2004), 297–8; see also Taylor's 'McKenzie Lectures', delivered at the University of Oxford in 2006 and his forthcoming book devoted to Edward Blount.

13 For further details, see, for example, Blayney 1996: xxviii.

14 This is how Blount describes himself in the dedicatory epistle prefaced to his edition of Marlowe's *Hero and Leander* (STC 17418, 1613, A2r 17).

15 Blount entered Jonson's *Sejanus* on 2 November 1604 and then transferred it to Thomas Thorpe on 6 August 1605; Blount seems to have declined to reclaim his rights on *Pericles*, which he registered on 20 May 1608, when this play was published for Henry Gosson the following year; similarly, Blount's entry for *A King and No King*, dated 7 August 1618, did not stop Thomas Walkley from publishing this play in 1619; Blount also registered two lost plays, *The Nobleman* and *The Twins' Tragedy* on 15 February 1612. The only exception is *Sir Giles Goosecap* (STC 12050, 1606), which Blount entered in *The Stationers' Register* on 10 January 1606.

16 Supporters of this theory include Peter Blayney (see, for example, Blayney 1991: 8). However, Gary Taylor has recently argued that Edward Blount was indeed the main agent responsible for the planning and publication of the First Folio (see Taylor, 'McKenzie Lectures').

17 In his edition of *Endymion*, David Bevington has for example observed that the first quarto from which Blount's edition was set 'is an excellent text, with very few printing errors ... It reads like a text prepared by the author himself for publication, with characters' names grouped at the beginning of each scene, in the literary and classically sanctioned "continental" style later adopted by Ben Jonson in his highly literary Folio of 1616. The sparsity of printing errors suggests that the manuscript was accurate and consistent ... The speech-headings are uniformly accurate and consistent, probably not because a "prompter" regularized them but because Lyly's own manuscript was a highly finished product. Stage directions are accordingly sparse yet practical and accurate' (Bevington 1996: 3). Similarly, G. K. Hunter and Bevington argue that Lyly's role as court dramatist and his association with boy rather than adult companies gave him more control over the publication of his plays. With reference to the quarto editions of *Campaspe*, Hunter and Bevington observe that 'Lyly had sold his play only to himself, since he himself controlled the acting company [the Paul's Boys] ... He seems to have decided to print *Campaspe* (and *Sappho and Phao*) soon after their court performances (to advertise that success, I assume). The publisher was thus made directly responsible to a somewhat formidable court figure; and this no doubt imposed a more than usual meticulousness in the printing ... These quartos are well printed, and require little emendation' (Hunter and Bevington 1991: 3).

18 Q1, B3v 1 '*Enter Iane*', Q2, B3r 2 '*Enter Susan*'; Q1, B3v 7 '*Iane*', Q2, B3r 8 '*Susan*'; Q1, B3v 10 '*Iane*', Q2, B3r 11 '*Sus*'; Q1, B3v 12 '*Iane*', Q2, B3r 13 '*Sus*'.; Q1, B3v 17 '*Iane*', Q2, B3r 18 '*Sus*'.; Q1, B3v 22 '*Iane*', Q2, B3r 23 '*Sus*'.; Q1, B3v 24 What '*Iane*', Q2, B3r 25 'Why *Sue*'; Q1, B3v 25 '*Iane*', Q2, B3r 26 '*Sus*'.; Q1, B4r 20 '*Iane*', Q2, B3v 26 '*Susan*'.

19 Q1, G1v 33 'Oh Susan', Q2, G4v 23 'O Sister'; Q1, G2v 13 'Neither Iane', Q2, H1v 16 'Neither Sister'.

20 Thomas Heywood's name or initials appear on the title page or in the paratext of all his known dramatic and non-dramatic publications dating from 1607–8 onwards. The only exceptions are *Life and Death of Elizabeth* (STC 7587, 1639) and *The Exemplary Lives* (STC 13316, 1640), which were published at the very end of Heywood's long career.

21 All of Heywood's dramatic and non-dramatic publications post 1607–8 include paratextual materials, except for *The Late Lancashire Witches* (STC 13373, 1634), *A Challenge for Beauty* (STC 13311, 1636), and *Life and Death of Elizabeth* (STC 7587, 1639).

22 Heywood's collaboration with the Okes seems to have extended beyond the publication of his own dramatic and literary works. The address to the reader which Heywood contributed to the 1614 edition of *Greenes Tu Quoque*, for example, suggests that he may have frequently visited Nicholas Okes's printing house: 'To gratulate the loue and memory of my worthy friend the Author, and my entirely beloued Fellow, the Actor, I could not chuse being in the way iust when this Play was to be published in Print, but to prefixe some token of my affection to either in the frontispire of the Booke' (STC 5673, A2r 2–7). Although the title page of this play does not specify the name of the printer, Greg established that Nicholas Okes printed it, except for quires G–K, which were probably printed by Edward Allde (1939–59: 464). Further evidence of the long-standing collaboration between Heywood and the Okes is provided by Heywood's biographer, A. M. Clark, who believes that Heywood may have acted as a literary and editorial agent for John Okes as late as 1638 (1927: 97–158, 166–7).

23 The imprint in Q2 identifies Nicholas Okes as its printer; although the imprint in Q1 only specifies the initials of the publisher – 'Printed at London for *I. W.* 1615' – the ornaments indicate that Nicholas Okes was also the printer of Q1 (Greg 1939–59: 475).

24 I am grateful to M. J. Kidnie for drawing this anomaly in Q1 to my attention and for pointing out that the solution offered by Q2 may suggest remedial rather authorial intervention.

25 Although both Edward Blount and Isaac Jaggard are mentioned in *The Stationers' Register* entry of 8 November 1623, only the former seems to have owned the copy of the sixteen plays first published in the First Folio, namely *The Tempest*, *Two Gentlemen of Verona*, *Measure for Measure*, *Comedy of Errors*, *As You Like It*, *All's Well That Ends Well*, *Twelfth Night*, *The Winter's Tale*, *1 Henry VI*, *Henry VIII*, *Coriolanus*, *Timon of Athens*, *Julius Caesar*, *Macbeth*, *Antony and Cleopatra* and *Cymbeline*, as suggested by a further entry in *The Stationers' Register* dated 16 November 1630, whereby Blount's rights were transferred to Robert Allot (Arber 1875–94: IV 209).

26 The third quarto was printed by John Windet for Smethwick in 1609 (Greg 1939–59: 235); the imprint of the fourth quarto omits to mention the name of the printer and the date of publication (for further details on the date of publication of the fourth quarto, see chapter 4, p. 120, and pp. 178–9 in this

chapter); the fifth and last quarto edition published by Smethwick was printed by Robert Young for Smethwick in 1637 (Greg 1939–59: 236).

27 Q3, for example, emends Q2's 'she will me rulde' at H2r 28 by replacing 'me' with 'be' and Q2's 'ottamie' at C2r 13 by replacing it with 'atomies'.

28 Improvements in the dialogue in Q3 occur at B1r 16 ('But he is owne affections counseller' in Q2 is replaced by 'But he his own affections counseller' in Q3), B2v 25 ('And shee agreed' in Q2 is replaced by 'And she agree' in Q3), E4v 35 (the nonsensical 'there' in Q2 is replaced by 'three' in Q3), H4v 26 (the equally inappropriate 'Bride' is replaced by 'Bridegroome'), I1r 31 (the obvious mis-reading 'liand' is emended to read 'allied'), I3v 33 ('walking' in Q2 is replaced by the more pertinent 'waking' in 'and he and I / Will watch thy waking' in Q3), and K4r 29 (the question 'Is it in so?' is effectively rectified to read 'Is it euen so?'). Q3 introduces two verbal substitutions at D1v 3 and L3v 21, by changing Q2's 'stirreth' into 'striueth', and 'vnthriftie' into 'vnluckie'.

29 For further details on the dating of Q4 and its relationship to F, see chapter 4, p. 120, and pp. 178–9 in this chapter.

30 For further details on the dating of Q4, see chapter 4, p. 120, and pp. 178–9 in this chapter.

31 See, for example, Q4 at L2v 7 and F at TLN 3061, where both editions identify a redundant direction and omit it, or Q4 at E3v 2 and F at TLN 1325, where both editions remove the wrong speech prefix '*M.*'.

32 Q4, for example, supplies no directions when F does at TLN 70, TLN 450, TLN 938, TLN 952, TLN 954, TLN 959, TLN 1556, TLN 2592, TLN 2785, TLN 3035, and TLN 3185, fails to expand directions when F does at TLN 1309, TLN 2338, TLN 2465, TLN 2477, and TLN 2758, and fails to intervene when F at least attempts to correct a direction at TLN 568.

33 According to R. Carter Hailey, paper evidence shows that Q4 was indeed published in 1623. For further details, see Hailey forthcoming.

6 PERFECTING SHAKESPEARE IN THE FOURTH FOLIO

1 Barbara Mowat has for example established that Rowe conflated the quarto of 1676 and the Folio of 1685. For further details, see Mowat 1988: 118.

2 According to Greg, 'the copy [underlying F4], apart from the preliminaries, was divided into three sections for, presumably simultaneous, printing at different presses, a single, double, and triple alphabet of signatures being allotted to each' (1939–59: 1120). The three sections, or divisions, do not coincide neatly with the three generic groupings of the plays into 'Comedies', 'Histories' and 'Tragedies'. *Coriolanus* falls into the second division, along with the 'Histories' and three other 'Tragedies', namely *Troilus and Cressida*, *Titus Andronicus*, and *Romeo and Juliet*. Still according to Greg, 'the printer of the Comedies appears from the ornaments used to have been Robert Roberts ... The printer or printers of the later sections have not been identified' (1939–59: 1120).

3 What follows is a list of the main emendations introduced in the text of *Richard II* as it appears in F4: 1. TLN 237 'vaded' (F3); 'faded' (F4). 2. TLN 732 'no men' (F3); 'no, men' (F4). 3. TLN 1767 'Jides' (F3); 'Jades' (F4). 4. TLN 1997 'A' (F3); 'As' (F4). 5. TLN 2240 'sights' (F3); 'sight' (F4). 6. TLN 2255 'Heart' (F3); 'Hearts' (F4).

4 The other publishers named in the variant imprints of F4 are Edward Brewster, Richard Chiswell, and Richard Bentley, who, according to Giles E. Dawson 'were probably small investors, each receiving a stipulated number of copies' (quoted in Murphy 2003: 55). The leading publisher behind F4 was clearly Herringman, who specialized in dramatic publication. Herringman was solely responsible for new dramatic collections, including Thomas Killigrew's *Comedies and Tragedies* (1664), William Davenant's *Works* (1673), and for dramatic or partly dramatic collections previously published by his predecessor, Humphrey Moseley, such as John Suckling's *Fragmenta Aurea* and *The Last Remains* (1676 and 1696) and Beaumont and Fletcher's *Fifty Comedies and Tragedies* (1679).

5 For more details, see Plomer 1907: 96–7, Wheatley 1909–11: 17–38, and Miller 1948: 292–306.

6 See, for example, Chancery Proceedings. PRO, Mitford, Bundle 298, MS 169.

7 For examples of Tate's shrewd corrections of mangled lines in Shakespearean passages which he retained unaltered in his adaptation of *King Lear*, see Bate and Massai 1997: 129–51.

CONCLUSION

1 This distinction is discussed at great length in William Jaggard's eloquent defence of his own practices against Ralph Brooke, whose *Catalogue and Succession of the Kings ... of this Realme* Jaggard had printed and published in 1619 (STC 3832). In his defence, appended to Augustine Vincent revision of Brooke's *Catalogue* (STC 24756, 1622), Jaggard explains the difference between 'literall faults, some of which kinde, might perhaps escape the Printer' (¶6r 41), and 'materiall faults ... [which] cannot slip through the fingers of a Compositor, or fall vpon the Printers score' (¶6r 14–15) because 'they rather sauour of Ignorance then Neglect' (¶6r 33). While the 'literall faults' accumulated during the printing process are regarded as 'pettie misprisions, where there was no feare that the meanest Reader were like to stumble' (¶6r 47–8), the author's 'materiall faults' are severely criticized.

2 John Kerrigan draws similar conclusions in his essay on 'The Editor as Reader: Constructing Renaissance Texts', where, among other things, he reflects on the extent and significance of editorial corrections carried out by early modern readers (2001: 115–37, esp. 126, 130). For further examples of appeals to the readers as correctors included in early modern printed books, see Bawcutt 2001: 15–18.

3 For a recent assessment of the impact of theories of authorial revision on current views on the origin of the printer's copy underlying the quarto and folio texts of *King Lear*, see Massai 2007: 252–77.

4 Sustained attention was, for example, devoted to Ralph Crane, the scrivener regularly employed by the King's Men towards the end of the 1610s and the beginning of the 1620s. Earlier studies on Crane, such as Wilson 1926: 194–215, were supplemented in the second half of the twentieth century by the extensive work of T. H. Howard-Hill (see, for example, Howard-Hill 1972 and 1992) and by several studies focused on specific plays set from a manuscript copy transcribed by Crane. Among these, see, for example, Jowett 1993: 107–20 and Howard-Hill 1988: 146–70.

5 I have adapted these terms from Richard Proudfoot's colourful description of the editorial strategies advocated by the un-editors as 'the new textual fundamentalism' (2002: 129).

References

Allen, Michael J. B. and Kenneth Muir (eds.) (1981) *Shakespeare's Plays in Quarto* (Berkeley, Los Angeles, and London: University of California Press)

Allen, P. S. (1913–15) 'Erasmus's Relations with His Printers', in *Transactions of the Bibliographical Society* 13, 297–321

Andreadis, A. Harriette (ed.) (1970) *Mother Bombie, by John Lyly* (Salzburg: Institut für Englische Sprache und Literatur, Universität Salzburg)

Arber, Edward (1875–94) *A Transcript of the Registers of the Company of Stationers of London, 1554–1640 A.D.*, 4 vols. (London)
  (1903–6) *The Term Catalogues: 1668–1709*, 3 vols. (London)

Axton, Richard (1979) *Three Rastell Plays: Four Elements, Calisto and Melebea and Gentleness and Nobility*, The Tudor Interludes Series (Cambridge and Totowa, NJ: Brewer and Rowan and Littlefield)

Baker, Howard (1939) *Introduction to Tragedy: A Study in the Development of Form in "Gorboduc", "The Spanish Tragedy" and "Titus Andronicus"* (University, LA: Louisiana State University Press)

Baldwin, T. W. (1944) *William Shakspere's Small Latine & Lesse Greeke*, 2 vols. (Urbana: University of Illinois Press)

Baskerville, Charles Read (1932–3) 'A Prompt Copy of *A Looking Glass for London and England*', in *Modern Philology* 30, 29–51

Bassi, Simonetta (1997) 'Editoria e Filosofia nella Seconda Metà del '500: Giordano Bruno e i Tipografi Londinesi', in *Rinascimento* 37, 437–58

Bate, Jonathan and Sonia Massai (1997) 'Adaptation as Edition', in D. C. Greetham (ed.) *The Margins of the Text* (Ann Arbor: University of Michigan Press)

Bawcutt, Nigel (2001) 'Renaissance Dramatists and the Texts of Their Plays' in *Research Opportunities in Renaissance Drama* 40, 1–24

Belting, Hans (2002) '*Utopia*: A Sometimes Hidden Exchange between Erasmus and Thomas Morus', unpublished paper presented at the 'Renaissance Go-Betweens: Cultural Exchange in Early Modern Europe' International Conference, held at the Shakespeare Library, University of Munich, 4–8 July 2002

Benbow, R. M. (ed.) (1968) *William Wager: The Longer Thou Liuest and Enough is as Good as a Feast* (London: Arnold)

Bennett, S. (1988) 'Jacob Tonson: An Early Editor of *Paradise Lost*', in *The Library* 10, 247–52

Berger, Thomas L. (1988) 'The Second Quarto of *Othello* and the Question of Textual "Authority"', in *Analytical and Enumerative Bibliography* 2, 141–59

Bevington, David (1968) *Tudor Drama and Politics: A Critical Approach to Topical Meaning* (Cambridge, MA: Harvard University Press)

Bevington, David (ed.) (1996) *John Lyly: Endymion*, The Revels Plays (Manchester: Manchester University Press)

Bevington, David and Eric Rasmussen (eds.) (1985) *Christopher Marlowe: Tamburlaine the Great, Parts I and II, Doctor Faustus, A- and B-Texts, The Jew of Malta, and Edward II* (Oxford: Clarendon Press)

Black, M. W. and M. A. Shaaber (1937) *Shakespeare's Seventeenth-Century Editors, 1632–1685* (New York: Modern Language Association of America)

Bland, Mark (1998) 'The Appearance of the Text in Early Modern England', in *Text*, 11, 91–154

Blayney, Peter (1990) *The Bookshops in Paul's Cross Churchyard*, Occasional Papers 5 (London: Bibliographical Society)

(1991) *The First Folio of Shakespeare* (Washington: Folger Shakespeare Library Publications)

(1996) 'Introduction', in *The Norton Facsimile, The First Folio of Shakespeare, Based on Folios in the Folger Shakespeare Library Collection*, 2nd edn (New York and London: Norton)

(1997) 'The Publication of Playbooks', in J. D. Cox and D. S. Kastan (eds.) *A New History of Early English Drama* (New York: Columbia University Press), 383–422

(2005) 'The Alleged Popularity of Playbooks', in *Shakespeare Quarterly* 56, 33–50

Boas, F. S. (1933) *An Introduction to Tudor Drama* (Oxford: Clarendon Press)

Bowers, Fredson (1978) 'Greg's "Rationale of Copy-Text" Revisited', in *Studies in Bibliography* 31, 90–161

(1973) *Christopher Marlowe: The Complete Works*, 2 vols. (Cambridge: Cambridge University Press)

(ed.) (1966–96) *The Dramatic Works in the Beaumont and Fletcher Canon*, 10 vols. (Cambridge: Cambridge University Press)

Brockbank, Philip (ed.) (1976) *Coriolanus*, The Arden Shakespeare (London and New York: Routledge)

Brooke, Tucker (1931) 'Elizabethan Proof Corrections in a Copy of *The First Part of the Contention, 1600*', in *The Huntington Library Bulletin* 2, 87–91

Brooks, Douglas A. (2000) *From Playhouse to Printing House: Drama and Authorship in Early Modern England* (Cambridge: Cambridge University Press)

Brown, Arthur (ed.) (1959) *The Lady Mother*, The Malone Society Reprints (Oxford: Oxford University Press)

Brown, John Russell (ed.) (1955) *The Merchant of Venice*, The Arden Shakespeare (London: Methuen)

Campbell, W. E. (ed.) (1927) *The Dialogue Concerning Tyndale by Sir Thomas More*, with an introduction by A. W. Reed (London: Eyre Spottiswoode)

Canzler, David G. (1968) 'Quarto Editions of "The Play of the Wether"', in *Papers of the Bibliographical Society of America* 62, 313–19

Cauthen, Irby B. (1962) '*Gorboduc, Ferrex and Porrex*: The First Two Quartos', in *Studies in Bibliography* 15, 231–3

  (ed.) (1970) *Gorboduc or Ferrex and Porrex*, Regents Renaissance Drama Series (London: Arnold)

Chambers, E. K. (1931) 'Dramatic Records: The Lord Chamberlain's Office', in *Malone Society Collections*, vol. II, part III, ed. W. W. Greg (Oxford: Oxford University Press)

Ciliberto, M. and N. Mann (eds.) (1997) *Giordano Bruno, 1583–1585: The English Experience* (Florence: Olschki)

Clark, A. M. (1927) 'A Bibliography of Thomas Heywood', in *Oxford Bibliographical Society: Proceedings and Papers*, vol. I, 1922–26 (Oxford: Printed for the Society at Oxford University Press), 97–153

Clark, W. G. and J. Glover (eds.) (1863) 'The Preface', in *The Works of William Shakespeare: Volume I* (Cambridge and London: Macmillan), 9–44

Clark, W. G., J. Glover, and W. A. Wright (1863–6) *The Works of William Shakespeare*, 9 vols. (Cambridge and London: Macmillan)

Coleman, Roger (ed.) (1971) *John Rastell, The Four Elements* (Cambridge: Cambridge University Press)

Cox, John and Eric Rasmussen (2001) *King Henry VI, Part 3*, The Arden Shakespeare (London: Thomson Learning)

Craven, Alan E. (1973) 'Simmes' Compositor A and Five Shakespeare Quartos', in *Studies in Bibliography* 26, 37–60

  (1974) 'Proofreading in the Shop of Valentine Simmes', in *Papers of the Bibliographical Society of America* 68, 361–72

Cunliffe, J. W. (1912) *Early English Classical Tragedies* (Oxford: Clarendon Press)

Davison, Peter (1977) 'The Selection and Presentation of Bibliographical Evidence', in *Analytical and Enumerative Bibliography* 1, 101–36

Dawson, G. E. (1951) 'Some Bibliographical Irregularities in Shakespeare's Fourth Folio', in *Studies in Bibliography* 4, 93–104

de Grazia, Margreta (1991) *Shakespeare Verbatim: The Reproduction of Authenticity and the 1790 Apparatus* (Oxford: Clarendon Press)

Devereux, E. J. (1975) 'Thomas More and His Printers', in *A Festschrift for Edgar Ronald Seary* (Memorial University of Newfoundland)

Dimsey, Sheila E. (1928) 'Giacopo Castelvetro', in *Modern Language Review* 23, 424–31

Duthie, George Ian (1951) 'The Text of Shakespeare's *Romeo and* Juliet', in *Studies in Bibliography* 4, 3–29

Dutton, Richard (1997) 'The Birth of the Author', in C. C. Brown and A. F. Marotti (eds.) *Texts and Cultural Change in Early Modern England* (Basingstoke: Macmillan), 153–78

Ellis-Fermor, Una (1930) *Tamburlaine the Great* (London: Methuen)

Erne, Lukas (2003) *Shakespeare as Literary Dramatist* (Cambridge: Cambridge University Press)

Evans, G. Blakemore (1962) 'The Douai Manuscript – Six Shakespearian Transcripts (1694–5)', in *Philological Quarterly* 41, 166–71

Farmer, Alan B. and Zachary Lesser (2005) 'The Popularity of Playbooks Revisited', in *Shakespeare Quarterly* 56, 1–32

(2005a) 'Structures of Popularity in the Early Modern Book Trade', in *Shakespeare Quarterly* 56, 206–13

Farmer, John S. (ed.) (1906) *The Dramatic Writings of Richard Edwards, Thomas Norton and Thomas Sackville* (London, Early English Drama Society)

Ferguson, W. Craig (1968) *Valentine Simmes: Printer to Drayton, Shakespeare, Chapman, Greene, Dekker, Middleton, Daniel, Jonson, Marlowe, Marston, Heywood and other Elizabethans* (Charlottesville: Bibliographical Society of the University of Virginia)

Forker, Charles (ed.) (1998) *King Richard II*, The Arden Shakespeare, 3rd series (London: Athlone)

Fuller, David (ed.), *Tamburlaine the Great* and Edward J. Esche (ed.) (1998) *The Massacre at Paris with the Death of the Duke of Guise*, in *The Complete Works of Christopher Marlowe*, vol. 5 (Oxford: Clarendon Press)

Geduld, Harry Maurice (1969) *Prince of Publishers: A Study of the Work and Career of Jacob Tonson* (Bloomington, IN, and London: Indiana University Press)

Giordano-Orsini, G. N. (1937) *Studi sul Rinascimento Italiano in Inghilterra* (Florence: Sansoni)

Goldberg, Jonathan (1994) ' "What? In a names that which we call a Rose,": The Desired Text of *Romeo and Juliet*', in *Crisis in Editing: Texts of the English Renaissance* ed. Randall McLeod (New York: AMS Press), 173–201

Gossett, Suzanne (ed.) (2004) *Pericles*, The Arden Shakespeare (London: Thomson Learning)

Gray, G. J. (1909) 'The Shops at the West End of Great St Mary's Church, Cambridge', in *Proceedings of the Cambridge Antiquarian Society*, vol. XIII, new series, vol. VII, 1908–1909 (Cambridge: Cambridge Antiquarian Society), 235–49

Gray, George J. and William Mortlock Palmer (1915) *Abstracts from the Wills and Testamentary Documents of Printers, Binders and Stationers of Cambridge from 1504 to 1699* (London: Bibliographical Society)

Greg, W. W. (1908a) 'On Certain False Dates in Shakespearian Quartos', in *The Library* 9, 113–31

(1908b) *The Interlude of Calisto and Melebea* (Chiswick: Charles Whittingham for the Malone Society)

(1911) *The Book of Sir Thomas More*, Malone Society Reprints (Oxford: Oxford University Press)

(1923–4) 'Massinger's Autograph Corrections in *The Duke of Milan*', in *The Library* 4, 207–18

(1924–5) 'More Massinger Corrections', in *The Library* 5, 59–91

(1932) *A Looking Glass for London and England*, Malone Society Reprints (Oxford: Oxford University Press)

(1939–59) *A Bibliography of English Printed Drama to the Restoration*, 4 vols. (London: Bibliographical Society)

(1942) *The Editorial Problem in Shakespeare: A Survey of the Foundation of the Text* (Oxford: Clarendon Press)

(1950–1) 'The Rationale of Copy-Text', in *Studies in Bibliography* 3, 19–36

(1955) *The Shakespeare First Folio: Its Bibliographical and Textual History* (Oxford: Clarendon Press)

(1967) *A Companion to Arber* (Oxford: Clarendon Press)

Gurr, Andrew (1990) *The Shakespearean Stage, 1574–1642*, 2nd edn (Cambridge: Cambridge University Press)

(1996) *The Shakespearian Playing Companies* (Oxford: Clarendon Press)

(1999) 'Maximal and Minimal Texts: Shakespeare v. the Globe', in *Shakespeare Survey* 52, 68–87

(2003) *King Richard II*, The New Cambridge Shakespeare (Cambridge: Cambridge University Press)

Halio, Jay L. (1992) *The Tragedy of King Lear*, The New Cambridge Shakespeare (Cambridge: Cambridge University Press)

Harbage, Alfred (ed.), rev. by S. Schoenbaum and S. S. Wagonheim (1989) *Annals of English Drama, 975–1700: An Analytical Record of all Plays, Extant and Lost, Chronologically Arranged and Indexed by Authors, Titles, Dramatic Companies, Etc.*, 3rd edn (London: Routledge)

Hayashi, Tetsumaro (1969) *A Textual Study of 'A Looking Glass for London and England by Thomas Lodge and Robert Greene'* (Muncie, IN: Ball State University)

Hinman, Charlton (1963) *The Printing and Proof-Reading of the First Folio of Shakespeare*, 2 vols. (Oxford: Clarendon Press)

(1968) *The First Folio of Shakespeare: The Norton Facsimile* (New York: Norton)

Hirsch, Rudolf (1978) *The Printed Word: Its Impact and Diffusion* (London: Variorum Reprints)

Hollan, Peter (ed.) (1994) *A Midsummer Night's Dream*, The Oxford Shakespeare (Oxford: Clarendon Press)

Honigmann, E. A. J. (1965) *The Stability of Shakespeare's Text* (London: Arnold)

(1996) *The Texts of 'Othello' and Shakespearian Revision* (London: Routledge)

(ed.) (1997) *Othello*, The Arden Shakespeare (Walton-on-Thames: Nelson)

Hoppe, Harry R. (1933) 'John Wolfe, Printer and Publisher, 1579–1601', in *The Library* 14, 241–89

Howard-Hill, T. H. (1972) *Ralph Crane and Some Shakespeare First Folio Comedies* (Charlottesville: University Press of Virginia)

(1980) 'New Light on Compositor E of the Shakespeare First Folio', *The Library* 2, 156–78

(1982) 'The Problem of Manuscript Copy for Folio *King Lear*', in *The Library* 4, 1–24

(1987) 'The Author as Scribe or Reviser? Middleton's Intentions in *A Game at Chess*', in *Text: Transactions of the Society for Textual Scholarship* 3, 305–18

(1988) 'Crane's 1619 "Promptbook" of *Barnavelt* and Theatrical Processes', in *Modern Philology* 86, 146–70

(1990a) 'The Evolution of the Form of Plays in English During the Renaissance', *Renaissance Quarterly* 43, 112–45

(ed.) (1990b) *A Game at Chess*, The Malone Society Reprints (Oxford: Oxford University Press)

(1992) 'Shakespeare's Earliest Editor, Ralph Crane', in *Shakespeare Survey* 44, 113–30

(ed.) (1993) *A Game at Chess*, The Revels Plays (Manchester: Manchester University Press)

Huffman, Clifford Chalmers (1988) *Elizabethan Impressions: John Wolfe and His Press* (New York: AMS)

Humphreys, A. R. (ed.) (1960) *The First Part of King Henry IV*, The Arden Shakespeare (London: Methuen)

Hunter, G. K. and David Bevington (eds.) (1991) *John Lyly: 'Campaspe' and 'Sappho and Phao'*, The Revels Plays (Manchester: Manchester University Press)

Hunter, Lynette (2001a) 'The Dating of Q4 *Romeo and Juliet* Revisited', in *The Library* 2, 281–5

(2001b) 'Why has Q4 *Romeo and Juliet* such an Intelligent Editor?', in *Re-Constructing the Text: Literary Texts in Transmission*, ed. by M. Bell et al. (Aldershot: Ashgate), 9–21

Ioppolo, Grace (2006) *Dramatists and Their Manuscripts in the Age of Shakespeare, Jonson, Middleton and Heywood: Authorship, Authority and the Playhouse* (London and New York: Routledge)

Jackson, William A. (1957) *Records of the Court of the Stationers' Company* (London: The Bibliographical Society)

Jardine, Lisa (1993) *Erasmus, Man of Letters: The Construction of Charisma in Print* (Princeton: Princeton University Press)

Jarvis, Simon (1995) *Scholars and Gentlemen: Shakespearian Textual Criticism and Representations of Scholarly Labour, 1725–1765* (Oxford: Clarendon Press)

Johnson, Gerald D. (1992) 'Thomas Pavier, Publisher: 1600–1625', in *The Library* 14, 12–50

Johnson, Samuel (1923) *Johnson's Proposals for his Edition of Shakespeare, 1756, Printed in Type-Facsimile* (Oxford and London: Oxford University Press and Humphrey Milford)

'The History of the English Language', quoted in *The Dialogue Concerning Tyndale by Sir Thomas More*, ed. W. E. Campbell (1927) with an introduction by A. W. Reed (London: Eyre Spottiswoode)

(ed.) (1765) *The Plays of William Shakespeare, in Eight Volumes, with the Corrections and Illustrations of Various Commentators, to which are added Notes by Sam. Johnson* (London)

Johnston, Alexandra F. (2004) 'Tudor Drama, Theatre and Society', in Robert Tittler and Norman Jones (eds.) *A Companion to Tudor Britain* (Oxford: Blackwell), 430–47

Jones, Emyr (1977) *The Origins of Shakespeare* (Oxford: Clarendon Press)

Jowett, John (1983) 'New Created Creatures: Ralph Crane and the Stage Directions in *The Tempest*', in *Shakespeare Survey* 36, 107–20

(1993) 'Johannes Factotum: Henry Chettle and *Greene's Groatsworth of Wit*', in *Papers of the Bibliographical Society of America* 87, 453–86

(1998) 'Henry Chettle and the First Quarto of *Romeo and Juliet*', in *Papers of the Bibliographical Society of America* 92, 53–74

(2007) 'Shakespeare Supplemented', in Douglas A. Brooks and Ann Thompson (eds.), *The Shakespeare Apocrypha, The Shakespeare Yearbook* 16, 39–75

(ed.) (2000) *Richard III*, The Oxford Shakespeare (Oxford: Oxford University Press)

Kastan, David Scott (1996) 'The Mechanics of Culture: Editing Shakespeare Today', in *Shakespeare Studies* 24, 30–7

(2001) *Shakespeare and the Book* (Cambridge: Cambridge University Press)

(ed.) (2002) William Shakespeare, *King Henry IV, Part 1*, The Arden Shakespeare (London: Thomson Learning)

Kerrigan, John (1982) '*Love's Labour's Lost* and Shakespearean Revision', in *Shakespeare Quarterly* 33, 337–9

(2001) 'The Editor as Reader: Constructing Renaissance Texts', in *On Shakespeare and Early Modern Literature: Essays* (Oxford: Oxford University Press), 115–37

Knafla, Louis A. (2004) 'John Boys', in *The Oxford Dictionary of National Biography* 7, 121

Lea, Kathleen M. (1939) [(1948)] *Mother Bombie*, Malone Society Reprints (Oxford: Oxford University Press)

Lee, Sidney (1895) 'An Elizabethan Bookseller', in *Bibliographica*, vol. 1 (London), 474–98

Lesser, Zachary (2004) *Renaissance Drama and the Politics of Publication: Readings in the English Book Trade* (Cambridge: Cambridge University Press)

Lievsay, John L. (1969) *The Englishman's Italian Books, 1550–1700* (Philadelphia: University of Philadelphia Press)

Lindley, David (2004) 'Thomas Campion', in *The Oxford Dictionary of National Biography* 9, 880

Logan, G. M., R. M. Adams and C. H. Miller (eds.) (1995) *Thomas More: Utopia. Latin Text and English Translation* (Cambridge: Cambridge University Press)

Long, William B. (1985) 'Stage-Directions: A Misinterpreted Factor in Determining Textual Provenance', in *TEXT: Transactions of the Society for Textual Scholarship* 2, 121–37

(1999) ' "Precious Few": English Manuscript Plays', in David Scott Kastan (ed.) *A Companion to Shakespeare* (Oxford: Blackwell), 414–33

Loewenstein, Joseph (2002) *Ben Jonson and Possessive Authorship* (Cambridge: Cambridge University Press)

Lynch, Kathleen Martha (1971) *Jacob Tonson: Kit-Cat Publisher* (Knoxville: University of Tennessee Press)

Maguire, Laurie E. (1996) *Shakespearean Suspect Texts: the "Bad" Quartos and their Contexts* (Cambridge: Cambridge University Press)

Marcus, Leah (1988) *Puzzling Shakespeare: Local Reading and Its Discontents* (Berkeley, Los Angeles, and London: University of California Press)

Malone, Edmond (ed.) (1790) *The plays and poems of William Shakspare, in ten volumes; collated verbatim with the most authentick copies, and revised: with the corrections and illustrations of various commentators* ... (London)

Massai, Sonia (2007) 'Working with the Texts: Differential Readings', in Andrew Murphy (ed.) *The Blackwell Companion to Shakespeare and the Text* (Oxford: Blackwell), 252–77

Masten, Jeffrey (1997) *Textual Intercourse: Collaboration, Authorship, and Sexualities in Renaissance Drama* (Cambridge: Cambridge University Press)

McCullough, P. E. (2004) 'Thomas Playfere', in *The Oxford Dictionary of National Biography* 44, 567

McKenzie, D. F. (1959) 'Compositor B's Role in *The Merchant of Venice* Q2 (1619)', in *Studies in Bibliography* 12, 75–90

McKerrow, R. B. (ed.) (1910) *A Dictionary of Printers and Booksellers in England, Scotland and Ireland, and of Foreign Printers of English Books, 1557–1640* (London: The Bibliographical Society)

McKinnon, Dana G. (1970) 'The Marginal Glosses in More's *Utopia*: The Character of the Commentator', in D. G. Donovan (ed.), *Renaissance Papers*, 11–19

McMillin, Scott (ed.) (2001) *The First Quarto of Othello* (Cambridge: Cambridge University Press)

Melnikoff, Kirk (2001) 'Richard Jones (fl. 1564–1613): Elizabethan Printer, Bookseller and Publisher', in *Analytical and Enumerative Bibliography* 12, 153–84

Miller, C. W. (1948) 'Henry Herringman, Restoration Bookseller–Publisher', in *The Papers of the Bibliographical Society of America* 42, 292–306

Montgomery, William (ed.) (1985) '*The Contention of York and Lancaster*: A Critical Edition', 2 vols. (unpublished D.Phil. thesis, University of Oxford)

Moore, J. K. (1992) *Primary Materials Relating to Copy and Print in English Books of the Sixteenth and Seventeenth Centuries* (Oxford: Oxford Bibliographical Society)

Mowat, Barbara (1988) 'The Form of *Hamlet*'s Fortunes', in *Renaissance Drama* 19, 97–126

(1994) 'Nicholas Rowe and the Twentieth-Century Shakespeare Text', in Tetsuo Kishi, Roger Pringle and Stanley Wells (eds.) *Shakespeare and Cultural Traditions: The Selected Proceeding of the International Shakespeare Association World Congress, Tokyo, 1991* (Newark: University of Delaware Press), 314–22

(1997) 'The Theatre and Literary Culture', in D. S. Kastan and J. D. Cox (eds.) *A New History of Early English Drama* (New York: Columbia University Press), 213–30

Moxon, Joseph (1958) *Mechanick Exercises on the Whole Art of Printing, 1683–4*, ed. by Herbert Davis and Harry Carter (London: Oxford University Press)

Mulryne, J. R. (ed.) (1989) *Thomas Kyd: The Spanish Tragedy*, The New Mermaids (London: A. and C. Black)

Murphy, Andrew (2003) *Shakespeare in Print: A History and Chronology of Shakespeare Publishing* (Cambridge: Cambridge University Press)

Mynors, R. A. B. and D. F. S. Thomson (trans.) and annotated by W. K. Ferguson (1975) *The Correspondence of Erasmus: Letters 142 to 297, 1501 to 1514*, vol. 2 (Toronto and Buffalo: University of Toronto Press)

(1976) *The Correspondence of Erasmus: Letters 298 to 445, 1514 to 1516*, vol. 3 (Toronto and Buffalo: University of Toronto Press)

(1977) *The Correspondence of Erasmus: Letters 446 to 593, 1516 to 1517*, vol. 4 (Toronto and Buffalo: University of Toronto Press)

Nelson, Alan H. (1980) *The Plays of Henry Medwall* (Woodbridge and Totowa, NJ: Brewer and Rowan and Littlefield)

Nicholl, Charles (2004) 'Thomas Nashe' in *The Oxford Dictionary of National Biography* 40, 242

Nicoll, A. (1924) 'The Editors of Shakespeare from First Folio to Malone', in *Studies in the First Folio* (London: Humphrey Milford for Oxford University Press), 157–78

Norland, Howard B. (1995) *Drama in Early Tudor Britain, 1485–1558* (Lincoln and London: University of Nebraska Press)

Orgel, Stephen (1999) 'What Is an Editor?', in *Shakespeare and the Editorial Tradition*, ed. by S. Orgel and S. Keilen (New York and London: Garland), 117–23

Osborn, J. M. (1940) *John Dryden: Some Biographical Facts and Problems* (New York: Columbia University Press)

Ottolenghi, Paola (1982) *Giacopo Castelvetro: Esule Modenese nell'Inghilterra di Shakespeare* (Pisa: ETS)

Papali, George Francis (1968) *Jacob Tonson, Publisher: His Life and Work, 1656–1736* (Auckland: Tonson Publishing House)

Patterson, Annabel (1984) *Censorship and Interpretation* (Madison, WI: University of Wisconsin Press)

Patterson, L. R. (1968) *Copyright in Historical Perspective* (Nashville: Vanderbilt University Press)

Paul, H. N. (1934) 'Quartos and Duodecimos of *Hamlet*', in *Modern Language Notes* 49, 369–75

Peters, Julie Stone (2000) *The Theatre of the Book, 1480–1880: Print, Text, and Performance in Europe* (Oxford: Oxford University Press)

Plomer, H. R. (1907) *A Dictionary of the Booksellers and Printers who were at work in England, Scotland and Ireland from 1641 to 1667* (London: Bibliographical Society)

Pollard, A. W. (1909) *Shakespeare Folios and Quartos: A Study in the Bibliography of Shakespeare's Plays, 1594–1685* (London: Methuen)

(1917) *Shakespeare's Fight with the Pirates, and the Problems of the Transmission of his Text* (London)

Pope, Alexander (ed.) (1725) *The works of Shakespear. In six volumes. Collated and corrected by the former editions, by Mr. Pope* (London)

Prosser, Eleanor (1981) *Shakespeare's Anonymous Editors: Scribe and Compositor in the Folio Text of '2 Henry IV'* (Stanford, CA: Stanford University Press)

Proudfoot, Richard (2002) 'New Conservatism and the Theatrical Text: Editing Shakespeare for the Third Millenium', in W. R. Elton and John M. Mucciolo (eds.) *The Shakespearean International Yearbook II: Where are We Now in Shakespeare Studies?* (Aldershot: Ashgate), 127–42

Rasmussen, Eric (1998) 'Anonymity and the Erasure of Shakespeare's First Eighteenth-Century Editor', in *Reading Readings: Essays on Shakespeare Editing in the Eighteenth Century*, ed. J. Gondris (Madison and London: Fairleigh Dickinson University Press, Associated University Presses), 318–22

(2001) 'The Date of Q4 *Hamlet*', in *Papers of the Bibliographical Society of America* 95, 21–9

Reed, A. W. (1923–4) 'The Editor of Sir Thomas More's English Works: William Rastell', in *The Library* 4, 25–49

Reid, S. W. (1982) 'The Editing of Folio *Romeo and Juliet*' in *Studies in Bibliography* 35, 43–66

Richardson, Brian (1994) *Print Culture in Renaissance Italy: The Editor and the Vernacular Text, 1470–1600* (Cambridge: Cambridge University Press)

(1999) *Printing, Writers and Readers in Renaissance Italy* (Cambridge: Cambridge University Press)

Rittenhouse, Jonathan (ed.) (1984) *A Critical Edition of 1 Sir John Oldcastle* (New York and London: Garland)

Robinson, Benedict Scott (2002) 'Thomas Heywood and the Cultural Politics of Play Collections', in *Studies in English Literature* 42, 361–80

Robinson, V. K. (1987) *A Critical Edition of "The Play of the Wether" by John Heywood* (New York and London: Garland)

Rose, Mark (1993) *Authors and Owners: The Invention of Copyright* (Cambridge, MA: Harvard University Press)

Rosenberg, Eleanor (1943) 'Giacopo Castelvetro: Italian Publisher in Elizabethan London and his Patrons', in *The Huntington Library Quarterly* 6, 119–48

Rowe, Nicholas (ed.) (1709) *The Works of Mr. William Shakespear* (London: Tonson)

Scragg, Leah (1995) 'Edward Blount and the History of Lylian Criticism', in *The Review of English Studies* 46, 1–10

(1997) 'Edward Blount and the Prefatory Material to the First Folio of Shakespeare', in *The Bulletin of The John Rylands Library of Manchester* 79, 117–26

(ed.) (2002) *Sapho and Phao (1584)*, the Malone Society Reprints (Oxford: Oxford University Press)

Seary, Peter (1990) *Lewis Theobald and the Editing of Shakespeare* (Oxford: Clarendon Press)

Seaton, Ethel (1932) 'Review of *The Works and Life of Christopher Marlowe. . . .* Volume II. *Tamburlaine the Great*, in two parts, ed. U. M. Ellis-Fermor ', in *Review of English Studies* 8, 467–8

Simpson, Percy (1935) *Proof-Reading in the Sixteenth, Seventeenth and Eighteenth Centuries* (London: Oxford University Press)

(1935–7) 'King Charles the First as Dramatic Critic', in *The Bodleian Quarterly Record* 8, 257–62

Sisson, Charles J. (ed.) (1928) *Believe as You List*, The Malone Society Reprints (Oxford: Oxford University Press)

Spencer, H. (1927) *Shakespeare Improved: The Restoration Versions in Quarto and on the Stage* (Cambridge, MA: Harvard University Press)

Stern, Tiffany (2004) *Making Shakespeare: From Stage to Page* (London and New York: Routledge)

Stern, Virginia F. (1980) *Gabriel Harvey: His Life, Marginalia and Library* (Oxford: Clarendon Press)

Strier, Richard (1995) *Resistant Structures: Particularity, Radicalism, and Renaissance Texts* (Berkeley, Los Angeles and London: University of California Press)

Surtz, E. and J. H. Hexter (eds.) (1965) *The Complete Works of St. Thomas More*, vol. 4 (New Haven and London: Yale University Press)

Taylor, Gary (1985) 'Folio Compositors and Folio Copy: *King Lear* and Its Context', in *Papers of the Bibliographical Society of America* 79, 17–74

(2004) 'Edward Blount', in *The Oxford Dictionary of National Biography* 6, 297–8

Theobald, Lewis (ed.) (1733) *The Works of Shakespeare*, 7 vols. (London)

Thompson, Ann (1999) '"I'll have grounds / More relative than this": The Puzzle of John Ward's *Hamlet* Promptbooks', in *The Yearbook of English Studies* 29, 138–50

Thomson, Leslie (1996) 'A Quarto "Marked for Performance": Evidence of What?', in *Medieval and Renaissance Drama in England* 8, 176–210

Trapp, Joseph Burney (1991) *Erasmus, Colet and More: The Early Tudor Humanists and Their Books* (London: The British Library)

Tricomi, A. H. (1986) 'Philip, Earl of Pembroke, and the Analogical Way of Reading Political Tragedy', in *Journal of English and Germanic Philology* 85, 332–45

Ure, Peter (ed.) (1966) *King Richard II*, The Arden Shakespeare (London: Routledge)

Wagner, Albrecht (1885) *Marlowes Werke. I. 'Tamburlaine'* (Heilbronn)

Walker, Greg (1998) *The Politics of Performance in Early Renaissance Drama* (Cambridge: Cambridge University Press)

Wall, Wendy (1993) *The Imprint of Gender: Authorship and Publication in the English Renaissance* (Ithaca and London: Cornell University Press)

Walsh, Marcus (1997) *Shakespeare, Milton, and Eighteenth-Century Literary Editing* (Cambridge: Cambridge University Press)

Walton, J. K. (1971) *The Quarto Copy for the First Folio of Shakespeare* (Dublin: Dublin University Press)

Weiss, R. (1964) *The Spread of Italian Humanism* (London: Hutchinson)

Wells, Stanley (ed.) (1969) *Richard II*, The New Penguin Shakespeare (London: Penguin)

Wells, Stanley (1997) 'The Copy for the Folio Text of *Love's Labour's Lost*', in *Review of English Studies* 33 (1982), 137–47, reprinted in F. H. Londré (ed.), *Love's Labour's Lost: Critical Essays* (New York and London: Garland), 277–87

Wells, Stanley and Gary Taylor, with John Jowett and William Montgomery (1987) *A Textual Companion* (Oxford: Oxford University Press)

Werstine, Paul (1990) 'Narratives about Printed Shakespeare Texts: "Foul Papers" and "Bad" Quartos', in *Shakespeare Quarterly* 41, 65–86

(1996) 'Editing After the End of Editing', in *Shakespeare Studies* 24, 47–54

(1999) 'A Century of "Bad" Quartos', in *Shakespeare Quarterly* 50, 310–33

Westfall, Suzanne R. (1990) *Patrons and Performance: Early Tudor Household Revels* (Oxford: Clarendon Press)

Wheatley, H. B. (1909–11) 'Dryden's Publishers', in *Transactions of the Bibliographical Society* 11, 17–38

Williams, George Walton (1965) 'The Printer and the Date of *Romeo and Juliet* Q4', in *Studies in Bibliography* 18, 253–4

Willoughby, Edwin Eliott (1934) *A Printer of Shakespeare: The Books and Times of William Jaggard* (London)

Wilson, F. P. (1926) 'Ralph Crane, Scrivener to the King's Players', in *The Library* 7, 194–215

(1969) *The English Drama, 1485–1585* (Oxford: Clarendon Press)

Wilson, John Dover (ed.) (1923) *Love's Labour's Lost*, The New Cambridge Shakespeare (Cambridge: Cambridge University Press)

(1924) 'The Task of Heminge and Condell', in *Studies in the First Folio Written for the Shakespeare Association in Celebration of the First Folio Tercentenary* (London and Oxford: Oxford University Press), 53–77

(ed.) (1949) *The First Part of King Henry IV*, The New Cambridge Shakespeare (Cambridge: Cambridge University Press)

(1955) 'The New Way with Shakespeare's Texts: II. Recent Work on the Text of *Romeo and Juliet*', *Shakespeare Survey* 8, 81–9

Winn, J. A. (1987) *John Dryden and His World* (New Haven and London: Yale University Press)

Woudhuysen, Henry, 'The Foundations of Shakespeare's Text', The Shakespeare Lecture, in *Proceedings of the British Academy* 125 (2004), 69–100

Yamada, Akihiro (c. 1994) *Thomas Creede: Printer to Shakespeare and His Contemporaries* (Tokyo: Meisei University Press)

Index

Alexander, William
  Monarchicke Tragedies 116, 161
  Alexandrean Tragedie 116
  Tragedie of Iulius Caesar 116
Alexander, Peter 145
Allde, Edward 231
Allen, Michael J. B. 24
Allen, P. S. 48, 211
Andreadis, A. Harriette 221
Apius and Virginia 83–4
Arber, Edward 186
Aretino, Pietro 69, 190
  Quattro Comedie 75, 76, 77, 79, 80
  Ragionamenti 75, 76, 77, 78, 79
Ariosto, Ludovico 69, 190
  Suppositi, I 73
Aspley, William 91, 158–9, 170–3, 225
Auerbach, Erich 211
Aurelio, Giovan Battista 76
Axton, Richard 60

Bade, Josse 44
Baker, Howard 215
Baldwin, T. W. 212
Bale, John 69, 212
Barley, William 133, 134
Barnes, Barnaby 80
Baskerville, Charles Read 13, 140, 208
Bassi, Simonetta 215
Bate, Jonathan 233
Bawcutt, Nigel 233
Beaumont, Francis and John Fletcher
  First Folio (1647) 4, 9, 11, 34, 92, 194, 198
  Second Folio (1679) 4, 9, 11, 179, 233
  King and No King, A 120, 222, 224, 225, 226, 230
  Maid's Tragedy, The 21, 22, 181, 222, 224
  Philaster 197–8, 226
  Wife for a Month, A 11, 14
  Wit Without Money 223
Belting, Hans 51–4
Bembo, Pietro 70

Benbow, Mark 83
Bennet, Stuart 186
Bentley, Richard 233
Berger, Thomas L. 2, 215
Berthelet, Thomas 69, 213
Bevington, David 85, 138–9, 161, 212, 213, 230
Black, M. W. and M. A. Shaaber 180, 182, 185
Blado, Antonio 78
Bland, Mark 76, 79
Blayney, Peter 33, 95, 101, 106, 118, 166, 220, 222, 223, 230
Blount, Edward 35, 113, 117–18, 119, 138, 150, 158–62, 170, 171, 210, 225, 230, 231
Boas, F. S. 210
Boccaccio, Giovanni
  Decameron 70, 78, 117, 162
Book of Sir Thomas More, The 43
Borghini, Vincenzo 70
Bowers, Fredson 4, 11, 31, 208, 218
Bracciolini, Poggio 42
Bradshaw, Thomas 95, 221
Breton, Nicholas 173
  Mothers Blessing, The 197
Brewster, Edward 222, 233
Brockbank, Philip 184
Brome, Henry 9
Brome, Richard
  Five New Plays 9
  Antipodes 110, 223
  Late Lancashire Witches, The 110
Brooke, Ralph
  Catalogue and Succession of the Kings 233
Brooke, William, tenth Baron Cobham 100
Brooke, Tucker 12
Brooks, Douglas A. 34, 165
Broome, Joan 99–100, 119
Broome, William 99–100, 119
Brown, Arthur 13
Brown, John Russell 121
Bruni, Leonardo 42
Bruno, Giordano 75

247

Buoni, Thommaso 171
Burby, Cuthbert 104, 210, 219
Busby, John 98–9, 115
Butter, Nathaniel 107, 112, 113

Cadman, Thomas 99–100
Cambridge editors, the (Clark, Glover, Wright) 136, 182, 193–4, 207
Cambridge editors, the (Logan, Adams, Miller) 49–51
Cammelli, Antonio 70
Campion, Thomas 97, 220
Canzler, David G. 67–8
Capell, Edward 183, 194
Carey, Elizabeth 100, 221
Carey, George, second Baron Hundson 100–1
Carey, Henry, first Baron Hundson 100
Carey, Robert, first earl of Monmouth 220
Carlell, Lodowick
    1 and *2 Arviragus and Philicia* 223
Cartwright, William
    Comedies, Tragedies, with other Poems (1651) 5
Castelvetro, Giacomo 70, 76, 77, 80
Castiglione, Giovanni Battista 70, 76
    Courtier, The 75
Cauthen, Irby B. 73, 215
Cavalcalupo, Domenico 71
Celestina 171
Cervantes, Miguel de 159
Chamberlain's Men, The 36, 95, 97–8, 101, 219
Chambers, E. K. 159
Chapman, George
    Bussy D'Ambois 171
    Chabot Admiral of France 223
    Conspiracy and Tragedy of Charles, Duke of Byron, The 21
    Divine Poem of Musaeus, The 117, 162
    Eastward-Ho 171, 173
    Sir Giles Goosecap 230
    Widow's Tears, The, A Comedy 6
Charles I 21, 181
Charlewood, John 75
Chartier, Roger 34
Chettle, Henry 98, 190
Children of Paul's, The 7, 98, 100, 230
Chiswell, Richard 233
Churchyard, Thomas 81, 218
Chute, Antony 80
Ciliberto, M. 215
Cinthio, Giovanni Battista Giraldi 69, 190
Clark, A. M. 231
Cokayne, Sir Aston
    Obstinate Lady, The 4, 10
    Small Poems of Divers Sorts 10

Tragedy of Ovid, The 10
Trappolin Suppos'd a Prince 4, 10
Coleman, Roger 61
Colet, John 211
Condell, Henry *see* Heminge
Constable, Francis 224
Cooke, John
    Greenes Tu Quoque 231
Cooke, William 224
Copland, William 69, 213
Cowley, Abraham
    Works 187, 188
    Cutter of Cole-man Street, The 187
Cox, John 121, 130
Crane, Ralph 2, 234
Craven, Alan E. 92–3, 208
Creede, Thomas 103–4, 115, 133, 134, 221
Cromwell, Thomas 212
Crooke, Andrew 9, 224
Cunliffe, J. W. 70, 71
Curtain, The 101

Daniel, Samuel 196
    Philotas 161, 225
Danter, John 190
Davenant, William
    Works 233
    Platonic Lovers, The 110
    Tempest, The 186
    Wits, The 223
Davenport, Robert
    King John and Matilda 197
Davison, Peter 219
Dawson, Giles E. 181, 233
Day, John 72–3, 75
de Grazia, Margreta 34, 137, 139, 194, 210
Dekker, Thomas
    Old Fortunatus 171
    Satiromastix 198
    Westward-Ho (see also Webster, John) 117
Devereux, E. J. 56
Devereux, Robert, second Earl of Essex 220
Devereux, Robert, third Earl of Essex 109–12, 222
de Worde, Wynkyn 41–2, 62
Dimsey, Sheila 76
Dolce, Lodovico 70, 213
    Didone 70
    Giocasta 73
Dorp, Martin 54
Douai Manuscripts 2
Downfall of Robert Early of Huntingdon, The 14, 16
Dryden, John 38, 185–6, 187–8, 190
Duthie, George Ian 141
Dutton, Richard 223

Edward VI 69, 212–13
Edwards, Richard 86
   Damon and Pithias 83, 86–7
Eglesfield, Francis 224
Eliot, John 80
Elizabeth I 36, 69, 70, 213
Ellis-Fermor, Una 85
Erasmus, Desiderius 35, 43–55, 64, 67, 68,
   73, 173
   Works
   Adagia 48
   Encomium Moriae 43, 54
   Lucubrationes 47–8
   Editions and translations
   Agricola, Rudolph *De inventione*
     dialectica 44
   Euripides, *Hecuba et Iphigenia in Aulide* 46
   Lucian *Dialogi* 43
   New Testament 44, 48
   Seneca, *Opera* 47
   St Jerome, *Omnium operum Divi Eusebii*
     Hieronymi (Book I) 44, 45–6
Erne, Lukas 31, 36, 95, 97–8, 100, 101, 105, 106, 112,
   206, 211, 212, 219, 223
Evans, G. Blakemore 2
Everyman 41

Farmer, Alan 33
Farmer, John S. 219
Fenton, Roger 171–2
Ferguson, W. Craig 208
Ficino, Marsilio 43
Field, Theophilus 97
Fisher, Thomas 107, 113
Fletcher, John
   Elder Brother, The 223
   Monsieur Thomas 223
   Night Walker, The 223
   Rollo Duke of Normandy 223
   Rule a Wife and Have a Wife 223
   Thierry and Theodoret 226
   Two Noble Kinsmen, The 223
Florio, John 70, 76, 159
Folio syndicate, the (Blount, Jaggard, Aspley,
   Smethwick) 108, 120, 139, 158–9,
   173, 179
Ford, John 111
   Broken Heart, The 223
   Fancies, The 223
   Love's Sacrifice 110
   Perkin Warbeck 110
   'Tis Pity She's a Whore 110, 198–9
Forker, Charles 221
Frankfurt Book Fair, The 79, 118
Froben, Johann 44, 48, 51

Gascoigne, George 73–4, 81–2
   Entertainment at Kenilworth (*see also* Jones,
     Richard) 6, 83
   Hundreth Sundrie Flowers, A 73–4, 81, 215
   Jocasta 73–4, 81
   Posies 73–4, 81, 215
   Supposes 73, 81
Gentili, Scipione 70, 76
Gerbel, Nicholas 47–8
Giglio, Giacomo 70
Giles, Peter 49–54
Gilbert, Humphrey 81–2
Giolito, Gabriele 70, 71, 77, 78, 213
Giordano-Orsino, G. N. 216
Giunti, The 70, 75–6
Glapthorne, Henry
   The Lady Matter 13
Goffe, Thomas
   Three Excellent Tragedies 115
Goldberg, Jonathan 2
Gossett, Suzanne 122, 129, 155
Gosson, Henry 113, 230
Gray, G. J. 95
Gray's Inn *see* Inns of Court, the
Greene, Robert
   Looking Glass for London and England, A
     (*see also* Lodge, Thomas) 104, 133, 140, 221
   Mother Bombie 104, 221
   Orlando Furioso 14, 19, 21
   Perimedes 80–1
Greg, W. W. 12, 31, 43, 67, 73, 91–2, 106, 109–10,
   112–13, 116, 137–8, 139, 141, 145, 150, 159, 174,
   195, 215, 231–2, 232
Griffith, William 72–3
Grove, John 224
Guarini, Giovanni Battista
   Pastor Fido, Il 75, 77
Gurr, Andrew 36, 92, 95, 146, 221, 222, 223

Halio, Jay L. 222
Hall, Joseph 119
Hailey, R. Carter 120, 225, 232
Hake, Edward 75
Hanmer, Thomas 191, 193–4
Harbage, Alfred 222
Harding, Samuel
   Sicily and Naples 197
Harvey, Gabriel, 80–1, 218
   New Letter of Notable Contents, A 76
Hawkins, Richard 197–8
Hayashi, Tetsumaro 221
Hayes, Lawrence 108, 114, 224
Hayes, Thomas 107, 108, 113–14
Heminge, John and Henry Condell 7–8, 32, 106,
   136–7, 139, 145, 150, 159, 229

Henry VIII 69, 212, 213
Henslowe, Philip 14
Herbert, Philip, fourth Earl of Pembroke and
    first Earl of Montgomery 21, 108–12, 159,
    222, 223, 224
Herbert, William, third Earl of Pembroke
    106–12, 159
Herringman, Henry 37–8, 185–8, 190, 233
Heywood, John 41, 59
    Four P's, The 69
    Gentleness and Nobility 64
    Play of Love, The 41, 67, 212
    Play of the Weather, The 41, 67, 212
Heywood, Thomas 111, 163–70, 224, 231
    Apology for Actors 117, 167
    Challenge for Beauty, A 110, 231
    1 & 2 Edward IV 99, 167
    English Traveller, The 111, 222
    Exemplary Lives 231
    Fair Maid of the Exchange, The 167
    Four Prentices of London, The 168, 170
    If You Know Not Me, You Know Nobody, Part I
    32, 166, 167
    *How a Man May Choose a Good Wife from a
    Bad* 167
    Late Lancashire Witches, The 110, 231
    Life and Death of Elizabeth 231
    Love's Mistress 110
    Maidenhead Well Lost, A 110
    Rape of Lucrece, The 165, 166, 168–9
    Royal King and the Loyal Subject, The 223
    Troia Britannica 117, 167
    Woman Killed with Kindness, A 117, 162–4,
    169–70
Hinman, Charlton 120, 121, 143, 158, 179,
    185, 222
Hirsch, Rudolf 211
Holbein, Ambrosius 50, 51
Holbein, Hans 51
Holland, Peter 121
Holland, Samuel
    Venus and Adonis 199
Honigmann, E. A. J. 105, 120, 200, 201–3,
    209, 222
Hoppe, Harry R. 79, 215
Howard, Robert
    Poems 186
Howard-Hill, T. H. 2, 30, 59–60, 143, 222, 234
Huffman, Clifford Chalmers 79, 215, 216
Humphreys, A. R. 104, 221
Hunsdon's Men, The 100
Hunter, G. K. 161, 230
Hunter, Lynette 174–5, 178–9
Hunter, William B. 229
Hyckescorner 41, 62

Inner Temple *see* Inns of Court, the
Inns of Chancery *see* Inns of Court, the
Inns of Court, the 36, 72, 74–5
    Gray's Inn 73, 171
    Inner Temple 81, 213; *The Tragedy of Tancred
    and Gismund* 70
    Inns of Chancery 75
    Middle Temple 81
Ioppolo, Grace 13, 219
Interlude of Youth, The 41, 62

Jack Drum's Entertainment 131–2
Jack Straw 133
Jackson, William A. 106, 113
Jaggard, Isaac 107–8, 116–19, 151, 158, 160, 161,
    162–70, 225, 231
Jaggard, William 12, 106, 107, 116–18, 137, 143, 151,
    158, 160, 167–8, 178–9, 225, 233
Jardine, Lisa 48, 54, 211
Jarvis, Simon 194
Johnson, Arthur 107, 112, 113
Johnson, Gerald D. 113, 222
Johnson, Samuel 56, 181, 191, 192, 207, 209
Johnston, Alexandra F. 212–13
Jones, Emyr 212
Jones, Richard 6–7, 35, 36, 74–5, 81–7, 139,
    178, 190
    Arbor of Amorous Devices 74, 218
    Bookes of Honor and Armes, The 218
    Brittons Bowre of Delights 82, 218
    Gorgious Gallery of Gallant Inuentions, A 218
    Handful of Pleasant Delites, A 218
Jonson, Benjamin 159, 165, 169, 196, 230
    First Folio (1616) 115, 119, 207
    Eastward-Ho 171, 173
    Sejanus 225, 230
Jowett, John 98, 103, 104, 114–15, 190, 219,
    225, 234

Kastan, David Scott 106, 154, 155, 203, 221, 225
Kerrigan, John 146, 148–9, 215, 233
Kidnie, Margaret Jane 231
Killigrew, Thomas
    Comedies and Tragedies 233
King's Men, The
    (Charles I) 109, 110–11
    (James I) 2, 37, 106–8, 112, 113, 114, 116, 117, 120,
    136, 137, 139, 140, 141, 150, 234
Kirschbaum, Leo 161
Knack to Know a Knave, A (*see also* Jones,
    Richard) 14, 17, 87
Knafla, Louis A. 171
Knight, Joseph 186
Kyd, Thomas
    Spanish Tragedy, The 133, 134

Lavender, Theophilus
  The Trauels of foure English men and preacher
    into Africa 6
Law, Matthew 95, 103, 120, 222
Lea, Kathleen M. 221
Lee, Sidney 117–18, 150, 159
Lefèvre, Jacques 45
Lesser, Zachary 33, 34, 120, 226
Lievsay, John L. 78, 215
Lindley, David 220
Ling, Nicholas 173
  Politeuphuia 5
Lodge, Thomas
  Looking Glass for London and England, A (*see*
    also Greene, Robert) 104, 133, 140, 221
  Works of Lucius Annaeus Seneca 196–7
Long, William B. 13, 219, 227
Loewenstein, Joseph 212
Lorenzini, Francesco 71
Lower, William
  Three New Plays 115
  Amorous Fantasm, The 115
  Enchanted Lovers, The 115
  Noble Ingratitude, The 115
Lyly, John 100, 138, 159, 230
  Six Court Comedies 119, 138, 160,
    161–2
  Campaspe 99, 119, 230
  Endymion, the Man in the Moon 7, 99, 119,
    138–9, 162, 230
  Gallathea 99, 119, 162
  Midas 99, 119, 162
  Sappho and Phao 99, 119, 230

McCullough, P. E. 220
McGann, Jerome J. 34, 203
McKenzie, D. F. 12, 34, 203
McKerrow, R. B. 91
McMillin, Scott 92, 226
Machiavelli, Niccolò 69, 72, 190
  Arte della Guerra 75, 76, 77
  Asino D'Oro, L' 75, 76, 77
  Discorsi, I 75, 76, 77, 78, 79, 80
  Historie 75, 76, 77, 78–79
  Mandragola, La 72, 75, 76, 77, 80
  Principe, Il 75, 76, 77, 78, 79, 80
Maguire, Laurie 166
Malone, Edmond 192–3, 194
Man, Thomas 99
Mann, N. 215
Manuali, Nicola 71
Manuzio, Aldo 44, 46–7, 70, 77
Marcus, Leah 34, 139, 210
Marlowe, Christopher 159, 161
  Hero and Leander 230

Jew of Malta, The 222
  Tamburlaine 14, 84–7, 139
Marmion, Shakerly
  Antiquary, The 223
Marston, John 196
  Works 132
  Dutch Courtesan, The 132
  Eastward-Ho 171, 173
  Malcontent, The 14, 20, 21, 171, 173, 198
  Sophonisba 198
Martens, Thierry 44
Martin Marprelate controversy, The 100
Mary I 69, 213
Massai, Sonia 233
Massinger, Philip 24, 30, 196
  Believe as You List 13
  Great Duke of Florence, The 223
  New Way to Pay Old Debts, A 222
  Picture, The 226
  Rollo Duke of Normandy 223
  Thierry and Theodoret 226
  Unnatural Combat, The 223
Massys, Quentin 51, 52, 53
Masten, Jeffrey 34, 207
Mayne, Jasper
  City Match, The 223
Medwall, Henry 211
  Fulgens and Lucrece 41, 61–64, 65, 66
  Nature 41
Melnikoff, Kirk 36, 75, 82, 215
Middle Temple *see* Inns of Court, the
Middleton, Thomas
  Game at Chess, A 30, 209
Middleton, William 69
Miller, C. W. 233
Millington, Thomas 12, 98, 100, 115, 219
Milton, John
  Paradise Lost 186, 190
Montaigne, Michel de 159
Montgomery, William 130, 154
Moore, J. K. 3, 208
More, Thomas 35, 41, 43, 49–59, 64, 67–8, 69,
  172, 210, 211
  Apologye of Syr T. More Knyght, The 55, 57
  Debellacyon of Salem and Bizance, The 57–8
  Dyaloge of Syr Thomas More, A 55, 56–7
  Eruditissimi viri . . . 56
  Utopia 49–55
  Translations
    Lucian *Dialogi* 43
Morton, John (Cardinal and Archbishop of
  Canterbury) 41, 211
Moseley, Humphrey 4, 5, 8–9, 11, 34, 92, 165,
  198, 233
Mowat, Barbara A. 181, 211, 232

Moxon, Joseph
    Mechanick Exercises on the whole Art of Printing
        11–12, 104, 208
Muir, Kenneth 24
Mulryne, J. R. 134
Munday, Anthony 80
Murphy, Andrew 106, 233

Nabbes, Thomas
    Covent Garden 223
    Hannibal and Scipio 223
    *Plays, Masks, Epigrams, Elegies, and
        Epithalamiums* 116
    Tottenham Court 223
Nashe, Thomas 100, 101, 218, 221
    Christs Teares over Ierusalem 96, 100
    Have with You to Saffron Walden 218
Nelson, Alan H. 64, 211
Nicholl, Charles 220
Nicoll, A. 180
Nobleman, The 230
Norden, John 171
Norland, Howard B. 59, 211–12
Norton, Thomas and Thomas Sackville (*see also*
        Sackville, Thomas)
    Tragedy of Ferrex and Porrex, The (*Gorboduc*)
        72–3

Okes, John 167, 231
Okes, Nicholas 117, 167–8, 231
Oliff, Richard 98, 100
Orgel, Stephen 199
Osborn, James 186
Ottolenghi, Paola 76, 216
Oxenbridge, John 99, 100
Oxford editors, the (Wells, Taylor, Jowett,
        Montgomery) 37, 138, 141, 143, 147–8, 150–1,
        152, 154, 179, 194

Palmer, William Mortlock 95
Passionate Pilgrim, The 117
Patterson, Annabel 209, 210
Pavier, Thomas 37, 106–8, 112–21, 132–5, 149,
        170–1, 178, 190
    'Pavier Quartos, The' 106–35, 153–4, 154–5
Pedlar's Prophecy, The 14, 15
Peele, George
    Edward I 21, 23
Pembroke's Men, The 98
Pepys, Samuel 186
Perrin, John 95
Peters, Julie Stone 3, 42, 59–60, 196, 200, 207
Petrarca, Francesco 42
Plautus, Titus Maccius 69, 212
Playfere, Thomas 95, 96, 100, 101, 221

Plomer, H. R. 233
Poliziano, Angelo 70
Pollard, A. W. 31, 32–3, 91–2, 101, 106, 137, 138,
        150, 180, 209–10
Pope, Alexander 193, 194
Prosser, Eleanor 153, 157
Proudfoot, Richard 148, 234
Purfoot, Thomas 120
Pynson, Richard 41, 56

Queen's Men, The
    (Anne) 111, 165–6
    (Henrietta Maria) 109, 110–11, 224

Racster, John 96
Rasmussen, Eric 85, 121, 130, 181, 225
Rastell, Joan 41, 67
Rastell, John 35, 41–2, 43, 55–68, 69, 83, 87, 210–11
    Nature of the Four Elements, The 59–64
Rastell, William 35, 41–2, 43, 55–68, 69, 87, 210–11
Red Bull, the 165
Reid, S. W. 141, 144
Rhenanus, Beatus 44, 47, 51
Richardson, Brian 69–70, 213
Rittenhouse, Jonathan 126
Roberts, James 97, 100, 107, 112, 117, 210, 220
Roberts, Robert 232
Robinson, Benedict Scott 115, 165
Robinson, V. K. 67
Rose, Mark 209
Rosenberg, Eleanor 76
Rowe, Nicholas 1–3, 38, 180–2, 183, 184, 189, 190,
        191–2, 194
Ruscelli, Girolamo 70, 71–2, 74, 80, 213
Rutter, Joseph 110
    Shepherds' Holiday, The 110

Sackville, Thomas 71, 72
Salisbury Court, The 223
Sandy, George
    Paraphrase Upon the Psalmes 209
Saunders, Francis 186–7
Scarlet, Thomas 104
Scragg, Leah 158–9, 160, 161, 162, 225
Seaton, Ethel 85–6
Seneca, Lucius Annaeus 69, 196, 212
Shadwell, Thomas
    Medall of John Bayes, The 185–6
Shakespeare, William 87, 91, 94–5, 100, 101–2,
        104–5, 219
    First Folio (1623) 1, 2, 7, 32, 34, 35, 37, 106–8, 115,
        116, 117–21, 136–79, 180, 182–4, 192, 207, 225
    Second Folio (1632) 1, 180, 182–4, 192–3, 207
    Third Folio (1663–4) 1, 182–4, 207
    Fourth Folio (1685) 1, 36, 37–8, 180–9, 193, 207

Fifth Folio 181
All's Well That Ends Well 225, 231
Antony and Cleopatra 186, 225, 231
As You Like It 225, 231
Comedy of Errors, The 2, 225, 231
Coriolanus 38, 138, 225, 231
Cymbeline 225, 231
Hamlet 101, 158, 173, 180, 186, 222, 225
1 Henry IV 11, 14, 36, 37, 91, 95, 96, 97, 101,
    102–3, 104, 115, 120, 137–8, 151–2, 153–5,
    158, 222
2 Henry IV 11, 14, 91, 153, 157, 171, 172
Henry V 99, 101, 107, 112, 113, 114, 115, 122, 130–1,
    134, 153–4
1 Henry VI 225, 231
2 Henry VI 12, 107, 122, 123, 124, 126–8, 130, 154
3 Henry VI 107, 122, 123, 124–5, 130
Henry VIII 225, 231
Julius Caesar 2, 225, 231
King John 225
King Lear 1, 107, 108, 112, 122, 123, 125, 188, 233
Love's Labour's Lost 137–8, 139, 140, 144–9, 151,
    152, 155, 158, 173, 174, 179
Macbeth 2, 225, 231
Measure for Measure 87, 225, 231
Merchant of Venice, The 12, 107, 108, 112,
    113–14, 121, 122–3, 124, 125, 128, 133
Merry Wives of Windsor, The 107, 112, 115, 122,
    123, 128–9
Midsummer Night's Dream, A 107, 108, 112, 113,
    121, 122, 124–5, 129
Much Ado About Nothing 11, 14, 91, 137, 151,
    156–8, 171, 172, 229
Othello 2, 24, 25–9, 120–1, 201–3, 226
Pericles 107, 121–2, 123, 129–30, 154–5, 222, 230
Richard II 11, 14, 36, 37, 91, 93–5, 96–7, 101, 102,
    104, 120, 185, 222, 233
Richard III 11, 14, 36, 37, 91, 95, 96, 97, 101, 102,
    103, 104, 120, 222
Romeo and Juliet 2, 101, 104, 120–1, 137–8,
    140–4, 149, 151, 152, 155, 158, 173, 174–9,
    190, 225
Taming of the Shrew, The 158, 173, 225
Tempest, The 186, 225, 231
Timon of Athens 225, 231
Titus Andronicus 138, 222
Troilus and Cressida 186
Twelfth Night 2, 225, 231
Two Gentlemen of Verona, The 225, 231
Winter's Tale, The 225, 231
Whole Contention, The (2 and 3 Henry VI) 107,
    113, 121
Sharpe, Lewis
    Noble Stranger, The 110
Sheares, William 132

Shirley, Henry
    Martyred Soldier, The 223
Shirley, James 111, 224
    Arcadia, The 223, 224
    Ball, The 223
    Bird in a Cage, The 110, 198
    Coronation, The 223
    Duke's Mistress, The 223
    Example, The 223
    Gamester, The 223
    Grateful Servant, The 224
    Hyde Park 223, 224
    Lady of Pleasure, The 223, 224
    Love's Cruelty 223
    Maid's Revenge, The 223
    Opportunity, The 223
    Royal Master, The 224
    School of Compliments, The 224
    Traitor, The 222
    Wedding, The 224
    Witty Fair One, The 222
    Young Admiral, The 223, 224
Short, Peter 104
Simmes, Valentine 12, 92–3
Simpson, Percy 24, 206, 208
Sir John Oldcastle 107, 112, 113, 115, 123, 124–5, 126,
    128, 130–1
Sisson, Charles J. 13
Smethwick, John 37, 120–1, 149, 158–9, 170,
    173–9, 222, 225, 231
Smith, Henry (Church of England clergyman)
    A Sermon of the benefite of Contentation 5–6
Smith, Henry (stationer) 95
Southwell, Robert
    Marie Magdalens Funeral Teares 77
Spencer, H 180
Stafford, Simon 104, 113, 222
Stansby, William 131–2, 174, 178
Stationers' Company, The 31–8, 80, 98, 106–8,
    109–10, 111, 112, 113, 121, 209–10, 223, 224
Statute of Anne, The 190
Stern, Tiffany 228
Stern, Virginia 80–1
Steevens, George 159, 194
Strier, Richard 188–9
Suckling, John
    Fragmenta Aurea 233
    Last Remains of Sr John Suckling, The
    8–9, 233
    Aglaura 110
    Sad One, The: A Tragedy 8–9

Taming of a Shrew, The 104, 158, 173, 225
Tapp, John
    Pathway to Knowledge, The 134–5

Tate, Nahum 38, 187–9, 190, 233
  History of King Lear, The 188, 233
  Ingratitude of a Common-Wealth, The 188–9
Taylor, Gary 35, 160, 222, 225, 230
Terence (Publius Terentius) 69, 212
  Andria 41
Theatre, The 101
Theobald, Lewis 192, 207
Thompson, Ann 180
Thomson, Leslie 13, 140, 208
Thorius, John 80
Thorpe, Thomas 225, 230
Tonson cartel 1, 206
Tonson, Jacob, 'the elder' 38, 186–7, 190, 206
Tottell, Richard 69, 213
  Miscellany, The 72
Tourneur, Cyril
  Play Booke 225
Tragedy of Tancred and Gismund, The see Inns of
  Court, The
Trapp, Joseph Burney 45, 211
Tricomi, A. H. 21
Trissino, Gian Giorgio 69, 190
  Sophonisba, La 71
Troublesome Reign of King John, The 225
Turner, Robert Kean 11, 208
Twins' Tragedy, The 230
Two Merry Milke-maids, The 140
Tyndale, William 57–8
  Answere vnto Sir Thomas Mores Dialoge, An 55

Ubaldini, Petruccio 70, 76, 216
  vite delle donne illustri, Le 77
Ure, Peter 221

Valla, Lorenzo 43, 45
Vettori, Pietro 70
Vincent, Augustine 233

Wager, William
  Longer Thou Livest, the More Fool Thou Art,
  The 83
Wagner, Albrecht 85
Walker, Greg 68, 211–12

Walkley, Thomas 120–1, 225, 230
Wall, Wendy 213–14, 215
Walton, J. K. 138, 141, 145
Warburton, John 225
Warning for Fair Women, A 171
Waterson, Simon 225
Weakest Goeth to the Wall, The 131–2
Webbe, William 70–1
Webster, John
  Westward-Ho 117
Weiss, R. 211
Wells, Stanley 145–6, 148–9, 221, 229
Werstine, Paul 31, 91–2, 138, 166, 200, 203, 205, 206
Westfall, Suzanne R. 212
Wheatley, H. B. 233
Whetstone, George 81, 218
  Promos and Cassandra (*see also* Jones, Richard)
   6–7, 83–4, 87
White, Edward 222
Whiter, George
  Hymnes and Songs of the Church 209
  Schollers Purgatory, The 209
Williams, George Walton 178
Williams, John 224
Willoughby, Edwin Eliott 113, 114, 117
Wilmot, Robert 70
Wilson, F. P. 234
Wilson, John Dover 137, 139, 141, 144–5
Wilson, Robert
  Three Lords and the Three Ladies of London,
  The 84
Windet, John 174, 231
Winn, James 186
Wise, Andrew 91, 94, 95–102, 104–5, 149
  'Wise Quartos, The' 11, 36–7, 91–105
Wolfe, John 36, 74–81, 87
World and the Child, The 41, 62
Woudhuysen, Henry 31

Yale editors, the (Surtz, Hexter) 53, 211
Yamada, Akihiro 221
Yorkshire Tragedy, A 107, 113, 115, 122, 125,
  128–9, 133
Young, Robert 232

CPSIA information can be obtained at www.ICGtesting.com
Printed in the USA
LVOW11*2254270616

494287LV00005B/34/P

9 780521 878050